Socrates' Children
The 100 Greatest Philosophers
Vol. IV: Contemporary Philosophers

Socrates' Children

The 100 Greatest Philosophers

Vol. IV: Contemporary Philosophers

Peter Kreeft

ST. AUGUSTINE'S PRESS
South Bend, Indiana

Manufactured in the United States of America.

2 3 4 5 6   25 24 23 22 21

Library of Congress Cataloging in Publication Data
Names: Kreeft, Peter, author.
Title: Socrates' children. Contemporary / Peter Kreeft.
pages cm. -- (The 100 greatest philosophers)
Includes index.
ISBN 978-1-58731-786-6 (paperback)
1. Philosophy, Modern--20th century. 2. Philosophy, Modern--19th century.
3. Philosophers, Modern. I. Title.
B804.K6446 2015
190--dc23   2015032106

St. Augustine's Press
www.staugustine.net

to William Harry Jellema,
Brand Blanshard,
Balduin Schwarz,
and W. Norris Clarke, S.J.

who taught me how to philosophize

Contents

A Salesman's-Pitch Introduction to This Book 1
A Very Short Introduction to Philosophy 9
A Personal Bibliography 13
A Few Recommended Histories of Philosophy 15

Introduction to Contemporary Philosophy 17

Existentialists

    73. Soren Kierkegaard * 21
    74. Friedrich Nietzsche * 32
    75. Martin Heidegger * 46
    76. Jean-Paul Sartre * 56
    77. Gabriel Marcel 72
    78. Marin Buber 79

Pragmatists

    79. William James * 84
    80. John Dewey 97

Positivists and Utilitarians

    81. Auguste Comte 107
    82. Jeremy Bentham 116
    83. John Stuart Mill * 124

Philosophers of Evolution 144

    84. Herbert Spencer 145
    85. Henri Bergson 149
    86. Pierre Teilhard de Chardin 160

"Analytic Philosophers" 173

87. G.E. Moore 177
88. A.J. Ayer 183
89. Bertrand Russell 192
90. Ludwig Wittgenstein * 206

Phenomenologists

91. Edmund Husserl * 228
92. Dietrich von Hildebrand 234
93. Paul Ricoeur 245
94. Emmanuel Levinas 251
95. Jacques Derrida 254

Thomists

96. Etienne Gilson 259
97. Jacques Maritain 261
98. Bernard Lonergan 268
99. W. Norris Clarke 272
100. G. K. Chesterton 276

Conclusion 304
Appendix I: A Doable Do-It-Yourself Course in the Classics of Philosophy 305
Appendix II: A Bibliography of Books on the History of Philosophy by the Author .. 308
Appendix III: Recommended Histories of Philosophy 309

* indicates especially important philosophers

A Salesman's-Pitch Introduction to This Book

Why the History of Philosophy Is the Best Introduction to Philosophy

There have been two very different conceptions of philosophy in the English speaking world for the last century. Traditionally, philosophy was about life, and it was something to be lived. Philosophers were looked up to as "wise men" rather than "wise guys." Philosophical reason was something computers simply did not have. But ever since (1) Russell and Whitehead's *Principia Mathematica,* in 1910, 1912, and 1913, (2) Wittgenstein's *Tractatus,* in 1921, and (3) Ayer's *Language, Truth and Logic,* in 1936, there has been a new conception of the task of the philosopher: (a) not to tell us what is, but to analyze the language of those who do; and (b) in so doing to imitate scientific and mathematical thinking, which is "digital," rather than ordinary language, which is "analog"; and, to that end, to use symbolic, or mathematical, logic (basically, computer logic) rather than traditional Aristotelian ordinary-language logic.

Indeed, this has been the "main line" conception of philosophy in English-speaking cultures for over half a century. It calls itself "analytic philosophy." It has moved far beyond the early, narrow, and dogmatic claims for it, such as Ayer's, but its *style* of philosophical writing is still easily identifiable: you can spot an "analytic philosopher" by reading just one paragraph.

Such philosophers are useful as vacuum cleaners and garbage collectors are useful, to identify and dispose of waste. They clean well. But they do not cook very tasty or interesting meals. I think large philosophy departments should have at least one and at most two of them, as restaurants should have cleaning crews.

The best way to teach philosophy is by a story: the dramatic story of the history of philosophy, the narrative of "the great conversation" which you find in "the great books." It's politically incorrect to say it, but there is indeed a canon or list of "great books." That's why Plato and Shakespeare never die. Of course the canon is arguable and not sacrosanct. It's only human. It's not a canon of sacred scriptures.

The most effective way to teach *anything* is by a story, a narrative. All the great teachers used stories, parables, examples, analogies, illustrations. It's really very easy to get ordinary human beings interested in philosophy: just put the picture back into the frame. The frame is the abstract, difficult questions that philosophers ask. The picture is the context of history, where they actually came from: the real, lived human conversations and arguments that passionately divided real individuals like Socrates and the Sophists, and whole cultures like ancient Rome or medieval Christendom and modern secular scientific democracies.

1

The primary reason why the history of philosophy works better than analytic philosophy, the primary reason why most students love it and often become philosophers and philosophy teachers through it, is embarrassingly simple: because the great masters of the past are more *interesting* than present day philosophers.

But we are too arrogant to admit that. We judge the past by the standards of the present; the opposite idea hardly ever even occurs to us. So we study the past not to learn from them but to teach them, to show how primitive they were compared to ourselves. I refute this "chronological snobbery" by three simple words: Socrates, Plato, Aristotle.

The sciences progress almost automatically; the humanities do not. Philosophy is one of the humanities, not one of the sciences.

Our ancestors made mistakes, just as we do, but different ones. Theirs are now usually obvious to us; our own are not, and therefore are much more harmful. They are the glasses through which we look rather than the things we look at. "To see ourselves as others see us" is to broaden our mind. We wonder how we will we appear to our remote descendants, but we cannot know. We cannot read the books that haven't been written yet. But we can know how we would look to our remote ancestors. For we can read their books.

The only alternative to listening to the many who have already spoken, and died, is listening to the few who are now alive and speaking: ourselves. The first, often called "tradition," is more democratic. It is what Chesterton called "the democracy of the dead": extending the vote to those who otherwise would be disqualified not by accident of birth but by accident of death.

A scientist studies the history of science as a series of instructive errors and gradual progress to enlightenment. And this is right in science, because in science the past really is inferior to the present, and has been proved to be that. But it is not right to do this in philosophy because philosophy is not science, and past philosophers have *not* been proved to be inferior to present ones. Here is a proof of that fact—or, rather, of the fact that at least unconsciously *we believe that* they were wiser than we are, and not vice versa: We do not speak of "modern wisdom" but of "ancient wisdom." The noun we spontaneously connect with "modern" is not "wisdom" but "knowledge." Knowledge is incremental, like a stairway: it naturally progresses. Wisdom is not. And philosophy is the search for wisdom.

The best way to learn philosophy, then, is through its history. This is true even if your eventual goal is to be an "analytic philosopher" and analyze the issues logically and not historically (which is a perfectly legitimate and necessary job). For you simply can't find any better teachers to begin with than the ancients, especially Socrates, Plato, and Aristotle, even if you want to move beyond them.

The history of philosophy is not a series of dead facts but living examples. It is not to be studied simply for its own sake. We should apprentice ourselves to the great minds of the past for our sakes, not for theirs; for the sake of the present and the future, not the past.

I have tried just about every possible way to introduce philosophy to beginners (and some impossible ways too), and by far the most effective one I have ever found is the "great books," beginning with the dialogs of Plato.

If Plato was the first great philosophical *writer,* Socrates, his teacher, was the first great *philosopher.* Plato was to Socrates what Matthew, Mark, Luke, John, and Paul were to Jesus. (Socrates, like Jesus and Buddha, wrote nothing. He was too busy *doing* it to publish it.) And Aristotle, Plato's prime pupil, is to the West what Confucius is to China: the archetype of common sense, the one whom subsequent thinkers either build on as a primary foundation or attack as a primary opponent.

So here is the story of philosophy. It's the story of a long, long series of arguments in a very large and dysfunctional family; and Socrates is its main patriarch, so I've called it "Socrates' Children."

Something about Passion

Most philosophy textbooks aren't fully human because they deliberately cut out all emotions, such as enthusiasm and wonder—even though Socrates, Plato, and Aristotle all said that wonder was the origin of philosophy! Most textbook authors try to imitate computers. I gladly announce that I am not a computer. I am a person, with both rational and irrational passions, and feelings. One of these is the passion for philosophy, and the conviction that philosophy should be exciting—rather, that it *is* exciting, and therefore should be taught that way. I am convinced that reason and passion, head and heart, are both very, very valuable and ought to be allies, not enemies.

The purpose of an introduction to philosophy is to introduce philosophy, that is, to lead-into (the literal meaning of "introduction") the-love-of-wisdom (the literal meaning of "philosophy"). To-lead-*into,* not merely to-see-and-analyze-from-afar. To be a door, not a microscope. And to lead the reader into the-love-of-wisdom, not the-cultivation-of-cleverness.

Love is a passion. Without blood from the heart, the brain does not work well. Without the will to understand, we do not understand. The brain is not merely a computer; it is a *human* brain. My ambition in this book is not just to inform and to summarize historical facts. I want to be your matchmaker. Jack and Jill, come up the hill and meet Plato. Fall in love with him. Struggle, be puzzled, get angry, fight your way out of the Cave. This book is not just *data,* this is drama.

Why This Book?

I decided to write this book when the umpteenth person asked me the following question: "Could you recommend just one book that covers the whole history of philosophy that beginners can understand and even get excited about?"

Since I could not answer that question in words, I decided to try to answer it in deeds. I write the books I want to read when nobody else will write them. Sometimes you have to write a book first in order to get the satisfaction of reading it.

Thirty-one features make this book distinctive.

(1) **It is "existential," practical, personal.** Philosophy is about human life and thought, so I concentrated on the ideas that *make a difference* to our experience, to our lives. That is William James' "pragmatic criterion of truth." His point is that if you can't specify *what difference it makes* if you believe or disbelieve an idea, then that idea is neither true nor false in any humanly significant sense.

(2) **It is selective.** It doesn't try to cover too much. For an "introduction" means, literally, a "leading-into" rather than a summary or survey. It is not the last word but a first word, a beginning; for it is for beginners. Little philosophers get only a page or two, great philosophers get only a dozen, medium sized philosophers get between 3 and 6.

(3) **It concentrates on "the Big Ideas."** (In fact, I thought of entitling it "What's the Big Idea?") This involves minimizing or omitting many "smaller" ideas. I think it is true of ideas, as of friends, that you can have too many of them. Better to have a few that are deeply understood and cherished than to have many that are not.

This book includes only what most students will find valuable. They will find valuable only what they remember years later. They will remember years later only those ideas that make a difference to their lives. And that's usually one Big Idea from each philosopher.

(4) **It covers 100 philosophers.** I chose them by two standards: (a) intrinsic excellence, wisdom, and importance, and (b) extrinsic historical influence and fame.

(5) **It gives much more space to the 'big nine': Socrates, Plato, Aristotle, Augustine, Aquinas, Descartes, Hume, Kant, and Hegel.** These are the most influential philosophers of all time.

(6) **It presents the history of philosophy as a story, a "great conversation."** A book about the history of philosophy is not about history but about philosophy; yet philosophers can be understood best historically: as partners in a dialog with other philosophers. The whole history of Western philosophy is a very long and complex Socratic dialog. The dialog is exciting, for thought-revolutions are more important than political revolutions, and battles between ideas are more important than battles between armies.

(7) On the other hand, **its point of view is not historical relativism.** I do not try to explain away any philosophers by reducing them to creatures of their times, as Marxists and Hegelians do. Though humans are rooted in *humus* (earth) like trees, yet like trees we also reach into the sky. Historians read the *Times* but philosophers try to read the eternities.

(8) **It is for beginners, not scholars.** It is not "scholarly" in style. It does not break new ground in content. It does not push any new philosophical theory.

(9) **It is not "dumbed down"** even though it is for beginners, for it is for intelligent beginners, not dumb beginners. (It is also appropriate for intelligent high school seniors and for graduate students in other departments than philosophy.)

(10) **It is for college courses** in the history of philosophy. **But it is also a "do-it-yourself" book** which does not require a teacher to interpret it.

(11) **Its point of view is traditional rather than fashionable.** It neither assumes nor tries to prove any one particular philosophical position. Though I try to be fair to all philosophers and get "into their heads" of each, I confess at the outset **a sympathy for common sense.** In philosophical terms, this usually (but not always) means, in one word, Aristotle rather than, e.g., Nietzsche, Marx, or Derrida.

(12) **It tries to be both clear and profound, both logical and existential.** For two or three generations philosophers have been divided into two camps separated by these two ideals. English speaking "analytic" philosophers have sought maximum clarity and logic, while Continental philosophers have sought a more "synthetic" "big picture" that is more profound and existential. The result is that the former sound like chirping birds while the latter sound like muttering witch doctors. I try to bridge this gap by going back to Socrates, who demanded both clarity and profundity. Many other philosophers today are also trying to bridge that gap by dialoging with each other across the Channel.

(13) Like Socrates, it takes logic seriously. Therefore **it summarizes not just conclusions but arguments,** and evaluates them logically. But it uses ordinary-language logic, common-sense logic, Socratic logic, rather than the artificial language of modern mathematical, symbolic logic.

(14) **It uses three kinds of logic,** as Socrates did:
It uses *inductive* logic by grounding and testing its abstract and general ideas in concrete and particular instances.
It uses *deductive* logic in tracing practices back to their principles and principles

back to their premises, and in following premises, principles, and practices out to their logical conclusions.

And it uses *seductive* logic as a woman would seduce a man by her beauty. For philosophy can be very beautiful.

(15) Many of the questions philosophers ask are also questions religion claims to answer, though the methods of these two enterprises are fundamentally different: philosophy uses human reason alone while religion relies on faith in something that is more than human. Therefore this book **naturally interfaces with religion** in its questions, but not in its methods. Neither religious belief nor unbelief is either presupposed or aimed at.

(16) **It is so unfashionable as to seek *truth*, of all things!** Much of contemporary philosophy looks like intellectual masturbation. But real philosophy ("the love of wisdom") seeks the fruit of truth, not just fun, play, or displays of cleverness. It is not mentally contraceptive.

(17) **It emphasizes the classical philosophers**, for two reasons.

We don't yet know which contemporary philosophers will be acknowledged as great and which will be forgotten. It takes time for history, like a sieve, to sort out the big and little stones. Every era makes mistakes about itself. "Our era is the only one that doesn't" is perhaps the stupidest mistake of all.

The questions contemporary philosophers typically ask are not the questions real people ask. They are questions like whether we can prove that we're not just brains in vats being hypnotized into seeing a world that isn't there. How many people do you know who worry about that question? I suspect even philosophers don't really worry about it if they're sane; they just pretend to. (In other words, they pretend to be insane.) Real people ask questions like: What are we? What should we be? Why were we born? Why must we suffer? Why must we die? Why do we kill? How should we live? Is there a God? An afterlife? Where does morality come from? What is the greatest good? How do you know?

(18) **It is full of surprises.** It emphasizes things readers probably do *not* already know, understand, or believe. It does not patronizingly pass off clichés as profundities. It emphasizes wonder, since "philosophy begins in wonder."

This does not contradict its preference for common sense (point 7 above), for common sense, when explored, turns out to be more wonderful than any cleverly invented ideologies. For real life is much more fantastic than any fantasy; for fantasy only imitates life, while life imitates nothing. (You can learn this, and similar things, from the most maverick pick among my 100 philosophers, G.K. Chesterton.)

(19) **It dares to be funny.** It includes humor whenever relevant, because reality does. Reality is in fact amazingly funny.

(20) **It includes visual aids** because we both learn and remember more effectively with our eyes than with our ears.

The treatment of each of the 100 philosophers usually contains **12 parts,** as follows:

(21) A photo, statue, or **portrait** of the philosopher

(22) A brief **bio,** including **the seven W's:**
    (a) **"Who":** his complete name
    (b) **"Where":** his place of birth and nationality
    (c) **"When":** his birth and death
    (d) **"What":** his job or career
    (e) **"Whimsy":** unusual, dramatic or humorous facts or legends about him
    (f) **"Which"** was his most famous book
    (g) **"Why"** he asked the questions he did, which is point (23) below:

Obviously, some philosophers' lives are much more interesting than others. Some philosophers are almost all life and hardly any theory (e.g. Diogenes the Cynic); others are almost all theory and almost no life (e.g. Hegel).

(23) His **historical situation** and problem, his dialog with previous philosophers

(24) His **Big Idea** or central insight or most important teaching

(25) His most **famous quotation(s)** (You will find the following piece of advice unusual but practical, I think. When you come to a quotation from a philosopher in this book, long or short, read it *aloud.* This helps you to remember and also to more deeply understand it, because this not only reinforces one sense [seeing] with another [hearing] but also brings into play your unconscious mind, your intuition and feelings.)

(26) A **diagram** or sketch whenever possible, translating the abstract idea into a visual image

(27) The **practical difference** the idea makes
    (a) to life—to *your* life;
    (b) to thought (the idea's logical implications); and
    (c) to history (to subsequent thinkers)

(28) The essential **argument(s) for** this idea

(29) The essential **argument(s) against** it

(30) Short recommended **bibliography,** both primary and secondary sources, but only when readable and helpful

(31) **Probable reading experience;** hints to make him come clear and alive.

A Very Short Introduction to Philosophy

The best introduction to philosophy is the history of philosophy. The best answer to the question "What is philosophy?" is not an ideal definition of it but real examples of it. If you want to know what philosophy is, read philosophers.

Start with Plato. Whitehead famously summarized the whole history of Western philosophy as **"footnotes to Plato."** (I thought of using that for the title of this book.). Plato is the first philosopher from whom we have whole books. He is the first great philosophical writer, *and the last.* For no philosopher has ever improved on his style.

Philosophy, according to its three greatest inventors, Socrates, Plato, and Aristotle, begins in wonder and ends in wisdom. It is, literally "the love *(philia,* friendship) of wisdom *(sophia)."*

"Wonder" means three things:

(1) It starts with *surprise* (e.g. "What a wonder!—that despite my deepest desire to live, I must die!"),

(2) It leads to *questioning* (e.g. "I wonder *why* I must die."),

(3) It ends with deepened *appreciation* (e.g. "How wonderful that my life, like a picture, has a frame, a limit! How wonderful that what I so deeply fear—death—I also deeply need!").

The first kind of wonder (surprise) leads to the second (questioning). We question only what we find remarkable. And the second kind of wonder (questioning), when successful, leads to the third kind (appreciation, contemplative wonder): we contemplate, and appreciate, and intellectually "eat," the truths we discover through questioning and investigating and reasoning.

What do philosophers ask questions about? These are the *divisions* of philosophy. They include 4 main parts:

(1) *metaphysics,* which is the study of the truths, laws, or principles that apply to all reality, not just physics but "beyond" *(meta)* those limits, though including them

(2) *philosophical anthropology,* or philosophical psychology, which is the philosophical study of human nature, or the self

(3) *epistemology,* which is the study of knowing and how we know; this can include logic and methodology

(4) *ethics,* which is the study of what we ought to do and be

In other words,

(1) What is real?

9

(2) What am I?

(3) How can I know?

(4) What should I do?

But philosophers also apply philosophy to many other areas, such as

(1) social and political philosophy

(2) philosophy of religion

(3) philosophy of education

(4) philosophy of art, or aesthetics

(5) philosophy of science

Etc. We can philosophize about anything: sexuality, sports, humor, even soup. E.g. I wrote a philosophy of surfing entitled *I Surf, Therefore I Am*

Why is philosophy important?

(1) Because it is distinctively human. Animals do not philosophize because they know too little, and God, gods, or angels do not philosophize because they know too much. To be human is to philosophize, for to be human is to wonder.

(2) Because it makes a difference to everything. Sometimes the difference is a matter of life or death. Wars are fought for philosophical reasons. The Civil War was fought over the rightness or wrongness of slavery. World War II was fought over Fascism, which was a philosophy. The Cold War was fought over a philosophy: Marxism, or Communism. The present "culture wars" are being fought throughout Western civilization over many related philosophical issues: religion, human nature, "natural laws," human sexuality, the meaning of marriage and family, whether human lives have absolute or relative value, just and unjust wars, and the role of the State in human life.

For a short but dramatic introduction to philosophy, I recommend you read four of the dialogs of Plato that center around the death of Socrates, the first great philosopher: *Euthyphro, Crito, Apology,* and *Phaedo.* Or—a very distant second best—read my *Philosophy 101 by Socrates: An Introduction to Philosophy via the "Apology" of Plato.*

The best way to learn philosophy is not through books *about* the philosophers— books like this one—but from the books written *by* the philosophers. Fortunately, most great philosophers wrote short, simpler books as well as long, harder ones; and almost always it was the shorter ones that became classics. For instance;

Philosopher	easy, short book	hard, long book
Plato	*Apology*	*Republic*
Augustine	*Confessions*	*City of God*
Boethius	*The Consolation of Philosophy*	*On the Trinity*
Anselm	*Proslogium*	*Monologium*
Bonaventure	*Itinerary of the Mind to God*	*many*
Machiavelli	*The Prince*	*Discourses*

10

Pascal	*Pensées*	*Provincial Letters*
Descartes	*Discourse on Method*	*Meditations*
Leibnitz	*Monadology*	(many)
Berkeley	*Three Dialogs between Hylas & Philonous*	(many)
Hume	*Enquiry on Human Understanding*	*Treatise on Human Nature*
Kant	*Grounding of Metaphysic of Morals*	*Critique of Practical Reason*
Heidegger	*Discourse on Thinking*	*Being and Time*
Sartre	*Existentialism & Human Emotions*	*Being & Nothingness*
Marx	*Communist Manifesto*	*Capital*
Kierkegaard	*Philosophical Fragments*	*Concluding Unscientific Postscript*
Marcel	*The Philosophy of Existentialism*	*The Mystery of Being*

Unfortunately, four of the most important philosophers—Aristotle, Aquinas, Hegel, and Nietzsche—never wrote a short, clear and simple book (though Aristotle wrote a long and simple one, the *Nicomachean Ethics,* Nietzsche wrote a few short but not simple ones, and Aquinas wrote a very long and clear but not simple one, the *Summa Theologiae).*

Philosophy and Religion

Philosophy is not religion and religion is not philosophy.

All religions, however diverse their content, originate in faith rather than pure reason, and their ultimate appeal is to divine authority, the authority of divinely revealed scriptures (e.g. Bible, Qur'an), or institutions (e.g. the Catholic Church), or mystical experiences (e.g. Buddhist "Nirvana").

Philosophy, classically conceived, originates in and is justified by appeal to reason. Medieval philosophers often used philosophical reason to justify religious faith (e.g. rational proofs for the existence of God). Ironically, modern philosophers, in reaction against medieval philosophy, often begin by questioning the validity of faith and end by questioning the validity of reason and substituting ideology, feeling, or will (e.g. Hobbes, Hume, Rousseau, Kant, Fichte, Schopenhauer, Nietzsche, Dewey, Derrida). Philosophers who make this move usually construe "reason" much more narrowly than classical (pre-modern) philosophers did. They think of "reason" as *scientific* reasoning. If medieval philosophy is in bed with religion, modern philosophy is in bed with science.

The greatest difference between philosophers and other human beings is probably not philosophy but religion. For everyone has a philosophy, whether well thought out or not, but not everyone believes in a religion. According to the polls, only 5-10% of Americans identify themselves as atheists, but 75% of philosophers do. That fact explains why most histories of philosophy do not understand religious philosophies very well. Religion, like sex, humor, and music, is something one understands from within much better than from without. Whenever I have my class argue about religion, I make the believers argue for atheism and the doubters, agnostics, and atheists argue for faith, and the result is always the same: the pretend atheists do a far better job than the pretend believers. Then we argue about whether this was because only the believers understood both sides or whether it was because the pretend believers had to argue for unarguable myths and superstitions.

This book is not about religion but about philosophy, but one of the primary questions of philosophy is whether something like God exists; for this idea makes more of a difference to everything else, both in life and in philosophy, than just about any other idea. It makes a difference to personal identity, death, morality, and "the meaning of life." The God-idea is almost certainly either the most important error and illusion or the most important truth in the history of human thought. So a book on philosophy cannot ignore the idea. Most great philosophers did not. However, it treats the idea philosophically (by reason) rather than religiously (by faith). It is no part of this book either to presuppose or to try to prove or disprove religious faith, either overtly or as a "hidden agenda." I have tried to be equally fair to all points of view, including philosophies I strongly disagree with such as nihilism, skepticism, Marxism, and even Deconstructionism, which I cannot help suspecting is not even serious but just "jerking our chain."

A Personal Bibliography

Please note: this is merely "*a* bibliography," one among many possible lists of recommended further reading, of other books I have written about these philosophers.

The very best books to read are, of course, the books of the great philosophers themselves, or the "great books." Why anyone would oppose "great books" blows my mind. Do they prefer tiny books, shallow books, or stupid books?

Most of the "great books" in the history of philosophy are surprisingly short and surprisingly clear, for they were written for intelligent, literate ordinary people, not for other philosophers. (This becomes increasingly rare as we approach the present time.) Seventeen of these classics are listed in the previous section, "A Very Short Introduction to Philosophy."

1. Solomon: *Three Philosophies of Life* (Ignatius Press)
2. Shankara: *Philosophy of Religion* (taped lectures, Recorded Books),
3. Buddha, *op. cit.*
4. Confucius, *op. cit.*
5. Lao Tzu, *op. cit.*
6. Presocratics, Greeks, and Moderns: *The Journey* (InterVarsity Press)
7. Socrates: *Philosophy 101 by Socrates: an Introduction to Philosophy via Plato's "Apology "* (St. Augustine's Press)
8. Plato: *The Platonic Tradition* (St. Augustine's Press)
9. Plato: *Socrates' Student* (an introduction to Plato's *Republic)* (St. Augustine's Press)
10. Aristotelian logic: *Socratic Logic* (St. Augustine's Press)
11. Jesus: *The Philosophy of Jesus* (St. Augustine's Press)
12. Jesus: *Socrates Meets Jesus* (InterVarsity Press)
13. Jesus: *Jesus Shock* (St. Augustine's Press)
14. Muhammad: *Between Allah and Jesus* (InterVarsity Press)
15. Augustine: *I Burned for Your Peace* (Ignatius Press)
16. Aquinas: *Summa of the Summa* (Ignatius Press)
17. Aquinas: *A Shorter Summa* (Ignatius Press)
18. Aquinas: an introduction (Recorded Books)
19. Aquinas: *Practical Theology* (Ignatius Press)
20. *Machiavelli:* Socrates Meets Machivevlli *(St. Augustine's Press)*
21. Pascal: *Christianity for Modern Pagans: Pascal's "Pensees"* (Ignatius Press)
22. Descartes: *Socrates Meets Descartes* (St. Augustine's Press)

23. Hume: *Socrates Meets Hume* (St. Augustine's Press)
24. Kant: *Socrates Meets Kant* (St. Augustine's Press)
25. Marx: *Socrates Meets Marx* (St. Augustine's Press)
26. Kierkegaard: *Socrates Meets Kierkegaard* (St. Augustine's Press)
27. Freud: *Socrates Meets Freud* (St. Augustine's Press)
28. Sartre: *Socrates Meets Sartre* (St. Augustine's Press)
29. Modern philosophers argued with: *Summa Philosophica* (St. Augustine's Press)
30. A history of ethics "What Would Socrates Do?" (Recorded Books)
31. Ethical classics: *Ethics for Beginners* (St. Augustine's Press)

A Few Recommended Histories of Philosophy

Here are a selected few histories of philosophy which do not duplicate mine but have somewhat different ends.

(1) Frederick Copleston, S.J. has written the most clear and complete multi-volume history of Western philosophy available, with increasing detail and attention as it gets more and more contemporary. It is not exciting or dramatic or "existential" but it is very logical and helpful.

(2) Will Durant's *The Story of Philosophy* is charmingly and engagingly written, though very selective and very personally "angled."

(3) Bertrand Russell, a major philosopher himself, has written a very intelligent, very witty, history of Western philosophy from the viewpoint of a modern, "Enlightenment" atheist. Don't expect fair and equal treatment of both sides.

(4) Francis Parker's one-volume history of philosophy up to Hegel, *The Story of Western Philosophy,* centers on the theme of the one and the many.

(5) Mortimer Adler's *Ten Philosophical Mistakes* is not a complete history but a diagnostic treatment of key errors in modern philosophy.

(6) Etienne Gilson's *The Unity of Philosophical Experience* does the same.

(7) William Barrett's *Irrational Man,* though only an introduction to existentialism, has some very powerfully written and engaging historical chapters on pre-existentialist philosophy from the existentialist viewpoint, as well as the best available one-chapter summaries of Kierkegaard, Nietzsche, Heidegger, and Sartre. His *The Illusion of Technique* thoughtfully compares James, Wittgenstein, and Heidegger.

Most philosophy texts today are anthologies of recent *articles* written by recent philosophers about recent systematic issues. Most of these are thin, dry, technical, dull, and lacking in "existential" bite, though all of them are very intelligent. They have their place. But usually, only Math and Science students, not English or History students, like them.

The very short "selected bibliographies" at the end of some of the chapters (only the important ones) are for beginners, not scholars. They are chosen for readability, for their power to interest and move the reader.

Introduction to Contemporary Philosophy

As in the previous volumes, my selection of which philosophers to include will probably be quite different from what most other philosophers' selections would be, but not very different from most ordinary people's. I did not ask merely which are the most profound or historically important (that too, of course) but also which are the most *interesting* and which are likely to make the biggest difference to your life.

This is one reason why an unusual amount of attention is paid to the "existential" philosophers, who are typically ignored, neglected, downplayed, or patronized in books about contemporary philosophy that are written by "analytic" philosophers.

This book—full disclosure here—assumes no preference for "continental" as opposed to "analytic" philosophy in *method*, but it does assume that preference in *content*, in the *questions* it considers primary. It assumes William James's commonsensical "pragmatic" definition of a meaningful philosophical question as one whose answer *makes a difference* to ordinary, everyday human lives. And by that definition, much (certainly not all) of contemporary "analytic" philosophy is trivial compared to the "existential" questions raised by "continental" philosophers: meaning, purpose, death, life, good, evil, identity, God, immortality, freedom, happiness, love, etc., which are also the questions raised by Socrates, Plato, Aristotle, Augustine, Aquinas, Descartes, Hume, and Kant.

The philosophical war that shot rockets of scorn across the English Channel from both sides for over half a century is winding down now, and both sides are constructively listening to and learning from each other. Continental philosophers are no clearer than they ever were, but analytic philosophers are more profound: many are dealing with the great questions rather than automatically dismissing them as meaningless. But there is still a significant gap, and the vast majority of beginners in philosophy are more interested in the questions of classical and continental philosophers than those of the "analysts." And this history of philosophy is designed for beginners.

Twentieth-century philosophers are on the whole less readable by the ordinary public than philosophers of any previous century except the late medieval Scholastics (whom, by the way, I almost totally omitted in Vol. II). For in the twentieth century, for only the second time in history (the first being in the late Middle Ages), many philosophers (though not all) began to write in highly specialized and technical terminologies, and to each other rather than to the general intelligent reading public. Most of this technicality comes from the quasi-mathematical "analytic" turn in English-speaking philosophy, though it is also true of many "phenomenologists." This focus on method seems to most people, especially to beginners, like an astronomer turning from star-gazing to telescope-making, or turning from looking at the world to looking at the eyes that did the looking: it is an honorable, useful, and necessary occupation but a secondary and relatively dull one.

We are still too close to twentieth-century philosophers to evaluate which ones will have lasting importance. Time and history will sift them out. Regarding the future we are guessers, not prophets, and my selection of philosophers is bound to be based somewhat on my personal guesses, which will be quite different from another writer's guesses. I have included some names not usually included in a list of the most important philosophers of the century, e.g., Marcel, Buber, Von Hildebrand, Clarke, Ricoeur, and Chesterton, and omitted some others, mostly mathematical and analytical philosophers, which are usually judged to be more important: Mach, Boole, Frege, Quine, and Goedel. The canon of lastingly great twentieth-century philosophers is far from set in stone. Already the reputation of at least one important twentieth-century philosopher, Heidegger, is so in doubt that some serious philosophers consider him the greatest fake, and others the most profound thinker, of our era, perhaps of all time. Opinions almost as opposite about Nietzsche, and even of Wittgenstein, can also be found.

My primary principle of selection among philosophers has been the depth of the reader's engagement. Which philosophers are most likely to strike us with their lightening, to magnetize our minds with theirs, to make the greatest difference to our thoughts and to our lives, and to spread the good infection and turn us into philosophers ourselves? That has been my main criterion of inclusion.

The order and outline is not strictly chronological, but grouped into schools of thought. Post-Hegelian philosophy does not have a single clearly defined plot line, as classical modern philosophy did from Descartes through Hegel.

Less needs to be said to introduce this volume (IV) than the other three (1) because it is a continuation of "modern philosophy" in volume III even when it is labelled "postmodern" and (2) because we are more confused and uncertain about what "post-modern" means and where it leads than we were at the beginning of any of the other three eras.

Hegel is the touchstone, the end of the classical modern era in philosophy and the philosophy against which almost all subsequent philosophical schools define themselves. They include:

(1) Marxism, which, in replacing "dialectical idealism" with "dialectical materialism," is Hegelian only in its form and the polar opposite in the content.

(2) Existentialism, which does the same thing as Marxism did to Hegel but in a very different direction (the individualistic, personal, and subjective, versus the universal, impersonal, and objective);

(3) Positivism and Utilitarianism, which opposes science and its method to Hegel's metaphysics;

(4) Pragmatism, which opposes a practical and experimental relativism to Hegel's theoretical and conceptual absolutism;

(5) Phenomenology, which takes an aspect of Hegel's method in a different, humbler and non-metaphysical direction, *viz.*, the analysis of ordinary experience;

(6) Analytic philosophy, the most extreme contrast of all to Hegel, which redefines philosophy itself as the analysis of language by the new mathematical logic;

(7) Neo-Thomism, which synthesizes the old Thomism with modern developments (Kantian, existential, personalistic, phenomenological, or analytic)

There are more philosophical schools, as well as more philosophers, in this period than in any other. One reason for this is obvious: there are more people in the world. Yet, paradoxically, as philosophy itself expands, its influence contracts. Philosophers are less important for their culture in this period than in the classical modern period, more in that period than in the Middle Ages, and more in the Middle Ages than in classical ancient times. How to explain and evaluate this is for from clear.

73. Soren Kierkegaard (1813–1855)

He is often regarded as the founder of existential[1] philosophy, and he profoundly influenced every twentieth-century existentialist. Yet Kierkegaard remained untranslated and unknown outside his provincial native Denmark for three-quarters of a century after his death. But he is, to my mind, by far the most brilliant Protestant thinker of all time. He had more strings to his bow, more areas of excellence—philosophical, psychological, literary, ethical, religious, and aesthetic—than any thinker I can think of since Augustine.

Like many geniuses, Kierkegaard was physically frail and funny-looking. (He also had a "funny" name (it means 'churchyard,' or 'graveyard' in Danish), so he is usually called simply "SK.") He had large, searching eyes, and was ungainly, skinny, scarecrowish and hunchbacked. In his controversial writings he was also such a troublemaker (he saw himself as a Christian Socrates) that mothers in his home town of Copenhagen warned their troublesome children, "Now don't be a little Soren." But unlike most philosophers, he had a fine, light and satirical sense of humor and a fascinating writing style. This is illustrated in the following satirical account of "How I Became an Author," and it explains why I quote him extensively, letting him largely speak his main points for himself rather than summarizing them.

It is now about four years since I got the notion of wanting to try my hand as an author. I remember it quite clearly; it was on a Sunday, yes, that's it, a Sunday afternoon. As usual I was sitting out-of-doors at the café in the Frederiksburg Garden, that wonderful garden which for the child was fairyland. . . . There I sat as usual and smoked my cigar.

I had been a student for ten years. Although never lazy, all my activity nevertheless was like a glittering inactivity, a kind of occupation for which I still have a strong predilection and perhaps even a little talent. . . . So there I sat and smoked my cigar until I lapsed into reverie. Among other thoughts I remember this: "You are now," I said to myself, "on the way to becoming an old man, without being anything and without really undertaking to do anything. On the other hand, wherever you look about you, in literature and in life, you see the celebrated names and figures, the precious and much heralded men who are coming into prominence and are much talked about, the many benefactors of the age, who know how to benefit

---

1   The term has no exact definition, and was not used until Sartre, a century later. But it means basically philosophizing about the fundamental issues of concrete, individual human existence: meaning, identity, choice, God, evil, despair, love, and death.

mankind by making life easier and easier, some by railways, others by omnibuses and steamboats, others by telegraph, others by easily apprehended compendiums and short recitals of everything worth knowing, and finally the true benefactors of the age who make spiritual existence easier and easier, and yet more and more significant. And what are you doing?"

Here my self-communication was interrupted, for my cigar was burned out and a new one had to be lit.[2] So I smoked again, and then suddenly there flashed through my mind this thought: "You must do something, but inasmuch as with your limited capacities it will be impossible to make anything easier than it has become, you must, with the same humanitarian enthusiasm as the others, undertake to make something harder." This notion pleased me immensely, and at the same time it flattered me to think that I, like the rest of them, would be loved and esteemed by the whole community.[3] For when all combine in every way to make everything easier and easier, there remains only one possible danger, namely that the easiness might become so great that it would be too great; then only one want is left, though not yet a felt want—that people will want difficulty. Out of love for mankind. . . . I conceived it my task to create difficulties everywhere. *(Concluding Unscientific Postscript)*

The Three Stages: Stages on Life's Way

SK worked this project out in a definite order. He divided the possible existential "points of view" into three: the "aesthetic," the "ethical," and the "religious." A "point of view" is not just a mental perspective or a practical "lifestyle" but a set of fundamental categories by which everything in your life is ultimately defined and judged. SK's three options are: (1) the pleasing or interesting vs. the unpleasing or boring (= the fundamental "aesthetic" categories), (2) moral right vs. wrong (= the fundamental "ethical" categories), and (3) faith vs. sin (= the fundamental "religious" categories, the two possible relationships with God).

The three "points of view" are also the three "Stages on Life's Way" (the title of SK's book about them). They constitute stages of inwardness, stages on a journey of self-discovery, from the periphery to the center of the self.

(1) The "aesthete" finds his meaning in his relationships to the world outside him, and in his own passions as attitudes to that world. God and other people are seen as means to this end, ingredients in this story. The small child is the natural "aesthete," but one can also be a sophisticated intellectual or artistic "aesthete" as an adult. The aesthete's absolute is pleasure, mental more than physical—pleasure in whatever interests rather than bores him.

2   Between these two cigars, modern Existentialism was born.
3   Just as Socrates was!

(2) The ethical person finds his ultimate meaning in his moral relationship to himself and to others. All the things of the world, including religion, for the ethical absolutist (like Kant), are relative to this ethical end. The ethical person's absolute is moral duty.

(3) The religious person finds his ultimate meaning in his relationship to God. His relationships to the world and to others (and even to himself) are relative to and determined by this new absolute, which is even more interior than self-consciousness—as in St. Augustine, who called God "more present to me than I am to myself." The religious person's absolute is God, and the faith-relationship with God.

Thus we have three possible absolutes the self can choose, as well as three possible answers to the question "know thyself," i.e., what this human self essentially is. Like many other sets of fundamental categories in the history of philosophy (such as Aristotle's "four causes"), this is a very useful device for distinguishing and categorizing something— in this case, ways of "existing"[4] as a human being. You can usefully label most of your friends, historical figures, fictional characters, and philosophers as fitting into one of these three "existential" categories.

SK's three stages form a Hegelian "dialectical" triad, a thesis (the aesthetic), an antithesis (the ethical), and a higher synthesis (the religious), which preserves in itself the positive points of both the aesthetic "thesis" (its concreteness and individuality, which is lacking in the ethical) and the ethical "antithesis" (its responsibility and self-transcendence, which is lacking in the aesthetic). When a philosopher defines himself so passionately against an opponent as SK did against Hegel, he seldom escapes being determined by him and his categories, even in the effort to escape them.

SK's Unifying Center: SK Interprets SK:
The Point of View for my Work as an Author

SK wrote in an astonishing variety of styles in exploring these three points of view, often using pseudonyms to identify the non-religious stages. What is the unity in this mass of diversity? SK himself tells us in his last complete book, The Point of View for my Work as an Author, where he prophetically foresaw that future admirers would studiously ignore this single ultimate point of his entire work:

The religious is present from the beginning . . . the author is and was a religious author. It might seem that a mere protestation to this effect on the part of the author himself would be more than enough, for surely he knows best what is meant. (And) now—now I am no longer interesting. That the problem of becoming a Christian, that this really should be the fundamental thought in my whole activity as an

4   Existentialists always mean by "existence" concrete human existence, or "a way of human living"—the "existing" of a human subject—rather than the abstract idea of the sheer factual existence of some object. In other words, it is a psychological, not a metaphysical, category.

author—how tiresome! And this thing of *The Seducer's* Diary, this tremendously witty production! Why, it seems now that even this belonged to the plan!

And here is the reason and the need for the plan. SK saw himself as a kind of spy, and his mission as what could be called a "new evangelization":

... an undertaking which means neither more nor less than proposing to reintroduce Christianity into Christendom ... "Christendom" is a prodigious illusion ... (but) an illusion is not an easy thing to dispel. Supposing now it is a fact that most people, when they call themselves Christians, are under an illusion—how do they defend themselves against an enthusiast? First and foremost, they do not bother about him at all ... next ... they make him a fanatic, his Christianity an exaggeration. ...

No, an illusion can never be destroyed directly, only by indirect means can it be radically removed. If it is an illusion that all are Christians, and if there is anything to be done about it, it must be done indirectly, not by one who vociferously proclaims himself an extraordinary Christian, but by one who, better instructed, is ready to declare that he is not a Christian at all ... one must let the prospective captive enjoy the advantage of being that rare thing, a Christian.[5] A direct attack only strengthens a person in his illusion, and at the same time embitters him. There is nothing that requires such gentle handling as an illusion, if one wishes to dispel it. If anything prompts the prospective captive to set his will in opposition, all is lost. And this is what a direct attack achieves; and it implies moreover the presumption of requiring a man to make to another person, or in his presence, an admission which he can make most profitably to himself privately ... alone before God—that he has lived hitherto in an illusion. The religious writer must therefore first get into touch with men. That is, he must begin with aesthetic achievement. ... If you can do that, if you can find exactly the place where the other is and begin there, you may perhaps have the luck to lead him to the place where you are.

As with Pascal, the whole of SK's work, though not all about religion, has a religious purpose. All his pre-religious works, even the clever "Diary of a Seducer," are a "setup" for the "leap of faith," as all of Pascal leads to the "wager." SK's unifying center is to be a philosophical and aesthetic missionary-spy whose ironic mission is to smuggle Christianity into Christendom.

Aesthetic vs. Ethical: *Either/Or*

In this, his first book and the one that made him famous, SK contrasts the life of the Epicurean calculating hedonist with that of the Stoic or Kantian morally responsible ethicist

---

5   Compare Socrates' method of assuming the point of view of his interlocutor: a kind of role reversal between student and teacher.

in a series of fictional letters written by the young "Johannes the Seducer" and the older "Judge William." In contrast to Plato's dialogs, which present Socrates as the more interesting as well as the more moral and intelligent speaker, SK divides up the goods, making Johannes much cleverer, funnier, and more interesting than the middle-aged moralist judge who, however, is in the right. Here is a sample of the "aesthetic":

Starting from a principle is affirmed by people of experience to be a very reasonable procedure; I am willing to humor them, and so begin with the principle that all men are bores. Surely no one will prove himself so great a bore as to contradict me in this. . . . Boredom is the root of all evil. . . . In the case of children, the ruinous character of boredom is universally acknowledged. Children are always well-behaved as long as they are enjoying themselves. . . .

All men are bores. The word itself suggests the possibility of a subdivision. It may just as well indicate a man who bores others as one who bores himself. Those who bore others are the mob, the crowd, the infinite multitude of men in general. Those who bore themselves are the elect, the aristocracy; and it is a curious fact that those who do not bore themselves usually bore others, while those who bore themselves entertain others. Those who do not bore themselves . . . keep themselves extremely busy; these people are precisely on this account the most tiresome, the most utterly unendurable. . . .

Everyone who feels bored cries out for change. . . .

I assume that it is the end and aim of every man to enjoy himself. . . .

The essence of pleasure does not lie in the thing enjoyed but in the accompanying consciousness. If I had a humble spirit in my service, who, when I asked for a glass of water, brought me the world's costliest wines blended in a chalice, I should dismiss him, in order to teach him that pleasure consists not in what I enjoy, but in having my own way.

That is the "Either." Here is the "Or," Judge William's basic response to this playboy. It is similar to Pascal's critique of "diversion":

You are outside yourself . . . you believe that only a restless spirit is alive, whereas all men of experience think that only a quiet spirit is truly alive. . . .

In fact you are nothing; you are merely a relation to others, and what you are you are by virtue of this relation. . . .

Do you not know that there comes a midnight hour when every one has to throw off his mask? Do you believe that life will always let itself be mocked? Do you think you can slip away a little before midnight in order to avoid this? Or are you not terrified by it? I have seen men in real life who so long deceived others that at last their true nature could not reveal itself . . . can you think of anything more frightful than that it might end with your nature being resolved into a multiplicity, that you really might become

many, become, like those unhappy demoniacs, a legion, and you thus would have lost the inmost and holiest thing of all in a man, the unifying power of personality?

. . . one is not tempted to pity you but rather to wish that some day the circumstances of your life may tighten upon you the screws of its rack and compel you to come out with what really dwells in you; that they may begin the sharper inquisition of the rack which cannot be beguiled by nonsense and witticisms.

The deepest point of *Either/Or*, however, is the choice, not between good and evil (the two essential categories of the ethical), or between pleasure and boredom (the two essential categories of the aesthetic), but between choice and no-choice, i.e., between the ethical itself and the aesthetic itself:

What is it, then, that I distinguish in my either/or? Is it good and evil? No, I would only bring you up to the point where the choice between the evil and the good acquires significance for you. . . . Here the question is under what determinants one would contemplate the whole of existence and would himself live. . . .

And this is the pitiful thing to one who contemplates human life, that so many live on in a quiet state of perdition . . . they live their lives outside of themselves, they vanish like shadows, their immortal soul is blown away, and they are not alarmed by the problem of its immortality, for they are already in a state of dissolution before they die.[6] They do not live aesthetically, but neither has the ethical manifested itself in its entirety, so they have not exactly rejected it either; they therefore are not sinning, except insofar as it is sin not to be either one thing or the other.

Ethical vs. Religious: Fear & Trembling

In the same year (1843) that SK published his contrast between the ethical and the aesthetic (*Either/Or*), he also published his contrast between the ethical and the religious (*Fear and Trembling*). This is a poetic and deeply moving exploration of the consciousness of Abraham, the hero of faith, in his willingness to sacrifice Isaac. SK bypasses the usual Jewish interpretation of the story in Genesis 22, that its main point was God's establishment of a new, distinctively non-pagan religion without human sacrifice. He also bypasses the usual Christian interpretation, that God stopped the sacrifice of Isaac because Isaac was only an image of the sacrifice of Christ. Instead, SK so sharply distinguishes "the religious" from "the ethical" that he calls Abraham's obedience a "teleological suspension of the ethical." God is forcing Abraham to choose between obedience to God's command to kill Isaac and obedience to the abstract, universal, impersonal moral law ("Thou shalt not murder"), between obedience to God's moral law and obedience to His concrete, individual, personal will. The "lesson" is that **the individual**

6   Compare Pascal on "indifference."

as the particular is higher than the universal, inasmuch as the individual as the particular stands in an absolute relation to the Absolute. He argues that if this is not so, then the believer is **wrong in not protesting loudly and clearly against the fact that Abraham enjoys honor and glory as the father of faith, whereas he ought to be prosecuted and convicted of murder**.

Fear and Trembling also sharply distinguishes the Biblical "knight of faith" from the pagan "knight of infinite resignation." The pagan hero sacrifices his most precious treasures to the gods, but without the hope of receiving them back again. Abraham, in contrast, is willing to sacrifice Isaac in the hope of receiving him back. In more traditional theological language, supernatural faith includes supernatural hope (in resurrection).

SK's "knight of faith" is also, like Christ, totally human, ordinary, and this-worldly at the same time as he is other-worldly, invisibly and interiorly "making the movements of infinity," the movements of faith—unlike the pagan religious hero who stands out, apart from and above his fellows. Thus even the choice of an ordinary Christian to take his family on an afternoon picnic is an act of faith made by a "knight of faith" because he does this "horizontal" deed "vertically," face to face with God. He has given up his whole world to God, as Abraham gave up Isaac, who was his whole world; and yet he possesses the whole world again through its sacrifice. It is a paradox that prefigures the "absolute paradox" of the Incarnation.

Transcending Natural Reason: Jesus vs. Socrates: *Philosophical Fragments*

SK's sharpest philosophical contrast is Socrates vs. Hegel, his most vs. least favorite philosophers. Hegel's offense, for SK, is not merely philosophical rationalism and absent-mindedness, but his claim that his supremely abstract philosophy is the true meaning of Christianity; that the Christianity of history, the Bible, the Church, and the masses is merely a kind of symbolic or mythic approximation to Hegelian philosophy. SK would have found Nietzsche's honest, passionate atheistic attack from without far less objectionable than this subversion from within.

Jesus and Socrates are probably the two most influential persons who ever lived, and SK made them the twin centers around which his thought revolves. Thus the comparison between these two, which SK makes in the first two chapters of *Philosophical Fragments,* is at the very center of SK's philosophy. (See my *Socrates Meets Kierkegaard* for a book-length Socratic dialog on these two short chapters.)

SK and Nietzsche, though poles apart on God, religion and morality, agree in judging Jesus and Socrates the two most important people in history. They differ on their value, but not on their importance. They are SK's two greatest heroes and Nietzsche's two greatest enemies, history's two greatest mistakes. For Nietzsche sees Socrates through the eyes of Plato's rationalism, while SK sees him as one who lived his philosophy and died for it, who existed it rather than writing it. (If you add the total number of words written by Jesus, Socrates, and Buddha, the three most influential humans who ever lived, you get the sum of zero.)

Nietzsche and SK are the only two philosophers of the nineteenth century who clearly saw the momentous existential consequences of the fact that Western civilization, which had for millennia revolved around Jesus and Socrates like planets around a double sun, had now detached themselves from their suns and were speeding into the emptiness of outer space; but this civilization was not yet aware of that fact. (See Nietzsche's famous "God is dead" speech on p. 37).

The Critique of Hegel: Truth as Subjectivity: *Concluding Unscientific Postscript*

The title of this work, like that of the *Philosophical Fragments,* is part of SK's satire on Hegel's claim to serve us a totally systematic, and complete philosophical system. It is SK's longest and most philosophically central work. In it, he critiques Hegel not only for his undermining of Christianity but also for his neglect of subjectivity and individual existence. SK pictures the Hegelian philosophy as an imposing castle which the disciple contemplates in wonder but cannot enter or live in because it has no doors.

One specific critique is directed against Hegel's claim to begin (like Descartes) with nothing, with no presuppositions:

The System's beginning . . . is itself reached by means of a process of reflection. . . . Reflection . . . cannot be stopped by itself. . . . But if a resolution of will is required to end the preliminary process of reflection, the presuppositionless character of the System is renounced. . . . What if, instead of talking or dreaming about an absolute beginning, we talked about a leap . . . ?

Another critique is of Hegel's claim to encompass everything, even concrete, individual, personal, subjective existence, within a philosophical system:

An existential system cannot be formulated. . . . Existence itself is a system—for God; but it cannot be a system for any existing spirit. System and finality correspond to each other, but existence is precisely the opposite of finality. . . .

Respecting the impossibility of an existential system, let us then ask quite simply, a Greek youth might have asked his teacher (and if the superlative wisdom can explain everything but cannot answer a simple question, it is clear that the world is out of joint): "Who is to write or complete such a system? Surely a human being; unless we propose again to begin using the strange mode of speech which assumes that a human being becomes speculative philosophy in the abstract. . . . Two ways, in general, are open for an existing individual: *Either* he can do his utmost to forget that he is an existing individual, by which he becomes a comic figure since existence has the remarkable trait of compelling an existing individual to exist whether he wills it or not. . . . *Or* he can concentrate his entire energy upon the fact that he is an existing individual. . . .

An actual emphasis on existence must be expressed in an essential form; in view of the elusiveness of existence, such a form will have to be an indirect form, namely the absence of a system. . . . The systematic Idea is the identity of subject and object, the unity of thought and being. Existence, on the other hand, is their separation.

SK proceeds to his famous definition of "truth as subjectivity," by which he does *not* mean a relativism ("my truth" vs. "your truth") in the cognitive or intellectual dimension, but a kind of truth that transcends that very dimension. It is not a truth I know but a truth I am. It is the Hebrew *emeth,* personal fidelity and authenticity:

When the question of truth is raised in an objective manner, reflection is directed objectively to the truth, as an object to which the knower is related. Reflection is not directed upon the relationship, however, but upon the question of whether it is the truth to which the knower is related. If only the object to which he is related is the truth, the subject is accounted to be in the truth. When the question of the truth is raised subjectively, reflection is directed subjectively to the nature of the individual's relationship: if only the mode of this relationship is in the truth, the individual is in the truth, even if he should happen to be thus related to what is not true. . . .

If one who lives in the midst of Christianity goes up to the house of God, the house of the true God, with the true conception of God in his knowledge, and prays, but prays in a false spirit; and one who lives in an idolatrous community prays with the entire passion of the infinite, although his eyes rest upon the image of an idol: where is there most truth? The one prays in truth to God though he worships an idol; the other prays falsely to the true God, and hence worships in fact an idol . . .

But the above definition of truth is an equivalent expression for faith. ("Faith" here means not "intellectual opinion" but "personal fidelity, trust.") **Without risk there is no faith. Faith is precisely the contradiction between the infinite passion of the individual's inwardness and the objective uncertainty. If I am capable of grasping God objectively** (rationally), **I do not believe, but precisely because I cannot do this I must believe. If I wish to preserve myself in faith I must constantly be intent upon holding fast the objective uncertainty, so that in the objective uncertainty I am out "upon the seventy thousand fathoms of water," and yet believe.**

Religious & Psychological Works

Since this is a history of philosophy rather than religion or psychology, I will merely summarize the single main point of SK's most influential religious and psychological works.

Works of Love distinguishes Christian love (charity, *agape)* from worldly love as will, duty, and commandment ("Thou *shalt* love . . .") are distinguished from the popular modern notion that love is a feeling: **To the Christian love is the works of love.** How can love be commanded by God's law yet be free? **Alas, we often think that it is the law which restricts freedom. However it is just the other way: without law freedom simply does not exist, and it is the law which gives freedom. . . . This "thou shalt" sets love free in blessed independence: such a love stands and falls not by some accidental circumstance of its object, it stands and falls by the law of eternity—but then it never falls.**

Training in Christianity answers SK's central question "what it means to be a Christian," and his answer is "contemporaneousness with Christ." What he means by this phrase is that Christianity is not merely knowing about and imitating Christ, it is His real presence in the Christian. So how can the historical Christ of the Gospels be really present now? And how can our eternal destiny depend on the temporal facts of the Incarnation, death and resurrection of Christ many centuries ago? (That is also the question of the *Fragments* and the *Postscript,* where it is treated more philosophically.)

The point of *Purity of Heart* is psychological and moral oneness, or, as its critics would say, narrowness and "fanaticism": **purity of heart is to will one thing . . . and he who in truth wills only one thing can will only the Good. . . . "Mary chose the better part." What is the better part? It is God, and consequently everything, but it is called the better part because it must be chosen; one does not receive everything as everything, that is not how one begins; one begins by choosing the better part, which is nevertheless everything.**

In contrast, *The Sickness Unto Death* is about the various forms of despair of this oneness, despair of one's self. SK here translates the idea of "sin" into psychological terms, and poses not virtue but faith as the alternative to sin (which is ultimately despair). This book has been very influential in "existential psychology" and "depth psychology."

A similar, and similarly influential, psychological study of "angst" or "existential anxiety" is *The Concept of Dread.* Ordinary dread, anxiety, or fear is over some finite object; angst is over everything.

SK as Critic of the Modern World: *The Present Age*

Existentialists in general, and SK in particular, are often criticized for being so individualistic that they ignore the community, so subjective that they ignore the world outside them, and so focused on the present that they ignore past and future history. This book shows how inaccurate that criticism is. As early as 1846 SK was seeing, prophetically, what dozens of observers came to see only later: modern secular, democratic civilization's dangerous "leveling":

The dialectic of antiquity tended towards *leadership* (the great individual and the masses—the free man and the slaves); so far the dialectic of Christendom tends toward *representation* (the majority sees itself in its representative . . .); the dialectic of the present age tends toward *equality,* and leveling. . . . The individual no longer

belongs to God, to himself, to his beloved, to his art or to his science; he is conscious of belonging in all things to an abstraction. . . . A demon is called up over whom no individual has any power . . . that phantom is *the public.* It is only in an age which is without passion, yet reflective, that such a phantom can develop itself with the help of the Press which itself becomes an abstraction. . . . The public is a concept which could not have occurred in antiquity because the people *en masse in corpore* took part in any situation which arose and . . . the individual was personally present . . . A generation, a people, an assembly of the people, a meeting, or a man are responsible for what they are and can be made ashamed if they are inconstant and unfaithful; but a public remains a public. . . .

The time has come for work to begin . . . every individual must work for himself, each for himself. No longer can the individual, as in former times, turn to the great for help when he grows confused. This is past; he is either lost in the dizziness of unending abstraction, or saved forever in the reality of religion. For the development is, in spite of everything, a progress, because all the individuals who are saved will receive the specific weight of religion, its essence at first hand, from God himself.

SK as Critic of the Modern Church: *Attack Upon Christendom*

SK's last published work was a series of pamphlets attacking the official state Danish Lutheran church for its Laodicean lukewarmness, mainline mediocrity, and comfortable conformities. Here is his main point:

I am not, as well-intentioned people represent, for . . . a Christian severity as opposed to a Christian leniency. By no means. I am neither leniency nor severity, I am—a human honesty. The leniency which is the common Christianity in the land I want to place alongside of the New Testament in order to see how these two are related to one another. Then, if it appears, if I or another can prove, that it can be maintained face to face with the New Testament, then with the greatest joy will I agree to it. But one thing I will not do, not for anything in the world. I will not, by suppression or by performing tricks, try to produce the impression that the ordinary Christianity in the land and the Christianity of the New Testament are alike.

SK died on the very day he withdrew the last of his inheritance from the bank. At his funeral one of his (few) admirers rudely interrupted the ceremony by reading Revelation 3:14–22. (Look it up!)

Select Bibliography:

Robert Bretall, ed., *A Kierkegaard Anthology*

74. Friedrich Nietzsche (1844–1900)

Nietzsche was probably the single most radical philosopher who ever lived.

This is true in the literal sense of "radical": he aimed his darts at the very "roots" *(radix)* of Western philosophy, religion, morality, and civilization. He called himself **"The Hammer"** and claimed to **philosophize with a hammer:** the hammer of Thor, not of a carpenter (like Jesus); a hammer of destruction (or "deconstruction"), not construction. Later "Deconstructionism' always harks back to Nietzsche. His claim was to be the undertaker to religion, morality, and nearly everything in the history of philosophy that began with Socrates.

Freud believed that Nietzsche "had a more penetrating knowledge of himself than any other man who had ever lived or was ever likely to live." He was certainly a genius and, as we shall soon see from some of his quotations, an astonishingly powerful rhetorician.

His father died when he was four, and he was raised by his mother, sister, grandmother, and two maiden aunts. (Perhaps that is why his writings are such pure verbal testosterone.) At the unthinkably young age of 24 he became Professor of Classics on the recommendation of his prestigious professor Ritschl, who was literally in awe at him.

His body was tragically less vigorous than his mind. Fragile since birth, he had to resign his professorship at 34 because of increasing problems with eyesight, stomach, and headaches. For the rest of his life he wandered around Europe seeking in vain a return to health. He died after ten years of insanity brought on physically by syphilis and mentally by a kind of martyrdom to his philosophy.

To explain and defend that last claim, we must state candidly that it is just about impossible to take a neutral, impersonal, observer's attitude toward Nietzsche. Those who write about him tend to fit into five classes.

Five Different Takes on Nietzsche

(1) The "gentle Nietzscheans" want to tame him and welcome him to the mainstream of Western thought, as its helpful critic. They see him as a sort of sheep in wolf's clothing, his rhetoric as an exaggeration. These people are mostly respectable establishment philosophers and scholars.

(2) The "screaming Nietzscheans" are mainly teenage rebels, some of them Neo-Nazi skinhead types, who use him to justify their own thoughtless rant against all existing order. The Nazis themselves did something like this, conveniently ignoring Nietzsche's attack on German nationalism and anti-Semitism and his admiration for intelligence and culture.

(3) Then there are the "neat Nietzscheans," the Deconstructionists, who play the Sophists' clever little games of applying the pins of "the hermeneutic of suspicion" to pop all the philosophical and cultural balloons of Western civilization, using Nietzsche as their main popper. These emphasize Nietzsche's prioritizing of appearance over "reality," so it is only fair to judge them by their appearance: it is that of a classic case of arrested development; adult academics who never got over the teenage thrill of rebellion and the thrill of the power to shock their elders.

(4) The "Nietzsche is nuts" people take Nietzsche seriously and literally, especially his immoralism and his claim to be "Antichrist." These people are usually honest, commonsensical, simple-minded moral and religious people, unlike Nietzsche himself; but I think Nietzsche would respect them more than the first three groups, even though they disagree with nearly everything he taught, because they at least take it all as seriously as he did. They fight him like a dragon instead of petting him like a puppy.

(5) This book takes a fifth approach. It sees Nietzsche as a prophetic "culture hero" whose example, both in word and in life, is a valuable warning to our entire culture and its Nietzschean "will to power." This approach is viable for theists as well as atheists; for looking face to face at all the existential consequences of a clear and consistent atheism can be the very best way to appreciate not only atheism but also theism and the difference it makes to everything.

A "culture hero" is a unique individual who lives out the deepest value of his culture in a more consistent, total, and costly way than his culture itself does, often to the point of sacrifice and martyrdom: e.g., Job, the hero of faith in ancient Hebrew culture, or Oedipus and Socrates, heroes of "know thyself" in ancient Athenian culture. The fundamental value Nietzsche lived out was the "will to power," in the vacuum of all other values that followed the "death of God," which he prophetically perceived as the most cataclysmic event in modern Western history.

This interpretation is the most sympathetic explanation of Nietzsche's tragic fate. William Barrett, in *Irrational Man,* commenting on Nietzsche's identification with the mythic figure of Dionysius in Greek mythology, says: "Dionysus was the god of the vine, the god of drunken ecstasy and frenzy, who . . . united miraculously in himself the height of culture with the depth of instinct, bringing together the warring opposites that divided Nietzsche himself . . . Dionysus reborn, Nietzsche thought, might become a savior-god for the whole race, which seemed everywhere to show symptoms of fatigue and decline. . . . But Dionysus is a dangerous as well as an ambiguous god. Those in antiquity who meddled with him ended up being torn to pieces. . . . So Dionysus himself, according to the myth, had been torn to pieces by the Titans, those formless powers of the subterranean world who were always at war with the enlightened gods of Olympus. The fate of his god overtook Nietzsche: he too was torn apart by the dark forces of the underworld, succumbing, at the age of 45, to psychosis. It may be a metaphor, but it is certainly not an exaggeration, to say that he perished as a ritual victim slaughtered for the sake of his god. . . . Nevertheless, the victim did not perish in vain; his sacrifice can be an immense lesson to the rest of the tribe if it is willing to learn from him."

In 1899 Nietzsche saw a horse cruelly beaten by its master in the street. From that moment on he fell into hopeless insanity for the last ten years of his life—ironically, not from any wild excess of Dionysian power, but from an attack of the thing he despised the most—pity.

Nietzsche's Personality: Dionysian vs. Apollonian

Some philosophers' personality has little to do with their philosophy (e.g., Aristotle); for others (e.g., Rousseau), it is everything. Nietzsche is clearly in the second class. He himself wrote that **in the end one experiences only oneself,** and: **I have come to realize what every great philosophy up to now has been: the personal confession of its originator, a type of involuntary and unaware memoirs.**

It is impossible to read Nietzsche logically, impersonally, and objectively. He is deliberately provocative, subjective, personal, and poetic rather than logical. In fact, it feels as if he is both shouting angry absurdities in your face and whispering prophetic profundities in your ear, sometimes simultaneously.

Nietzsche's little autobiography, *Ecce Homo,* is a late work, three years before his death, written when psychosis was already taking strong hold of him; yet it can be a key to the whole of Nietzsche. The ego-inflation is deliberate, and the inflated balloon is about to pop. Its chapter titles include **Why I Am So Wise, Why I Am So Clever,** and **Why I Write Such Good Books.** He writes: **I am not a man; I am dynamite.** His self-portrait is clearly at odds with his reality: he was frail, ugly, sick, perpetually suffering, resentful, and angry, starved for ordinary human emotions, and lonely—surely one of the loneliest men who ever lived. We can see Nietzsche himself in the "dwarf" image that occurs in a number of his own writings, especially in his masterpiece *Thus Spake Zarathustra;* and he tried in vain to overcome this dwarf. He called himself **an old artilleryman,** though he never saw combat, and a Don Juan with women, though his only lady friend, Lou Salome, quickly rejected him for his friend Paul Rees; and there is some evidence that he was either impotent or homosexual. His attitude toward women was ambiguous but it certainly was not healthy or happy or welcoming. He wrote: **Are you going to see a woman? Bring a whip.** And still many modern "feminists" adore Nietzsche! Go figure.

The title "Ecce Homo" ("Behold the man") refers to Pontius Pilate's parading the soon-to-be-crucified Christ before the Jews at his trial. Having called himself "the Antichrist" (the title of one of his books), Nietzsche now identifies himself as the new Christ. His last letters, from the asylum, were signed **"The Crucified One."**

But this living in denial was consistent with one of the earliest and most famous ideas of his own philosophy, the contrast and conflict between "the Apollonian" and "the Dionysian." These referred mainly to the contrast between reason and instinct, light and heat, truth and life, which he made famous in *The Birth of Tragedy from the Spirit of Music* (where he applies his "Dionysianism" to art) and *The Use and Abuse of History for Life* (where he applies it to history).

34

These two psychic forces, symbolized as two Greek gods, also could be seen as symbolic versions of the two fundamental forces of life according to Schopenhauer; "idea" and "will." Nietzsche was deeply affected by reading Schopenhauer's *The World as Will and Idea* early in his life. He lastingly imbibed Schopenhauer's atheism and anti-rationalism, but struggled all his life to avoid his cynicism, nihilism, and pessimism. Whether this struggle was successful or unsuccessful divides Nietzsche's interpreters. . . . Although Nietzsche's ideal was the synthesis of these two forces rather than the suppression of either one, yet because of what Nietzsche took to be Apollo's "decadent" triumph over Dionysus in Socrates and in all subsequent Western culture, the first task he devoted himself to was the rebirth of Dionysus; and in practice this often meant an attack on the Apollonian.

Questioning "The Will to Truth"

For the sake of "life," then, "truth" had to be demoted. There is no simpler or surer definition of insanity in theory, and no surer prediction of its presence in practice, than this demotion of truth, the preference for fantasy or even lies over reality, and the subsequent confusion of the objective and subjective worlds. Here is what may well be Nietzsche's most radical idea of all, an idea not one philosopher before him ever dared to toy with, the Pandora's box no one before him had ever dared to open. He called his questioning of **the will to truth** the most dangerous of all questions: **What is the value of this will? . . . Why not rather untruth?** All philosophers had claimed they taught the truth, and questioned the truth of their opponents' teachings, but none had ever questioned this "will to truth" itself, or called it a "prejudice":

ABOUT PHILOSOPHERS' PREJUDICES. The will to truth! That will which is yet to seduce us into many a venture, that famous truthfulness of which all philosophers up to this time have spoken reverently—think what questions this will to truth has posed for us! What strange, wicked, questionable questions! . . . we become suspicious. . . . We asked "What is the value of this will?" Supposing we want truth: *why not rather untruth?* **. . . It may be unbelievable, but it seems to us in the end as though the problem had never yet been posed—as though it were being seen, fixed, above all** *risked,* **for the first time. For there is a risk in posing it—perhaps no greater risk could be found. . . .**

The falseness of a given judgment does not constitute an objection against it, so far as we are concerned. It is perhaps in this respect that our new language sounds strangest. The real question is how far a judgment furthers and maintains life. *(Beyond Good and Evil)*

"Why truth?" is a very strange question, for any possible answer to it *presupposes* "the will to truth." For it says that "The *true* answer to the question 'Why truth?' is . . ."

On what possible foundation can one base that "truth" which is the foundation for everything? It is not a conclusion but a premise, which is either a self-evident and indubitable necessity or a personal choice, a "prejudice"; and what can we say to one who questions that "prejudice"?

But this demand to deny or hide himself from the truth for the sake of "life" does not just appear for no reason in a soul as brilliant as Nietzsche's. It has a cause. And its cause is very clear from his own writings. It is the consequence of the death (i.e., the *murder)* of God. We killed God, said Nietzsche, because we could not bear that He see the truth of our own dwarf, our own dark side. He wrote: **I will now *disprove* the existence of all gods. If there were gods, how could I possibly bear not to be a god? *Consequently,* there are no gods.** Whatever else you say about that passage, it is shatteringly candid.

There is a startlingly similar passage in Sartre's autobiographical *The Words:* "Only once did I have the feeling that He existed. I had been playing with matches and burned a small rug. I was in the process of covering up my crime when suddenly God saw me. I felt His gaze inside my head and on my hands. I whirled about in the bathroom, horribly visible, a live target. Indignation saved me. I flew into a rage against so crude an indiscretion, I blasphemed, I muttered like my grandfather: 'God damn it, God damn it, God damn it.' He never looked at me again."

The Death of God and Its Consequences

If this "death of God" is the deepest source of the rest of Nietzsche's distinctive radical ideas, we must explore it first. What does it mean?

It means not, of course, a biological death, for "God" does not mean a biological being. Nor does it mean that God once actually existed. No atheist believes that. But *faith* in God, and the consequences of that faith, once not only lived but dominated Western civilization, as the sun dominates the solar system. For over a thousand years, civilization was "the God system." It was called "Christendom." What would happen to the solar system if the sun went dark? The "God" whose death Nietzsche announces is the Christian God, of course, but also all others (thus the title of his book *The Twilight of the Idols*—more literally translated as *The Twilight of the Gods),* including not only all religions but also all transcendent, eternal truths, absolute goods, categorical imperatives, Platonic Ideas, and even Aristotelian substances, forms, final causes, and objective order: everything meant by that incredibly rich Greek concept of *logos.* (Today's Nietzscheans, especially Deconstructionists, routinely rail against "logocentrism.") But *logos* means no less than "the nature of things" or "the order of being." Really, for Nietzsche *there is no being.* There is only becoming. And *there is no truth.* There is only lying. Language and reason are inherently self-deceptive. Words are hypocritical masks painted on the face of the Will to Power. Unlike most of those who breezily quote him, Nietzsche actually believed and lived this philosophy, to the bitter end. For them it is a pleasant breeze; for him it was a tornado. For his academic admirers, it is fashionable; for him it was fatal.

Here is the most famous and powerful passage in all of Nietzsche. It is probably the greatest atheist manifesto ever written, by the most brilliant and passionate atheist who ever lived. Notice especially the *consequences* of this event, which Nietzsche calls the greatest of all events in history, the death of God:

The madman.—Have you not heard of that madman who lit a lantern in the bright morning hours, ran to the market-place and cried incessantly: "I am looking for God! I am looking for God!"—As many of those who did not believe in God were standing together there, he excited considerable laughter. Have you lost him then? said one. Did he lose his way like a child? said another. Or is he hiding? Is he afraid of us? Has he gone on a voyage? Or emigrated? —thus they shouted and laughed.

The madman sprang into their midst and pierced them with his glances. "Where has God gone?" he cried. "I shall tell you. *We have killed him*—you and I. We are all his murderers.

"But how have we done this? How were we able to drink up the sea? Who gave us the sponge to wipe away the entire horizon? What did we do when we unchained this earth from its sun? Whither is it moving now? Whither are we moving now? Away from all suns? Are we not perpetually falling? Backward, sideward, forward, in all directions? Is there any up or down left? Are we not wandering as through an infinite nothing? Do we not feel the breath of empty space? Has it not become colder? Is more and more night not coming on all the time? Must not lanterns be lit in the morning? Do we not hear anything yet of the noise of the gravediggers who are burying God? Do we not smell anything yet of God's decomposition?—goods, too, decompose.

"God is dead. God remains dead. And we have killed him. How shall we, the murderers of all murderers, console ourselves? That which was holiest and might-iest of all that the world has yet possessed has bled to death under our knives—who will wipe this blood off us? With what water could we purify ourselves? What fes-tivals of atonement, what sacred games shall we need to invent? Is not the greatness of this deed too great for us? Must we not ourselves become gods simply to seem worthy of it? There has never been a greater deed—and whoever shall be born after us, for the sake of this deed he shall be part of a higher history than all history hith-erto."

Here the madman fell silent and again regarded his listeners; and they, too, were silent and stared at him in astonishment. At last he threw his lantern to the ground and it broke and went out. "I come too early," he said then; "my time has not yet come. This tremendous deed is still on the way, still travelling—it has not yet

reached the ears of men. Lightning and thunder require time, deeds require time after they have been done before they can be seen and heard. This deed is still more distant from them than the most distant stars—*and yet they have done it themselves.*"

It has been related further that on that same day the madman entered divers churches and sang a *requiem aeternam deo.* Led out and quieted, he is said to have retorted each time, "What are these churches now if they are not the tombs and sepulchers of God?" (*The Joyful Wisdom*)

For Nietzsche the death of God is profoundly ambivalent. It is neither merely negative nor merely positive, but both terrifying and exhilarating, like the death of a feared father to a precocious child. Nietzsche actually praises God more powerfully than many believers do by showing the size of His absence. A silhouette can be more striking than a portrait.

The consequences of the death of God go far beyond religion. They include the death of objective truth, which, Nietzsche would likely say, is only "God without a face." He famously wrote: **There are no facts, only interpretations.** Most especially, there are no objective values or ends or goods. And therefore, if there are no objective goods, there are no objective evils: as Dostoyevski said, "If God does not exist, everything is permissible." There is, in fact, no being, no *logos,* nothing that withstands or resists "the hermeneutic of suspicion." Picasso drew the consequence of this "postmodernism" in painting, Giacometti in sculpture, Schoenberg and John Cage in music: chaos replaces cosmos. Not only Exodus 20 (the Ten Commandments, the order of human life) but also Genesis 1 (the order of the cosmos) comes undone. The sweater unravels into a tangle of yarn.

> Humpty Dumpty sat on a wall.
> Humpty Dumpty had a great fall.
> And all the King's horses and all the King's men
> Couldn't put Humpty together again.

The "Superman": *Thus Spake Zarathustra*

This is Nietzsche's masterpiece, and his most poetic book. Perhaps no book ever written contains such a plethora of Jungian archetypes straight out of the collective unconscious. Here is how Nietzsche described the spell of inspiration under which he wrote it: **the feeling that one is utterly out of hand . . . everything occurs quite without volition, as if in an eruption of freedom, independence, power and divinity . . . one loses all perception of what is imagery and simile.** It is put forth as a demonic parody of divine inspiration.

Its central theme is the new man, the "Overman" or "super-man" *(Übermensch),* the man without God or traditional morality. Nietzsche sees modern man as a tightrope walker suspended between the Overman above and ahead and "the Last Man" below and behind. Notice especially, in the following excerpt, the similarity of Nietzsche's "Last Man" to the citizens of Huxley's *Brave New World*—and to our world. We resort to quotation rather than summary once again, for how can one "summarize" a great poem?

I teach you the Overman. **Man is something that shall be overcome. What have you done to overcome him?**

All beings so far have created something beyond themselves; and do you want to be the ebb of this great flood and even go back to the beasts rather than overcome man? What is the ape to man? A laughing-stock or a painful embarrassment. And man shall be just that for the overman: a laughing-stock or a painful embarrassment. You have made your way from worm to man, and much in you is still man. Once you were apes, and even now, too, man is more ape than any ape. . . .

Behold, I teach you the Overman. The Overman is the meaning of the earth. Let your will say: The Overman *shall be* the meaning of the earth. I beseech you, my brothers, *remain faithful to the earth,* and do not believe those who speak to you of otherworldly hopes! Poison-mixers are they, whether they know it or not. Despisers of life are they, decaying and poisoned themselves, of whom the earth is weary; so let them go.

Once, the sin against God was the greatest sin; but God died, and these sinners died with him. To sin against the earth is now the most dreadful thing. . . .

When Zarathustra had spoken these words he beheld the people again and was silent. "There they stand," he said to his heart; "there they laugh. They do not understand me; I am not the mouth for these ears. Must one smash their ears before they learn to listen with their eyes? Must one clatter like kettledrums and preachers of repentance? Or do they believe only the stammerer?

"They have something of which they are proud. What do they call that which makes them proud? Education they call it; it distinguishes them from goatherds. That is why they do not like to hear the word 'contempt' applied to them. Let me then address their pride. Let me speak to them of what is most contemptible: and that is the *Last Man.*"

And thus spoke Zarathustra to the people: "The time has come for man to set himself a goal. The time has come for man to plant the seed of his highest hope. His soil is still rich enough. But one day this soil will be poor and domesticated, and no tall tree will be able to grow in it. Alas, the time is coming when man will no longer shoot the arrow of his longing beyond man, and the string of his bow will have forgotten how to whir!

"I say unto you: one must still have chaos in oneself to be able to give birth to a dancing star. I say unto you: you still have chaos in yourselves.

"Alas, the time is coming when man will no longer give birth to a star. Alas, the time of the most despicable man is coming, he that is no longer able to despise himself. Behold, I show you *the Last Man.*

Is this fantasy? I once assigned Huxley's *Brave New World* to a class of freshmen with no preliminary guidance or explanation, and most of them thought it was not a dystopia but a utopia.

"'What is love? What is creation? What is longing? What is a star?' thus asks the Last Man, and he blinks.

"The earth has become small, and on it hops the last man, who makes everything small. His race is as ineradicable as the flea-beetle; the last man lives longest.

"'We have invented happiness,' say the Last Men, and they blink. . . .

"One still works, for work is a form of entertainment. But one is careful lest the entertainment be too harrowing. One no longer becomes poor or rich: both require too much exertion. Who still wants to rule? Who obey? Both require too much exertion.

"No shepherd and one herd! Everybody wants the same, everybody is the same: whoever feels different goes voluntarily into a madhouse.

"'Formerly, all the world was mad,' say the most refined, and they blink.

"One is clever and knows everything that has ever happened; so there is no end of derision. One still quarrels, but one is soon reconciled—else it might spoil the digestion.

"One has one's little pleasure for the day and one's little pleasure for the night; but one has a regard for health.

"'We have invented happiness,' say the Last Men, and they blink."

Here ended Zarathustra's first speech, which is also called "the Prologue," for at this point he was interrupted by the clamor and delight of the crowd. "Give us this Last Man, O Zarathustra," they shouted. "Turn us into these Last Men!"

Socrates

Kierkegaard and Nietzsche both saw all of Western civilization orbiting around the double stars of Jesus and Socrates. But while they were Kierkegaard's two great heroes, they were Nietzsche's two great villains, or two great tragedies for Western civilization, even though he grudgingly admired the cleverness and posthumous success of both in persuading the world to meekly and sheepishly conform to nonexistent Gods or Goods. Nietzsche, more consistently than anyone else, attacked both halves of the medieval faith-reason synthesis, which could be summarized as a synthesis of Jesus and Socrates.

Nietzsche's charge against Socrates was that he had persuaded mankind to bow down to Reason, of all things, and Reason's highest power was supposedly the power of knowing this highest fiction, this eternal, absolute Good, whether it had a face (as in Christianity) or not (as in Plato). For Nietzsche, **"Reason" is the cause of our falsification of the evidence of the senses. In so far as the senses show becoming, passing away, change, they do not lie. . . . Heraclitus will always be right in this: that 'being' is an** empty fiction. The "apparent" world is the only one; the "real" world has only been *lyingly added...*

(And this "lie" included) **all supreme values ... all the supreme concepts—"that-which-is," "the unconditioned," "the good," "the true," the "perfect"—all that cannot have become ... thus they acquired their stupendous concept "God" ... the last, thinnest, emptiest ... the brain-sick fancies of morbid cobweb-spinners!**

(This) **error has ...** *language* **as a perpetual advocate ... we find ourselves in the midst of a rude fetishism when we call to mind the basic presuppositions of the metaphysics of language—which is to say, of** *reason*. **It is** *this* **which sees everywhere deed and doer; this which believes in will as cause in general; this which believes in the "ego," in the ego as being, in the ego as substance, and which** *projects* **its belief in the ego-substance on to all things—only thus does it** *create* **the concept "thing" ...**

"Reason" in language: oh what a deceitful old woman! I fear we are not getting rid of God because we still believe in grammar. ...

For heaven's sake, do not throw Plato at me ... Plato is a first-rate decadent in style. ... To be attracted to the Platonic dialogue, this horribly self-satisfied and childish kind of dialectic, one must never have read good French writers— Fontenelle, for example. Plato is boring ... so moralistic, so pre-existently Christian—he already takes the concept 'good' for the highest concept ... the culture of the Sophists ... (is) the culture of the realists ... amid the moralistic and idealistic swindles let loose on all sides by the Socratic schools. ... Plato is a coward before reality, consequently he flees into the ideal. ...

Socrates' decadence is suggested ... by the hypertrophy of the logical faculty ... I seek to comprehend what idiosyncrasy begot that Socratic equation of reason, virtue and happiness: that most bizarre of all equations. ...

With Socrates, Greek taste changes in favor of dialectics. What really happened there? Above all, a *noble* **taste is thus vanquished; with dialectics the plebs come to the top ... the philosophers are the decadents of Greek culture, the counter-movement to the ancient, noble taste ... to the value of race, to the authority of descent.**

Everyone says that Nietzsche was not a racist like the Nazis. He was not a *pseudo-scientific* racist, but ...

In one sense Nietzsche's attack on Christianity is a logical consequence of his attack on Plato (though in another, deeper, more existential sense it is the opposite causal order); for he described Christianity as **Platonism for the people.** (Where Kierkegaard interpreted Plato through the lens of Socrates, Nietzsche interpreted Socrates through the lens of Plato.)

The deepest reason Nietzsche despised Socrates will come clear in the next section: Socrates represented "slave morality" instead of "master morality." **Socrates belonged by origin to the lowest rung of the people; Socrates was rabble. We know, we can even still see, how ugly he was** (the pot is calling the kettle black here) **... Ugliness is often**

enough the expression of a stunted development, hampered by cross-breeding.... Before Socrates, dialectical (logical) **manners were disapproved of in polite society.... Whatever needs first to have itself proved to be believed is of little value. Wherever it is still good manners to have authority, and people do not 'reason' but command, the dialectician is a kind of buffoon: he is laughed at, he is not taken seriously. Socrates was the buffoon who** *got himself taken seriously.*

Master Morality vs. Slave Morality

Nietzsche's philosophy of morality is essentially that of Thrasymachus in Plato's "Republic" and Callicles in Plato's "Gorgias." He distinguishes two moralities, "master morality" and "slave morality." "Master morality" is natural and healthy. In it, "good" meant merely "aristocratic rather than plebian, noble rather than vulgar." Its values are heroism in battle, the joy of expressing the "will to power" over inferiors, selfishness, and self-glorification. In "master morality," nothing is forbidden. For "slave morality," by contrast, unselfishness is the supreme value; and selfishness, injustice, cruelty, and hate are forbidden. Thus the values of "slave morality" are not only unnatural and artificial but "decadent." It prizes justice and equality, kindness and charity, and peace rather than war. Nietzsche warns his disciples: **Resist all sentimental weakness. Life is essentially appropriation, injury, conquest of ... the weak, suppression, severity ... and at the least, putting it mildest, exploitation.**

You can see why the Nazis loved Nietzsche. Whether he would have loved them is another question. (Nietzsche was neither an anti-Semite nor a German nationalist.) Mussolini, who was much more of a philosopher than Hitler, was an adoring student of Nietzsche. When they met, Hitler presented him with the collected works of Nietzsche. The Fascists constantly used the Nietzschean slogans of "the will to power," "the triumph of the will," and "the superman." Nietzsche came to be regarded as the voice of Fascist philosophy both by the Fascists and their opponents.

Nietzsche refutes "slave morality" not by argument but by its "genealogy." Thus the title *The Genealogy of Morals*. He says it originated in envy and resentment (Nietzsche uses the French word *ressentiment* to "stick it to" the Germans) against their "natural superiors" on the part of weaker and inferior peoples, the slaves, the sheep, especially the Jews and most of all the Christians. Their resentment led them to invent the unnatural artifice of a universal moral conscience, and "conscience doth make cowards of us all." That is why **the bite of conscience is indecent.** This "slave morality" was similar to the Socratic exaltation of the Apollonian against the Dionysian, of reason and conscience against desire and instinct. The sheep persuaded the wolves to feel guilty about their superiority and to obey the sheep's unnatural ideals like justice and equality, democracy and the common good, compassion and kindness, altruism and love, (which Nietzsche called **the greatest danger)** and to obey the sheep's artificially invented laws like the Ten Commandments or the Golden Rule, which the sheep claimed came from God or

42

"pure reason" and rational duty, as in Kant. (Nietzsche hated Kant almost as much as he hated Socrates and Jesus.)

Another name for Nietzsche's ideal, almost equivalent to "the Overman," is "the Antichrist." (Since Nietzsche called himself "the Antichrist" but never "the Overman," we should probably see "the Antichrist" as the *prophet* of "the Overman.") In his book by that title he sees Christianity as the master heresy, the synthesis of all errors:

I condemn Christianity. I raise up against the Christian Church the most terrible accusations that have ever passed the lips of any accuser. She is, for me, the greatest of all imaginable corruptions . . . it has made a counter-value of every value, a lie of every truth, a perversion of everything that is honest . . . I regard Christianity as the most fatal and seductive lie that has ever yet existed . . . the most repugnant kind of degeneracy that civilization has ever brought into existence. . . . This eternal accusation against Christianity I would inscribe on every wall wheresoever there exists a wall to write it on. I call Christianity the sole great damnation, the sole greatest inner perversion, the sole great revenge instinct in which no means are poisonous enough, stealthy enough, subterranean or petty enough; I call it the only unquenchable infamy of mankind. (Come on, Nietzsche, don't be polite; tell us what you *really* feel.)

Nietzsche admired Darwin's idea of nature as war, as a power struggle producing "the survival of the fittest" at the expense of the unfit and inferior; and he saw this as the basis for the only true, natural morality. Necessarily, then, he condemned the Christian idea of each individual person having the same intrinsic and absolute worth as a deadly, decadent and devolutionary idea, because it impeded evolution's next step: the merciless evolution of man into super-man (Overman).

This step, unlike previous evolutionary steps, would be done by will, not nature; and it would produce not a biologically new race but a new kind of individual, or at most a few of these new individuals. These wolf-men are necessarily at war (spiritually) with the sheep-men, who are the majority. Equality among men always meant leveling down rather than up for Nietzsche; therefore for him there could be **no such thing as a "common good,"** as there had been in all previous social and political philosophies.

The main point of *The Genealogy of Morals* is to deflate the pretentions of morality by exposing its origin in inferiority and resentment. Once we see that morality is not objective, universal, and eternal but an invention of subjective resentment, we are freed from its slavery. And the cure is to transcend this artificial "slave morality" with its dualism of good vs. evil, i.e., to go *Beyond Good and Evil.* (That title is the flip side of the coin, the practical corollary of *The Genealogy of Morals.)* The will of the Overman does not discover or acknowledge good; it creates it in willing it. He does not will it because it is good; it is good simply because he wills it. What Plato's Euthyphro believes about God, Nietzsche believes about man. (So does Sartre.)

This is to exactly and entirely reverse the movement from Kierkegaard's pre-moral or amoral "aesthetic" stage into the "ethical" stage and, above all, the "religious." Nietzsche is almost a perfect negative mirror image of Kierkegaard.

All this is not only philosophical but personal for Nietzsche. He despised ordinary people. He said that **books for common people always smell bad, for the odor of little people clings to them.**

Though Nietzsche's defenders disagree, I see no essential difference between this and Nazi morality if we omit their pseudo-scientific racism. After Nietzsche died, his sister Elizabeth, a rabid German nationalist and anti-Semite, produced a Nazi version of Nietzsche, published as *The Will To Power,* by cutting out all the passages inconvenient to Nazi propaganda. What remained, however, was indeed Nietzsche, and it includes plenty of passages that glorify the war of the strong against the weak. The potential Overman must free himself from all weakness, most especially the weakness of Christian morality with its condemnation of egotism and its cultivation of charity. Since this Christian morality is the exact opposite of Nietzsche's morality, his term for himself, "The Antichrist," is quite accurate.

The Eternal Return

We have seen that there is for Nietzsche no being, only becoming. But Nietzsche thought he had discovered the pattern or map of this becoming in the idea of **the eternal return of the same.** This seemed to follow from two premises. (1) Matter is only finite, and therefore the number of possible universes is only finite. (2) But since there is no God, no Creator, and no moment of creation, time is infinite. Thus there must have been enough time for every possible universe to have come into existence already, in fact an infinite number of times, including ones containing the "last man" and the "overman" and Nietzsche himself. Everything that ever happened has happened before and will happen again.

In the face of such a meaningless and hopeless future, it takes what Nietzsche mislabeled as supreme "courage" to affirm life despite its meaninglessness. In Nietzsche, passion has conquered reason. Life has prevailed over truth, Dionysus over Apollo.

Nietzsche naively thought this was psychologically possible. Was his psychosis the penalty he paid for this naïveté?

Evaluation

I have written imaginary dialogs in which Socrates converses with Machiavelli, Descartes, Hume, Kant, Marx, Sartre, Freud, and Kierkegaard, and I tried to write one with Nietzsche, but it proved quite impossible. For Socrates is logic on two legs, but Nietzsche is a centipede on fire. He is the most difficult of all philosophers to evaluate logically. For he impugns the very enterprise of logical argument as "decadent dialectics," which he says were invented by Socrates out of his resentment at his own ugliness and weakness in order to take revenge on the "noble," wolfish Sophists by getting them to play his "decadent," sheepish game of reason rather than theirs—and, of course, Socrates always wins at that game. Nietzsche denies the most basic presuppositions of logical evaluation: the reality of objective truth, the "will to truth," and the rules of fairness.

He offers no *evidence* for his position—deliberately. His practice is consistent with his belief that life is power, not dialectics. The essence of life is the will to power, and therefore Nietzsche uses words as weapons, not as labels, for the sake of their power, not their truth. As Nietzsche's Deconstructionist disciples say, words are not "intentional" signs pointing to any objective truth; the "text" does not intend or mean "the world" but *constructs* the world. Words are not labels on things telling us what is inside or beyond the label. Words are not signs but things. As Archibald MacLeish wrote, "A poem should be palpable and mute/ Like globed fruit. / A poem should not mean but be." Words are not maps to guide us to real places; they are little dynamite sticks that speakers or writers make to explode in your mind. It's all "the will to power."

Unfortunately for Nietzsche, it was his own mind that was destroyed by the dynamite. The most fateful question for Western civilization is whether it will follow in his footsteps. "Socrates vs. the Sophists," "Christ vs. Antichrist"—those options are not "ancient" or "medieval," they are quintessentially modern.

Nietzsche is not popular among farmers, but he is very popular among philosophers. In fact Nietzsche is the single most popular philosopher in the Western world today among those who write doctoral dissertations, essays, and scholarly articles. Let us call that Fact #1. Fact #2 is that in the Western world there were ten times as many farmers as philosophers 100 years ago, but there are now ten times as many philosophers as farmers. What conclusion about the future of our civilization seems to follow from juxtaposing these two facts?

Selected Bibliography:

"Nietzsche" chapter in William Barrett's *Irrational Man*
Nietzsche, *Thus Spake Zarathustra*; *The Twilight of the Idols*

75. Martin Heidegger (1889–1976)

For many serious thinkers who read him, as for most of his enthusiastic students who heard him, Heidegger is the most profound philosopher of the century, perhaps of all time. No twentieth-century thinker has been more influential among continental philosophers. But for many other equally serious thinkers, especially English-speaking "analytic" or scientific philosophers, Heidegger is a great fake, a peddler of pretentious nonsense or, worse, dangerous pseudo-mysticism.

The best evidence for both opinions is his own writings, rather than any "explanation" of them. So I decided to introduce this controversial figure by plunging the reader directly into two excerpts from his own words.

The first is about the single question that haunted all his writings, the question of Being. It is perhaps the greatest of all questions; and even if Heidegger has no adequate answer to it, he could be seen as a profound and passionately single-minded questioner like Socrates, though with metaphysical rather than ethical interests.

The second set of writings is about a positive "existential" answer that Heidegger gave in his own life as well as in his thoughts and writings, an answer which nearly all readers will regard as one of the worst answers ever given. It is not an overt answer to the question "What is Being?" but to questions closely associated with it for Heidegger, like "What is authenticity?" and "What is truth?" and "What is the destiny of Western civilization?" The answer was Nazism. Heidegger is the only major philosopher who was an enthusiastic, Hitler-loving member of the Nazi party. And even after the War, he never uttered the dreaded W-word and said "I was wrong." The coexistence of these two things in the same man is more than puzzling. It is astonishing.

The first excerpt is from ch. 1 of *Introduction to Metaphysics,* "The Fundamental Question of Metaphysics."

Why are there beings at all instead of nothing? That is the question.

. . . it is not the first question in the chronological sense. Individuals as well as peoples ask many questions in the course of their historical passage through time . . . before they run into the question "Why are there beings at all instead of nothing?" Many never run into this question at all, if running into the question means not only hearing and reading the interrogative sentence as uttered, but asking the question, that is, taking a stand on it, posing it, compelling oneself into the state of this questioning.

And yet, we are each touched once, maybe even now and then, by the concealed power of this question, without properly grasping what is happening to us. In great despair, for example, when all weight tends to dwindle away from things and the

sense of things grows dark, the question looms. Perhaps it strikes only once, like the muffled tolling of a bell that resounds into Dasein (human existing, human life) and gradually fades away. The question is there in heartfelt joy, for then all things are transformed and surround us as if for the first time, as if it were easier to grasp that they were not, rather than that they are, and are as they are. The question is there in a spell of boredom, when we are equally distant from despair and joy, but when the stubborn ordinariness of beings lays open a wasteland in which it makes no difference to us whether beings are or are not—and then, in a distinctive form, the question resonates once again: Why are there beings at all rather than nothing? . . .

(When we ask about Being,) we are now asking about something that we hardly grasp, something that is now no more than the sound of a word for us, and that puts us in danger of falling victim to the mere idolization of words . . . we are not able to lay hold of the *Being of* beings directly and expressly. . . .

A few examples should help. Over there, on the other side of the street, stands the high school building. A being. We can scour every side of the building from the outside, roam through the inside from basement to attic, and note everything that can be found there: hallways, stairs, classrooms, and their furnishings. Everywhere we find beings, in a very definite order. Where now is the Being of this high school? It *is,* after all. The building *is.* The Being of this being belongs to it if anything does, and nevertheless we do not find this Being within the being.

Moreover, Being does not consist in our observing beings. The building stands there even if we do not observe it. We can come across it only because it already *is.* . . .

A distant mountain range under a vast sky—such a thing "is." What does its Being consist in? When and to whom does it reveal itself? To the hiker who enjoys the landscape, or to the peasant who makes his daily living from it and in it, or to the meteorologist who has to give a weather report? Who among them lays hold of Being? All and none. Or do these people only lay hold of particular aspects of the mountain range under the vast sky, not the mountain range itself as it "is," not what its real Being consists in? Who can lay hold of this? Or is it nonsensical . . . to ask about what is in itself, behind those aspects? Does Being lie in the aspects? . . .

A painting by Van Gogh: a pair of sturdy peasant shoes, nothing else. The picture really represents nothing. Yet you are alone at once with what *is* there, as if you yourself were heading homeward from the field on a late autumn evening, tired, with your hoe, as the last potato fires smolder out. What is the being here? The canvas? The brushstrokes? The patches of color?

In everything we have mentioned, what is the Being of beings? . . . Everything we have mentioned *is,* after all, and nevertheless, if we want to lay hold of Being it is always as if we were reaching into a void. . . . So in the end (it seems) Nietzsche is entirely right when he calls the "highest concepts" such as Being "the final wisp of evaporating reality. . . . In fact, nothing up to now has been more naively persuasive than the error of Being." (*Twilight of the Idols*)

Does Nietzsche speak the truth? Or is he himself only the final victim of a long-standing errancy and neglect, but as this victim the unrecognized witness to a new necessity?

Is it Being's fault that Being is so confused, and is it the fault of the word that it remains so empty? Or is it our fault, because in all our bustling and chasing after beings, we have nevertheless fallen out of Being? What if the fault is not our own, we of today, nor that of our immediate or most distant forebears, but rather is based in a happening that runs through Western history from the inception onward, a happening that the eyes of all historians will never reach, but which nevertheless happens—formerly, today, and in the future? What if it were possible that human beings, that peoples in their greatest machinations and exploits, have a relation to beings but have long since fallen out of Being, without knowing it, and what if this were the innermost and most powerful ground of their decline?

There is something compelling about Heidegger's questioning, and something canny about his focus on Nietzsche. Surely our Nietzschean "will to power" over beings, manifested by our spectacular technological success, is a leading cause (and effect) of our forgetfulness of Being.

Perhaps that was the connection between Heidegger's fascination with Nietzsche and his fascination with Nazism. In this same book, *Introduction to Metaphysics,* published in 1953, Heidegger repeated without retraction what he had written in 1935 in the original lecture course that this book was taken from, praising **the inner truth and greatness of this movement** (National Socialism) and then adding the parenthetical explanation **(namely, the encounter between global technology and modern humanity).** Perhaps Heidegger meant "greatness" to refer not to great *goodness* but to great *tragedy.* He clearly meant to juxtapose Nazism and Western civilization in general, and not to allow us to use Nazism as our scapegoat and escape the hidden common sources of both its culture and our own. For Hitler's politicization of the Nietzschean "will to power" and our own technological "conquest of nature" surely have connecting underground tunnels. A democratic "soft totalitarianism" (to steal a term from De Tocqueville) is surely preferable to a Nazi hard one; yet both are totalitarianisms that worship power.

Even if this is Heidegger's point, and even if it is both profound and true, it is impossible to explain away or excuse what Heidegger publicly said in 1933:

The National Socialist Revolution is not simply the taking of power in the state by one party from another, but brings a complete revolution of our German existence. . . .

Doctrine and "ideas" shall no longer govern your existence. The Fuehrer himself, and only he, is the current and future reality of Germany, and his word is your law. . . .

Now there is a sharp battle to be fought in the spirit of National Socialism, which must not stifle on account of humanistic, Christian notions that hold us down. . . .

We first understand the glory and the greatness of the Hitler revolution when

we carry implanted deep within us this reflection: **Everything that is great is in the midst of the storm.** . . .

Danger never came of working for the State, but only from indifference and resistance. . . .

There exists only one single German "way of life" . . . **The lame, the complacent, the halfhearted will go into the Hitler Labor Service.** . . .

. . . **through the National Socialist State our entire German reality has been altered, and that means altering all our previous ideas and thinking too. The words "knowledge" and "scholarship" have acquired a different meaning.** . . .

The student body of the University of Freiburg announces that it is determined to carry the fight against Jewish-Marxist undermining of Germany to the bitter end, to the complete annihilation of the foe. The public burning of Jewish-Marxist writings on May 10, 1933, served as a symbol of this fight. Germans, rally to this fight! Make your participation public too. From the publishers and bookstores send us all books and writings that deserve burning. . . . **The fire of destruction is to us like a blazing up of the German spirit.** . . .

Would Nietzsche be scandalized at this? At National Socialism?

Would he not be more scandalized at "the Last Man," and at the Brave New World that we have chosen as its alternative?

Is there a third option? There has to be.

If so, does it have something to do with our relationship with Being? Necessarily.

If so, cannot Heidegger, like Nietzsche, help us to see this? Perhaps. Let's look.

Heidegger's Project

Rarely has any philosopher been more passionately single-minded than Heidegger. Everything he wrote is about one thing—or perhaps two things: Being, and man's estrangement from Being. He wrote: **To think is to confine oneself to a single thought that one day stands still like a star in the world's sky.**

This is one of many similarities between this "atheist" (or, perhaps, agnostic) and passionate theists. If we substitute "God" for "Being" (something Heidegger explicitly forbade us to do), we almost have St. Paul, Augustine, or Kierkegaard. Just as the primal sin for theists is idolatry, the substitution of *a* god—any god—for God—which is the violation of the very first commandment—so the primal sin of philosophy for Heidegger is the reduction of Being to beings, and the reduction of thinking-of-Being (which is rare and difficult) to thinking-about-beings (which is common and easy).

And this reduction began, according to Heidegger, with Socrates and Plato. (Significantly, Nietzsche too focused on Socrates as the primary agent of the philosophical equivalent of the Fall of Man.) This happened when Reason replaced Thinking: **Thinking only begins at the point where we have come to know that Reason, glorified for centuries, is the most obstinate adversary of thinking.** Reason's contents and objects are concepts, propositions, and arguments. These are excellent tools for knowing and manipulating beings. But Heidegger insists that Being itself cannot be reached by any of them.

This attack on Rationalism is not a form of Irrationalism, however, like Rousseau's, or Hume's emotive theory of morality, or Nietzschean voluntarism. Irrationalism and Rationalism share a common error: the reduction of thinking to Reason (and perhaps also the reduction of Reason to *reasoning,* or at least conceptualizing). Heidegger does not suggest abandoning thinking for intuition, sentiment, will, or emotion, but a more fundamental and primordial kind of thinking, out of which all these other, more "rational" alternatives, arose in our history, especially with the Greeks.

Since Western man has reduced Being to beings, according to Heidegger, he has lived increasingly in a "will to power" relationship with these beings. But one cannot have this "will to power" relationship to Being, only to beings. What would be our alternative fundamental relationship to Being? What kind of thinking is Heidegger calling for, in order to think Being? In the title of a suggestive dialog (translated into English as "Discourse on Thinking"), he calls it **Gelassenheit**—literally, "releasement," letting-be, letting Being be. This is the polar opposite to "the will to power." It is the open palm rather than the closed fist—a kind of surrender, or "islam." That word also means "peace." It is cognate to "shalom."

Thus Heidegger is often interpreted as turning to an Oriental, as opposed to an Occidental, metaphysic. What he means by "Being" is at least very similar to what Lao Tzu means by "Tao" in the *Tao Te Ching.* A student once saw Heidegger reading a book by D. T. Suzuki, who first introduced the West to Zen Buddhism, and Heidegger reportedly said to him, "If I understand this man correctly, he is saying what I've been trying to say about Being in all my writings." Even if the story is mythical, it may be an illuminating and appropriate myth. It is no accident that ever since the end of World War II Japanese students have been more interested in Heidegger than any other Western philosopher. And it is certainly no accident that both rational philosophy and science arose mainly in the West, not in the East. Nor can this be labeled a genetic accident or a simple superiority of the Western mind.

Thus Heidegger offers us a "regressive" theory of history, as we find in Genesis and in all the world's myths, rather than a typically modern "progressive" one, as in all thinkers who take science as their touchstone. The "Fall of Being" in Heidegger parallels the Fall of Man in Genesis. Heidegger takes very seriously the pre-Socratic thinkers, especially Parmenides and Heraclitus, and the poets, ancient and modern (especially Hölderlin, who was also a favorite of Nietzsche's), as being closer to Being than "rational" philosophers. Those who deride pre-Socratic philosophers as "primitive," Heidegger says, **forget that what is under discussion is philosophy, one of man's few great achievements. But what is great can only begin great.**

Heidegger's first attempt to recapture Being from the "forgetfulness of Being" caused by the philosophers was his most famous work, *Being and Time,* in which he tried to find a path to Being by mapping the **existentialia,** the basic categories or structures of human existence. He sharply distinguishes human existence (which he calls **Dasein,** "being-there") and its categories, from beings in the universe **("Seiendes")** and their categories; and he maintains that the Greek philosophers who laid the foundations for future Western thought, especially Aristotle, failed to make that distinction. Heidegger argues that the exploration of **Dasein** should be a more adequate path to **Sein** (Being itself) since Dasein is the only being in the universe for whom Being is an issue. And he tries to do this mapping by using the method of phenomenology invented by his mentor Husserl. (See ch. 91.)

But after writing the first half of *Being and Time,* he pronounced the project a failure and left it unfinished, turning in his later works to a more direct and immediate method, one that might be called "poetic" or perhaps even "mystical." This "turn" ("Kehre") in Heidegger is so sharp that scholars sometimes distinguish "Heidegger I" from "Heidegger II" as if they were almost two different persons.

It is clear that there is a parallel or analogy (but not an identity) between Heidegger's triad of fundamental metaphysical terms and the three fundamental realities of traditional theism. For theism there is (1) God, the Being greater than man, (2) man, and (3) the material universe, the beings lesser than man. For Heidegger there is (1) *Sein* (Being itself, Existence itself), (2) *Dasein* (Being-there, Being-in-the-world, human existing, the human mode of being, what Kierkegaard called "subjectivity" (but not subjectivism)), and (3) *Seiendes* (beings, things, entities, objects). These correspond to (but are not to be identical with) God, man, and the universe. Heidegger studiously avoids using either the word "God" or even the word "man." (He uses "Dasein" instead.) Why? Because they are rational concepts, which are appropriate only for objects, entities, things in the universe. And neither God nor man nor the universe itself, for that matter, are *things* in the universe like rocks or rabbits.

But *What Is* Being?

Our very language in asking that question reveals why we have no answer to it. "What is it?" was the great Socratic-Platonic question, and it was the foundation of a great thing: rational, logical Western philosophy, and the science that is its spinoff, and the technology that is science's spinoff. But the price we paid for this great thing was the forgetfulness of another great thing, which for Heidegger was an even greater thing, the thing that is *not* any kind of "thing" at all, namely Being. The question "What is it?" assumes two things: ontologically it assumes an "it," *a* being, a thing with a definable essence; and epistemologically it assumes a "what," i.e., a concept that reveals the essence or definable nature of this "it." But Being does not reveal itself through a concept.

It does reveal itself, however, though in different ways. For instance, see Heidegger's three existential "moods" in the third paragraph of *Introduction to Metaphysics* above, "The Fundamental Question of Metaphysics."

Being is not a Platonic Form or essence like Justice, or even The Good. Each of the Platonic dialogs seeks to grasp and define one of the Forms. But Being is not a Platonic Form; and when Plato comes to write a dialog about Being (the "Parmenides") his dramatic art fails, for the only time in the Platonic dialogs, as does his fictional Socrates. In this dialog it is Parmenides who instructs Socrates rather than vice versa.

One way of approaching Heidegger's central point is a grammatical clue. "Being" in English is a participle, which can be used both as a noun and as a verb. Nouns designate things, entities, with clear definitions. Verbs are different. They designate acts. Being, or existence, can be treated either as a noun or as a verb, as a fact or as an act, as essence or as existence (or, rather, the act of existing). Heidegger's point is that ever since Plato we have focused on the first and forgotten the second. We have reduced Being to what is common to all facts, and forgotten that it is the most distinctive of all acts. The first is the most abstract of all concepts, the second is more concrete than any concept. We live it; we exist it; we are it (or it is us); we are immersed in it. We do not understand it precisely because we are not set apart from it, as we are set apart from things and from the concepts we use to know things. Perhaps the best word for it would be "presence." It is a "mystery" rather than a "problem." (See Marcel, ch. 77.)

Heidegger apparently did not know the Gilsonian, "existential" interpretation of Aquinas's metaphysics, which centers on exactly what Heidegger says we have all forgotten: *esse,* the very act of existing. But, then, according to Gilson, nearly all Thomists forgot it too! (See ch. 96.)

The Phenomenology of *Dasein* in *Being and Time*

The phenomenological method Heidegger used In *Being and Time* meant, for its inventor Husserl, an attempt at a purely descriptive rather than explanatory, argumentative, or evaluative analysis of what is immediately given to us in common experience, without any assumptions or preconceptions or hypotheses. Husserl's motto was: "to the things themselves." Even the question of whether these objects of experience were noumenal or phenomenal, as Kant would say, i.e., independent of or dependent on our experience, objective or subjective, was to be "bracketed." Neither the pre-Kantian ("realist") nor the post-Kantian ("idealist") epistemological answer was to be either assumed or proved by this purely phenomenological analysis. Thus both opponents and proponents of Kant's "Copernican Revolution in philosophy" could equally participate in phenomenological analysis.

Phenomenology involves a more primordial notion of Truth than "the correctness of a proposition." Heidegger blames Plato for forgetting this primordial kind of Truth and starting philosophy on the road to Rationalism. In light of works like the "Symposium," the "Phaedrus," and the "Seventh Letter," all of which could almost be called mystical, that critique seems almost as unfair as Nietzsche's critique of Socrates.

Always alert to hidden wisdoms in words, Heidegger makes much of the fact that the Greek word for "truth" is *aletheia,* literally "unhiddenness" or "revelation," or "not-forgetfulness." (The river *Lethe* was the River of Forgetfulness in Greek mythology.) In Plato's *Meno,* truth is known by "remembering," or "recollection," which seems to be something like Jung's "collective unconscious." For *aletheia* means also

Whether or not Heidegger is right in blaming Plato for forgetting this more primordial and preconceptual and perhaps unconscious notion of truth, the notion allows Heidegger to understand the "truth" of a work of art, or of a fateful event like Caesar's crossing of the Rubicon—or, perhaps, Hitler's assumption of power and transformation of German life. Heidegger, like Hegel, had a propensity to see not only the hand of Fate but the historical revelation of Being in contingent historical events, somewhat as Jews and Christians see the hand of God revealed in history. Heidegger went to seminary, after all, and wrote his doctoral dissertation on Duns Scotus. Ex-Christians tend to use many hidden Christian categories and assumptions.

Heidegger tried to apply his phenomenological method to ordinary human existing, or be-ing-in-the-world, or human living. He called it "Dasein" (literally, "being-there"), but we might call it "life." But it is not "life" in a biological, scientific, objective sense, because we are not objects but subjects. This is why Heidegger does not use the term "man" at all.

Dasein is always individual **(in each case *mine*).** It is not public and impersonal **(Das Man).** And it is intrinsically finite: its being is a **being-toward-death (Sein-zum-Tode).** This notion of "being-towards death" is the most well-known and popular "existentialist" aspect of Heidegger's thought. It means that death is not merely a future event but a present orientation. "They give birth astride a grave," writes Samuel Beckett in "Waiting for Godot." The best way to see Heidegger's point about death is to read Tolstoy's little masterpiece "The Death of Ivan Ilyitch," and to note that Ivan's surprise and incomprehension at his own mortality mirrors that of Western civilization.

Dasein is **in each case mine,** but it is more like a *field* than a *thing*: a field of consciousness—yet not primarily intellectual, speculative, theoretical consciousness but personal "care" **(Sorge)** and concern. Think of Einstein's Relativity Theory with its "field theory of matter" as opposed to the Newtonian notion of a material thing as existing only within its surface boundaries. Now apply this to human consciousness rather than matter. We are whatever we find our identity in, and we find our identity in whatever we identify with, i.e., whatever we care about. A two-year-old whose name is Peter and who "identifies" with his parents, when asked where Peter is, might point at Daddy or Mommy, until he is corrected, i.e., until he is taught to forget the field of Be-ing ("Dasein") and focus on beings and their clear distinctions from each other. He has to unlearn this earlier consciousness of Being as a field in which he is immersed, and replace it with the consciousness that lets him cope conceptually with the objects and other persons in the world. (one might use the concepts of "ground" and "figure" in Gestalt psychology as an analogy.) Thus he comes to see the limits of his identity no longer as the limits of his care, which are dynamic and shifting, but of his epidermis, if he is materialistic, or of his concepts, if he is rationalistic. In contrast, "Dasein" is ecstatic, always beyond-itself, always into-something. It is "intentional" in a more than merely intellectual way.

Heidegger lists three "existentialia" or structures of "Dasein," all of which reveal Being itself ("Sein"), or are about Being: (1) mood, or feeling, (2) understanding, and (3) speech, or language. Mood is not merely subjective; it permeates one's whole world. Understanding is not merely conceptual: it is the reception of the whole world, as it reveals itself as soon as we open our mind and our eyes every morning. And language is **the house of Being,** not merely a means of manipulating and communicating things: **words and language are not wrappings in which things are packed for the commerce of those who write and speak. It is in words and language that things first come into being and are. For this reason the misuse of language in idle talk, in slogans and phrases, destroys our authentic relation to things.** Confucius said something quite similar about the importance of language: see Vol. I, ch. 5.

Heidegger's theory of language is a path to his thinking of Being. All language begins in listening, in silence. only out of silence can speech emerge. When we silently listen to the world, we "hear" not only things (beings) but also the "background energy," so to speak, of Being. But we hear this only when we silence all other noise. Silence is not just negative. Silence can be the profoundest language between friends or lovers. And thoughtful silence is the only language that can hear Being. (We might call this Heidegger's Oriental orientation.) It is "letting-be," or letting Being be. It is "Gelassenheit," "releasement" of our ordinary cares and concerns about things.

The very method of phenomenology is more typically Oriental than Occidental in that it is psychologically the opposite of the Nietzschean Will to Power, whether this power over the object is theoretical (using the tool of concepts and propositions to "conquer" the object mentally) or practical (technological). It attempts simply to let its object of attention be, letting it reveal itself. *Being and Time* is the result of applying this method to "Dasein." But the analysis of "Dasein" was not Heidegger's end, only his means. His end was applying it to Being itself, and he confessed that he did not attain that end, at least in *Being and Time.*

Thus Heidegger left his masterpiece unfinished. One could compare this to Kierkegaard's point that since "existence is not a system," the only faithful expression of it is not, as in Hegel, its inclusion in a system but the very absence of a system. It is even a little reminiscent of Thomas Aquinas's refusal to finish the *Summa* because compared with what he saw in mystical experience all he had written seemed to him only "straw." Is it too fanciful to wonder whether perhaps Heidegger so thirsted for the vision of the God that St. Thomas saw that he fastened onto the first interesting idol that appeared on his empty horizon, the pseudo-Overman called Hitler?

It is certainly significant that Heidegger never wrote about ethics, the division of philosophy that most deeply affects most people's lives, especially when faced with choices like Nazism. The only other great philosopher who never wrote about ethics was Hegel. And Hegel, like Heidegger, though from a remoter historical distance, also enthusiastically embraced a kind of German nationalism and even totalitarianism (see ch. 67).

Heidegger's philosophy is in a sense deeply religious. It is often described as a holy temple waiting for a new god. This, together with his lack of an ethics, could help explain why he welcomed Hitler as the new god, of course. But the lack of an ethics could also explain why he remained outside religion all his life despite the strong parallels between God and Being, his one philosophical obsession. For, as Kierkegaard showed with his three "stages on life's way," the ethical is the necessary preliminary to the religious. Heidegger remained in what Kierkegaard would call the aesthetic stage, an intellectual aesthete—which is how Kierkegaard described Hegel. There is a kinship here between Heidegger and Hegel as well as between Heidegger and Nietzsche.

Selected Bibliography:

Heidegger, *Introduction to Metaphysics*, ch. 1
Discourse on Thinking
William Barrett, *What Is Existentialism?*

76. Jean-Paul Sartre (1905–1980)

Life and character

The historian Paul Johnson says: "Certainly no philosopher this (20th) century has had so direct an impact on the minds and attitudes of so many human beings, especially young people, all over the world." Yet the thought of no major philosopher has ever been so nihilistic, pessimistic, and insulting to the dignity of mankind. (What conclusion do you come to when you put those two premises together?)

Like many philosophers, Sartre was a child genius. He was a totally "spoiled" only child. His father died when he was one, and his mother doted on him. (He said of his father that **If he had lived, my father would have laid down on me and crushed me. Fortunately, he died young.**) His mother was there only **to wait on me. . . . My mother was mine. . . . There was no question of rebelling since no one else's whim ever claimed to be my law.** His definition of **progress** was **that long and arduous road which led to myself.** When he became a schoolteacher he used the same philosophy with his students: total permissiveness, no grades, no tests, no rules, no responsibilities.

His writing style is powerful, clear, and remarkably dexterous. His whole life was words. Thus the title of his autobiography was "The Words." He read 300 books a year. He wrote millions of words: e.g., a 700-page defense of a public thief and liar *(Genet),* which is a celebration of incoherence and antinomianism. His conversations were uninterrupted and uninterruptable. If you left the room in the middle of one, he did not notice, and went on talking.

He was short (5'2"), frog-faced, ugly, and with a grotesque-looking crooked eye. He was habitually dirty and seldom bathed. He wrote that he became a seducer **to get rid of the burden of my ugliness.** Like Rousseau, he picked quarrels with all the men he ever met, including Camus, whose good looks, honesty, and moral common sense he envied, and drove them away if they dared argue with him, as most women did not. Women fawned on him, and he seduced most of his students when he taught school. At his funeral, 50,000 adoring young people, mostly women, followed his body to his grave, one of them falling onto his coffin. (Another parallel to Rousseau. There are many.)

World War II made Sartre famous. He had no interest in the rise of Hitler or in politics until anti-anti-Communism became fashionable among the young radical Left, after the War. He spent the war teaching and writing philosophy in Paris, under the approving eyes of the occupying Nazi censors. He wrote not a word and lifted not a finger to help the Jews. Yet he later wrote stirring and heroic things about the Resistance, calling them "we." After the War he joined the Communist Party and extolled "the proletariat," although, like

Marx, he never personally knew one proletarian nor made any effort to. Visiting Stalin's Russia in 1954, he extolled it: **There is total freedom of criticism in the USSR.** Asked why citizens were forbidden to travel, he explained that no one had any desire to leave their paradise. He was not an idiot, he was a liar, and he freely admitted it years later.

The only civilizations he hated were Europe and America, which he compared to the Nazis. He extolled violence and terrorism. He encouraged Blacks to **shoot down a European.** He had himself photographed with many African and Asian dictators, called Castro's Cuba **a direct democracy** and praised Mao Zedong, the greatest mass murderer in history. In 1970 he joined a French movement called Proletarian Left which tried to export Mao's violent Cultural Revolution to Europe. Pol Pot's genocide of about a third of all Cambodia's citizens was inspired by Sartre's lectures in Paris, which were attended by a small group of Cambodian intellectuals who called themselves "The Higher Organization." They had absorbed Sartre's philosophy in France and, unlike Sartre himself, transferred it to the real world by action in Cambodia's "killing fields." Ideas have consequences. Genocide is one of them.

"No Exit" was the play that made Sartre and his "existentialism" suddenly and passionately famous, in 1944. The word "existentialism" was coined by the Press, but Sartre co-opted it. Once he did, most of the other philosophers whom the world classified as existentialists publicly announced that they were *not* existentialists, including Heidegger, Jaspers, and Marcel.

Sartre was wildly popular in France, especially among the young. Mobs attended his abstract, technical lectures. Women fainted. Furniture was smashed. The Press loved it, and him.

His lifelong mistress, Simone de Beauvoir, was the author of the early "feminist" manifesto *The Second Sex.* It is a screed against everything feminine. Simone let herself be the object of Sartre's lifelong emotional abuse, infidelities, lies, deceptions, and insults. He bragged to her of his sexual conquests of many other women. He secretly proposed marriage to other girls, and he legally adopted one of his mistresses and left to her, not to Simone, all his money. Yet Simone adored him, and provided him with sexual and emotional victims from among her own students, herself as the first among them. What can one say? Perhaps only the French can understand the French.

One of his biographers estimates that his daily intake amounted to a quart of alcohol, two packs of cigarettes, several pipes, 200 mg. of amphetamines, 15 grams of aspirin, several grams of barbiturates, plus large quantities of coffee and tea.

A thinker's thoughts are not reducible to his character. If we discovered that Einstein was a secret cannibal or a Nazi spy, that would not prove that E did not equal MC squared. But philosophers are related to their philosophies differently than scientists are related to their sciences. Philosophies—especially "existential" philosophies—are about human existence, human life. They are proved—or disproved—not in equations but in life. These personal facts, therefore, are not just muckraking gossip but relevant *data* in understanding and evaluating Sartre's philosophy.

"Nausea" and "Absurdity"

The central insight, vision, or "big idea" that animates all of Sartre, according to his own writings, is what he calls "absurdity" or "the absurd." It is the stunningly simple point that the answer to the great and universal philosophical question "What is the meaning of life?" is: "Nothing." The meaning of life is nothing but the meanings and values we freely and arbitrarily choose to give it. And all these meanings are unjustifiable by anything other than our own free choice to invent them. (Compare Justice Anthony Kennedy's "mystery" passage in *Casey* v. *Planned Parenthood.)*

Sartre could be called a "nihilist" or "nothing-ist." Not that he believes that nothing *exists,* which is absurd and self-contradictory. (Cf. Descartes' simple and obvious argument "I think, therefore I exist.") But his main point is that there is no real meaning or purpose, no *logos,* to human life. Sartre practiced what he preached: that life is only speaking, not listening.

This fundamental point is expressed in two ways: (1) immediately, imaginatively, intuitively and affectively, with concrete images, in his fiction, especially his novel *Nausea (La Nausee),* and (2) conceptually and rationally, especially in his philosophical analysis of the relation between ***ens-pour-soi*, being-for-itself,** or human existence, and ***ens-en-soi*, being-in-itself,** or the being of objects. What is lacking is any "being itself" to unify the two modes of being in any common field. There is only being-for-itself versus being-in-itself; *there is no Being.*

We begin with the intuitive imagery. Roquentin, the anti-hero protagonist of *Nausea,* is contemplating the irrationality of a knobby tree root

It was useless to repeat to myself: This is a root. It did not click in my mind. Its function did not explain anything. . . . The function explained roots in general, but this particular root, with its color, its shape, its arrested movement, was beneath all explanation. Every one of its qualities leaked from it a little, overflowed, became partly solid, became almost a thing; every one of them was unnecessary in a root.

This contingency and inexplicability applies not only to the being of objects ("being-in-itself") but also to "being-for-itself," the being of human subjects:

There we were, the whole lot of us, awkward, embarrassed by our own existence, having no reason to be here rather than there;[7] confused, vaguely restless, feeling superfluous to one another. Superfluity was the only relationship I could establish . . . I thought vaguely of doing away with myself, to do away with at least one off

---

7 It is instructive to contrast Pascal's interpretation of and reaction to the same experience: see Vol. III, 51, par. 4.

these superfluous existences. But my death—my corpse, my blood poured out on this gravel, among these plants, in this smiling garden—would have been superfluous as well. I was superfluous to all eternity.

The more emotional word for this is "nausea." The more intellectual word is "absurdity," or meaninglessness. But even this abstract concept is rooted in a feeling so concrete that it seems like a *thing:*

Absurdity was not an idea in my head nor the sound of a voice, it was this long, dead, wooden snake curled up at my feet, snake or claw or talon or root, it was all the same. Without formulating anything I knew that I had at last found the clue to my existence, to my nausea, to my life. And indeed, everything I have ever grasped since that moment comes back to this fundamental absurdity.

To those who are tempted to take an attitude of patronizing pity to Sartre, dismissing this "nausea" as nothing more than "unhealthy-minded" personal depression, William Barrett gives a reason for the "healthy minded" to take it seriously: "to those who are ready to use this as an excuse for tossing out the whole of Sartrean philosophy, we may point out that it is better to encounter one's existence in disgust than never to encounter it at all." (Is it, really? If so, why? Is it because "It is better to be Socrates dissatisfied than a pig satisfied" (to slightly misquote John Stuart Mill)? Or is that Socratic sentiment very different from Sartre's?)

Atheism

It is not clear whether Sartre's atheism is derived from the fundamental principle of "absurdism" or whether the absurdism derives from his atheism. For he also writes:

(My) **Existentialism is nothing else but an attempt to draw the full conclusions from a consistently atheistic position. . . .**

God does not exist and we have to face all the consequences of this. The existentialist is strongly opposed to a certain type of secular moralism which would like to abolish God with the least possible expense . . . something like this:—God is a useless and costly hypothesis; we are discarding it; but, meanwhile, in order for there to be an ethics, a society, a civilization, it is essential that certain values should be taken seriously, and that they be considered as having an *a priori* existence. It must be considered obligatory, *a priori,* to be honest, not to lie, not to beat your wife, to have children, etc., etc. So we're going to try a little device which will make it possible to show that values exist all the same, inscribed in a heaven of ideas, though . . . God does not exist. We shall find ourselves with the same norms of honesty, progress, and humanism, and we shall have made of God an outdated hypothesis which will peacefully die off by itself.

The existentialist, on the contrary, finds it very distressing that God does not exist, because all possibility of finding values in a heaven of ideas disappears along with Him; there can no longer be an *a priori* Good since there is no infinite and perfect consciousness to think it. Nowhere is it written that the Good exists, that we must be honest, that we must not lie; because the fact is we are on a plane where there are only men. Dostoyevsky said, "If God didn't exist, everything would be possible (permissible)." That is the very starting point of existentialism. Indeed everything is permissible if God does not exist, and as a result man is forlorn, because neither within him nor without does he find anything to cling to. . . . If God does not exist we are not provided with any values or commands that could legitimize our behavior.

One cannot help wondering how honest Sartre is in professing to be "distressed" at God's non-existence. It certainly seems, from everything else he wrote, that he would be much more profoundly distressed at God's *existence,* which would threaten his primary value, namely his own absolute freedom and autonomy.

Notice how similar Sartre's point in this quotation is to the traditional moral argument for God's existence. That argument begins with the same Dostoyevskian premise that Sartre uses:

If God does not exist, everything is permissible. It then adds the second premise:
Not everything is permissible, and concludes, logically, that
Therefore God exists.

Sartre simply exchanges the second premise and the conclusion, and negates both:

If God does not exist, everything is permissible;
God does not exist;
Therefore everything is permissible.

Both arguments are logically valid. But—assuming the truth of the first premise—one of the two arguments must have a false second premise. The difference between (A) the traditional moral argument for God's existence and (B) Sartre's argument is thus the difference between (A) being more certain of your morality or (B) of your theology; i.e., it is the difference between (A) Dostoyevski's assuming that the reality of morality is more certain than the unreality of God and (B) Sartre's assuming that the unreality of God is more certain that the reality of morality. Since most people claim to be more certain of morality than of theology, Sartre's argument could almost be satirized as a *reductio ad absurdum* argument against atheism, with Sartre as a theistic spy planting a logical time bomb in the camp of the atheists.

It is not clear whether Sartre's atheism is meant as a rational metaphysical claim to objective truth or only something purely subjective and irrational, either emotional (the feeling of nausea and absurdity) or volitional (as in Nietzsche's demand "If there were gods, how could I bear not to be a god? *Consequently* there are no gods"). The second, subjective option is more consistent with Sartre's insistence on absolute freedom. But it is inconsistent with any claim to objective truth and does not give any reason for others to share it; it is mere personal confession or spiritual autobiography, and thus loses its claim or existential bite on the reader, who, after all, is not Sartre himself.

Existence and Essence; Being-for-itself and Being-in-itself

Sartre is a metaphysical dualist: there are two totally opposite kinds of reality. He calls them

(1) "existence" and "essence." He also calls them

(2) "being-for-itself" and "being-in-itself." They amount to

(3) subjectivity and objectivity, i.e., subjective being and objective being; or

(4) "man" and "nature"; or

(5) the kind of being that has self-consciousness and freedom and the kind that does not; or

(6) to be a subject of consciousness and choice and to be an object of consciousness and choice.

(7) This is analogous to and historically influenced by Descartes's dualism between thinking substance and extended substance, or consciousness and matter. But it is not the same, because being-in-itself includes mental objects (essences and concepts) as well as physical objects; and being-for-itself includes body-consciousness.

These seven dualisms are not exactly identical, but they are so similar that the parallels are a useful approach for beginners to what otherwise would appear a very abstract and difficult concept. It is because this central concept is so crucial to Sartre's philosophy that we begin with this compromising oversimplification.

Let's now try to explain a little more exactly what Sartre means by these two terms. Being-in-itself is perfect, and positive. It is full of itself, of its own essence. It is purely and simply what it is. It has no inwardness, no self-consciousness, no freedom, no choice, no anticipated future. Its essence cannot change. It does not shape its own essence, and it cannot fail to be what it is. We never call dogs un-doggy, or rocks non-rocky, nor can triangles be non-triangular. But we can call some humans "inhuman." For man is conscious and free; and that means that his being-for-itself contains negativity, or non-being. It is not simply what it is; it starts out by being nothing, and it only *becomes* what it is, it makes itself what it is, it constructs its own nature by its choices.

Aristotle said that we construct our own "second nature," our character, by our habits, which we construct by our repeated choices. But Sartre says that we construct our very essence, our "first nature."

The reason Sartre calls this "negative" is that self-consciousness and free choice both imply a gap, a space, a difference, a *not-that,* between subject and object. The very nature of consciousness and freedom is that it is perpetually beyond itself, going "out" into its objects, creating its thoughts and choices, thus "identifying with" what is not itself.

The point may be clearer in the concrete example than in the abstract formula. Here is Sartre's famous analysis of the waiter in the café:

Look at this waiter who is serving us. His gestures are lively, insistent and a little too precise. He comes to get his orders a little too quickly, he bends down a little too readily; his voice, his glance are a little too solicitous. Now he is coming back with the drinks, carrying his tray with the agility of the conjurer, keeping it in a state of precarious equilibrium which he restores by a flick of his wrist and arm. His whole manner is a performance. His movements are linked together like the parts of a mechanism, even to his expression and his voice; he affects the incredible neatness and swiftness of inanimate objects. He is play-acting, he is enjoying himself. What then is his role? Whom is he impersonating? The answer is simple: he is impersonating a waiter in a café.

This being-for-itself is trying to turn himself into a being-in-itself, to disappear into his role, to be nothing but this perfect essence "the waiter." But of course he cannot, because he is *trying,* willing, designing to do so, which is an act of being-for-itself.

So being-for-itself can never escape itself because the very act of escape is an act of being-for-itself. On the other hand, being-in-itself can never escape itself either, any more than a triangle can grow a fourth side.

Here is Sartre's explanation, from his most accessible, short and popular book, *Existentialism and Humanism* (also called *Existentialism and Human Emotions),* of the same dualism in terms of "essence" and "existence." The terms are not meant in the same way as in St. Thomas Aquinas's metaphysics; for "existence," for Sartre, means not the objective metaphysical co-principle with essence, the ontological actualization of an essence, but only *human* existence, or subjectivity, self-consciousness. That is what the term "existence" means for most Existentialists.

"Existence precedes essence." Just what does that mean? Let us consider some object that is manufactured, for example a book or a paper-cutter: here is an object which has been made by an artisan whose inspiration came from a concept . . . and . . . a specific use. One cannot postulate a man who produces a paper-cutter but does not know what it is used for. Therefore let us say that, for the paper-cutter, essence—that is, the . . . properties which enable it be both produced and defined—precedes existence.

When we conceive God as the Creator, he is generally thought of as a superior sort of artisan . . . we always grant that will more or less follows understanding, or, at the very least, accompanies it, and that when God creates He knows exactly what

He is creating. Thus, the concept of man in the mind of God is comparable to the concept of the paper-cutter in the mind of the manufacturer....

In the 18th century, the atheism of the *philosophes* discarded the idea of God, but not ... the notion that essence precedes existence. To a certain extent, this idea is found everywhere ... (that) man has a human nature....

Atheistic existentialism, which I represent, is more coherent. It states that if God does not exist, there is at least one being in whom existence precedes essence, a being who exists before he can be defined by any concept, and that this being is man.... What is meant here by saying that existence precedes essence? It means that, first of all, man exists, turns up, appears on the scene, and only afterwards defines himself. If man, as the existentialist conceives him, is indefinable, it is because at first he is nothing. Only afterward will he be something, and he himself will have made what he will be. Thus there is no human nature, since there is no God to conceive it....

Man is nothing else but what he makes of himself. Such is the first principle of existentialism.

This follows from atheism:

If God does not exist, there is no such thing as human nature.
God does not exist.
Therefore there is no such thing as human nature.

But just as with his argument that "If God does not exist, everything is permissible," Sartre's logic here may easily be turned upside down and used as a *reductio ad absurdum* argument *for* the existence of God:

If God does not exist, there is no such thing as human nature.
There is such a thing as human nature.
Therefore God exists.

For just as it seems much more obvious to most people that not everything is permissible than that God does not exist, so it seems much more obvious to most people that there is such a thing as a human nature, or a human essence, or a human meaning, than that God does not exist. For surely *we* are more knowable and accessible objects to ourselves than God is! It is obvious, even to most atheists, that there is a human nature, just as it is obvious, even to most atheists, that not everything is permissible.

This theistic argument from human nature to God (the second argument above) is a version of the "argument from design." The more usual form of the "argument from design" appeals to design in nature, or being-in-itself, but here it appeals to design in man, or being-for-itself. Thus Sartre seems to have unwittingly invented a new argument for the existence of God.

Sartre's metaphysics of being-in-itself vs. being-for-itself is connected with his athe-ism in this way: there is no God because there is no Being, for Sartre; there is only being-in-itself and being-for-itself. Being-in-itself and being-for-itself in Sartre correspond, functionally, to *Seiendes* (beings) and *Dasein* (our be-ing) in Heidegger. Subtract Being from Heidegger and you get Sartre. "Being" in Heidegger corresponds, functionally, to God, as the ultimate unifier of the fundamental dualism of our experience. Thus "There is no God" corresponds to "There is no Being." Heidegger is not a theist, but he is not a nihilist either. Sartre is. For him "There is no God" means that "There is no Being."

Another way to explain the connection between Sartre's metaphysical dualism and his atheism would be the following: Being-in-itself is perfect, with a complete, timeless essence, but it is impersonal; while being-for-itself is personal but imperfect, always *en passant,* "on the way," in process of making itself what it is. But God would be the im-possible synthesis of perfection and personhood; God would be a perfect person; and that is self-contradictory for Sartre. (Compare the similar argument for Brahman's im-personality in Shankara's Vedanta Hinduism, Vol. I, ch. 3.)

Once these two categories of "being-in-itself" and "being-for-itself" are set up as both exclusive (they cannot meet, overlap, or participate in each other) and exhaustive (there can be no third), atheism necessarily follows. For God would be the impossible and self-contra-dictory synthesis or identity of being-in-itself and being-for-itself, both object and subject, both impersonal and personal, both necessary and free, both essence and existence.[8]

It is unclear whether Sartre begins with these two categories, derived from an analysis of human experience, and then logically deduces atheism from it, or whether he begins with atheism as a personal demand and then erects his two metaphysical categories to explain and justify it.

Sartre's analysis of being-for-itself and being-in-itself is relevant to the question of God also in another way. Man, says Sartre, always wants to achieve the synthesis of being-in-itself and being-for-itself; he wants to be both perfect and personal, like the waiter in the café. In other words, **man is the being who seeks to divinize himself. Man is the being whose project is to be God. But the idea of God is self-contradictory, and we lose ourselves in vain. Man is a useless passion.**

Thinking about this last quotation, we come up with a fascinating paradox: what Sartre says here is almost what St. Augustine said: that our hearts are restless until they rest in God. Our very being contains a demand for the impossible! For Augustine, it is only a personal impossibility—to lift ourselves up by our own bootstraps, without divine grace, to union with God. For Sartre it is a metaphysical impossibility. But both the pas-sionate theist and the passionate atheist see at the heart of human existence the desire for God. Subtract divine grace from Augustine and you almost get Sartre. (It's not the same

8   In Aquinas God's essence *is* existence, but this is not a logical self-contradiction, as it would be in Sartre, because Aquinas means by "existence" and "essence" not "subject" and "object," as Sartre does, but "that it is" and "what it is," or the actuality or act of being and the poten-tiality or ability to be.

thing, of course, since for Sartre, it's the desire to *be* God, while for Augustine it's the desire for *union* with God.)

My Being = My Life

Another conclusion that most people would find depressing follows from Sartre's analysis of human existence: that since I have no essence that transcends my existence, no being-in-itself but only being-for-itself, I therefore have no being that transcends my life. My being is merely my life, the sum total of my choices and acts, nothing more. (Contrast Marcel's explicit alternative to this, ch. 77, point 3.) **Man is nothing else but what he makes of himself . . . nothing else but the sum of his actions, nothing else but what his life is. Hence we can well understand why some people are horrified by our teaching. For many have but one resource to sustain them in their misery, and that is to think, ". . . I was worthy to be something much better than I have been."** But no: that dull, depressing, limp-spirited person is not a potential poet, saint or genius, but simply a dull, depressing, limp-spirited person. There are no hidden potentialities there, there is only the sum total of his actions. I am my behavior, nothing more.

And since we are nothing but our life, since we cannot transcend our life, since we cannot identify with or judge from the standpoint of anything that transcends our life, therefore we cannot objectify our life, judge our life and find it wanting or fulfilling, bad or good.

Like reality itself, for Sartre a person is far less, not more, than we think. Sartre entitled his book "Existentialism is a Humanism." Does this reductionist philosophy of man deserve that title?

Sartre's Male Chauvinism

Sartre applies this reduction of life to actions to everything, even literature, which for him is not contemplative or receptive at all (that would compromise our freedom) but exclusively active. Literature is a mode of intellectual action, in fact political action. Sartre did not concern himself with politics at all during the War, but after the war he absolutized politics and political activism. His theory of literature as action applies to himself, at least: he himself did only one thing with his life: he talked and wrote furiously every minute of every day, taking no time to listen or to be silent. There is nothing of the poet in him, no wonder, no contemplation, and no sense of mystery.

In terms of the classical archetypes (which many moderns declare to be only social stereotypes), Sartre's mind is exclusively masculine. All the images of the feminine in his novels and plays are images of the disgusting: the viscous, the gluey, the formless, the pregnant, the entrapping, the overflowing, "too much, too fat." Both matter and thought are *de trop,* superfluous, absurd.

The opposite vision of reality—as not absurd and *less* than rational but gloriously *more* than the clean, bright rationality of clear and distinct ideas—the vision which inspired and gave joy to all the great poets and mystics—is for Sartre not a Heaven but a Hell; not a feast but a diarrhea. In contrast, look at his almost erotic description of "the black boulevard" in *Nausea:*

A street of iron. . . . It is inhuman like a mineral or a triangle. It is fortunate that there should be such a street in Bouville. . . . Nausea has been left behind under the yellow lights. I am happy: this cold, this darkness are so pure; am I not myself a wave of frozen air? To have no blood, no lymphatic tissue, no flesh. To flow along this canal towards that pale light. To be nothing but the cold.[9]

It is no accident that Sartre's only lifelong companion was Simone de Beauvoir, whose *The Second Sex* is a screed against everything archetypically feminine (intuition, sympathy, mystery, poetry, wombs, pregnancy, children, family, relationships, receptivity, softness) in favor of everything archetypically masculine (reason, choice, freedom, individualism, autonomy, activism, hardness). The woman one finds in this book is not the ordinary woman in all times, places, and cultures; it is only the modern Western deracinated, artificial, protesting, rootless, randy, over- intellectualized, trousered turkey hen who is like Simone herself. I suppose it is French logic to call such male chauvinism "feminism." Do they also call cannibals "chefs"?[10]

Sartre's Ethics

Sartre is an ethical subjectivist and relativist. Moral values, for him, are totally dependent on our choice. They are created, not discovered. He says: **My freedom is the unique foundation of values. And since I am the being by virtue of whom values exist, nothing—absolutely nothing—can justify me in adopting this or that value or scale of values. As the unique basis of the existence of values, I am totally unjustifiable. And my freedom is in anguish at finding that it is the baseless basis of values.**

One must honestly ask: is it more likely that the reaction of the young, hedonistic rebels who constitute most of Sartre's followers will be "anguished" at this rather than feeling comfortable relief, freedom from guilt, and license?

If "ethics" is, as Kant says, fundamentally about the experience of moral duty or obligation, then Sartre has no ethics at all. For his radical claim is that *no* value or system of values impinges on our mind or will or conscience as a moral obligation. To use the categories of the phenomenologist Von Hildebrand (ch. 92), there is no such thing as "value-response." For our free choice is the sole creator, cause, foundation and justification of the values we choose. We judge values, values do not judge us.

Therefore all choices by definition are good. **We can never choose evil . . . to choose between this and that is at the same time to affirm the value of that which is chosen**

9   Compare the negative half of Plotinus (ch. 33), who was "ashamed of having a body."
10   Please do not report me to the thought-police for "hate speech." It's a joke.

. . . **we are unable ever to choose the worse. What we choose is always the better** . . . **it has value only because it is chosen.**

The logical consequence of this seems to be that even the Holocaust was good because Hitler chose it. For Sartre says that **One can choose anything, but only if it is upon the ground of free commitment.**

He answers the objection that **"your values are not serious, then, since you chose them yourselves." To that I can only say that I am very sorry that it should be so, but if I have excluded God the Father, there must be somebody to invent values. We have to take things as they are.**

The only thing that is intrinsically valuable, then, the only absolute value, is freedom. **We will freedom for freedom's sake.** What Nietzsche did to power (changing it for a means to an end, *the* end), Sartre does to freedom. Freedom is not relative to values, values are relative to freedom. It is *not* true, for Sartre, that freedom is misused and evil if it is used to affirm wrong values. Nothing judges freedom, no other values judge freedom; freedom judges everything, freedom judges all values. There are no values to justify choices; it is choices that justify values. There are no principles to justify actions; it is action that justify principles: the action of freely choosing them.

Another radical but logical consequence of the idea that there are no objective values is that **we do not believe in progress. Progress is betterment.** "Progress" means "a real better"; and "a real better" presupposes "a real best," and thus "a real good." You can't judge one runner as closer to the goal line if there is no goal line. You can't grade student papers if there is no standard except the students' own standards for themselves, because they will all give themselves A's. (This was exactly what Sartre's students did.) In other words, if there is no absolute good, there is nothing for relative goods to be relative to; and if there is nothing for relative goods to be relative to, then one person or deed cannot be better, nearer to this absolute, than another person or deed; and in that case, moving from one goal to another cannot be called progress, only change. Change is movement in time, forward, in a horizontal direction; progress is movement also upward, in a vertical direction, toward the good.

It might seem that this "ethics" must be purely individualistic, and not at all communal. Yet Sartre says that **when we say that man is responsible for himself, we do not mean that he is responsible for his own individuality, but that he is responsible for all men . . . nothing can be better for us unless it is better for all.** But *why,* if there is no such thing as a universal human nature, and no such thing as an objectively real universal moral law or a divine Lawgiver? The only reason Sartre can give for this universalism is that this is what he chooses. He cannot say the alternative choice is "wrong."

Freedom

In a single word, the reason Sartre believes he has to deny objective values is freedom. It is an either/or for him: If values are objective, they are imposed on me, as light is imposed on the eyes; and then I am not free.

Freedom, for Sartre, is absolute. It cannot be compromised, cannot be limited, cannot be finite, and cannot be judged or determined by its end. It cannot be freedom to do or attain this or that. It is not relative to truth. It is not the truth that makes you free; it is freedom that makes you true.

Freedom is always negative for Sartre: it can only be the freedom to say No, not the freedom to say Yes. Good or value cannot come both from my will and from God's will, or be determined by both my choice and objective moral truth. Even if I should freely will to obey God's will, I would be unfree because I am then willing to obey another's will rather than my own. I cannot unite my will to another's will any more than I can unite my being-for-itself with another's being-for-itself. There can be no "we," only "I."

To common sense this sounds absurd and childish. It is the philosophy of a totally spoiled, egotistical child dressed up in fancy adult philosophical clothes.

Because of this extreme notion of freedom, Sartre's moral philosophy not only denies any real objective values but includes a strongly negative judgment on what to most ordinary people are the three most passionately important moral values in human life: religion, altruistic love, and family. For all three threaten his freedom.

We have seen why Sartre is anti-religious. Why is he anti-family and anti-altruism?

Take family first. All Sartre's images of family, pregnancy, women, and children are images of something threatening and gluey. They are *traps,* like spider webs. For instance, in *Nausea* the protagonist Roquentin sees in a museum a painting with a moral that he hates:

... it was entitled "A Bachelor's Deathbed." Naked to the waist, the torso a little green as befits a corpse, the bachelor lay prone on a untidy bed; the disordered blankets and sheets showed that the agony had been long and painful. ... The man had lived for himself alone, his punishment—a lonely deathbed—was as severe as it was deserved. This picture was a warning to me to retrace my steps while there was still time. And if I disregarded it I was to remember this: with the exception of the Reverend Mother of an orphanage and of a few young men whose premature deaths were mourned by their families, there was not a single celibate among all the hundred and fifty notables whose portraits hung on the walls of the great gallery which I was about to enter. Not one of them had died without leaving children and a will; not one of them had died without the last sacraments. On good terms with God and the world on that day as on all the others, those men had gone to claim the part of eternal life to which they had a right.

The words drip with sarcasm, not with praise. Sartre has a negative view not only of family but also of the very idea of parenthood and, in fact, of social order as such. Sartre's view of a parent is the same as his view of the waiter in a café: it is someone who is play-acting, identifying with his part, his role, trying to submerge his being-for-itself, his freedom, into his impersonal social role, his being-in-itself. That would be "inauthentic" because it would require him to stick fast, to be pinned down, to be less free than a bird in the air. Sartre did much of his writing in cafes, where there is total freedom to watch the world go by, with no responsibilities. Like Rousseau, he could not imagine himself married with children: they would interfere with his freedom and his work. But at least Sartre did not have five children and then do what Rousseau did to them.

(Only a small minority of ten famous philosophers ever did what the vast majority of other people did: had families.)

To have a family and children is to sacrifice very much of one's individual freedom and convenience, i.e., to practice unselfish love. Sartre's philosophy of human relationships makes genuine unselfish love not only rare, and not only undesirable, but metaphysically impossible. To see this, let us look at his analysis of the structure of human relationships, from *Being and Nothingness*.

Imagine yourself walking in a public garden toward a row of chairs. Suddenly you see another man looking at and walking toward the same chairs. He is necessarily your rival. Not that he would physically fight you for a seat; there are plenty of chairs there. But his gaze is not yours. It is alien and other. To you, you are the one unique center of the universe, as the sun is the unique center of the solar system, and those chairs are objects of *your* unique subjective consciousness, as the planets of our solar system belong to the sun. But that other man is like another star entering your solar system and claiming your planets for himself. There is a kind of spiritual gravity emanating from his gaze that pulls the chairs— *your* chairs, *your* planets—toward him. (I cannot help identifying Sartre with the seagulls in "Finding Nemo": to everything in the universe each one squawks the same word: "Mine!") To Sartre, encountering another, alien consciousness feels like your world is slipping away from you in a landslide, drawn away from you and down to him. Sartre writes:

The appearance of others coincides with a kind of frozen landslide of the universe, or with a shifting of its center which undermines the centralization operated by myself. . . . It is as if the world had a sink-hole (like a "black hole" in contemporary cosmology) **in the middle and were continually emptying itself through that hole.**

Even worse, the other man then notices you, and you suddenly become one of his planets, an object in his universe, thereby losing your freedom and your uniqueness. In exactly the same way, he becomes that to you. Thus you are ontological rivals. Each is the unique "I," the subject, the "being-for-itself," and each sees the other as an object. *There can be only one "I. "* He calls himself "I" and calls you "you" or "he." But "I" is your name for yourself and yourself only. To him, you are an object: you stand on that lawn in exactly the same way as the chair does. He is the author of the drama of his life, and you are only a character in it, a walk-on in his play. But for you, it is he who is the character and you are the unique author. In other words each of you plays God, and there can be only one God, so you are necessarily rivals.

And there is nothing anyone can ever do to change this situation. It is not an attitude or a choice, it is the very metaphysical structure of the relation between any human self and an other. However friendly you may act to each other, you are metaphysical enemies. This is the reason for the famous "punch line" of "No Exit," that "Hell is other people."

Thus there is a little ordinary word that is strictly meaningless for Sartre, though it is a word which almost everyone else finds meaningful and which lovers find profound and delightful. It is the word "we."

There is a character in Sartre's *Sursis* named Daniel who experiences this gaze of the other upon him without feeling it as threatening. It is the gaze of God. Daniel is converted by this gaze. But for Sartre the atheist, this conversion is what apostasy is for a believer. It is a kind of damnation. If the traditional concept of Heaven means being known by God, being in the presence of the Absolute Other, and if Hell means not being in this presence, then Sartre would call the traditional Heaven his Hell and the traditional Hell his Heaven. Sartre would hate Heaven: there are too many children there. He would call it an obscenely large family.

In "No Exit" three people find themselves in Hell, but it is a Hell without demons to torture them because each of them tortures the others simply by knowing them as what they are. For you are only what you have done, and they have all committed crimes. They cannot hide and they cannot love. No two of them can enter a love relationship with each other because the third is there to know them. Being known and being loved are mutually exclusive for Sartre. For to be loved is to be affirmed in your freedom and your own unique subjectivity, but to be known is, for Sartre, to be deprived of your freedom and reduced to an object.

Love is the gift of self to another. This is impossible, for Sartre. In fact, even giving a material gift out of genuine generosity and unselfish love is impossible. Here is his analysis of gift-giving (remember this the next time someone you think loves you gives you a Christmas present): **To give is to appropriate by means of destroying and to use this act of destruction as a means of enslaving others.** What Sartre means by this is that in giving you a gift I destroy my ownership of it, and by doing this I put you in my debt, I control you, I rob you of your freedom. Now you are my object, and you owe me.

It gets even more shocking. Since freedom is only the freedom to say No, the freedom to refuse, therefore **Freedom coincides at its roots with the non-being** (the "No") **which is at the heart of man. For a human being, *to be* is to choose himself; nothing comes to him either from without or from within himself** (thus Sartre denies also the very existence of the subconscious) **that he can receive and accept** (without selling his freedom).

Marcel, Sartre's closest critic, comments about this sentence: "I do not believe that in the whole history of human thought grace, even in its most secularized forms, has ever been denied with such audacity or such impudence."

Such a notion of freedom is not only profoundly anti-love; it is also anti-freedom. For it cannot admit half of freedom: the freedom to say Yes instead of No. If Sartre is right, Yes always compromises your freedom, so that you cannot be free to say Yes, only No. And that means you are not free to choose between Yes and No. And if you are not free to choose that, you are not free.

What good can we say about Sartre? What compliment can we give to him and his philosophy, as distinct from his brilliant and arresting writing style? Sartre would regard a compliment as a threat to his freedom. (Perhaps that is part of the reason he refused the Nobel Prize when he won it.) An insult would not be a threat to his freedom, because he would recoil against it, he would say No to it, and No is the word of freedom; but a compliment would be a kind of glue that would tempt him to stick to the one who gave it by accepting it. Similarly, to be hated would not compromise his freedom, but being loved would. That is another reason why Heaven would be his Hell and Hell would be his Heaven.

Sartre's argument for his view of freedom is that it gives man not only the dignity of not being an object, but also gives him responsibility, so that we cannot blame anyone but ourselves for anything we are or do. The response may be made that if it is true that our freedom means that we cannot blame others, does it not also, for the same reason, mean that we cannot praise and thank others, either human or divine? It is true that we should not blame others (e.g., our parents) for what we are—that is indeed a cop-out and an abdication of one's own freedom and responsibility. But can we not praise them and thank them for anything that we are? Does all praise and all thanks compromise the freedom of both its giver and its receiver? Has anyone ever come up with a gloomier philosophy than that?

Yet, as with Nietzsche, Sartre's very extremism, consistency and clarity can be very useful and instructive, like a warning sign at the edge of an interior abyss.

And more than that: even if one passionately disagrees with the negative and nihilistic dimensions of Sartre, one can find not only a negative warning but also at least one profoundly positive insight at the very center of his thought: the insight that each person, as a free subject, is a radically different kind of being than any object; so that even if God exists and man is a created object, an object of creation to his Creator, yet this Creator has given him the dignity and incredible responsibility of being his own co-creator. Even if God creates our "what," our common human nature, we create our own "who," our unique personality, through our free choices. Even if God is our Creator, He is a playwright rather than a novelist; and it is not only the Author but also the actors who are necessary to complete the play. Even if the Author is the unique "I AM," so is each character in the play. So in some mysterious way "I-ness" is communicable after all. Thus even though only by contrast and against his will, Sartre helps define the idea that man is made in "the image of God."

Selected Bibliography:

Sartre, *Existentialism and Humanism*
"No Exit"

77. Gabriel Marcel (1889–1973)

Marcel is the anti-Sartre, the alternative to Sartre, point by point. That is not accidental; the two met and informally argued on a number of occasions.

Marcel is one of the most unclassifiable of philosophers. Existentialist, Humanist, Personalist, Jamesian "Radical Empiricist," phenomenologist, Catholic philosopher—all these labels are true in one sense and false in another, and he has resisted them all. He prefers "Neo-Socratic." It is an obscure, surprising, and slippery term—like his philosophy itself, to most readers. One never gets the sense of finality and finished clarity in reading Marcel; one is always exploring unmarked, original paths. Philosophy to him is not construction work or architecture; it is more like archeological excavation or cave spelunking. It explores mysteries rather than solving problems. Yet one gets a stronger sense of assurance and authenticity and fidelity to experience from Marcel than from nearly any other philosopher. He is confusing, but he is trustable.

He was an accomplished pianist and composer, drama critic, and playwright. The music of Bach was the deepest source of his religious life, until his conversion to Catholicism in 1929. His mother died when he was 3, and he says her presence haunted his whole life and thought, accounting for his typical dialectic between the seen and the unseen, the physical and the spiritual. His experience during World War I of informing families that their sons were missing in action gave him a deep sense of interior personal drama. Rare among philosophers, he was happily and faithfully married.

If there is one typical tendency in his thought, it is to push the exploration of the light by which the dramas of ordinary human life are illuminated; to look back at the light rather than forward toward objects. He calls the light "Being," and sometimes "value" or "the good." Though he does not call it "God," he pretty obviously believed that it is.

His most oft-quoted teaching is the distinction between **problems** and **mysteries,** a distinction many other philosophers have found useful:

(1) Problems can be fixed objectively, mysteries cannot. They surround us and involve us. The object of a problem is absent and external to the self, but the object of a mystery is something I am inextricably involved in, or something that is inextricably involved in me.

(2) A problem admits of a solution, because it can be fixed and finitized. A mystery does not, because there is something unlimited about it, because it is internal to a *person,* a free subject.

(3) The self that thinks about a problem is an impersonal rational mind. But a mystery always invokes a uniquely personal response.

(4) And the attitude of the mind confronting a problem is intellectual curiosity, while the attitude of mind in the face of a mystery is wonder (which Socrates, Plato and Aristotle all labeled the beginning of philosophy).

Marcel criticizes modern culture as well as modern philosophy for prioritizing problems over mysteries.A key example of the distinction between mystery and problem is the distinction between my **being** (which is a mystery) and my **having** (which can be seen as a problem). For instance, I do not have my body, I am my body. My body is a mystery rather than a problem because I participate in a world of bodies. (**Participation** is perhaps Marcel's most central and pervasive concept.) I am also a person because I participate in a world of persons. Persons are related to each other by fidelity (trust), hope, and communion (love). These are three modes of personal "participation." I become a self only in relationship to other selves, like one of two foci of an ellipse. (Compare Buber's *I And Thou* on this in ch. 78.)

One naturally asks of Marcel the same question one naturally asks of Heidegger: "But what *is* my Being?" The impatient question cannot be answered, because Being is not an object, and therefore not an object of reason. It does not have an essence, like a number or a rock. In the last analysis, only persons have Being, or *are* Beings, because to have Being is to have intrinsic value, and only persons (whether human or divine) have intrinsic value. Persons cannot be defined by any list of attributes because no list of attributes can ever define the one who *has* these attributes. (See also Clarke on "Person and Being," ch. 99.)

Like Sartre and other existentialists, Marcel sees a self as a subject and not an object. Telling truths *about* a self makes it an absent object, a third-person "he" or "she." But we always begin not there but "here," with a first-and-second-person presence, the presence of a "you" to an "I," which for Marcel (as *not* for Sartre) can make a "we." The "I" emerges from the "we" as much as the "we" from the "I."

Unlike most philosophers, Marcel has provided us with a very useful, short and simple summary of his seven most important themes, in an essay entitled "On the Ontological Mystery." These themes are related more like musical themes that interplay than like theses in a dialectical argument. Quoting from this work will present Marcel's unique style, personality, and method better than an abstract summary. It gives you something of the very "presence" of Marcel rather than pointing to him as an absent object; and this very "presence" is one of his seven central themes.

(1. Being) **Rather than begin with abstract definitions and dialectical arguments . . . I should like to start with a sort of global and intuitive characterization of the man in whom . . . the sense of being is lacking. . . . Generally speaking, modern man is in this condition.**

The characteristic feature of our age seems to me to be what might be called the misplacement of the idea of function. . . . The individual tends to appear both to himself and to others as an agglomeration of functions. . . . As for death, it becomes

... functionally, the scrapping of what has ceased to be of use and must be written off as total loss. I need hardly insist on the stifling impression of sadness produced by this functionalized world. ...

In such a world the ontological need, the need of being, is exhausted in exact proportion to the breaking up of personality on the one hand and, on the other, to the triumph of the category of the "purely natural" and the consequent atrophy of the faculty of *wonder*. ...

As for defining the word "being," let us admit that it is extremely difficult. I would merely suggest this method of approach: being is what withstands—or what would withstand—an exhaustive analysis bearing on the data of experience and aiming to reduce them step by step to elements increasingly devoid of intrinsic or significant value. (An analysis of this kind is attempted in the theoretical works of Freud.)

(2. Mystery) At this point we can begin to define the distinction between mystery and problem. A mystery is a problem which encroaches upon its own data, invading them, as it were, and thereby transcending itself as a simple problem. A set of examples will help us to grasp the content of this definition.

It is evident that there exists a mystery of the union of the body and the soul ... always inadequately expressed by such phrases as *I have a body, I make use of my body, I feel my body,* etc. ...

This distinction is particularly clear in the case of the problem of evil. In reflecting upon evil, I tend inevitably to regard it as a disorder which I view from outside and of which I seek to discover the causes. ... In reality, I can only grasp it as evil in the measure in which it *touches* me—that is to say, in the measure in which I am *involved,* as one is involved in a lawsuit. ... This brings out how the distinction between what is *in me* and what is only *before me* can break down. ...

But it is, of course, in love that the obliteration of this frontier can best be seen. ...

(3. Recollection) And this at last brings us to recollection. ... The word means what it says—the act whereby I re-collect myself as a unity. ... It is within recollection that I take up my position—or, rather, I become capable of taking up my position—in regard to my life: I withdraw from it in a certain way, but not as the pure subject of cognition; *in this withdrawal I carry with me that which I am and which perhaps my life is not.* (Contrast Sartre here.) This brings out the gap between my being and my life. I am not my life; and if I can judge my life—a fact I cannot deny without falling into a radical skepticism which is nothing other than despair—it is only on condition that I encounter myself within recollection beyond all possible judgment. ... Recollection ... does not consist in looking at something. ...

(4. Hope.) Let us take despair. I have in mind the act by which one despairs of reality as a whole, as one might despair of a person. This appears to be the result,

or the immediate translation into other terms, of a kind of balance sheet. Inasmuch as I am able to evaluate the world of reality. . . . I can find nothing in it that withstands that process of dissolution at the heart of things which I have discovered and traced. I believe that at the root of despair there is always this affirmation: "There is nothing in the realm of reality to which I can give credit—no security, no guarantee. It is a statement of complete insolvency. As against this, hope is what implies credit. . . .We have now come to the centre of what I have called the ontological mystery, and the simplest illustrations will be the best. To hope against all hope that a person whom I love will recover from a disease which is said to be incurable is to say: It is impossible that I should be alone in willing this cure; it is impossible that reality in its inward depth should be hostile or so much as indifferent to what I assert is in itself a good. It is quite useless to tell me of discouraging *cases* or *examples:* beyond all experience, all probability, all statistics, I assert that a given order shall be reestablished, that reality *is* on my side in willing it to be so. I do not wish, I assert: such is the prophetic tone of true hope. . . .

The correlation of hope and despair subsists until the end; they seem to be inseparable. I mean that while the structure of the world we live in permits—and may even seem to counsel—absolute despair, yet it is only such a world that can give rise to an unconquerable hope. If only for this reason, we cannot be sufficiently thankful to the great pessimists in the history of thought: they have carried through an inward experience which needed to be made and of which the radical possibility no apologetics should disguise; they have prepared our minds to understand that despair can be what it was for Nietzsche. . . .

Just as long as my attitude towards reality is that of someone who is not involved in it, but who judges it his duty to draw up its minutes as exactly as possible (and this is by definition the attitude of the scientist), I am justified in maintaining in regard to it a sort of principle of mistrust, which in theory is unlimited in its application; such is the legitimate standpoint of the workman in the laboratory, who must in no way prejudge the result of his analysis. . . . It would be a profound illusion to believe that I can still maintain this same attitude when I undertake an inquiry, say, into the value of life; it would be a paralogism to suppose that I can pursue such an inquiry as though my own life were not at issue. . . .

This brings us to a nodal point of our subject, where certain intimate connections can be traced. The world of the problematical is the world of fear and desire, which are inseparable; and the same time, it is that world of the functional, or of what can be functionalized, which was defined at the beginning of this essay; finally, it is the kingdom of technics of whatever sort. Every technique serves, or can be made to serve, some desire or some fear; conversely, every desire, as every fear, tends to invent its appropriate technique. From this standpoint, despair consists in the recognition of the ultimate inefficacy of all technics, joined to the inability or the refusal to change over to a new ground, a ground where all technics are seen to be incompatible with the fundamental nature of being, which itself eludes our grasp (in so far as our grasp is limited to the world of objects and to this alone). It is for this reason that we seem nowadays to have entered upon the very era of despair; we have not ceased to believe in technics, that is, to envisage reality as a complex of problems; yet at the same time the failure of technics *as a whole* is as visible as its *partial* triumphs. To the question: what can man achieve? We continue to reply: He can achieve as much as his technics; yet we are obliged to admit that these technics are unable *to save man himself,* and even that they are apt to conclude the most sinister alliance with the enemy he bears within him.

I have said that man is *at the mercy of his technics.* This must be understood to mean that he is increasingly incapable of controlling his technics, or rather of *controlling his own control....*

The more the sense of the ontological tends to disappear, the more unlimited become the claims of the mind which has lost it to a kind of cosmic governance, because it is less and less capable of examining its own credentials to the exercise of such dominion.

(5. Creative fidelity) **Fidelity is, in reality, the exact opposite of inert conformism. It is the active recognition of . . . a presence, or . . . something which can be maintained within us and before us as a presence but which, *ipso facto,* can be just as well ignored, forgotten, or obliterated . . . the menace of betrayal. . . .**

It may perhaps be objected that we commonly speak of fidelity to a principle. But it remains to be seen if this is not an arbitrary transposition of the notion of fidelity. A principle . . . is a mere abstract affirmation. . . . Fidelity to a principle is idolatry in the etymological sense of the world. . . .

So little is fidelity akin to the inertia of conformism that it implies an active and continuous struggle against the forces of interior dissipation, as also against the sclerosis of habit. . . .

We must, I think, go much further into the notion of fidelity and of presence.

(6. Presence) **If presence were merely an *idea* in us whose characteristic was that it was nothing more than itself, then indeed the most we could hope would be to maintain this idea in us or before us, as one keeps a photograph on a mantelpiece or in a cupboard. But it is of the nature of presence as presence to be uncircumscribed; and this takes us once again beyond the frontier of the problematical. Presence is mystery in the exact measure in which it is presence. Now fidelity is the actual perpetuation of presence. . . .**

Here again we may be helped by the consideration of aesthetic creativeness; for if artistic creation is conceivable, it can only be on condition that the world is present to the artist to a certain way. . . .

This seems to me to have almost inexhaustible consequences, if only for the

relationships between the living and the dead. . . . We are here at the opening of a vista at whose term death will appear as the *test of presence.* . . .

In saying, "It depends upon us that the dead should live on in our memory," we are still thinking of the idea in terms of a diminution or an effigy. We admit that the object has disappeared, but that there remains a likeness which it is in our power to keep. . . . But it is altogether different in the case where fidelity is creative. . . . A presence is a reality; it is a kind of influx; it depends upon us to be permeable to this influx, but not, to tell the truth, to call it forth. Creative fidelity consists in maintaining ourselves actively in a permeable state; and there is a . . . gift granted in response to it. . . .

. . . fidelity raises up its voice: "Even if I cannot see you, if I cannot touch you, I feel that you are with me; it would be a denial of you not to be assured of this." *With* me: note the metaphysical value of this word, so rarely recognized by philosophers, which corresponds neither to a relationship of inherence or immanence nor to a relationship of exteriority. . . .

(7. Availability *(Disponibilité))* It is an undeniable fact, though it is hard to describe in intelligible terms, that there are some people who reveal themselves as "present"—that is to say, at our disposal (the word means "openness" rather than a kind of garbage "disposal")—when we are in pain or in need to confide in someone, while there are other people who do not give us this feeling, however great is their goodwill. It should be noted at once that the distinction between presence and absence is not at all the same as that between attention and distraction. The most attentive and conscientious listener may give me the impression of not being present; he gives me nothing, he cannot make room for me in himself, whatever the material favors which he is prepared to grant me. The truth is that there is a way of listening which is a way of giving, and another way of listening which is a way of refusing, of refusing *oneself;* the material gift, the visible action, do not necessarily witness to presence. . . . Presence is something which reveals itself immediately and unmistakably in a look, a smile, an intonation or a handshake . . . the person who is at my disposal is the one who is capable of being with me with the whole of himself when I am in need, while the one who is not at my disposal seems merely to offer me a temporary loan raised on his resources. For the one I am a presence; for the other I am an object. . . .

But it is above all the sanctity realized in certain beings which reveals to us that what we call the normal order is, from a higher point of view, from the standpoint of a soul rooted in the ontological mystery, merely the subversion of an order which is its opposite. In this connection, the study of sanctity with all its concrete attributes seems to me to offer an immense speculative value; indeed, I am not far from saying that is the true introduction to ontology.

Has anyone in the history of philosophy ever made a claim that is either more philosophical (i.e., more pregnantly profound) or more unphilosophical (i.e., more outrageously non-"rational") than that one?

Selected Bibliography:

Kenneth Gallagher's *The Philosophy of Gabriel Marcel* is one of the most clear secondary source summaries of one of the least clear philosophers that I have ever read. Marcel's *magnum opus* is *The Mystery of Being* in two volumes, but readers should begin with the four short essays in *The Philosophy of Existentialism,* which includes a short autobiography and a critique of Sartre. Other Marcel classics are *Creative Fidelity* and *Homo Viator* (Man the Traveler). Marcel's plays, while not as striking as Sartre's, are more realistic, i.e., true to lived human experience. The characters are people you actually know.

78. Martin Buber (1878–1965)

Born in Vienna, Buber was a Jew, eventually a rabbi (arguably the most famous in the world). He was traumatically separated from his parents, and this experience probably inspired his philosophy of human relationships as a response. He studied in Vienna, Zurich, Leipzig, and Berlin, and was influenced by his reading of Kierkegaard and Nietzsche. After a period of rebellion he rediscovered his Jewish faith through Eastern European mystical Hasidism, which he popularized to the West. He was a cultural but not political Zionist, and criticized Israel for its treatment of the Arabs, fighting all his life for dialog between alienated peoples.

I classify Buber as a philosopher even though his method is more poetic and suggestive than rigorous, either in the analytic or the phenomenological way. Yet it is a kind of easy-to-read phenomenology. In fact *I and Thou,* one of the *least* difficult of philosophy classics, is perhaps the best introduction to the central idea of Levinas, who is also a phenomenologist and a "personalist" but one of the *most* difficult of all philosophers to read. (See below, ch. 94.)

I and Thou is one of the most popular, enduring, and beloved books of philosophy of the twentieth century. Unlike most modern philosophy texts, it is both strikingly simple and profound at the same time. Though clear on first reading, it rewards much reflection and repeated rereadings. I present typical excerpts from it here without comments.

To man the world is twofold, in accordance with his twofold attitude.

The attitude of man is twofold in accordance with the twofold nature of the primary words which he speaks.

The primary words are not isolated words, but combined words.

The one primary word is the combination *I-Thou.*

The other primary word is the combination *I-It*. . . .

Hence the I of man is also twofold.

For the *I* of the primary word *I-Thou* is a different *I* from that of the primary word *I-It.*

Primary words do not signify things, but they intimate relations.

Primary words do not describe something that might exist independently of them, but being spoken they bring about existence. . . .

If *Thou* is said, the *I* of the combination *I-Thou* is said along with it.

If *It* is said, the *I* of the combination *I-It* is said along with it.

The primary word *I-Thou* can only be spoken with the whole being.

The primary word *I-It* can never be spoken with the whole being. . . .

There is no *I* taken in itself, but only the *I* of the primary word *I-Thou* and the *I* of the primary word *I-It*. . . .

When *Thou* is spoken, the speaker has no thing for his object. For where there is a thing there is another thing. Every *It* is bounded by others; *It* exists only through being bounded by others. But when *Thou* is spoken, there is no thing. *Thou* has no bounds. . . . This human being is not *He* or *She,* bounded from every other *He* and *She,* a specific point in space and time within the net of the world; nor is he a nature able to be experienced and described, a loose bundle of named qualities. But with no neighbor, and whole in himself, he is *Thou* and fills the heavens. This does not mean that nothing exists except himself. But all else lives in *his* light. . . .

The spheres in which the world of relation arises are three.
First, our life with nature. There, the relation sways in gloom, beneath the level of speech. . . .
Second, our life with men. There the relation is open and in the form of speech
Third, our life with spiritual beings . . . it does not use speech, yet begets it . . . we feel we are addressed and we answer. . . .
. . . in each *Thou* we address the eternal *Thou* . . .

The *Thou* meets me through grace—it is not found by seeking. . . .

All real living is meeting. . . .

Spirit is not in the *I,* but between *I* and *Thou.* It is not like the blood the circulates in you, but like the air which you breathe.

The present, and by that is meant not the point which indicates from time to time in our thought merely the conclusion of "finished" time . . . but the real, filled present, exists only in so far as actual presentness, meeting, and relation exist. The present arises only in virtue of the fact that the *Thou* becomes present. . . .

Feelings accompany the metaphysical and meta-psychical fact of love, but they do not constitute it. The accompanying feelings can be of greatly differing kinds. The feeling of Jesus for the demoniac differs from his feelings for the beloved disciple; but the love is the one love. Feelings are "entertained"; love comes to pass. Feelings dwell in man; but man dwells in his love. That is no metaphor, but the actual truth. Love does not cling to the *I* in such a way to have the *Thou* only for its "content," its object; but love is *between I* and *Th o u.* . . .

But this is the exalted melancholy of our fate, that every *Thou* in our world must become an *It* . . . an object among objects—perhaps the chief, but still one of them. . . .

In the beginning is relation.

Consider the speech of "primitive" peoples, that is, of those that have a meager stock of objects, and whose life is built up within a narrow circle of acts highly charged with presentness. . . . We say "far away"; the Zulu has for that a word which means, in our sentence form, "There where someone cries out: 'O mother, I am lost.'" The Fuegian soars above our analytic wisdom with a seven-syllabled word whose precise meaning is, "They stare at one another, each waiting for the other to volunteer to do what both wish, but are not able to do." . . .

It is simply not the case that the child first perceives an object, then, as it were, puts himself in relation with it. But the effort to establish relation comes first— the hand of the child arched out so that what is over against him may nestle under it . . . the thing, like the *I,* is produced late, arising after the original experiences have been split asunder and the connected partners separated. In the beginning is relation. . . .

The development of the soul in the child is inextricably bound up with that of the longing for the *Thou,* with the satisfaction and disappointment of this longing, with the game of his experiments and the tragic seriousness of his perplexity. . . .

. . . without *It* man cannot live. But he who lives with *It* alone is not a man. . . .

Spirit is not in the I, but between *I* and *Thou.* It is not like the blood that circulates in you, but like the air which you breathe. . . .

. . . in general, the world of objects in every culture is more extensive than that of its predecessor . . . the progressive augmentation of the world of *It* is to be clearly discerned in history. . . .

But that which has been so changed into *It,* hardened into a thing among things, has had the nature and disposition put into it to change back again and again . . . again and again that which has the status of object must blaze up into presentness and enter the elemental state from which it came, to be looked on and lived in the present by man. . . .

(Modern man) has divided his life with his fellow-men into two tidily circled-off provinces, one of institutions and the other of feelings—the province of *It* and the province of *I.* Institutions are "outside". . . . Feelings are "within". . . . But the separated *It* of institutions is an animated clod without soul, and the separated *I* of feelings an uneasily fluttering soul-bird. Neither of them knows man. . . .

That institutions yield no public life is realized by increasing numbers. . . . That feelings yield no personal life is understood only by a few. . . .

The men who suffer distress in the realization that institutions yield no public life have hit upon an expedient: institutions must be loosened, or dissolved, or burst asunder, by the feelings. . . . But it is not so. The true community does not arise through peoples having feelings for one another (though not indeed without it), but through, first, their taking their stand in living mutual relation. . . . Living mutual relation includes feelings, but does not originate with them. . . . This (unity) is the metaphysical and metaphysical factor of love to which feelings of love are mere accompaniments. . . .

True public and true personal life are two forms of connexion. In that they come into being and endure, feelings (the changing content) and institutions (the constant form) are necessary; but put together they do not create human life; this is done by the third, the central presence of the *Thou*. . . .

He who takes his stand in relation shares in a reality . . . that neither merely belongs to him nor merely lies outside him. . . .

At times the man, shuddering at the alienation between the *I* and the world, comes to reflect that something is to be done. . . . And thought, ready with its service and its art, paints with its well-known speed one—no, two rows of pictures, on the right wall and on the left. On the one there is . . . the universe. . . . On the other wall there takes place the soul. . . . Thenceforth, if ever the man shudders at the alienation, and the world strikes terror in his heart, he looks up (to right or left, just as it may chance) and sees a picture. There he sees that the *I* is embedded in the world and that there really is no *I* at all—so the world can do nothing to the *I*, and he is put at ease; or he sees that the world is embedded in the *I*, and that there is really no world at all—so the world can do nothing to the *I*, and he is put at ease. . . . But a moment comes, and it is near, when the shuddering man looks up and sees both pictures in a flash together. And a deeper shudder seizes him.

The extended lines of relations meet in the eternal *Thou*.

Every particular *Thou* is a glimpse through to the eternal *Thou;* by means of every particular *Thou* the primary word addresses the eternal *Thou* . . . the *Thou* that by its nature cannot become *It*. . . .

God is the Being that . . . may properly only be addressed, not expressed. . . .[11]

To look away from the world, or to stare at it, does not help a man to reach God; but he who sees the world in Him stands in His presence. "Here world, there God"

11 Read *Job* in this light, especially 42:7.

is the language of It; "God in the world" is another language of It; but to eliminate or leave behind nothing at all, to include the whole world in the *Thou,* to give the world its due and its truth, to include nothing beside God but everything in Him—this is full and complete relation. . . .

This does not mean a giving up of, say, the *I,* as mystical writers usually suppose; the *I* is as indispensable to this, the supreme, as to every relation, since relation is only possible between *I* and *Thou.* . . .

He who approaches the Face has indeed surpassed duty and obligation—but not because he is now remote from the world; rather because he has truly drawn closer to it. Duty and obligation are rendered only to the stranger; we are drawn to and full of love for the intimate person. . . .

Man receives, and he receives not a specific "content" but a Presence . . . the man can give no account at all . . . (yet) Meaning is assured. Nothing can any longer be meaningless. The question about the meaning of life is no longer there. But were it there, it would not have to be answered. You do not know how to exhibit and define the meaning of life, you have no formula or picture for it, and yet it has more certitude for you than the perceptions of your senses. . . .

79. William James (1842–1910)

Life and Personality

James is America's most influential and popular philosopher, and his philosophy, Pragmatism, is the most typically American. But, like many other philosophers (Kierkegaard comes to mind) he is very commonly misunderstood by those who have heard about him but have never read him.

Few philosophers give the impression of being complete human beings, open and honest, trustable and commonsensical, and capable of lasting, faithful friendships and marriage. This is probably because extreme intelligence often comes at the expense of these other things. Yet James, despite being a child prodigy, and despite being vulnerable to various physical, mental, and emotional disorders (he had bouts of depression), and despite having the eccentricities typical of geniuses, was precisely that exception. Extreme intelligence is often paid for by narrowness of focus, like laser light, but not in the case of James. Very few philosophers' ideas are as commonsensical as his. Perhaps the best initial impression of his writings is that they are at the polar opposite from Hegel's.

James was born into a cultured, brilliant, and famous family. His grandfather was a stern Calvinist, his father a "black sheep" Swedenborgian mystic. His brother, Henry, was one of the greatest of American novelists. Both studied psychology, and it is said that William wrote psychology like fiction while Henry wrote fiction like psychology. William received an M.D. from Harvard Medical School in 1870, and taught there until his death (1910): first anatomy, then psychology, then philosophy.

His *Principles of Psychology* (1890) is still regarded as a masterpiece, and it almost singlehandedly invented the science of empirical psychology. James was also an accomplished artist.

Like many sensitive psychologists and artists, he suffered all his life from serious depression as well as physical ailments (vision, back pain, gastric disruption, irritability). The virtues he preached (courage and hard work; cheerfulness and hope; openness, sympathy, and tolerance; both strenuousness and "relaxation") were the virtues he practiced. In fact, he distrusted any philosophical ideas or ideals that were not derived from or proved in practice, in experience.

Pragmatism, in James's hands (and Dewey's too), means *not* the Machiavellian, amoral thing it means in popular discourse, but merely the commonsensical principle that "By their fruits you shall know them." In the simplest possible terms, "pragmatism" means "practicalism." Like America itself, it embraces both what James calls "tough-mindedness" (facts and science) and "tender-mindedness" (personal religious and moral values), as parts of the totality of human experience.

That is what he called his "radical empiricism." It does not mean the reduction of experience to the sensory; in fact, it means *not* reducing experience to anything but itself, in all its unpredictable, raucous, smack-in-your-face reality. "Radical empiricism" was both a method and a world-view. The method was to test everything abstract by concrete, lived experience, to test all theories not by their premises but by their results in experience. As a world-view it affirmed the universe as not a monistic "block universe" of either spirit (Hegelian pantheism) or matter (scientistic determinism) but a pluralistic, ever-changing, and unpredictably adventuresome place.

It is fitting to apply to our treatment of James himself his advice to a student of philosophy: **Building up an author's meaning out of separate texts leads nowhere unless you have first grasped his centre of vision by an act of the imagination.** What is imagined is always a concrete particular, so here is one from James himself that goes to the very heart of the matter, to the heart of William James. It is his reaction to an ideal utopian community that sounds like "The Truman Show" or *Brave New World,* where "everybody's happy now." It is from an essay entitled "What Makes a Life Significant?"

A few summers ago I spent a happy week at the famous Assembly Grounds on the borders of Chautauqua Lake. The moment one treads that sacred enclosure, one feels one's self in an atmosphere of success. Sobriety and industry, intelligence and goodness, orderliness and ideality, prosperity and cheerfulness, pervade the air. It is a serious and studious picnic on a gigantic scale. Here you have a town of many thousands of inhabitants, beautifully laid out in the forest and drained, and equipped with means of satisfying all the necessary lower and most of the superfluous higher wants of man. You have a first-class college in full blast. You have magnificent music—a chorus of seven hundred voices, with possibly the most perfect open-air auditorium in the world. You have every sort of athletic exercise from sailing, rowing, swimming, bicycling, to the ball field and the . . . gymnasium. You have kindergartens and model secondary schools. You have general religious services and special houses for the several sects. You have perpetually running soda-water fountains, and daily popular lectures by distinguished men. You have the best of company. . . . You have no zymotic diseases, no poverty, no drunkenness, no crime, no police. You have culture, you have kindness, you have cheapness, you have equality, you have the best fruits of what mankind has fought and bled and striven for under the name of civilization for centuries. You have, in short, a foretaste of what human society might be were it all in the light, with no suffering and no dark corners.

I went in curiosity for a day. I stayed a week, held spell-bound by the charm and ease of everything, by the middle-class paradise, without a sin, without a victim, without a blot, without a tear.

And yet what was my own astonishment, on emerging into the dark and wicked world again, to catch myself unexpectedly and involuntarily saying: "Ouf! What a relief! Now for something primordial and savage, even though it were as bad as an Armenian massacre, to set the balance straight again. This order is too tame, this culture too second-rate, this goodness too uninspiring. This human drama without a villain or a pang, this community so refined that ice-cream and soda-water is the utmost offering it can make to the brute animal in man, this city simmering in the tepid lakeside sun, this atrocious harmlessness of all things—I cannot abide them. Let me take my chances again in the big outside worldly wilderness with all its sins and sufferings. There are the heights and depths, the precipices and steep ideals, the gleams of the awful and the infinite. . . ."

So I meditated. And, first of all, I asked myself what the thing was that was so lacking in this Sabbatical city . . . (it) is the everlasting battle of the powers of light with those of darkness, with heroism . . . snatching victory from the jaws of death. But in this unspeakable Chautauqua there was no potentiality of death in sight anywhere, and no point of the compass visible from which danger might possibly appear. . . . But what our human emotions seem to require is the sight of the struggle going on.[12]

It will come as no surprise that James was a New Yorker. If you hate a great city, you will not understand James. As Samuel Johnson famously said: "He who hates London, hates life."

"The Tender-Minded vs. the Tough-Minded"

To understand James's Pragmatism in its historical context, and to see how he proposed it as an answer to the basic dilemma of modern philosophy, we need only summarize his own essay on the subject entitled "The Present Dilemma in Philosophy."

James is one of the very few philosophers in this book whose words we will quote extensively, simply because he is such a good writer. I quote James on James because James's own explanations of James are usually much clearer than those of people who write books explaining James. For instance, I have read six different summaries of James's essay "The Will to Believe" and not one of them is nearly as clear or even as succinct as the essay itself.

James begins "The Present Dilemma in Philosophy" by asserting that philosophies are chosen by temperament more than by argument. He then distinguishes two basic and opposite temperaments in every field:

In manners we find formalists and free-and-easy persons. In government, authoritarians and anarchists. In literature, purists or academics and realists. In art,

---

12 James is saying the same thing another, later, philosopher put in one sentence: "If this world was perfect, it wouldn't be." His name is Yogi Berra.

classics and romantics. You recognize these contrasts as familiar. Well, in philosophy we have a very similar contrast expressed in the pair of terms "rationalist" and "empiricist," "empiricist" meaning your lover of facts in all their crude variety, "rationalist" meaning your devotee to abstract and eternal principles. No one can live an hour without both facts and principles, so it is a difference rather of emphasis; yet it breeds antipathies of the most pungent character.

He calls these two temperaments "the tender-minded" and "the tough-minded" and lists their differences as follows:

THE TENDER-MINDED	THE TOUGH-MINDED
Rationalistic (going by "principles")	Empiricist (going by "facts")
Intellectualistic	Sensationalistic
Idealistic	Materialistic
Optimistic	Pessimistic
Religious	Irreligious
Free-willist	Determinist
Monistic	Pluralistic
Dogmatical	Skeptical

The dilemma seems impossible to solve. For the two minds **have a low opinion of each other. . . . The tough think of the tender as sentimentalists and soft-heads. The tender feel the tough to be unrefined, callous, or brutal.**

But James wants both, like his description of the typical American: **He wants facts, he wants science; but he also wants a religion. . . .You want a system that will combine both things, the scientific loyalty to facts and willingness to take account of them, the spirit of adaption and accommodation, in short, but also the old confidence in human v a l u e s . . . . I offer the oddly-named thing pragmatism as a philosophy that can satisfy both kinds of demands.**

What Pragmatism Means

This is the key section. To understand it, we will first try to probe the spirit of it, the heart of it, before defining it more exactly. A good way to do this is to look at a particular example from James's own experience. (You will probably remember this example longer than anything else in this chapter.)

Some years ago, being with a camping party in the mountains, I returned from a solitary ramble to find everyone engaged in a ferocious metaphysical dispute. The *corpus* **of the dispute was a squirrel—a live squirrel supposed to be clinging to one side of a tree-trunk, while over against the tree's opposite side a human being was imagined to stand. The human witness tries to get sight of the squirrel by moving**

rapidly around the tree, but no matter how fast he goes, the squirrel moves as fast in the opposite direction, and always keeps the tree between himself and the man, so that never a glimpse of him is caught. The resultant metaphysical problem now is this: *Does the man go round the squirrel or not?* He goes round the tree, sure enough, and the squirrel is on the tree; but does he go round the squirrel? In the unlimited leisure of the wilderness, discussion had worn threadbare. Everyone had taken sides, and was obstinate.

James used a pragmatic standard to solve the question. "Which party is right," I said, "depends on what you *practically* mean by 'going round.' If you mean passing from the north of him to the east, then to the south, then to the west, and then to the north of him again, obviously the man does go round him, for he occupies these successive positions. But if on the contrary you mean first being in front of him, then on the right of him, then behind him, then on his left, and finally in front again, it is quite obvious that the man fails to go round him, for by the compensating movements the squirrel makes, he keeps his belly turned towards the man all the time. . . ."

I tell this trivial anecdote because it is a peculiarly simple example of what I wish now to speak of as *the pragmatic method.* The pragmatic method is primarily a method of settling metaphysical disputes that otherwise might be interminable. Is the world one or many? Fated or free? Material or spiritual? . . . The pragmatic method in such cases is to interpret each notion by tracing its respective practical consequences. What difference would it practically make to any one if this notion rather than that notion were true? If no practical difference whatever can be traced, then the alternatives mean, practically, the same thing, and all dispute is idle.

G. E. Moore, the Oxford "ordinary language" analytic philosopher, gives as an example of the kind of metaphysical dispute James is talking about the claim, in Kant, that "time is not noumenal but phenomenal"—i.e., not an objectively real "thing in itself" but projected from within ourselves by the inherent structure of our human consciousness. Moore asks: "Does this mean that I didn't really eat my lunch after I ate my breakfast, but only seemed to?" If so, it is nonsense. If not, it says nothing different than its apparently contradictory idea (that time is noumenal), because it means that I *really did* eat my lunch after my breakfast.

Meaning, for James, is not a timeless and abstract quality inherent in an idea. The meaning of an idea is the concrete difference it makes to our experience. If it makes no difference, it has no meaning.

James was not the first to teach this simple central idea (let's call it "the pragmatic criterion of meaning"). **It was first introduced into philosophy by Mr. Charles Pierce** (pronounced "purse") **in 1878. In an article in the *Popular Science Monthly* for January of that year entitled "How to Make Our Ideas Clear," Mr. Pierce, after pointing out that our beliefs are really rules for action, said that, to develop a thought's meaning, we need only determine what conduct it is fitted to produce. . . .**

It is astonishing to see how many philosophical disputes collapse into insignificance the moment you subject them to this simple test of tracing a concrete consequence. There can *be* no difference anywhere that doesn't *make* a difference elsewhere—no difference in abstract truth that doesn't express itself in a difference in concrete fact and in conduct consequent upon that fact. . . . The whole function of philosophy ought to be to find out what definite difference it will make to you or me, at definite instants of our life, if this world-formula or that world-formula be the true one.

There is absolutely nothing new in the pragmatic method. Socrates was an adept at it. Aristotle used it methodically. Locke, Berkeley and Hume made momentous contributions to truth by its means. . . .

At the same time it does not stand for any special results. It is a method only. . . . It appears less as a solution, then, than as a program for more work. . . . *Theories thus become instruments, not answers to enigmas in which we can rest.*

Truth, James says, is not a timeless property of an idea but **happens to an idea** when it is verified. Instead of seeking truth through the logical *origin* of an idea in *theory,* in its premises, James seeks it *in practice,* in the idea's *consequences.* Pragmatism **shifts the emphasis and looks forward.** It is not a doctrine but a method and an attitude, **the attitude of looking away from first things, principles, categories, supposed necessities, and of looking towards last things, fruits, consequences, facts.**

The third famous member of the pragmatic school, John Dewey, following Pierce and James, then took pragmatism a step farther as a theory of *truth:* **Messers Schiller and Dewey appear with their pragmaticistic account of what truth everywhere signifies. Everywhere, these teachers say, "truth" in our ideas and beliefs means the same thing that it means in science. It means, they say, nothing but this,** *that ideas (which themselves are parts of our experience) become true just so far as they help us to get into satisfactory relationship with other parts of our experience.* . . .

James makes the same point more simply: that **truth is one** *species of good* **and not, as is usually supposed, a category distinct from good and co-ordinate with it.** *The true is the name of whatever proves itself to be good in the way of belief.*

The technical, logical adequacy of this definition of truth may be problematic, but the upshot or "cash value" of the theory is clear. It is a practical program and method rather than a doctrine: **pragmatism . . . has in fact no prejudices whatever, no obstructive dogmas, no rigid canons of what shall count as proof. She is completely genial. She will entertain any hypothesis, she will consider any evidence. It follows that in the religious field she is at a great advantage both over positivistic empiricism, with its anti-theological bias, and over religious rationalism, with its exclusive interest in the remote, the noble, the simple, and the abstract.** . . .

By this standard James is more "genial" and "pragmatic" than Dewey, who, as we shall see, is (1) anti-religious, (2) anti-metaphysical, (3) ideologically committed to everything "leftist" in politics, and (4) tends to scientistic naturalism.

James's notion of truth is not a subjectivism or relativism. It is, he contends, nothing but common sense. **Truth, as any dictionary will tell you, is a property of certain of our ideas. It means their "agreement," as falsity means their disagreement, with "reality." Pragmatists and intellectualists** (i.e., rationalists) **both accept this definition as a matter of course. They begin to quarrel only after the question is raised as to what may precisely be meant by the term "agreement," and what by the term "reality"** . . . **the great assumption of the intellectualists is that truth means essentially an inert static relation.** . . . **Pragmatism, on the other hand, asks its usual question. "Granted an idea or belief to be true," it says, "what concrete difference will its being true make in any one's actual life? How will the truth be realized? What experiences will be different from those which would obtain if the belief were false? What, in short, is the truth's cash-value in experiential terms?"**

Truth is indeed an "agreement" with reality, James says, but it is not a static "correspondence" (often called "the picture theory of truth"). An idea *becomes* **true, it is made true by events, by the actions it calls forth. Our mental interests, hypotheses, postulates, so far as they are bases for human action—action which to a great extent transforms the world—help make the truth which they declare.** Mental acts are just as real and just as causally influential in the world, as physical acts. We are participants in life, not spectators of it. (Compare Marcel's distinction between "problem" and "mystery" here.)

James's point is not primarily theoretical ("What *is* truth?") but practical, a rule for practice. He is asking for what scientists often call "operational definitions." For instance "hard" means "what cannot be scratched by most other things" and "heavy" means "what will fall if we let go of it." It is especially, but not only, scientific ideas that are verified in this way.

A concrete example of James's principle that actions can *make* truth is his own financial support of his friend Charles Sanders Peirce. Peirce was unable to support himself, and James knew he would not accept charity, so he invented many nonexistent "anonymous donors" through whom he channeled his own money to Peirce. Was that *lying?* or was that *true?*

"The Will to Believe"

James's most famous and most controversial application of his pragmatic method is the essay with the title above. It is essentially a defense of Pascal's Wager against rationalism, especially against "Clifford's Rule," named after an Oxford philosopher, which says that "If a belief has been accepted on insufficient evidence . . . it is sinful. . . . It is wrong always, everywhere and for everyone, to believe anything on insufficient evidence." Against this, James writes **an essay in justification of faith, a defense of our right to adopt a believing attitude in religious matters in spite of the fact that our merely logical intellect may not have been coerced.** If we accept the few simple practical principles that James sets out below, he claims, **Pascal's argument, instead of being powerless, then seems a regular clincher** even though it is our passions rather than our reason that move us to believe. For *our passional nature not only lawfully may, but must, decide an option between propositions, whenever it is a genuine option that cannot by its nature be decided on intellectual grounds.* To explain this, he defines "a genuine option" as follows:

He begins by three distinctions among beliefs, or "hypotheses." **Let us give the name of** *hypothesis* **to anything that may be proposed to our belief. . . . Options** (choices between rival hypotheses) **may be of several kinds. They may be (1)** *living or dead, (2) forced or avoidable; (3) momentous or trivial;* **and for our purposes we may call an option a** *genuine* **option when it is of the forced, living, and momentous kind.**

(1) . . . just as the electricians speak of live and dead wires, let us speak of any hypothesis as either *live* **or** *dead.* **A live hypothesis is one which appeals as a real possibility to him to whom it is proposed. If I ask you to believe in the Mahdi** (the Shi'ite Muslim Messiah), **the notion makes no electric connection with your nature. . . . This shows that deadness and liveness in an hypothesis are not intrinsic properties, but relations to the individual thinker. They are measured by his willingness to act. . . .**

(2) If I say, "Either accept this truth or go without it," I put on you a forced option, for there is no standing place outside of the alternative. Every dilemma based on a complete logical disjunction, with no possibility of not choosing, is an option of this forced kind. . . .

(3) The option is trivial . . . when the stake is insignificant or when the decision is reversible. . . .

James then explains why he disagrees with Clifford (and, implicitly, also with Descartes's famous method of universal doubt): **There are two ways of looking at our duty in the matter of opinion . . . (1)** *We must know the truth, and* **(2)** *we must avoid error*—**these are our first and great commandments as would-be knowers . . . and by choosing between them we may end by coloring differently our whole intellectual life . . . Clifford . . . exhorts us to the latter course (2). Believe nothing, he tells us, keep your mind in suspense forever, rather than by closing it on insufficient evidence incur the awful risk of believing lies. . . . For my own part I have also a horror of being duped; but I can believe that worse things than being duped may happen to a man in this world; so Clifford's exhortation has to my ears a thoroughly fantastic sound. It is like a general informing his soldiers that it is better to keep out of battle forever than to risk a single wound. . . .**

James then applies his principle to religious beliefs: **we see, first, that religion offers itself as a** *momentous* **option. . . . Secondly, religion is a** *forced* **option, so far as that good** (religious good) **goes. We cannot escape the issue by remaining skeptical and waiting for more light, because, although we do avoid error in that way** *if religion be untrue,* **we lose the good** *if it be true,* **just as certainly as if we positively chose to** disbelieve it. **It is as if a man should hesitate indefinitely to ask a certain woman to marry him because he was not perfectly sure that she would prove an angel after he brought her home . . . what proof is there that dupery through hope is so much worse than dupery through fear?**

Faith entails trust. Life contains many situations—marriage proposals, military attacks, believing in your ability to perform some difficult or dangerous task, neighborly goodwill, and being promised something are some of the most obvious—in which only if we begin with an unproven trust will we see the result we desire. **There are cases where a fact cannot come at all unless a preliminary faith exists in its coming. And where faith in a fact can help create the fact, that would be an insane logic which would say** (as Clifford does) **that faith running ahead of scientific evidence is the "lowest kind of immorality" into which a thinking being can fall.**

James closes with a quote from Fitz-James Stephen: "In all important transactions of life we have to take a leap in the dark. . . . We stand on a mountain pass in the midst of whirling snow and blinding mist, through which we get glimpses now and then of paths which may be deceptive. If we take the wrong road we shall be dashed to pieces. We do not certainly know whether there is any right one. What must we do? 'Be strong and of a good courage.' Act for the best, hope for the best, and take what comes. . . . If death ends all, we cannot meet death better."

That was the philosophy of the "good guys" in *The Lord of the Rings*. It worked.

James's *Varieties of Religious Experience* is still, over a century later, an all-time classic of the study of religious mysticism and comparative religions. The basic conclusion from the mass of psychological data in this book is **that we can experience union with *something* larger than ourselves and in that union find our greatest peace.** James was both a believer and an agnostic. His last words, found on his desk when he died, were typically open-minded: **There is no conclusion. What has concluded, that we might conclude in regard to it?** But he also had written: **When I tell you that I have written a book on men's religious experience which on the whole has been regarded as making for God, you will perhaps exempt my own pragmatism from the charge of being an atheistic system. I firmly disbelieve, myself, that our human experience is the highest form of experience extant in the universe** (i.e., in objective reality). **I believe rather that we stand in much the same relation to the whole of the universe** (reality) **as our canine and feline pets do to the whole of human life.**

James draws essentially the same pragmatic conclusion about morality as he draws about religion, by comparing the human moral consequences of the two philosophies of religion and irreligion, or spiritualism and materialism. For in **all the delicate consequences which their differences entail, lie the real meanings. . . . Materialism means simply the denial that the moral order is eternal, and the shutting off of ultimate hopes . . .** (spiritualism) **means the affirmation of an eternal moral order and the**

letting loose of hope. Materialism's ultimate consequences are **utter wreck and tragedy.** (Cf. Bertrand Russell's famous quotation from "A Free Man's Worship," ch. 89.)

Moral belief proves itself in practice. It is a self-fulfilling prophecy. The belief that the meaning of life is to be a saint (which even the atheist Camus believed) "works," if and only if we believe in it. Saintliness actually "works," but only if we *do* it. **If things are ever to move upward, someone must be ready to take the first step, and assume the risk of it. No one who is not willing to try charity, to try** (Christ's and Ghandi's) **non-resistance, as the saint is willing, can tell whether these methods will or will not succeed. When they do succeed, they are far more powerfully successful than force or worldly prudence. Force destroys enemies; and the best that can be said of prudence is that it keeps what we already have in safety. But non-resistance, when successful, turns enemies into friends; and charity regenerates its objects. These saintly methods are . . . creative energies. . . .**

James is saying what Abraham Lincoln said: "The best way to destroy your enemy is to make him your friend."

James's affirmation of (1) religion, of (2) morality, which is one of its essential ingredients, and (3) therefore also of free will, which is one of morality's essential presuppositions, all follow from his "radical empiricism," which judges all hypotheses by the totality of human experience. Experience appears to us as full of wildness, passion, variety, and unpredictability. James criticizes ordinary empiricism (e.g., Hume's) for its over-neat packaging of experience into tidy little atomistic bits, and says it is essentially the same error as that of the apparently-opposite philosophy, rationalism: it reduces the universe to a **block universe.** (James means by "the universe" not merely matter but the sum total of reality.)

Free Will vs. Determinism

James defines determinism as the belief that all events in the universe, mental as well as physical, are determined—i.e., caused and made *necessary*—by previous events. Thus every event is totally predictable if only we know all its causes, all previous events. Free will contends that we can add new and unpredictable events to the universe. For determinism, every thing that is, must have been, and all alternatives are in the last analysis impossible. Determinism, if it is logically consistent, identifies reality with necessity and denies the existence of any possibilities that do not become actualities.

Those who believe determinism usually do so because they think science proves it. After all, science can explain and predict causal chains remarkably well, even in human behavior. However, James argues, science cannot, in principle, prove determinism because **Science professes to draw no conclusions but such as are based on matters of fact, things that have actually happened; but how can any amount of assurance that something actually happened give us the least grain of information as to whether another thing might or might not have happened in its place?**

Just as James did not believe God's existence could be conclusively either proved or disproved, he believed that neither free will nor determinism (fatalism, the denial of free will) could be either proved or disproved. He says: **I disclaim openly ... all pretension to prove to you that the freedom of the will is true.** He tells a story of a philosopher in the middle of a Boston street with philosophy clubs on both sides. On one side there is The Determinists' Club and on the other side The Free-Willers' Association. Since the philosopher respects science, and many people claim there are scientific arguments for determinism, he chooses to join them. He knocks on the door of The Determinists' Club and asks admission. They ask him why he came. He replies that he came of his own free will. So they shut the door in his face. He then crosses the street and asks admission to the Free-Willers' Association. They ask him why he came. He replies, "They threw me out of the other place, so I had no choice in the matter." So they also shut the door in his face, and he is left homeless in the street.

It is his pragmatic method which leads James to believe in free will. In the absence of conclusive arguments, James *chooses* to believe in free will, thus *making* the belief in free will true. **In other words, our first act of freedom, if we are free, ought ... to be to affirm that we are free. .... At any rate, I will assume ... that it is no illusion. My first act of free will shall be to believe in free will.**

His pragmatic argument against determinism is the human consequences of the mechanistic world-view it teaches: **It professes that those parts of the universe already laid down absolutely appoint and decree what the other parts shall be. The future has no ambiguous possibilities hidden in its womb; the part we call the present is compatible with only one totality. ... The whole is ... an iron block.** Such a universe may not be disprovable, but it is unlivable. And the main reason is our *moral* experience. **If this ... murder was called for by the rest of the universe ... what are we to think of the universe? ... it is nothing short of deliberately espousing a kind of pessimism. The judgment of regret calls the murder bad. Calling a thing bad means, if it means anything at all, that the thing ought not to be, that something else ought to be in its stead. Determinism, in denying that anything else can be in its stead, virtually defines the universe as a place in which what ought to be is impossible.**

The argument is similar, though not identical, to Aquinas's: if free will does not exist, all moral language, all praising, blaming, counseling, commanding, rewarding, and punishing, is strictly meaningless. It is meaningless to blame or punish a machine when it fails to work properly, no matter how complex the machine is. We do not have priests who hear confessions from non-performing vending machines.

In "The Dilemma of Determinism" James argues that determinism entails either moral pessimism (reality could not possibly be better than it is; even murders *have* to happen) or moral optimism (everything is justified because it is necessary); but pragmatism entails a middle view that he calls moral **meliorism**. This alone puts the responsibility on us, not on the world, for the moral state of the world. It contends that we *can* make the world better, and ought to. Again, James sides with common sense.

So like the pragmatic conception of truth and like the defense of "the will to believe," the rejection of determinism is necessitated by James's refusal to believe in a single **block universe,** unbending, invulnerable and inflexible, closed to any real novelty. Instead, he argues, our experience shows that the universe is open and pluralistic and vulnerable— more like ourselves. It is fit for human habitation.

Accepting this world of risk instead of the "block universe" is a choice. **Suppose the world's author put the case to you before creation, saying: "I am going to make a world not certain to be saved, a world the perfection of which shall be conditional . . . the condition being that each several agent does its own "level best." I offer you the chance of taking part in such a world. Its safety, you see, is unwarranted** (not guaranteed). **It is a real adventure, with real danger, yet it might win through. . . . Will you join the procession? Will you trust yourself and trust the other agents enough to face the risk?** Those who answer Yes write the world's great novels. Those who answer No write no fiction—except dull defenses of "Brave New World" like the determinist-behaviorist B. F. Skinner's *Walden Two.*

For my own part, I do not know what the sweat and blood of this life mean if they mean anything short of this. If this life be not a real fight, in which something is eternally gained for the universe by success, it is no better than a game of private theatricals from which we may withdraw at will. But it *feels* **like a real fight—as if there were something really wild in the universe which we, with all our idealities and faithfulnesses, are needed to redeem; and first of all to redeem our own hearts from atheisms and fears.**

Like Frodo Baggins, James says "I will take the Ring, though I do not know the way."

Critique

A logical problem in James is that he seems to confuse the two questions of an idea's *meaning* and its *truth.* The pragmatic criterion of meaning does not seem to contain any internal self-contradiction, but the pragmatic criterion of truth does. For if we apply the pragmatic criterion of truth to itself, we find that it "works" and is thus "true" in the pragmatic sense only if it is "true" *in the non-pragmatic, old sense* of "objective truth." Even moral and religious beliefs "work" only if we believe them to be *really, objectively and factually* true. The only kind of God one can believe in effectively and practically, so as to make a real difference to one's life, is a God who is objectively real. We cannot believe merely in a belief, or in a fiction created by our belief. I think this is what Chesterton meant when he said that "man's most pragmatic need is to be more than a pragmatist."

Not only practically but also logically, the pragmatic criterion of truth seems self-contradictory. For it says that it is really true that ideas become true only by belief and practice. If the idea that an idea becomes true only by belief and practice itself becomes true only by belief and practice, we have an infinite regress.

Insofar as pragmatism is a doctrine, a theory, it seems to reduce truth to something *less* than common sense believes it is; and all reductionisms and skepticisms seem self-contradictory, whether they are simple or complex: Is it true that there is no truth? Is it objectively true that truth is not objective? Is it certain that truth is only probable, not certain? Is it universally true that truth is not universal? Is it absolutely true that truth is not absolute? Etc.

However, if we remember James's initial insistence that pragmatism is *not* a doctrine, a theory, but only a practical method, it then is not reductionist and self-contradictory, but is often very useful in practice, like the scientific method itself as a mere method as distinct from the theory of scient*ism* that claims that there is no truth outside the scientific method—which is self-refuting because it cannot be proved by the scientific method!

Selected Bibliography:

It is usually pointless to list books about great philosophers who are also great writers, for it is always better to read the philosophers themselves. However, William Barrett's *The Illusion of Technique* is recommended as a creative and challenging look at James, Heidegger and Wittgenstein as three very different allies against modern technologism and reductionism.

80. John Dewey (1859–1952)

Though James has had the most influence on American philosophers, Dewey has had more influence on non-philosophers, especially in education. He is the main founder of "progressive education," which could briefly be described as more experiential, permissive, student-centered, and informal as opposed to classical, traditional, bookish, or authoritarian methods. A vague but accurate generalization is that on every issue Dewey is "liberal" rather than "conservative." He is the polar opposite of a rationalistic and religious philosopher like Aquinas or a popular apologist for traditional, pre-modern ideas like C. S. Lewis or G. K. Chesterton.

Life

His mother was a devout Calvinist. He was happily married, with seven children, one adopted. He was born (in Burlington, Vermont) during the Civil War and died during the Korean War, and lived through enormous changes in America. This is reflected in his philosophy, which is essentially a philosophy of change. His favorite object of attack is the idea of any realm of changeless truths. He is probably the most influential philosopher of education since Plato. He was a public figure of influence, advising China, Japan and Turkey as well as America on education. He visited Stalin's Russia in the 1920s and was favorably impressed by its schools. He taught at the Universities of Michigan, Minnesota, Chicago, and Columbia, and published over 1000 articles and books. He co-founded the New School for Social Research in New York City in 1919.

Darwin was his master influence. He wrote that **"The Origin of Species" introduced a mode of thinking that in the end was bound to transform the logic of knowledge, and hence the treatment of morals, politics, and religion . . . an intellectual revolt (against) . . . the conceptions that had reigned in . . . philosophy . . . for two thousand years, the conceptions that had . . . rested on the assumption of the superiority of the fixed and final.** Like Spencer (ch. 84), Dewey tried to work out the consequences of Darwinian evolutionism and naturalism in all areas of philosophy, including metaphysics, philosophy of history, epistemology, ethics, religion, politics, and education, as we shall see point by point.

Metaphysics

Since a philosopher's metaphysics (or anti-metaphysics) determines everything else in his philosophy, we must begin with Dewey's metaphysics, which in a word is *Naturalism,* the

97

denial of any reality to the supernatural, which for him meant above all the timeless: **The discovery that natural science is forced by its own development to abandon the assumption of fixity and to recognize that what . . . is actually universal is process . . . is the most revolutionary discovery yet made.**

Dewey thus parts company with the assumption of Plato and Aristotle which had dominated nearly all previous philosophy, namely the idea that things have essential natures that are unchangeable. In this philosophy **the conception of *eidos,* a fixed form and final cause, was the central principle of knowledge. . . . Genuinely to know is to grasp a permanent end. . . .** The new philosophy instead **forswears inquiry after absolute origins and absolute finalities.** Such philosophy is a wild goose chase after nonexistent absolutes, what Aristotle called "formal causes" and "final causes." There is no such thing. The only thing that is unchanging is change.

Instead of the classical ideal of knowing the truth for its own sake, Dewey substitutes the Baconian program of "knowledge for *power,*" for "man's conquest of nature." **The brain is primarily an organ of a certain kind of behavior, not of knowing the world. . . . The essential point in all response is the desire to control the environment. The problem of philosophy is not how we can come to know an external world but how we can learn to control it and remake it. . . . To idealize and rationalize the universe at large is after all a confession of inability to master the courses of things. . . . Ever-renewed progress is to Bacon the test as well as the aim of genuine logic. Where, Bacon constantly demands, where are the works, the fruits, of the older logic? What has it done to ameliorate the evils of life, to rectify defects, to improve conditions? . . . A true logic or technique of inquiry would make advance in the industrial, agricultural and medical arts . . .** (instead of) **the errors of our ancestors, musty with antiquity and organized into pseudo-science through the use of the classic logic. . . . Aristotle thought of reason as capable of solitary communion with rational truth. . . . To Bacon, error had been produced and perpetuated by social influences, and truth must be discovered by social agencies organized for that purpose . . . the Empire, as he says, of Man over Nature.**[13]

This naturalistic metaphysics of Dewey's has immediate consequences. Its anthropology sees man as totally embedded in time, process, and nature, with no remainder, no "transcendence." Its epistemology gives up the quest for certainty. Its ethics does the same. Good and evil are not relatively absolute but absolutely relative. The good is not the end but the process and the progress: **The bad man is the man who, no matter how good he has been, is beginning to deteriorate, to grow less good. The good man is**

---

13 See C. S. Lewis's *The Abolition of Man*, ch. 3, and his *Brave New World*-like novel *That Hideous Strength* for a critique of this new Baconian *summum bonum*, and also Walter M. Miller, Jr.'s classic science fiction novel *A Canticle for Leibowitz*, for a non-Deweyan treatment of the relation between morality and technology.

the man who, no matter how morally unworthy he has been, is moving to become better.

Dewey's naturalism even revolutionizes logic, somewhat as Hegel's historical relativism did. (Like Marx, Dewey began as a Hegelian and abandoned the Hegelian content, especially the talk about an "absolute," while borrowing the historicism and progressivism of Hegel's dialectical logic.) It does this by denying the law of excluded middle, the "either A or non-A" principle that is a corollary of the law of non-contradiction itself.

This is possible because Dewey's logic is not formal and abstract, but relative to its ever-changing content. For instance, Dewey would call himself neither an atheist nor a theist nor an agnostic since the very question "Does God exist?" is a question not to be answered but to be "abandoned," not for logical reasons but for psychological reasons of "attitude" and "preference." And the ultimate reason for this, in a word, is Darwin:

The conviction persists—though history shows it to be a hallucination—that all the questions that the human mind has asked are questions that can be answered in terms of the alternatives that the questions themselves present. But in fact intellectual progress usually occurs through sheer abandonment of questions together with both of the alternatives they assume—an abandonment that results from their decreasing vitality and a change of urgent interest. We do not solve them; we get over them. Old questions are solved by disappearing, evaporating, while new questions corresponding to the changed attitude of endeavor and preference take their place. Doubtless the greatest dissolvent in contemporary thought of old questions . . . is the one effected by the scientific revolution that found its climax in *The Origin of Species*.

All philosophies of the classic type have made a fixed and fundamental distinction between two realms of existence. One of these corresponds to the religious and supernatural world of popular tradition, which in its metaphysical rendering became the world of highest and ultimate reality. . . . This is the trait which, in my opinion, has affected most deeply the classic notion about the nature of philosophy. Philosophy has arrogated to itself the office of demonstrating the existence of a transcendent absolute. . . . It has therefore claimed that it was in possession of a higher organ of knowledge than is employed by positive science . . . and that it is marked by a superior dignity and importance.

This entails also a revolution in morals and values, a repudiation of the Greek and Christian notion of hierarchy that subordinated the "how" questions of technology and physical science, which deal with changing things, to standards of ethics that were believed to be timeless values. Plato, for instance, asks, **Who would put the art of the shoemaker on the same plane as the art of ruling the state? Who would put even the higher art of the physician in healing the body upon the level of the art of the priest in healing the soul? Thus Plato constantly draws the contrast in his dialogues. The shoemaker is a judge of a good pair of shoes, but he is no judge at all of the more important question, whether and when it is good to wear shoes; the physician**

is a good judge of health, but whether it is a good thing or not to be well or better to die, he knows not. While the artisan is expert as long as purely limited technical questions arise, he is helpless when it comes to the only really important questions, the moral questions as to values. Consequently, his type of knowledge is inherently inferior and needs to be controlled by a higher kind of knowledge which will reveal ultimate ends and purposes, and thus put and keep technical and mechanical knowledge in its proper place.

Naive readers, note: Dewey is not describing this as something obvious and true but as an error, even a "hallucination." He could write this in 1920, after the bloodbath of World War I, and he did not repudiate it even after Hiroshima and Auschwitz.

Dewey does not try to *prove* naturalism or refute supernaturalism, but to *undermine* it, as Nietzsche did, by exposing its questionable origins: **This course of lectures** *(Reconstruction in Philosophy,* Dewey's most succinct and comprehensive work) **will be devoted to setting forth this different conception of philosophy in . . . its main contrasts to . . . the classic conception . . .** (by tracing the origin of classical philosophy to) **an authoritative tradition originally dictated by man's imagination working under the influence of love and hate and in the interest of emotional excitement and satisfaction. . . . It seems to me that this genetic method of approach is a more effective way of undermining this type of philosophic theorizing than any attempt at logical refutation . . . philosophy originated not out of intellectual material but out of social and emotional material . . . under disguise of dealing with ultimate reality, philosophy has been occupied with the . . . values embedded in social traditions. . . .**

This can be a very convenient way of ignoring honest questions that you don't want to answer. Instead of refuting an idea, you "undermine" it by finding its psychological origins in emotions and desires. Logicians used to call that "the genetic fallacy": attacking an idea not because it is false but because of its psychological origin. It is a fallacy. Even if Newton had come to believe that F=MA because he hated his mother, who denied it, F would still equal MA.

Epistemology

Dewey named his theory of knowledge **instrumentalism,** which means that thinking is not an end but a means, an instrument for the end of solving practical problems.

Both rationalism and empiricism separate knower and known, while Dewey joins them from the beginning in "experience." The knower does not stand apart from the known world as a spectator, but is an active part of it and its processes. The knower does not transcend the known. Dewey claims that this solves modern epistemology's primary problem, how to bridge the gap between knowing subject and known object, or reason and nature; how to return to the world once it had been Cartesianly doubted. The solution is that there is no gap. In the words of the Zen *koan,* the solution to how you get the goose out of the bottle is that it's already out.

Both rationalism and empiricism separate reason and sense experience; instrumentalism joins them. Reason does not transcend experience, hovering over it and judging it, but emerges from it, as part of it.

Both rationalism and empiricism separate thinking and doing; instrumentalism sees thinking as a stage of doing. Thinking and learning does not transcend doing but is a kind of doing, or a part of doing. As the educational maxim puts it, "you learn by Deweying."

This may sound commonsensical to some, but to others it entails a shocking denial of objective truth independent of the mind. It denies **the assumption that the true and valid object of knowledge is that which has been prior to and independent of the operations of knowing.** Concepts, for Dewey, do not reveal "the real world," even if there is any such thing; they are merely our instruments for solving problems. They are instruments for action, not for knowledge of objective truth. (And that idea also is only an instrument and not an objective truth.)

All learning, says Dewey, is problem-solving. All problems are practical problems, problems of practice and behavior. Theory is strictly an instrument for practice. And since problems arise only when our emotions and desires are frustrated, it follows that all concepts are relative to our emotions and desires, our interests. Concepts and hypotheses are merely instruments, tools that we use to serve our purposes, and which we discard when our purposes change.

Dewey sees Science as only one way (though the most reliable way) of solving problems. He attacks materialistic "scien*tism*" as not relativistic enough: **There is no inquiry which has a monopoly on the . . . title of knowledge . . . the statesman, educator and dramatist may know human nature as truly as the professional psychologist; the farmer may know soils and plants as truly as the botanist and mineralogist. For the criterion of knowledge lies in the method used to secure consequences and not in metaphysical conceptions of the nature of the real.** It is useful to compare Aristotle here: he would agree with Dewey's conclusion (the first sentence) but not with his premise (the second).

Ethics

Dewey's ethics is a revised Utilitarianism. Like the Utilitarians, Dewey believes (1) that goodness is not an essence inherent in things, (2) that it is not the same for all individuals or all generations, (3) that it must be discovered by trial and error, (4) that the methods of science are the best way of discovering it, and (5) that an act is good if it produces satisfactory consequences. But unlike the Utilitarians, he also held that values are not wholly relative to subjective desires; that the desired and the desirable, or wants and needs, are not the same. What distinguishes them is intelligence. But (and here he resembles Utilitarianism again) this means not theoretical intelligence but intelligence calculating the action's likely consequences, and not just individually but socially.

Dewey identifies the primary crisis about values in modern philosophy as parallel to the crisis in epistemology: the gap between rationalism and empiricism. Ethical rationalists like Kant see goodness as an a priori, as non-empirical, as something beyond nature, and theists see it as rooted in the will or the supernatural and eternal character of God. This is ethical supernaturalism. Empiricists like Hume see goodness as purely subjective, not derived from nature but added to nature or imposed on nature by our feelings or will rather than God's. The common error of both, Dewey says, is the gap between values and nature, the assumption that nature is value-free.

This assumption he traces to modern science, which succeeded in conquering nature only when it excluded teleology (ends, purposes, "final causes," goods, values) from nature and reduced it to a machine. In pre-modern philosophy ethics had an objective foundation in nature. Aquinas, e.g., begins the ethics section of his *Summa* with the thesis that man, like nature, always acts for an end, and identifies the first problem of ethics as that of man's ultimate end, or "summum bonum." Dewey says that **In such a context there was no call and no place for any *separate* problem of valuation and values, since what are now termed values were taken to be integrally incorporated in the very structure of the world. But when teleological considerations were eliminated from one natural science after another, and finally from the sciences of physiology and biology, the problem of value arose as a separate problem.**

Dewey's solution is a wholly naturalistic ethics but not a wholly subjective one. He wants to overcome what most "analytic philosophers" call the "fact-value distinction" (which is their way of identifying the same crisis). **The problem of restoring integration and cooperation between man's beliefs about the world in which he lives and his beliefs about the values and purposes that should direct his conduct is the deepest problem of modern life . . . science and traditional morals have been at complete odds with one another. . . . Hence a deep and impassable gulf is set up between the *natural* subject-matter of science and the *extra-* if not supra-natural subject matter of morals** Dewey's solution is a **change in point of view which will render the methods and conclusions of natural science serviceable for moral theory and practice. All that is needed is acceptance of the view that moral subject matter is also spatially and temporally qualified** (i.e., purely naturalistic). Science is not to be enlarged to include spiritual values; values are to be reduced to space and time to conform to naturalistic science.

Dewey's methodological solution to this gap between nature and moral values is the utilitarian version of the pragmatic method, **defining value by enjoyments which are the consequences of intelligent action.**

But "enjoyments" are totally subjective. What overcomes subjectivism, and the reduction of moral values to personal desires? Only **the intervention of intelligence.** And this means not perceiving objective values but calculating consequences. **Not stern moralists alone but everyday experience informs us that finding satisfaction in a thing may be a warning, a summons to be on the lookout for consequences.** (Drug use is an obvious example here.)

But it is not the *morally* bad consequences that determine good or bad for Dewey, but the consequences for our pleasure and enjoyment. So like the Utilitarians, Dewey is essentially a Hedonist.

Thus Dewey claims to make science and ethics not opposite but cooperative ventures, since science provides us with the best method for calculating consequences. (Does it?) And facts and values are not opposites, since values are based on facts about these consequences. They are predictions about future human satisfactions, as science predicts nature's future behaviors. So value judgments can be objectively true or false, and can be verified by science, which is not an alien and inhuman thing but only ordinary intelligence perfected by a more controlled method.

Though Dewey is not a *subjectivist*,[14] he is a *relativist* rather than an absolutist. Not only are goods relative to our enjoyments, but they are also relative to time and change. There is no absolute good. There are no ends in themselves. Every end is but a provisional means to a further end, or **ends-in-view. If the notion of some objects as ends-in-themselves were abandoned, human beings would for the first time in history be in a position to frame ends-in-view and form desires on the basis of empirically grounded propositions.**

Dewey sees this change as radical and revolutionary: **for the first time in history** we should now learn to do ethics as we have learned to do science, and learn to treat our moral values as we now treat our scientific ideas. If we did that, then all **standards, principles, rules . . . and all tenets and creeds about good and goods would be recognized to be hypotheses. Instead of being rigidly fixed, they would be treated as intellectual instruments to be tested and confirmed—and altered—through consequences. . . . The change would do away with the intolerance and fanaticism that attend the notion that beliefs and judgments are capable of inherent truth and authority. . . . Men, instead of being proud, and accepting and asserting beliefs and "principles" on the ground of loyalty, will be as ashamed of that procedure as they would now be to confess their assent to a scientific theory out of reverence for Newton.**

This is indeed radical and revolutionary, for it seems to logically entail that all the saints of past history, including secular saints, be regarded as practicing **intolerance and fanaticism,** while *un*-principled ethical compromisers and experimenters be regarded as moral pioneers. Does this theory account for the common human experience of moral obligation and duty? Does it account for the historical fact of the influence for good of "fanatics" like Jesus, Socrates, Buddha, Gandhi, Mother Teresa, and Martin Luther King?

Politics

Like most anti-religious naturalists, Dewey sees politics as crucially important. Much of what the Church used to do for man, the State must now do. But this should not be a

14 He *claims* not to be; but since pleasure is subjective, must not all Hedonists be relativists?

totalitarian state. Dewey's political liberalism strongly supported democracy, freedom, and open experimentation, but also tended to socialism and collectivism. The paradox is resolved by a free, populist and pluralist collectivism rather than expanded governmental control. Collectivism yes, totalitarianism no. A multiplicity of voluntary associations would reconcile individualism with common action.

Thinking itself is social, for Dewey; it is conditioned by its cultural milieu. Individuals are largely products of society; yet they are also called on to be creative innovators to change society and culture. (We find this same tension in a more radical form in Marx.) Even apparently a priori logical as well as moral categories are for Dewey merely the product of the cultural transmission of certain evolved mental habits of thinking. Nothing is rigid in human nature, everything is flexible.

Like most "liberals" as distinct from "conservatives," Dewey believed man was naturally good and not evil. He was an optimist in an optimistic time, a time of great growth in every field in America. He had an instinctive faith in ordinary people to solve great problems, in students to design their own educational experiences, in common people rather than elites, and in the future rather than the past, in the new rather than the old. And this applied also to his politics.

Education

Dewey's greatest influence and success was in education. His is the name most associated with "progressive education" as opposed to "classical" or "traditional" education. What does this difference mean? Here is Dewey's definition of the classical theory of education that he wants to replace, point for point:

(1) **The subject-matter of education consists of bodies of information and of skills that have been worked out in the past; therefore, the chief business of the school is to transmit them to the new generation.**

(2) **In the past, there have also been developed standards and rules of conduct; moral training consists in forming habits of action in conformity with these rules and standards.**

(3) **Finally, the general pattern of school organization . . . constitutes the school as a kind of institution sharply marked off from other social institutions.**

(4) **Since the subject-matter as well as standards of proper conduct are handed down from the past, the attitude of pupils must, upon the whole, be one of docility, receptivity, and obedience.**

(5) **Books, especially textbooks, are the chief representatives of the lore and wisdom of the past. . . .**

(6) **The traditional scheme is, in essence, one of imposition from above and from outside. It imposes adult standards, subject-matter, and methods upon those who are only growing slowly toward maturity . . . the gulf between the mature or adult**

products and the experience and abilities of the young is so wide that the very situation forbids much active participation by pupils. . . .

(7) **Moreover, that which is taught is thought of as essentially static. . . . It is to a large extent the cultural product of societies that assumed the future would be much like the past.**

(1) In contrast, Dewey called for education by experiment, trial and error, as in a laboratory

(2) To encourage self-learning, he encouraged rather than discouraged nonconformist behavior. He admitted that **visitors to some progressive schools are shocked by the lack of manners they come across.**

(3) He wanted the school to be a miniature industry in an industrial society, with **shops, kitchens, and so on in the school. . . .**

(4) It was also to be a miniature democracy in a democratic rather than hierarchical and authoritarian society. Thus **the teacher loses the position of external boss or dictator but takes on that of leader of group activities It is his business to arrange for the kind of experiences which, while they do not repel the student but rather engage his activities are . . . enjoyable since they promote having desirable future experiences. . . .**

(5) Dewey wanted more experiments and fewer books, more laboratories and less literature, for **the philosophy in question is, to paraphrase the saying of Lincoln about democracy, one of education of, by, and for experience.**

(6) **When education is based upon experience and educative experience is seen to be a social process, the situation changes radically . . . when education is conceived in terms of experience, anything which can be called a study . . . must be derived from materials which at the outset fall within the scope of ordinary life-experience. In this respect the newer education contrasts sharply with procedures which start with facts and truths that are outside the range of the experience of those taught.** Instead of Dante going to Hell, Purgatory, and Heaven, Dick and Jane go to the supermarket.

(7) **The educational system must move one way or another, either backward to the intellectual and moral standards of a pre-scientific age or forward to ever greater utilization of scientific method . . . in all subjects . . . (For) scientific method is the only authentic means at our command for getting at the significance of our everyday experiences of the world in which we live.**

Evaluation

It's a good rule of thumb (though not an infallible criterion) that philosophers are right in what they affirm and wrong in what they deny, right in what they see and wrong in what they fail to see. If we apply this rule to Dewey, we must admit two things.

On the one hand, even his opponents cannot quarrel with his call for progress, innovation, creativity, and change; or with the utility of questions about utility, or with the practicality of the pragmatic method; or with the call to learn from the scientific method; or with the emphasis on the social; or with the need to overcome the polarities of rationalism vs. empiricism and morality vs. science.

On the other hand, even his disciples must admit there is something troubling and problematic about his reductionisms. The contrast with James is striking: James agrees with almost all of Dewey's positive points but not his negative ones, except their common attack on abstract rationalists like Hegel.

It may also be instructive in this connection to compare Dewey with Marcel regarding each of the seven points Marcel (ch. 77) used to summarize his own philosophy: the sense of being (and not only becoming); of mystery (and not only problems); of self-knowledge by individual "recollection" (and not just social and cultural conditioning); of a "hope" that depends on something ontologically real that is more than ourselves (not just optimism about humanity and the future); of the "creativeness" of "fidelity" (and not just of science); and of the "presence" of a person and an "availability" that is open to personal charity (and not just to "experience"). Of course, Dewey is a naturalist and a secularist; but one need not derive these Marcelian values from religion alone; one can derive them from experience. "Experience"—that was Dewey's favorite word, but it was not broad enough to include these additional "existential" dimensions, as it was for James.

81. Auguste Comte (1798–1857)

Comte is often called "the father of Positivism." He popularized the term "positive philosophy," but did not invent it. John Stuart Mill said that positivism was "the general property of the age." The essential meaning of the term "positivism" is the "ism" or ideology that takes modern science as the medievals took divine revelation: as the single absolute criterion and ideal for judging all human knowledge. Indeed, a good case could be made for saying that even though Positivism always strongly disagrees with the truth-claims of religion, yet the ultimate foundation and presupposition of Positivism is religious rather than scientific: a presupposed rather than proved *faith* in Science as the absolute. Not only do positivists take a scientific attitude to religion: they also take a religious (i.e. absolutistic) attitude toward science.

John Stuart Mill classified himself as a Positivist and defined Positivism as the doctrine that "we have no knowledge of anything but Phenomena (sense impressions), and our knowledge of phenomena is relative, not absolute. We know not the essence, nor the real mode of production (cause) of any fact, but only its relations to other facts in the way of succession or of similitude . . . . The constant relations which link phenomena together, and the constant sequences which unite them as antecedent and consequent, are termed their laws. The laws of phenomena are all we know respecting them. Their essential nature, and their ultimate causes, either efficient or final, are unknown and inscrutable to us."

The late medieval Nominalists had eliminated formal causes (universal essences). Descartes had eliminated final causes (purposes) from nature. Hobbes had eliminated material causes (potentialities). Hume had eliminated efficient causes. What was left? For the Positivist, nothing but appearances.

Positivism changed its character in the twentieth century from an ideology to a logic, and called itself "Logical Positivism," in the words of A. J. Ayer. It was later broadened and softened to the more generic "analytic philosophy," and as such is still the single most popular philosophy, at least as a method, everywhere in the English-speaking world. We will explore four nineteenth-century Positivists (Comte, Bentham, Mill, and Spencer) and four twentieth-century "analytic philosophers" (Ayer, Moore, Russell, and Wittgenstein).

Comte was born, lived, and wrote in France. He never held a university teaching post, and supported himself by private tutoring. Like many modern philosophers, he grew up in a religious home and left his Catholic faith early, as a precocious 14-year-old. He befriended the socialist Saint-Simon, from whom he picked up his most famous idea, the three stages of human history. Like many philosophers, Comte had difficulty keeping four things: friends (he quarreled with his teacher acrimoniously, ending a 7-year friendship), money (he had to be financially supported by others even after he became famous), marriage (he had a brief, unhappy one), and happiness (overwork caused a mental breakdown and a suicide attempt). One wag said: "I keep trying to be philosophical, but happiness keeps breaking in." Many philosophers could say the opposite: "I keep trying to be happy, but philosophy keeps breaking in." However, this seems typical only of modern philosophers: Socrates, Plato, Aristotle, Augustine, Anselm, and Aquinas all seemed quite happy.

The Meaning of "Positivism"

"Positivism" is Comte's affirmative word for a negative enterprise, a kind of reductionism: the reduction of all meaningful ideas and theories to those that are in principle empirically verifiable or falsifiable by their ability to coordinate data observed by the senses. Only what can be empirically tested counts as knowledge. The only real knowledge we have, according to Comte, is (1) our sense observation of visible facts and (2) science, which coordinates these facts under more general laws. These laws merely describe phenomena rather than causally explain them. Such science is the *only* valid form of knowledge. Everything else is only pretended knowledge. Thus at one stroke Positivism excludes most of the most important and interesting questions asked by philosophers in the past and by ordinary people at all times, e.g., What is a good person and a good life? Do God, free will, and life after death exist? What are my moral obligations? What is beauty? Does human life have an objective purpose or end?

This is a more radical empiricism than even Hume's. For Hume, like Locke and Berkeley, argued for his empiricism by tracing all ideas back to sense impressions, as their copies. Comte refuses to argue for his empiricism in this or any other way. It is an absolute starting point, a non-negotiable, non-provable and non-refutable faith, a "posit." As "positive laws" are laws posited by human wills (like "Drive on the right side") while both "natural laws" and "divine laws" are discovered rather than created by man; and as Positivism in ethics admits only positive laws, and not natural or divine laws; so Comte's epistemological Positivism simply "posits," or asserts, as an act of will rather than a thesis to be proved by premises, that all knowledge is to be reduced to empirical scientific knowledge. It is not established by logic or proof but "posited" by "ideology." Its justification is not premises or evidence but its use, its effects, its power in transforming both science and society into forms which Comte assumes are better.

We can see this if we imagine how Comte would view an argument between a theist and an atheist, who would both give *reasons* for their conclusions. For instance, the theist might argue that design or causality in the universe proves a Designer or First Cause, and the atheist might argue that the existence of evil in the universe disproves a God who is both all-good and all-powerful. Comte would not *argue* for atheism. He would simply exclude the idea of God rather than disprove it. Although Comte insists he is *not* an atheist, he is actually much more atheistic than classical atheists because the idea of God cannot, for him, even rise to the level of meaningful error. It is meaningless because it is not empirical. (The same is true for final causes, formal causes, essences, Platonic Forms, souls, spirits, free will, life after death, and real moral values as distinct from felt desires.)

The point is that Comte does not think "backward," so to speak, to find premises to justify his Positivism, but only "forward" to use it as a weapon to destroy all non-scientific ways of thought, all theological and metaphysical ideas, and, most importantly of all, societies and social organizations based on those ideas. He wants to create a new mind, which will refuse to think in unscientific terms, so that this new mind can create a new society. This is why it is an "ideology": the only justification he gives for it is the political and social change it concretely aims at. It is not a philosophy at all if "philosophy" means, as it did for Socrates, an open-minded "love of wisdom."

The parallel above between the medievals' faith in divine revelation and the modern Positivist's faith in science is misleading, because the medieval reveled in giving *reasons* for their faith. In this sense they were much more scientific, and less fideistic or fundamentalistic, than the Positivists.

The Three Stages

The most famous of Comte's ideas is his philosophy of history. It is that Man has passed through three fundamentally different intellectual stages, the "theological," the "metaphysical," and the "positive scientific." ***The law of human progress . . . is this: that each of our leading conceptions—each branch of our knowledge—passes through theoretical conditions: the Theological, or fictitious; the Metaphysical, or abstract; and the Scientific, or positive. . . .***

In the theological stage, the human mind, seeking the essential nature of beings, the first and final causes (the origin and purpose) of all effects—in short, Absolute knowledge—supposes all phenomena to be produced by the immediate *(sic!)* **action of supernatural beings.**

Comte subdivides this stage into three: (1) In the animistic or fetishistic stage, all things in nature are thought to have life and will; (2) in the polytheistic stage, these forces are located in supernatural gods and goddesses who manipulate these natural things; and (3) in the monotheistic stage, the gods are condensed into a single deity.

Next, **In the metaphysical stage, which is only a modification of the first, the mind supposes, instead of supernatural beings, abstract forces . . . personified abstractions inherent in all beings and capable of producing all phenomena** such as "essences," "potentialities," "tendencies" and "natures"; or energy, force, attraction and repulsion. In place of the Mind and Will of God or the gods, the metaphysician posits an impersonal universal *Logos* or Reason as the ordering principle of the universe, as in Plato, the Stoics, and Hegel.

In the final, the positive, state, the mind has given over the search for Absolute notions, the origin and destination of the universe, and the causes of phenomena, and applies itself to the study of their laws, that is, their invariable relations of succession and resemblance. Reasoning and observation, duly combined, are the means of this knowledge. Instead of trying to understand and explain things, positive science enables us to predict and control them, as Bacon called for.

This theory of history is also a theory of individual psychological development, for **the phases of the mind of a man correspond to the epochs of the mind of the race. Now each of us is aware, if he looks back on his history, that he was a theologian in his childhood, a metaphysician in his youth, and a natural philosopher** (scientist) **in his manhood.**

Each of the three stages, or acts of the human play, has a culminating and unifying scene. **The Theological system arrived at the highest perfection of which it was capable when it substituted the single action of a providential Being for the various operations of numerous divinities which had been before imagined. In the same way, in the last stage of the Metaphysical system men substitute one great entity (Nature) for the cause for all phenomena instead of the multitude of entities at first supposed. In the same way again, the ultimate perfection of the Positive system would be . . . to represent all phenomena as particular manifestations of a single general fact, such as Gravitation, for instance.**

The first stage is "organic," conservative, and stable. The second is revolutionary and progressive. The third stage, into which we are now moving, is peaceful and combines endless progress in scientific knowledge with stable and unrivalled scientism since the remaining vestiges of the Theological and Metaphysical stages are destined to soon die off forever, like vestigial organs rendered useless by Natural Selection.

Each the three stages manifests itself in a different society or social organization. At the Theological stage, society is authoritarian, hierarchical, and monarchical, with kings ruling by divine right. It is also a militaristic order, which maintains authority from above. The Middle Ages represented the culmination of this society. In the Metaphysical stage, belief in abstract Justice and Rights critiques the former regime, and the royal and military authority is replaced by the rule of abstract law. Though there are foreshadowings of this in ancient times, as in Plato and Aristotle, this comes to typify society only in modern times. The Enlightenment represented the culmination of this kind of society. Finally, the positive scientific stage produces a society governed by industry and economics, which is ruled by a scientific elite, which imposes a rational scientific organization on all of society.

Comte insists that this third kind of society alone is inherently peaceful rather than warlike. But it is future rather than present (though it is in the process of being born), and it cannot develop until the most important science emerges, the super-science Comte himself invented and named "Sociology" or "social physics." This uses science to control mankind and his industrial society perfectly and peacefully. Since the culmination of this

110

society is still in the future, the deepest purpose of Comte's Positivistic philosophy is to bring it about. It is a new kind of religion, a way of salvation, a gospel or "good news," with Comte as its Messiah, evangelist, missionary and prophet.

Comte regarded himself as living and thinking wholly in the "positive scientific" stage, which is why he claims to be neither an atheist (since the very question of God presupposes "theological stage" thinking) nor a materialist (since that very question presupposes "metaphysical stage" thinking).

Sociology as the Supreme Science

Comte lists the basic sciences as mathematics, astronomy, physics, chemistry, physiology and biology, and then Sociology,[15] or "social physics," with one more offshoot of Sociology to come, which he calls ethics. They develop in that historical order, from the most abstract (mathematics) to the most concrete (Sociology and ethics).

Each science has a distinct method and cannot be reduced to each other. (Comte is not a reductionist *within* the sciences, only *to* the sciences.) Biology, e.g., cannot be reduced to mathematics; yet only when the laws and relationships of biological phenomena are measured mathematically can biology become a real, exact science.

Comte does not believe one science can be deduced from another. Like Bacon, he relies on sense observation and induction, not deduction. He is an empiricist, not a rationalist.

Psychology is not a distinct science, but is divided between its physiological-biological part and its Sociological part. Physiology-biology studies man as an individual phenomenon, while Sociology studies human nature and behavior as social phenomena.

Ethics meant for Comte not a normative science of duties, obligations, laws, rules, or commandments, but only a study of how man in fact can be observed to behave in social groups. Its purpose is to discover general laws, as in all other sciences, which will enable us to predict and control future behavior, as in 20th century Behaviorism (e.g., B.F. Skinner). It is the culmination of Sociology.

Sociology is the master science, the queen of the sciences, the summit of human knowledge to Comte, as revealed theology was to the Middle Ages, because in it alone we achieve a synthesis of all the sciences by looking at everything from the point of view of the needs of man as a social being (and not, any longer, as an individual being).

He distinguishes a "static" and a "dynamic" component in Sociology. The dynamic component is the progress defined by the law of the three stages. The static component is the unchanging elements of society, especially the family, private property, language, and some sort of religion, all of which flow from human nature and needs. Unlike Marx, Comte did not demand to abolish any of these, except only supernatural religion.

---

15 Comte always capitalizes "Sociology" as the supreme science, as a theist would capitalize "Divine Revelation."

The unification of all the sciences is not a theoretical unification but a practical one: it is to foster **the immense social revolution in the midst of which we are living and to which the totality of preceding revolutions has really contributed only a necessary preliminary.** Theory exists not for its own sake but for practice, as with Bacon ("knowledge for power").

Political Philosophy

Comte believed that the perfect society was not a democracy but a rule by a scientific elite, especially those who are mastering the supreme science of Sociology. He classified democracy under the "metaphysical" stage of history because of its belief in invisible essences such as "equality," "natural rights," and "popular sovereignty."

He also disbelieved in the democratic premise of any essential equality among human beings, because of his Positivism. For science sees no such equalities, and science is the only valid knowledge. What science does see is innumerable inequalities.

In his politics, Comte had no sympathy with the liberal doctrine of the inherent rights of man, i.e., of individuals. He could not admit that individuals had any rights over against society, since he believed that "humanity" was more real than individuals. Like Hegel, he called the idea of an individual human being "a bare abstraction." He wrote: **the word *right* should be as much erased from the true language of politics as the word *cause* from the true language of philosophy . . . nobody possesses any other right than that of always doing his duty** (to "Society" or "Humanity").

Comte favored a paternalist government rather than a representative one, and thought "the will of the people" to be a mere abstraction that should not determine the direction of society. In fact, his thought, though beneficent and humanistic in intention and certainly in no sympathy with tyranny or violence, was more simplistically totalitarian than Hegel's. It looks suspiciously close to the dystopia of Huxley's *Brave New World,* or of C. S. Lewis's *That Hideous Strength,* or the supposed utopia of Skinner's *Walden Two*— a "soft totalitarianism" rather than the "hard totalitarianism" of Orwell's *1984.*

Comte's Positivism is a Messianic dream, a "gospel," a call to action, a religion, a way of (social) salvation. And this makes it inspiring, like Marxism, with which it has many affinities. It diagnoses a cause and cure of all social ills: **Now the existing disorder is abundantly accounted for by the existence, all at once, of three incompatible philosophies, the theological, the metaphysical, and the scientific . . . This general revolution of the human mind is nearly complete. We have only to complete the Positive Philosophy by bringing Social phenomena within its comprehension. . . . It is time to complete the vast intellectual operation begun by Bacon, Descartes, and Galileo by constructing the system of general ideas which must henceforth prevail among the human race. This is the way to put an end to the revolutionary crisis which is tormenting the civilized nations of the world.**

The Religion of Humanity

As with Nietzsche, the religion Comte repudiated in his youth took revenge on him in his later life. He literally turned his Positivism into a religion, which he called "the religion of Humanity," in which Man was "The Great Being" to be worshipped. He created a Positivist Church, with its high priest (himself), its own creeds and catechism (which he wrote), its own saints and bishops (they were scientists and positivist philosophers), and its own liturgy, feast days, and hymns. (Chesterton quips that turning the hymn "Nearer, My God, to Thee" into the Humanist "Nearer, Mankind, to Thee" makes it sound like a crush on the subway.) He called his young mistress, Clotilde de Vaux, the patron saint of his new religion. He also became quite jealous and paranoid about any criticisms of his religion. All this has not, needless to say, helped his reputation among atheists and secular humanists.

Comte came to believe that religion was the final key to the whole social system, with Man replacing God as "the Great Being" to be worshipped. He often referred admiringly and nostalgically to the Middle Ages as the time when religion and society were in perfect harmony, when there was a common religion which ordered and harmonized all areas of society: family, property, and government. He wanted to return to this form, only with a very different content, a different religion. This synthesis alone, he thought, could overcome the anarchy of the nineteenth century. The Middle Ages had the right kind of society but the wrong kind of religion, Comte thought; and his century had the right kind of religion (scientific positivism, naturalism and humanism) but the wrong kind of society. His Utopia was to be a kind of Catholic Church without God.

Clotilde's tragic death after a two-year affair with Comte suddenly and radically changed his Positivist outlook. Instead of worshipping scientific reason, he now said that **Where the moral excellence of true Religion is illustrated, feeling takes the first place.** Like Rousseau, he lamented **the disastrous revolt of Reason against Feeling,** defined love as the supreme feeling, and said that **in the construction of a really complete synthesis, love is the one universal principle.**

Critique

(1) A very simple question about the idea of automatic progress: why must the newer be automatically better? Why could there not be regress as well as progress? Why could not, in principle, the theological stage be more "advanced" than the "positive scientific" stage?

(2) Comte has to be an elitist and scorn the opinions of the vast majority of mankind, who have always thought and lived, and continue to think and live, in the theological stage. Traditional religion, or religious tradition, has always been the strongest force in human thought and life, in every place and time outside modern Europe and its "Enlightenment." That is simply a fact, whether good or bad. To say that traditional religion is

mankind's greatest illusion is to write off as fantasy or ignorant primitivism the most important convictions of the vast majority of all human beings who have ever lived, including Socrates, Plato, Aristotle, Moses, Solomon, Akhenaton, Zoroaster, Jesus, Muhammad,
Augustine, Aquinas, Confucius, Lao Tzu, and Buddha. Owen Barfield calls this "chronological snobbery."

(3) Comte's prediction, shared by nearly all anti-religious thinkers of modern times,
that all traditional religions, especially Christianity, are doomed to die off, has been and
is being empirically refuted everywhere in the world except in Europe and North America. Science has not in fact replaced religion.

(4) Nor has it refuted it. The "war between Science and Religion" is an ideological
construct, not a scientific observation. Not a single discovery of a single science has ever
refuted a single essential dogma of a single Western religion. That is fact; the "war" is
ideology.

(5) Comte's lack of sympathy for concrete individuals, for freedom and human rights,
for democracy, and for the entire moral and ethical dimension of human life has to count
seriously against his claim to be the philosopher of "Humanity."

(6) Comte's assertion that modern industrial society is necessarily more peaceful
than the two preceding stages has been empirically refuted by "the century of genocide,"
in which modern industry and technology has not in fact produced peace but has vastly
magnified war and violence. Two words rather spectacularly refute Comte's optimism
here: Hiroshima and Auschwitz.

(7) Comte's worship of Humanity or Mankind or Society seems a perfect example
of metaphysical thinking. It is a hypostatized abstraction. Whitehead would call it an example of "the fallacy of misplaced concreteness." It is certainly not *scientific*

(8) Positivism seems to be logically self-contradictory, self-refuting. For there is no
scientific proof possible of any ideology, including the ideology of Positivism, which
disallows all proofs except scientific proofs. How could there be empirical evidence for
the non-empirical, abstract idea that the only evidence is empirical evidence? How could
one prove *by the scientific method* that no proofs are possible outside the scientific
method? Comte's reductionism succumbs to the self-contradiction of all skepticisms: its
standard is so narrow that it eliminates itself.

Comte's apparent answer to this logical critique would be to classify it as an example
of metaphysical thinking instead of positive scientific thinking; that it is a philosophical,
not a scientific, argument. If this is so, and if Positivism is simply "posited" by the will
rather than argued for by the reason, as a Socrates would argue for it, then it is a sword,
not a pen; a weapon, not an argument; an act of spiritual warfare and violence, not an act
of calm, peaceful reasoning. Both Hobbes and Hume openly admitted that the primary
purpose of their philosophies was to be used as intellectual weapons in the great spiritual
war against the superstitions of "the Kingdom of Darkness," the enemy, which is supernatural religion, i.e., religion that is not reduced to myth or moralism. This confession of
Positivism as ideology rather than philosophy disqualifies Positivism itself from both

scientific and philosophical argument. Spiritual warfare may indeed be much more important than philosophy, *whichever* side is right in this war. But it is not philosophy.

An enlightening, wide-ranging, interesting and unusual critique of Comte as a pioneer of the typically modern imperialism of one method over all others is to be found in Gilson's *The Unity of Philosophical Experience.*

82. Jeremy Bentham (1748–1832)

Bentham invented what has proved to be the single most popular ethical and social philosophy in the English-speaking world. But it was his successor, John Stuart Mill, who refined and perfected this philosophy and popularized the name ("Utilitarianism") for it.

Since any idea is best understood first in its simple origins rather than in its more complex later forms, we will spend almost as much time on Bentham as on Mill, even though Mill is a much more popular, intelligent and defensible philosopher.

Utilitarianism's popularity is based largely on its clarity and simplicity. It is simple because it contains a single moral principle: *Do whatever promotes the greatest happiness of the greatest number.* It is simple also because it identifies happiness simply with pleasure. The main distinction between Bentham's earlier "simple utilitarianism" and Mill's later more sophisticated form is that Bentham denies, and Mill affirms, that pleasures can be qualitatively and not just quantitatively different, and that some pleasures can be qualitatively better, or "higher," than others.

Utilitarianism and Positivism

Unlike Comte's Positivism, Utilitarianism's program can be summarized by the single ideological term "liberalism." That is a notoriously slippery term, but its central meaning is the maximization of individual liberty, or freedom, as the greatest social and political good.

Utilitarians did not follow Comte in his utopian socialism. They were individualists who were suspicious of the power of the State, of the collective, and of elites. They believed in *laissez-faire* government, which means essentially "let it be," or "let it alone," the "it" here meaning individuals and their lives. Today this ideology is often called "libertarianism."

But in many other ways, the Utilitarians followed Comte's Positivism.

(1) Like Comte, the Utilitarians were ideologists. Philosophy's ultimate end was not truth but social change. Utilitarianism, like Comte's Positivism, is an "ideology"; that is, the epistemology of the Utilitarians is a means to their ethical end, and their ethics is in turn a means to their social program.

(2) And they were epistemologists first, basing their ethical philosophy and their political ideology on their epistemology.

(3) In their epistemology, they were total empiricists and scientific Positivists, i.e., they believed, like Comte, that science was the only valid human knowledge. Thus they rejected all metaphysics as scientifically unverifiable.

(4) In ethics, their epistemology also led them to agree with Hume's absolute distinction between facts and values. Thus, they denied that any "natural moral law," any objective, universal, absolute moral values, could be known by man. They therefore embraced a cultural or social relativism of values.

(5) This put them in conflict with traditional religion.

For Positivism, and therefore for utilitarianism too, ethics, like every other kind of human knowledge, must be based on science, on empirical observation and calculation, and not on religion, on the will of God or divinely revealed Commandments. Nor must it be based on "pure (non-empirical) reason," as Kant taught, or on duty, or on a "categorical imperative." Nor must it be based on a "natural law" that assumed a human reason that could know objective reality, do metaphysics, and know man's essential nature and end. For positive science knows nothing about essences (Aristotelian "formal causes") or ends ("final causes").

Bentham's Life

Like most philosophers, Bentham was a child prodigy. He mastered Latin grammar at 4, and entered Oxford at 12. He studied for a career in law until he heard the lectures of the world's most famous law professor, Blackstone, a conservative "natural law" theorist, and immediately rejected Blackstone's idea of "natural rights" as "rhetorical nonsense." He therefore viewed the American Declaration of Independence as absurd, jumbled, groundless dogmatism. Reading Hume, on the other hand, made scales fall from his eyes. He became a social reformer and developed his new morality of utilitarianism as an ideological basis for liberal social reform. This reform was critically needed in England at the time, in the wake of the dehumanizing social conditions triggered by the Industrial Revolution.

Bentham used his Principle of Utility as the basis for all social reforms. Wherever he found that social conditions were not promoting "the greatest happiness for the greatest number of people," which was his single principle, he called for reform of those conditions. Thus he blamed the aristocratic, class-conscious society of his day for being concerned only for their own happiness, and said that to reform such a society we had to create an identity between the rulers and the ruled by putting rule into the hands of the masses. This necessitates democracy and the abolition of the monarchy.

Bentham believed this structural political change rather than appealing to individuals' reason and free choice was the *only* effective way to reform society because we all acted not out of rational wisdom and charity but for our own pleasure. Like Machiavelli and Hobbes, he saw men as egotists by nature and not altruists. Thus traditional calls for the moral reform of society through the cultivation of personal moral virtue, love and altruism, such as was called for by Christianity and by classical moral philosophers like Aristotle, would always prove ineffective; but identification of one's own interests with others' interests would be effective because it would give altruistic behavior an egotistic "hook."

The most important fact about Bentham's life is that he was a close friend of James Mill, John Stuart Mill's father, and was the main teaching influence on John Stuart Mill, who made Utilitarianism famous. But the most interesting fact about Bentham is that his fully dressed, mummified body still presides over all trustees' meetings of university College in London, since Bentham left his fortune to the college only under the condition that he be able to attend all their meetings. (This was the only form of life after death that Bentham believed in.)

The Principle of Utilitarianism

The single principle and point of Utilitarianism is that **good = the greatest happiness for the greatest number.**

One cannot prove one's first principle. That would make it second (to its premises) rather than first. So Bentham admits that his fundamental principle, the Principle of Utility, cannot be proved: **Is it susceptible to any proof? It should seem not, for that which is used to prove everything else cannot itself be proved; a chain of proofs must have their commencement somewhere.**

Most moralists say that that "somewhere" is either (1) in the nature of God, or (2) the will of God, or (3) a priori in what Kant called "pure reason," or (4) in the self-evidence of "Do good and avoid evil," or in (5) a rational intuition" (you just "see" it), or (6) in the nature of man and his real needs (not just felt wants) as known by reason. But Positivists reduce "reason" to what is verified by sense experience or logical calculation, so all of these foundations for ethics are not available options for them. So what did Bentham base his first principle on? (He did admit a "basis" for it, though not a deductive *proof* of it.) On the only reliable epistemic basis for a Positivist, namely scientific data, on empirical observation of actual human behavior. For Bentham this was the supposed fact of observation that Freud called "the pleasure principle": the "fact" that all men do in fact not only seek pleasure but seek it always and as their ultimate good. (Do they? Do you?) The desire for pleasure and the fear of pain are the universal gravity of the whole human moral universe:

Nature has placed mankind under the governance of two sovereign masters, *pain* and *pleasure*. It is for them alone to point out what we ought to do, as well as determine what we shall do.

Thus Bentham is not only a *psychological* hedonist (pleasure and pain *do in fact* determine what we aim at) but also an *ethical* hedonist (pleasure and pain *ought to be* what we aim at). This single principle, composed of two quite different parts which are often confused, is called "the pleasure principle," or Hedonism.

Sometimes "the pleasure principle" is *identified* with the fundamental Utilitarian "happiness principle" or "principle of utility"; and sometimes it is said to be its *basis*.

It is called "the principle of utility" (usefulness) because it says that utility in achieving the end of pleasure (which is the only absolute end) is the standard, touchstone, or criterion for all moral good and evil: "good" means "whatever is useful to maximize pleasure or minimize pain." For the end justifies the means. (Of course it does; that's what a "means" *means*. But not any end justifies any means.)

The obvious ethical problem with hedonism is that it seems to entail egotism. For pleasure and pain are private feelings of the single individual. Yet everyone believes that altruism, and the overcoming of egotism, is essential to ethics. Bentham claimed to include altruism in his hedonistic ethics by enlarging the meaning of pleasure and pain to include the pleasure and pain of other people. Thus his "principle of utility" or "utilitarian principle" is: *Act always to promote the greatest happiness for the greatest number.* (But *why,* if it does not increase *my* pleasure? His only consistent answer is that)

Bentham claimed that all other, supposedly "higher" ethical principles, even religious principles, could be reduced to this one. For instance, **the principle of theology refers everything to God's pleasure. But what is God's pleasure? God does not . . . either speak or write to us. How then are we to know what is his pleasure? By observing what is our own pleasure, and pronouncing it to be his.** (But isn't that exactly what tyrants do, identifying their own pleasure with God's will, as the absolute?)

Applying the Principle: the Hedonic Calculus

Since Bentham wanted to make ethics a science, he had to appeal only to empirical observation and mathematical calculation. He did this in what he called his **hedonic calculus.** This was a way of introducing mathematical measurement into the empirical data of the "pleasure principle."

He identified seven elements that determine the quantity of any pleasure or pain:

(1) Intensity (how strong is it?)
(2) Duration (how long will it last?)
(3) Propinquity (how soon will it occur?)
(4) Certainty (how likely is it that it will occur?)
(5) Fecundity (how likely is it to produce more pleasure?)
(6) Purity (how much pain will accompany the pleasure, or how much pleasure will accompany the pain?)
(7) Extent (how many other people will be affected by it?)

Bentham proposed giving positive numerical "units" to pleasure and negative "units" to pain. This would enable us to calculate mathematically whether any proposed act is good or evil, positive or negative; and which of two acts would be the most positive, i.e., the best.

The standard of goodness, therefore, is purely quantitative, not qualitative. Pleasures are not ranked "higher" or "lower" in quality, only quantity. Bentham referred to this as a **moral thermometer.** Just as a thermometer measures only the quantity of heat, irrespective of whether it was produced by coal, oil, or wood, Bentham's "hedonic calculus" measures good and evil by the strictly scientific criterion of the quantity of pleasure, irrespective of its source or its quality. He famously said that **push-pin is of equal value with the arts and sciences of music and poetry. If the game of push-pin furnishes more pleasure, it is more valuable than either.** (Push-pin was a simple child's game, also played in pubs.) Mill would later disagree with this, insisting that "it is better to be Socrates dissatisfied . . . than a pig satisfied."

To the obvious objection that no one sits down to calculate units when confronted with an ethical choice such as whether or not to rush into a burning building to try to save a child, Bentham replied that we do indeed sometimes choose immediately and instinctively, but what motivates our choices is not only our present conscious calculations but also our habits that we have cultivated by repeated past choices, and that these, in turn, have always been made by some sort of calculation of pleasures and pains, so that we need never go outside the hedonic calculus. For pleasure and pain are our only motivators, whether they work immediately or mediately.

The Egotistic Foundation of Social Altruism

Bentham explained the fact that most men seem to have innate altruistic as well as egotistic impulses—an empirical fact that seems to refute his egotistic psychology—by replying that when I care about others it is always defined by how others affect me and my pleasant and painful feelings. What motivates me to do good, i.e., to give pleasure, to those who give pleasure to me is not conscience or duty or altruistic love of the other for the sake of the other in a self-forgetful way, but only the principle that motivates all human behavior, the pleasure principle: I always seek to maximize my own pleasure, and giving pleasure to those who give me pleasant feelings gives me more pleasant feelings.

Note also, by the way, that it is feelings rather than reason or will that Bentham appeals to and implicitly locates at the center of the self. As for Hobbes, for Bentham reason is "the slave and scout for the passions." Pleasure and pain are the masters. Reason is not a master but a servant. It is the tool whose purpose is to calculate the most likely consequences of an act in terms of the hedonic calculus of future pleasures and pains.

Thus moral education should appeal to "enlightened self-interest" rather than unselfish moral absolutes like justice or charity, or even compassion. If we only learn that we will always find more pleasure in doing good by making others happy than by giving them pain (but will we?), we will automatically become saints without any distinctive moral effort (will we?). We need only the intellectual effort of "enlightenment." Here Bentham agrees with Plato's idea that all evil is due to ignorance and all good is due to knowledge. But his cure for evil is scientific knowledge rather than philosophical knowledge.

But education cannot *show* us that altruistic behavior will make us happier if it is not *true* that it will. And Bentham argued that it is up to those who govern society to *make* it true, by identifying everyone's best interest with everyone else's, by egalitarianizing society. This is why the social order needs radical reform.

Law

Classical pre-modern theories of law (e.g., Thomas Aquinas') said that the purpose of law was "to make men good," since "the common good of the state cannot flourish unless the citizens are virtuous." Classical modern theories of law find their purpose in justice or defending human rights. Utilitarianism rejects both of these philosophies, since it finds these ends too metaphysical. In order to be consistent with the principle that happiness is the only end-in-itself, Utilitarianism sees the purpose of law simply as maximizing happiness (which is identified as pleasure) in the whole community. That is the only justification for inflicting on lawbreakers some punishment, which is *un*pleasure: that it achieves a greater sum of pleasure for all by deterring potential lawbreakers from acts which would cause much pain to many others.

Consistent with the Positivism of Utilitarianism, there is no appeal to anything non-empirical such as the intrinsic value of the person, or even justice. Punishment is meted out not because it is justly deserved but because of its consequences: greater happiness (pleasure) for more individuals. But if this principle is not modified somehow, it would justify *anything* that would attain that end in that society, e.g., many cannibals eating a single missionary, or punishing an innocent man if that would make the whole society happy.

Bentham admitted that if governments used only the principle of utility in making and enforcing laws, this would require a radical reclassification of public human behavior. Many acts that were illegal in his time would have to be decriminalized, especially in the area of sexual morality. E.g., there would be no justification for laws against prostitution or even bestiality. Utilitarians, and today's libertarians, usually oppose laws against such things as assisted suicide, private drug use, or driving without seat belts. They make liberty, or "free consent," and "no removal of others' liberty" the only two criteria of legal acceptability. A few years ago a cannibal in Germany advertised on the Internet for freely consenting victims and he got 28 volunteers. The government had a legal crisis: did it have any principled reason for forcibly preventing this?

Critique

The obvious and commonly-offered critiques of Bentham's "simple Utilitarianism" are:

(1) The denial that there are any other ends than happiness seems to demean all such candidates as knowledge, wisdom, virtue, justice, salvation, truth, beauty, God (union with God, love of God, obedience to God's will, and/or becoming more like God), or meaning and purpose (cf. Viktor Frankl's *Man S Search for Meaning).*

(2) The identification of happiness with pleasure ("hedonism") seems to deny the

difference in kind between men and animals, and to reduce man to a clever animal. (To answer this, Mill had to distinguish pleasures qualitatively, not just quantitatively, as Bentham did.)

(3) *Ethical* hedonism (the claim that pleasure *should* be our only final end) does not logically follow from *psychological* hedonism (the claim that all men do in fact seek pleasure as their final end).

(4) Psychological hedonism seems to be an unwarrantedly simplistic psychology. Men do in fact seek other things as ends, and often sacrifice pleasure for them, such as the ends mentioned in point (1) above. These are not just *worthy* ends in themselves, they are also psychologically *effective* ends for many. Those who seek them insist that they are *not* seeking them merely as means to pleasure. If this is true, Utilitarianism is not as empirical and experiential as it claims.

(5) Hedonism seems essentially egotistic and selfish, which no one regards as ethically good. Bentham's "egotistic hook," even if it works to motivate altruistic behavior, still reduces all supposedly altruistic *motives* to egotistic ones: I work for your pleasure only because it gives me pleasure. I use you for me.

(6) In concentrating on consequences alone, Bentham ignores the morality of motives. Kant taught that a good motive in the will (duty, or respect for moral law) is the *only* thing that makes an act good; but even if this is an exaggeration, motives must count too.

(7) Connected with this point, Bentham ignores the *person* in ignoring motives and good or bad wills, and concentrates only on the external deed and its consequences. He would not be able to justify Kant's second "categorical imperative," to respect persons as ends rather than using them as means.

(8) Bentham's "consequentialism," the claim that an act is good if and only if it produces good consequences, sounds like *"the end justifies the means"* which nearly everyone regards as an *un*ethical rather than ethical principle. Utilitarianism allows for no intrinsically good or bad acts, so that the end of happiness (pleasure) would seem to justify *any* means at all, as long as it produces the most happiness for the most people. It seems to have no moral "bite." In fact it seems to be not an inferior morality but not a morality at all, only a theory of selfish calculation of pleasures. The whole moral *dimension* is missing, as color is missing from a color-blind person.

(9) Closely connected with this point, the only psychological demand it makes is calculation, not conscience.

(10) "Conscience," in turn, if it means anything more than this calculation, is reduced to an unfree *feeling,* not a free knowing or willing. But doing good is a matter of will and choice, not of feeling. That is what makes us *responsible* for our actions.

(11) Bentham makes no room for justice or rights. Utilitarianism seems to justify a surgeon murdering one innocent man to harvest seven viable organs from his body to save the lives of seven patients who would die without them, or murdering one innocent man to quell a riot and save many lives (exactly what Caiaphas did to Jesus: see John

11:47–53). The murderous act has good consequences, and produces "the greatest happiness for the greatest number," but it is obviously morally wrong, unjust, and a violation of the innocent victim's rights.

(12) Utilitarianism is based on the fact that "all (human) action is for the sake of some end" Mill, *Utilitarianism).* But "end" can mean three things, not just one: (a) the *act* that is willed or desired, (b) the *motive* for willing it, and (c) the *consequences* desired. For a human act to be morally good, all three aspects of it must line up as good, not just one. Legalists focus on the act alone, Kant on the motive alone, and Utilitarians on the consequences alone.

(13) The claim that ethics can be reduced to a quantitative science, that the only criterion of moral good and evil is the *amount* of pleasure for any individual, and the *number* of individuals who get it, would make computers more ethical than people. Though Mill was grateful to Bentham for his basic idea, he called him "a one-eyed man" who sees clearly but narrowly.

(14) Missing from Utilitarian "ethics" are all the essentials of morality:

(a) "Doing the right thing just because it is the right thing" as the proper moral motive

(b) The notion that there is any such thing as "the right thing," i.e., actions which are by their nature morally right or wrong

(c) The dignity, intrinsic value, or rights of the person

(d) Love, not in the sense of feeling but goodwill, self-forgetfully willing the good of the other person, as an intrinsic moral good

Fourteen is a very large number of objections to such a simple theory. Mill will give reasonable answers to many of these objections to Utilitarianism with his more complex and sophisticated version of it. Whether he answers all of them is something philosophers are still arguing about.

83. John Stuart Mill (1806–1873)

Life

Bentham was John Stuart Mill's godfather and the closest friend of his father, James Mill. On the advice of Bentham, James undertook the educational experiment of home-schooling John at a very early age, producing a prodigy who learned Greek at 3, Latin at 7, algebra at 11, logic and philosophy at 12, economics at 16, and how to have a nervous breakdown at 20.

In his *Autobiography* he described his mother as one who **only knew how to pass her life drudging.** His parents were "emotionally divorced," **as far apart, under the same roof, as the north pole from the south.**

His relation to his father was a loveless master-slave relationship. **My father's older children neither loved him nor with any warmth of affection anyone else. . . . I thus grew up in the absence of love and in the presence of fear.** His father **resembled most Englishmen in being ashamed of the signs of feeling.** But his **temper was constitutionally irritable.**

Mill was forbidden to make friends or play with other children. He was thus robbed of his childhood. He was raised to be **a mere thinking machine,** with no **genuine benevolence or sympathy with mankind.** A friend described him as "a 'made' or manufactured man." He wrote: **The only thing that I believe I am really fit for is the investigation of abstract truth, and the more abstract the better.**

He was taught to think for himself (his father, like Socrates, gave him questions and puzzles, not answers), but not to morally choose for himself: **I acquired the habit of leaving my responsibility as a moral agent to rest on my father and my conscience never speaking to me except by his voice.**

He was raised **from the first without any religious belief. . . . I am thus one of the very few examples, in this country, of one who has not thrown off religious belief but never had it.**

His philosophy, as well as his conscience, came from his father and Bentham, though through his own discovery. As soon as he read Bentham, he says, **the feeling rushed upon me that all previous moralists were superseded, and that here indeed was the commencement of a new era of thought. . . . I now had opinions, a creed, a doctrine, a philosophy, in one among the best senses of the word a religion, the inculcation and diffusion of which could be made the principal outward purpose of a life.**

This discovery of Bentham was to him like Socrates' encounter with the Delphic Oracle, or Augustine's encounter with God in the garden, or Descartes's dream by the stove, snowbound, returning from the Thirty Years' War: one "big idea" that changed a whole mind, a whole life, and much of the world.

He described his nervous breakdown and depression, at age 20, in terms strikingly similar to that of Leo Tolstoy in his *Confession:* **In this frame of mind it occurred to me to put the question directly to myself: "Suppose that all your objects in life were realized; that all the changes in institutions and opinions which you are looking forward to could be completely effected at this very instant: would this be a great joy and happiness to you?" And an irrepressible self-consciousness distinctly answered, "No!" At this my heart sank within me.**

Four things freed him from this depression. First, he was **moved to tears** by reading a story about the death of an author's father. Second, he read Wordsworth's Romantic poetry. Third, his father died, in 1836. Fourth, and most important, he fell in love, in 1830, at 24, with a married woman, Harriet Taylor. He kept up an apparently-Platonic "soul-mate" relationship with her until her older husband died, then he married her, 21 years later, in 1851. (She died only 7 years after that.) He credits her with everything humane in his life and thought: **What was abstract and purely scientific was generally mine; the properly human element came from her.**

Works

Rarely if ever, since Plato and Aristotle, has any philosopher produced more works of lasting popularity and influence than Mill. They include:

Autobiography

Utilitarianism (a short, densely written defense of his ethics against objections to it)

Liberty (his social and political philosophy, his single most influential book)

Theism (his case against natural theology and supernatural religion)

Nature (his argument against natural law morality)

The Subjugation of Women

System of Logic (This is Mill's most complete philosophical system, and it includes far more than formal logic, e.g., his psychology of determinism.)

Metaphysics

Mill was an empiricist and a positivist, though not a materialist, since materialism is a metaphysic and Mill does not believe metaphysics is possible. **What the mind is, as well as what matter is, or any other question respecting Things in themselves, as distinguished from their sensible manifestations, it would be foreign to our mind's power and impossible for us to try to discover.**

Yet everyone necessarily has a metaphysic, at least implicitly. Mill's can be found mainly in his essay *Nature,* although that essay's point is not a metaphysical one but an ethical one. It is an attack on the traditional idea of a "natural moral law," the idea that we should "follow nature" and not violate it by "unnatural acts." In this essay, Mill reveals his metaphysics of Naturalism and his denial of anything supernatural.

Judged by theistic standards, this seems to make Mill an atheist. However, in *Theism* he argues that it is possible that there is a God, as the cause of Nature, although he argues that (1) this is impossible for us to know, and (2) that this could logically be only a finite God, limited in either power or goodness, who either cannot or will not solve the problem of evil by making everything good, since evil does exist. (This is the most popular and powerful argument for atheism.)

He begins *Nature* by distinguishing two meanings of "nature." In its broadest sense, **Nature means the sum of all phenomena** that appear to our sense experience, exterior or interior. **Nature, then, in this its simplest acceptation, is a collective name for all facts.** Mill's strictly Empiricist epistemology reduces Nature to what is able to be sensed, either exteriorly or interiorly (thoughts, feelings, or desires). Like most Empiricists, Mill does not admit a distinction in kind between these two sources of experience: for him, concepts are not radically different from percepts, nor spiritual feelings or desires from physical ones.

Nature thus is a collection of things, not a single thing such as "the force that makes a thing move and act and grow from within in a way specific to its essence," which is what the ancients meant by it. "Nature" for Mill means only phenomena, not anything beyond or behind or invisibly present in phenomena such as essences or substances or ends (final causes). The opposite of the "natural" in this sense is the "supernatural," which for Mill is simply the mythical or imaginary, since "nature" equals all of the "facts." Mill is thus a metaphysical Naturalist as opposed to a Supernaturalist. (In this sense, all religions are supernaturalist.)

In a second, narrower sense, "nature" means that subdivision of Nature in the broad sense that has not been altered by man; and its opposite would be the artificial.

Mill then argues that "following nature" in either sense is morally nonsensical, as we shall see in the Ethics section. For if Nature is all there is (sense #1), everything always follows nature willy-nilly; and if Nature means what is "untouched by human hands" (sense #2), then "following nature" means imitating brute animals instead of human reason, which is obviously *not* moral or wise.

Cosmology

If only nature exists, what is in it? What are the things that make up the cosmos? They are bodies, some of which (ourselves) have minds. Mill defines a body as **the external cause to which we ascribe our sensations.** (For Mill, we cannot know anything beyond our sensations. He limits knowledge to phenomena.)

Hume, who was also a phenomenalist and an Empiricist, denied that we could know either (1) causality or (2) substance; and Mill follows his lead here in (1) reducing causality to something to which **we ascribe** (thus phenomenalism) **our sensations** (thus Empiricism); and (2) he also denies that we can know the answer to the metaphysical

126

question whether there is a material substance underlying the sensed phenomena: **All we know of objects is the sensations which they give us.** (See Vol. III, ch. 60 for Locke's similar critique of "substance.")

He denies that we can know that there really is an external world, and says **that the belief in an external world is not intuitive** (innate) **but an acquired product** conditioned in us by our education. How then does he account for our belief that physical objects do not disappear when we stop seeing them, e.g., that a piece of paper on a table is still there when we leave the room? He says this means only that if we re-enter the room we will see the paper again. External bodies are thus defined merely as **possibilities of sensation.** This is the phenomenalist definition of material bodies: **Matter, then, may be defined: a Permanent Possibility of Sensation.** Sensation is not defined relative to bodies; bodies are defined relative to sensation.

(Note that this is *not* what we usually mean by "bodies." Mill is not really empirical in his implied philosophy of language: he does not tell us what people do in fact mean but what he thinks they ought to mean or should have meant. He does not confine himself to *linguistic* Empiricism.)

Anthropology

Mill applies his radical Empiricism and phenomenalism to mind as well as matter. He says we have **no conception** of mind in itself **as distinct from its conscious manifestations.** We believe, but we do not know, that our mind continues to exist even **when it is not feeling, nor thinking, nor conscious of its own existence.** As he defines bodies merely as enduring possibilities of external sensations, he defines minds merely as enduring possibilities of internal sensations. Like Hume, he analyzes the self into nothing but successive mental and sensory states, without any real substance, or substantial self, to hold them together. Like Buddha and unlike Descartes, he says that I do not exist, only "my" mental acts. (*Whose?*)

Mill has no answer to the question of how this mere bundle of mental states or succession of mental acts can have self-consciousness, memory, and a permanent sense of identity—in other words he cannot account for the meaning of the simple little word "I." He admits this problem and candidly calls it **inexplicable.** He says we are aware only of **a certain "thread" of consciousness . . . a series of feelings, that is, of sensations, thoughts, emotions, and volitions** but not of any entity called a self.

How odd to say that *"I* do not have an 'I'" or that "*I* know or think that there is no 'I' behind 'my' knowing or thinking." This seems not only logically self-contradictory, as Descartes argued, but also dogmatic, an imposition of Mill's peculiar lack of self-consciousness upon the rest of the human race, who testify that they have it—like a color-blind man insisting that the colors the rest of us see are only illusions. Or, closer to home, like a Utilitarian moral relativist insisting that the common experience of absolute moral obligation that most people have is really only a mask for hedonistic pleasure-seeking.

Mill admits that we experience mental as well as physical phenomena (e.g., the thought of a tree as well as the sense perception of a tree), but claims that we do not know whether or not these are caused by independently real entities in an independently real world of nature (i.e., whether there are real trees out there independent of our thoughts and perceptions). Perhaps we just get phenomenal apples from phenomenal trees. Nor do we know the nature of bodies or minds. All metaphysics is strictly out of bounds for Mill's phenomenalism.

There is, however, a science (though only an inexact one) of human nature, which Mill calls "Psychology." **The phenomena with which this science is conversant being the thoughts, feelings, and actions of human beings, it would have attained the ideal perfection of a science if it enabled us to foretell how an individual would think, feel, or act throughout life with the same certainty with which astronomy enables us to predict the places and the occultations of the heavenly bodies.** He says that the only reason this exactness is not possible is *not* that man is distinctive in having a soul, free will, or a mind, but merely that we do not have data that are complete enough and exact enough regarding the causes of human interior and exterior acts. (Thus, Mill is a determinist, not a "free-willer.") These data would be all the causes, both internal (which Mill calls "character") and external (which he calls "circumstances"), that determine our actions.

Mill admits an irreducible difference in kind between states of mind and states of body, which are studied by two different sciences, Psychology and Physiology; and he says that mental phenomena cannot in principle be deduced from physiological phenomena. In other words, even if I knew *everything* about your brain activity, I could not predict exactly what you would think or say.[16]

Epistemology and Logic

Like most modern philosophers, Mill views epistemology as the most important and determinative division of philosophy. It certainly was that for him: the reasons for his conclusions in all the other areas of his philosophy come from the limitations on human knowledge that are set by his epistemology.

Though he is not as skeptical as Hume, he agrees with Hume's **doctrine of the Relativity of Knowledge to the knowing mind.** Like Kant, he denies that we can know any "things in themselves."

Perhaps the most original feature of his epistemology is his teaching that deduction is totally dependent on induction. He argues that the deductive syllogism is really a kind of fake. When we argue that "All men are mortal, and Socrates is a man, therefore Socrates is mortal," we seem to start with a universal ("all men are mortal") and deduce from it a particular ("Socrates is mortal"). But it is impossible for us to really do that,

16 See also the Mill quotation in the second paragraph of ch. 81.

according to Mill, because the only way we could possibly know that "all men are mortal" is to first know that Socrates, and every other individual, is mortal. In other words, universals can only be collections of particulars which we arrive at through inductive generalization. For Mill, we have no knowledge of universals that is different in kind from our knowledge of particulars, no knowledge of essences or kinds or natures. So we cannot know that "all men are mortal" by examining the universal concept "man" and finding *in* it, as part of its meaning, the concept of a material body which, as an animal organism, is in principle always able to lose its organic life by the failure of its organs. We thus cannot be absolutely *certain* that all men are mortal. (Life insurance companies, take note!)

This follows from Mill's Nominalist metaphysics and his Empiricist epistemology. There are no universal essences (that is what Nominalism means), therefore we cannot know them. All we can know is particulars, because that is all that is real. And particulars are known by sense experience. Universals, if they existed, would be known by intellectual intuition, if it existed. Thus Mill, like Hume and Kant, denies that there is any such thing as intellectual intuition, the understanding of the nature of a thing. The question of every Platonic dialog, "What is it?" cannot really be answered. We cannot do metaphysics; we can give only nominal definitions, i.e., empirical observations of how people use a certain word, not real definitions; for there are no universal essences to define. In other words, Mill's Nominalistic metaphysics forbids him to do metaphysics.

Even this purely inductive knowledge, however, raises a problem for Mill. How can we can know or prove the principle on which all induction depends, *viz.* "the uniformity of nature"? This requires a bit of explanation.

Mill says that induction **consists in inferring from some individual instances in which a phenomenon is observed to occur, that it occurs in all instances of a certain class, namely in all which** *resemble* **the former.** Thus induction must presuppose **that the course of nature is uniform.** But how can we know that a priori, *before* we make our predictions? The belief **that the course of nature is uniform is the fundamental principle, or general axiom, of Induction,** but this assumption **is itself founded on prior generalizations,** i.e., on induction; so it begs the question: it presupposes the thing it wants to prove.

So it cannot be a certainty, but only a practical working assumption, a postulate. Yet without it *no* inference is possible, since all deduction depends on induction and all induction depends on it.

One of Mill's great contributions to logic is his five methods for determining causes. They are only probable, and (of course) inductive, but they are very practical. They are:

(1) **The Method of Agreement: If two or more instances of the phenomenon under investigation have only one circumstance in common, the circumstance . . . is** (probably) **the cause.** If the passengers who got sick *all* chose steak rather than chicken, the steak probably caused the sickness.

129

(2) **The Method of Difference: If an instance in which the phenomenon under investigation occurs, and an instance in which it does not occur, have every circumstance in common save one, that one occurring only in the former, that circumstance . . . is** (probably) **the cause. . . .** If the *only* passengers who got sick were the ones who ate the chicken, not the ones who ate the steak, and all the side dishes were the same, then blame the chicken.

(3) **The Joint Method of Agreement and Difference: If two or more instances in which the phenomenon occurs have only one circumstance in common, while two or more instances in which it does not occur have nothing in common save the absence of that circumstance, the circumstance . . . is** (probably) **the cause . . .** (Combining (1) and (2) adds to the probability.)

(4) **The Method of Residues: Subduct** (subtract) **from any phenomenon such part as is known by previous inductions to be the effect of certain** (other) **antecedents, and the residue of the phenomenon is** (probably) **the effect of the remaining antecedents.** Weigh your squirming cat at the vet's office by subtracting your weight alone from your weight plus the cat's when you step on the scale holding the cat.

(5) **The Method of Concomitant Variations: Whatever phenomenon varies in any manner whenever another phenomenon varies in some particular manner, is** (probably) **either a cause or an effect of that phenomenon. . . .** If tides rise more and more as the moon gets closer and closer and recede more and more as the moon recedes more and more, the moon probably causes the tides.

Freedom and Determinism

Mill is a determinist. He holds that all human actions, including those we think are free, are really just as necessarily determined as purely physical acts like rainfall. But in us it is not an external, purely material determinism, but one that also works from within the individual, from "motives" and "character." He claims **that, given the motives which are present to an individual's mind, and given likewise the character and disposition of the individual, the manner in which he will act might be unerringly inferred.** (This has, of course, never actually been done "unerringly," or infallibly.)

Mill says this determinism is *not* "fatalism," which he defines as the idea that **there is no use in struggling against** what is happening and **that it will happen however we may strive to prevent it.** He says that one **has, to a certain extent, a power to alter his character.** He says that a person's **character is formed by his circumstances** totally and deterministically, yet **his own desire to mould it in a particular way is one of those circumstances.**

This is not *"pure* fatalism" Mill says, because pure fatalism **holds that our actions do not depend on our desires** but only on external circumstances. In contrast, Mill's **Modified fatalism holds that our actions are determined by our will, our will by our desires, and our desires by the joint influence of the motives presented to us and of our individual character.**

This position is today called *"compatibilism"* since it maintains that some kind of freedom (though not what people ordinarily mean by "free will") and determinism are both true, and are logically compatible.

On the one hand, it is a determinism, and a denial of what people usually mean by free will. Mill says that an act of will or volition is totally and necessarily caused: **A volition is a moral** (psychological) **effect, which follows the corresponding moral causes as certainly and invariably as physical effects follow their physical causes.** Mill denies that we ever *can* do anything different from what we *do* do—or, more exactly, that we can never know what we can do, or are able to do, or have a potentiality or possibility to do: **we are conscious of what is, not of what will or can be. We never know that we are able to do a thing except from having done it.**

On the other hand, one of the causes of our actions is from within: desire, character, feeling, and will. But not "free will." Mill is very strong on freedom, but it is only political freedom—perhaps as a compensation for denying personal, inner free will.[17] What determines our will is only desire, or feeling. Like both Rousseau and Hobbes, Mill sees man as determined by feelings, not by reason and will, which have no power to contradict desire. He does not deny that we have a will, but he says that **the will can only be educated through the desires**.

This psychology determines his ethics: **The difference between a bad man and a good man is not that the latter acts in opposition to his strongest desires; it is that his desire to do right, and his aversion to doing wrong, are strong enough to overcome . . . any other desire.**

The strongest argument against determinism is that it removes personal responsibility in removing free will. If I couldn't help doing what I did, I am no more to blame than a broken machine. Mill tries to answer this objection by affirming personal responsibility, but he identifies it merely with fear of punishment, and classifies it as only a feeling: **When we are said to have the feeling of being morally responsible for our actions,** we are not experiencing a fact but a feeling, **the feeling of liability to punishment**.

Mill thinks that determinism follows from the principle that nothing happens without an adequate cause, which is a basic principle of reason and science. He sees the only alternative to determinism as the absurd idea that there are acts of free will that have no cause. But "free-willers" do not usually hold this. They hold that they are self-caused. But Mill cannot say this because, like Hume, he denies that we can know that we have any substantial self to cause them, only "states of character" without a substantial "I" or person behind them.

17 Englishmen and Americans are often struck by the traditional German intellectual habit of combining inner mental freedom and political and social subservience. Perhaps Germans are struck by the opposite combination in us.

Ethics: Relativism

I give an unusually large amount of space to Utilitarian ethics (1) because ethics is the division of philosophy that affects everyone, and affects them most personally and practically and passionately, (2) because Utilitarianism is the most popular ethical philosophy in the Western world today, and (3) because this popularity is the most radical philosophical change in the history of ethics. Perhaps as many people *lived* Utilitarianism in the past, but very few *justified* it philosophically.

Utilitarian ethics in a way is a kind of relativism, but in another way it is a kind of absolutism.

On the one hand, it is relativistic because it attacks the notion of any moral absolutes. There are no *intrinsically* good or evil acts, good or evil in themselves, of their own nature. For Utilitarianism is Nominalistic and suspicious of claims to know the universal natures of things, including human acts.

Utilitarianism is relativistic also because it identifies good with happiness, and happiness with pleasure, and pleasure is a feeling, and feelings are relative to the one who feels them. Thus the moral good is as relative as personal feelings, because it is relative *to* personal feelings: x is good if it makes people feel happy, non-x is bad if it makes them feel unhappy.

Thus Mill opposes what he calls "the intuitive school" of ethics, which claims that **the principles of morals are evident *a priori* through reason,** as was held by Plato, Aquinas, and Kant. As an Empiricist, Mill insists that moral knowledge, like all other knowledge, comes only inductively, from experience, not deductively, from principles.

On the other hand, Mill seems to be a kind of ethical absolutist because there is for Mill one absolute moral principle, one good-in-itself that makes all other goods relative *to it*. And that is happiness, which Mill identifies with pleasure. So even though Utilitarianism is hedonistic (pleasure = the only good), it is not wholly unprincipled, for it has one moral principle, though only one: "the happiness principle," or "the pleasure principle."

The simplicity of Utilitarianism (that there is only one principle) makes its ethics a quasi-scientific art. For **every art has one first principle, or general major premise, not borrowed . . . that which enunciates the object aimed at and affirms it to be a desirable object.**

But if Mill's epistemology requires that we learn *everything* by experience and nothing a priori, this must apply to the happiness principle too. We must learn it inductively and empirically. And that is just what Mill says: when we observe ourselves and others, we find that happiness is the one and only thing that everyone does in fact desire all the time.

The logical problem here is how we move from fact to value, from is to ought; how the premise that we do desire happiness proves the conclusion that we *ought* to do that.

Ethics: Happiness

Mill enunciates his "happiness principle" in quasi-religious terms, since it is his one and only absolute, calling it a "creed": **The creed which accepts as the foundation of morals Utility or the Greatest Happiness Principle, holds that actions are right in proportion as they tend to promote happiness, wrong as they tend to produce the reverse of happiness.**

How does Mill prove this most important principle of his ethics?

In the first place, he argues that a first principle, by definition, cannot be proved. For instance, the first principle of logic, the Law of Non-contradiction, cannot be proved because all logical proofs *presuppose* it. And to presuppose your conclusion in your premises is to commit the fallacy of "begging the question."

Secondly, he says it is known in the same way everything is known: empirically, and inductively, by generalization from repeated experience. How a principle about what actions are "right" can be known empirically is not clear, since "right" is not an empirical concept at all.

Thirdly, he explains how we come to know it (this is not the same thing as claiming to prove it is true, by the way) by an analogy. This analogy has become a famous example of something quite rare: a brilliant philosopher committing not only a logical fallacy but one that is quite obvious. Mill writes: **The only proof capable of being given that an object is visible is that people actually see it. The only proof that a sound is audible is that people hear it; and so of the other sources of our experience. In like manner, I apprehend, the sole evidence it is possible to produce that anything is desirable is that people do actually desire it.**

This is clearly an example of the fallacy of a false analogy, since "visible" and "audible" mean simply "can be seen" and "can be heard," but "desirable" means not merely *"can* be desired" but *"should* be desired." Cocaine, revenge, or genocide are often desired, but they are not desirable.

Why didn't Mill see this fallacy? For a reason much more important than the fallacy itself: because he is "color blind" to the whole moral dimension of duty, oughtness, or moral responsibility.

This is much more than just a logical fallacy for another reason. Here is where Empiricism seems to break down. We can empirically observe what is desired, but not what is desirable. We can observe what is in fact desired but not what ought to be desired. We can observe facts empirically, but not values. Strict Empiricism makes it impossible to speak of the whole dimension of moral values at all.

To put the same essential point in still another way, Mill cannot validate his "happiness principle" as the supreme moral value simply by observing the empirical fact that all men seek happiness. To do so would be to forget the distinction between is-statements and ought-statements. To get to an ought-conclusion, you need an ought-premise, since it is a fallacy to put more in your conclusion than you have in your premises. So either

(1) you have a self-evident ought-premise or moral absolute like Kant's "categorical imperative" or Aquinas's "Good must be done and evil avoided," from which you can then deduce ought-conclusions when you add a fact-premise like "stealing violates the categorical imperative" or "stealing is evil"; or

(2) you deduce your ought-conclusions from ought-premises that are not self-evident but need justification by other ought-premises—and such a regress must eventually stop at a moral absolute, as in (1); or

(3) you cannot justify any ought-conclusions at all, since you have only is-premises. Mill, as an Empiricist, is limited to is-premises. So he cannot justify any moral argument at all. Like Hume, he must then reduce morality to feelings. But feelings are merely facts, not values. The *fact* that Hitler hates Jews, the fact that killing them makes him very happy, does not make it good, right, just, or of any moral value. It takes a "one-eyed" genius like Mill to miss such an obvious point.

Ethics: Hedonism

Mill is often classified as a "eudaemonist," since he teaches that the end of human life and action, the supreme human good, is *eudaimonia,* which is the Greek word for happiness. This is what Aristotle taught too. But there is a very important distinction here. What Aristotle (and Aquinas) meant by "happiness," and the meaning of the word *eudaimonia* in ancient Greek, was something quite different from what the English word "happiness" means to most people today. It was something that by definition included moral virtue. For it was not just a subjective feeling but objectively real human perfection, the actualizing of our human potentialities for completeness, like a complete work of art, which acts as the end or final cause of the process of creating that work of art. (The artist adds these notes, or brush strokes, or words precisely in order to make the music or painting or poem perfect, i.e., complete.) To subtract the whole dimension of final causality from ethics is to make this natural, meaningful, and popular analogy (between morality and art) impossible.

To see how the meaning of the word "happiness" has changed, imagine telling someone today that "You think you're happy, but you're really not." It sounds like nonsense. But that is exactly what pre-moderns could say, e.g., to a self-satisfied tyrant. Modern "happiness" is purely the subjective feeling of contentment; ancient "happiness" *(eudaimonia)* is also objective blessedness.

And therefore not only do nearly all pre-modern thinkers deny that happiness is simply pleasure, but they insist that it must include some pain and suffering! Suffering, far from being the *opposite* of happiness, actually was thought to be *necessary* for happiness, for without it we cannot be wise, and without wisdom we cannot be perfectly human, and that is what happiness means.

They argued that pleasure is *not* the same as human happiness because it is not specifically human, it is something we share with the irrational animals.

They also argued that pleasure is not the same as happiness because it is the subjective *effect* of objective happiness, i.e., of our true good. Whatever that good may consist in, it cannot be pleasure, because we are pleased only *because* of it, because we have the real good. Pleasure is the smell of the rose, not the rose.

Mill argues for his hedonism in the same way he argues for his Happiness Principle: inductively. We learn it from experience, he says. We observe that pleasure is in fact what all people do desire as the meaning of their happiness. But this "fact" can be challenged on Mill's own empirical grounds. Nietzsche, who despised the English as "a nation of shopkeepers" and Utilitarianism as "the pig philosophy," argued that "man does not strive for pleasure, only the Englishman does." Viktor Frankl observed, in the Nazi concentration camps, that Freud (who was also a Hedonist) was empirically wrong: man does not seek pleasure above all things, but meaning, and therefore can endure great suffering if and only if he has this greater thing, a real meaning and purpose to his life. He quotes Nietzsche on this: "A man can endure almost any *how* if only he has a *why*."[18]

Mill answers the charge that his Hedonism is an animalistic philosophy by asserting, as did Epicurus, that pleasure does not mean merely physical or animal pleasures; that there is a qualitative difference between "higher" (distinctively human) pleasures and "lower" ones. This was his most important correction of Bentham's version of Utilitarianism. He argues: **It would be quite absurd that, while in estimating all other things quality is considered as well as quantity, the estimation of pleasure should be supposed to depend on quantity alone.**

But the standard for judging some pleasures "higher" or "better" than others cannot itself be simply the standard of pleasure itself. Whatever that standard is, it judges pleasure rather than pleasure judging it; therefore it, rather than pleasure, must be the ultimate meaning and standard of the degree of goodness. Mill is being more human and less "animalistic" than Bentham here, but less logical; for in introducing a qualitatively new *dimension* into ethics other than pleasure, he is implicitly transcending and judging pleasure by a higher standard and rejecting Hedonism.

Mill's answer to this problem, consistent with his epistemological principles, is entirely empirical. He says the standard is the empirically observed judgment of people who test different pleasures: **If I am asked what I mean by difference in quality in pleasures, or what makes one pleasure more valuable than another . . . except its being greater in amount, there is but one possible answer. Of two pleasures, if there be one which all or almost all who have experience of both give a decided preference, irrespective of any feeling of moral obligation to prefer it . . . we are justified in as-**

18 Ironically, Nietzsche, the virulently anti-Christian "immoralist" and proto-Nazi, is in a way closer to Christian morality than Mill is. One can more easily imagine Nietzsche converting and becoming a saint than Mill. He is at least fighting the moral war, even if on the wrong side.

cribing to the preferred enjoyment a superiority in quality. In other words, all or nearly all who have tested and compared bodily and mental pleasures find the latter higher and better; therefore they are. That conclusion is only probable, of course, since human judgment is not infallible; but it is reasonable. And it is still a strictly empirical criterion. And it helps us to decide practical, empirical matters like whether to use the surplus money in the city budget for a library or a roller coaster.

But this too is quantitative: "all or almost all" rather than "some or a few." In explaining his qualitative amendment to Bentham's merely quantitative hedonism, Mill too reduces his version to quantity. He is not quantifying pleasure-experiences, but he is quantifying pleasure-experiencers.

Suppose the tastes of the majority change from books to roller coasters? Or from poetry to push-pin? Mill seems to have to go back to Bentham here.

Ethics: Altruism

Pleasure is by its essential nature an individual and subjective thing, and therefore Hedonism seems bound to egotism. But nearly everyone, including Mill, admits that egotism is morally bad, and that altruism, concern for the good of others, is morally good. If there is nearly universal agreement on any moral principle at all among all the individuals, cultures, religions, and philosophies of the world, there is agreement on that one. (Ayn Rand is the only exception I can think of.) To make his Utilitarianism an acceptable moral theory, Mill has to include altruism in it. How does he do this?

Bentham's answer was the "egotistic hook" of enlightened self-interest: my reason tells me that I can attain my own happiness best if I work for society, for others, for the common good. The three main weaknesses of this answer are (1) that it is not usually a psychologically effective motivator, even if it is true; (2) that it is often *not* true for the individual alone: e.g., it is not myself but my descendants who benefit from my taking the trouble to care for the environment; (3) and above all, the *motive* remains purely egotistic, so the actor remains just as selfish a *person* inside as he was before; he only changes his external *actions* because he is "enlightened" enough to know that his egotistic self-interest is best served by working for others. It is not the others that he loves as ends, but only himself.

Mill explains why his Utilitarianism is altruistic and not egotistic by the principle of the equality of value between the individual's happiness and that of others. He says that no one person's happiness is more or less important than any other person's: **the happiness which forms the utilitarian standard of what is right in conduct is not the agent's own happiness but that of all concerned. As between his own happiness and that of others, utilitarianism requires him to be as strictly impartial as a disinterested and benevolent spectator.**

But *why* be impartial? Why are others as important as me? Mill cannot give a metaphysical answer like "They are human persons with the same essence and the same intrinsic value and/or the same rights as you."

Impartiality is a principle of *justice,* but Mill does not call it that, for that would be introducing another standard of value than happiness.

If Mill says that we should be altruistic because our own happiness really *is,* in objective fact, of no greater value than that of others, even if we desire it more than we desire others' happiness—if Mill says that, then he is once again transcending his Empiricist premise in judging what is valuable in objective fact and not just in our subjective experience; he is doing ethics metaphysically instead of empirically.

Mill also argues for altruism logically in a second way: **Each person's happiness is a good to that person, and the general happiness, therefore, a good to the aggregate of all persons.** This may be true, but altruism does not follow from this. Each person's happiness is a good to someone but it does not follow that your happiness is a good *to me.* Nor does it follow that collective happiness, or the common good, is my happiness and my good. That is an example of the fallacy of composition and division: applying to the whole what is true of each part or applying to each part what is true of the whole. "Large bricks" and "a large pile of bricks" do not imply each other.

How does Mill account for the fact that we admire individuals who sacrifice their own personal happiness for that of others? He interprets this in hedonistic terms: **After all, this self-sacrifice must be for some end; it is not its own end; and if we are told that its end is not happiness but virtue, which is better than happiness, I ask: Would the sacrifice be made if the hero or martyr did not believe that it would earn for others immunity from similar sacrifices** (i.e., less pain and more pleasure)?

Mill assumes here that it is inconceivable that one would sacrifice his own pleasures for another's *moral* improvement rather than for the other's pleasure. But this assumption is not empirically true. Good parents would often rather have their children be virtuous than happy, if it came to that choice. E.g., suppose their son was a soldier who was captured by a wicked enemy and given the choice between being a martyr or being a coddled collaborator with the enemy in torturing his fellow soldiers.

Mill admits that some people, like Kant, do in fact seem to prize virtue over happiness. But he interprets this to mean that virtue has become, in their minds, an essential ingredient in happiness itself. He says that the virtue which **was once desired as an instrument for the attainment of happiness, has come to be desired for its own sake. In being desired for its own sake, it is, however, desired as** *part* **of happiness.** One wonders whether this answer is anything more than a shuffling of the verbal cards.

Mill was a genuinely altruistic, humanitarian person. But it does not answer the logical question of *why* altruism is good, *why* it should be inculcated.

Ethics: Sanctions

It is not quite true that Mill has no answer to the question: *Why* seek the greatest happiness for the greatest number, what is the *ground* or reason or premise or justification for that one moral absolute? He does have an answer, or what he thinks is one. He calls these grounds "sanctions."

Mill means by a "sanction" something subjective and psychological: whatever rewards or punishments may in fact work to motivate you because of your desires or fears.

But there is linguistic confusion there: these are not "grounds" because "grounds" means "objective, logical reasons," not just "subjectively effective feelings."

Mill says there are two kinds of sanctions. **Sanctions are either external or internal.** The external sanctions are our desire for rewards and our fear of punishments, whether from nature, from other men, or from God. The internal sanction is **a feeling in our own mind** that gives us guilt and remorse (thus mental pain) for bad acts and moral satisfaction (thus mental pleasure) for good ones. This is what he calls **the essence of Conscience.**

So conscience is a *feeling.*

To see how influential Mill has been, note that this is exactly what most people today mean by "conscience": a feeling. That is *not* what philosophers before Mill usually meant by conscience. Kant, e.g., *contrasts* conscience's moral experience of duty, or obligation, with inclination, or feeling. Our conscience often tells us to ignore or defy our feelings, since our feelings are often *temptations.* But if you say and believe slogans like "If it feels good, do it," or "It can't be wrong if it feels so right," then feelings cannot possibly be temptations. (Do you think that people who say that really believe it, deep down?)

Mill asks where this internal sanction comes from, whether the **feeling of duty is innate or implanted** in us by Society. His answer is that **moral feelings** (which is all that he means by Conscience) **are not innate but are acquired.**[19] This is similar to Freud's reduction of conscience to the social "super-ego," a kind of reflection, in the individual mirror of our own psyche, of Society's rules for behavior. It is an illusion, according to Freud and Mill, that the images in the mirror come from within; they come from without, a posteriori, inductively, and empirically.

However, Mill says we are born with the capacity to develop conscience, as we are born with the innate capacity to learn languages. (Does this contradict his "not innate" answer above? If we have an innate capacity for language, is not the linguistic dimension as such, as distinct from particular languages, innate in us? Why is not the same true of the moral dimension?)

Ethics: Justice and Human Rights

An obvious objection to Utilitarianism is that applying the Happiness Principle would be unjust. E.g., if there were ten cannibals and one non-cannibal in a room, the greatest happiness (pleasure) for the greatest number might well be for the ten cannibals to kill and eat the one non-cannibal. But surely that would not be just. It would violate the non-cannibal's rights.

19 But where did it come from in the first place? Why did the first human who felt guilt or obligation feel it?

Imagine a society of extraterrestrials on another planet who are totally happy, peaceful, and altruistic only because a machine transmits good spiritual "vibes" to everyone. It gets this energy from the continued exquisite torture of one innocent victim, whose negative spiritual energy is transformed by the machine into positive spiritual energy for everyone else. This system has great happiness for great numbers of people (everyone except one), but it is clearly *unjust*. We are morally outraged by it. (There is an actual science fiction story by Ursula LeGuinn with exactly this plot.)

How does Mill include justice in Utilitarianism? He says that justice is simply the name we give to certain kinds of acts which, we discover, are almost always morally good, i.e., which produce happiness—e.g., obeying the Ten Commandments. But there are always exceptions: *Les Miserables'* Jean Valjean "stealing" bread to feed his family; or saving innocent lives by "killing" an aggressor; or Dutchmen "lying" to the Nazis about where the Jews were hiding. (By what principles would you justify these choices, by the way?) Justice is not an absolute for Mill, only happiness is; but most of the time they coincide; that is why we call these general rules "just": simply because they usually produce the most happiness. (But what if and when they don't? And is this what we mean by calling something "just"? Isn't Mill simply ignoring a whole other *dimension* of human experience here?

Morality versus Nature

Mill's essay "Nature" attacks the traditional idea of a "natural moral law," the idea that morality means following nature and that "unnatural acts" are intrinsically immoral. Mill says that **Conformity to nature has no connection whatever with right and wrong. The idea can never be fitly introduced into ethical discussions at all.** Why? Here is how he sums up his argument:

It will be useful to sum up in a few words the leading conclusion of this Essay.

The word Nature has two principal meanings: it either denotes the entire system of things, with the aggregate of all their properties (Mill here assumes Naturalism as vs. Supernaturalism), or it denotes things as they would be apart from human intervention.

In the first of these senses, the doctrine that man ought to follow nature is unmeaning, since man has no power to do anything else than follow nature; all his actions are done through, and in obedience to, some one or many of nature's physical or mental laws. (Mill here assumes Determinism as well as Naturalism.)

In the other sense of the term, the doctrine that man ought to follow nature, or in other words ought to make the spontaneous course of things the model of his voluntary actions, is equally irrational and immoral.

Irrational, because all human action whatever consists in altering, and all useful action in improving, the spontaneous course of nature.

Immoral, because the course of natural phenomena being replete with everything

which when committed by human beings is most worthy of abhorrence, anyone who endeavoured in his actions to imitate the natural course of things would be universally seen and acknowledged to be the wickedest of men. . . .

If the artificial is not better than the natural, to what end are all the arts of life? To dig, to plough, to build, to wear clothes, are direct infringements of the injunction to follow nature. . . . [20]

Mill uses his notion of "nature" here also to challenge one of the most interesting arguments for the existence of God and immortality, the argument from the natural desire for them:

Some people . . . maintain that every natural inclination must have some sphere of action granted to it, some opening left for its gratification. All natural wishes, they say, must have been implanted for a purpose; and this argument is carried so far that we often hear it maintained that every wish which it is supposed to be natural to entertain must have a corresponding provision in the order of the universe (objective reality) for its gratification; insomuch (for instance) **that the desire of an indefinite prolongation of existence is believed by many to be in itself sufficient proof of the reality of a future life.**

The argument is that all other natural hungers imply real foods; why not the hunger for God, Heaven, immortality, and the supernatural? But Mill's Empiricism, Positivism, and anti-metaphysical skepticism are assumptions that prevent him from perceiving even a probability in this argument: **I conceive that there is a radical absurdity in all these attempts to discover, in detail, what are the designs of Providence.**

The argument is not refuted but forbidden by Mill's metaphysical premises. They are metaphysical premises, for anti-metaphysical assumptions are also metaphysical assumptions, just as prejudices against philosophy are philosophical prejudices. If you say "I will not philosophize," that is your philosophy.

Social and Political Philosophy

Though he shared Comte's Positivism, Empiricism, and suspicion of religion, Mill did not share his "soft totalitarianism," his love of central social planning by a scientific elite. Mill was a Libertarian. Thus his famous work on politics is entitled On Liberty. It is the classic work of "liberal" or "libertarian" political philosophy.

What does this mean? It means that classical political philosophy is wrong when it says that the end of the state is to make its citizens good. Instead, **the sole end for which mankind are warranted, individually or collectively** (notice: the same standard for

---

20 How would defenders of traditional "natural law" morality answer this? What third meaning would they have for "nature"? Do they mean by "nature" the cosmos, or *human* nature? If the latter, why isn't selfishness "natural," since is it common?

both individuals and governments), **in interfering with the liberty of action of any of their number, is self-protection. That the only purpose for which power can be rightly exercised over any member of a civilized community, against his will, is to prevent harm to others. His own good, either physical or moral, is not a sufficient warrant** (for public interference). . . . **The only part of the conduct of any one for which he is amenable** (responsible) **to society is that which concerns others. In the part which merely concerns himself his independence is, of right,**[21] **absolute. Over himself, over his own body and mind, the individual is sovereign**.

In other words, no paternalist state. If a drug-addicted, sadomasochistic necrophiliac rides his motorcycle helmetless round and round his own room alone, shouting obscene, racist "hate speech," sells his soul to Satan, and plans to commit suicide, that should be of no concern to the State.

Mill defined freedom, or liberty, this way: **The only freedom which deserves the name is that of pursuing our own good in our own way, so long as we do not attempt to deprive others of theirs.**

Mill did not deny that government was necessary for protection of our liberties, or even for utility when the greatest happiness could be served best by government activity, e.g., if private post offices and roads would be very inefficient. But he defined three principles that should limit government's action: (1) Governments should not do what individuals can do as well or better. (2) Even when governments can do it more effectively, they should not do it when it is better for individuals to grow into self-reliance by doing it themselves. (3) Governments should not interfere when too much power would accrue to them.

Mill was especially strong on free speech, which he regarded as the very best social condition for the discovery and testing of truth. Truth is not determined by conformity to popular opinion, past (tradition) or present (the "Zeitgeist"). **If mankind were one, were of one opinion, and only one person were of the contrary opinion, mankind would be no more justified in silencing that one person than he, if he had the power, would be justified in silencing mankind. . . . Truth gains more even by the errors of one who . . . thinks for himself than by the true opinions of those who only hold them because they do not suffer themselves to think**.

Mill regarded lifestyles in the same way he regarded truth: something best discovered by maximum freedom to experiment in different ways, **without hindrance, either physical or moral, from their fellow-men, so long as it is at their own risk and peril** rather than endangering others. **It is useful . . . that there should be different experiments in living**. Social nonconformity really serves society, while tradition and custom, which he called a despotism ("**the despotism of custom**") is an obstacle to progress. Thus tradition

21 Now, Mill speaks not of "happiness" but of "right." Before, he spoke not of right, or rights, or justice, but of happiness. Why?

was to him not an aid to knowledge and wisdom, or to progress, but an obstacle. (Would he have to include family, local, and religious traditions in this critique too?)

Mill thought a republic or representative democracy was the best form of government. He warned against the tyranny of majorities over minorities in a direct democracy, and thought minorities should have proportional representation.

He also pioneered the full equality of women in his essay *The Subjugation of Women.* He wrote that **the legal subordination of one sex to the other is wrong in itself, and now one of the chief hindrances to human improvement . . . it ought to be replaced by a principle of perfect equality, admitting no power or privilege on the one side, nor disability on the other.**

Mill's libertarian political philosophy has become widely accepted in the West, especially in America.

Religion

Mill approached religion from the same positivistic, empirical, and utilitarian point of view as everything else.

As an Empiricist, he insisted that we had no concept of any divine attribute beyond our experience. He insisted that religious language be univocal, not analogical; that is, that it have the same meaning when speaking of God as when speaking of things in our experience. This eliminates any meaningful language about a transcendent being, and reduces religious language to the human level. Mill is adamant about this reductionism: **I will call no being good who is not what I mean when I apply that epithet to my fellow-creatures; and if such a being can sentence me to hell for not so calling him, to hell I shall go.** In *Three Essays on Religion,* Mill argues that the evils of the world make it much more probable that a Creator, if He exists at all, is limited in either goodness or power or both. If God is good, and wills our happiness, then He is not omnipotent, Mill argued, for **in our corner of the universe, at least,** he is **an ignominious failure.**

In *Theism,* he argued that polytheism is **immeasurably more natural to the human mind than monotheism's belief in one author and ruler of nature.** He ascribes the rise of monotheism not to religion but to science!

After investigating all the arguments for God's existence and finding that each one of them claimed more in its conclusion than its premises warranted, his final judgment is neither atheism nor theism but agnosticism: that there is **no more than a probability** of an intelligent Creator.

Yet Mill maintained that religion, though not intellectually defensible, could have a good utilitarian moral value. And this, he was honest and perceptive enough to see, led to a serious problem about the conflict inherent in the human heart between truth and goodness: **It is a most painful position to a conscientious and cultivated mind to be drawn in contrary directions by the two noblest of all objects of pursuit—truth and the general good.** Having to choose between the two, Mill himself chooses truth and agnosticism rather than social goodness and religion. But he was happy that most others chose the opposite.

This is not quite the "double truth" theory of Siger of Brabant and Averroes in the Middle Ages, or the double morality of Nietzsche; but it is a doubleness between truth and morality.

Mill also admitted that religion provided significant consolation to suffering people, but he ascribed this to emotion rather than truth: **The essence of religion is the strong and earnest direction of the emotions and desires toward an ideal object, recognized as the highest excellence.** But he thought a "Religion of Humanity" could do this as well as supernatural religion and could dispense with the non-scientific and therefore rationally-indefensible baggage.

Mill was as agnostic about immortality, or life after death, as he was about God. He defended our right **to hope for a future state** as a possibility, but saw no good reason to support that hope. Most of the philosophical arguments for it, he noted, assumed that the individual soul was a single substance. But Mill, like Hume, saw this as a metaphysical claim beyond our experience. Instead, like Hume, he reduced the soul to a bundle of successive acts, states, or attributes. (Acts *of what*? States *of what*? Attributes *of what*?)

He lived as he thought and died as he lived. When he knew he was dying, he wrote of his belief in **the cessation of our consciousness when our earthly mechanism ceases to work.** In fact he spoke of immortality not as a hope for him but as "tedious" and a "burden." (There is a psychological puzzle here: the puzzle is not why someone would disbelieve in Heaven but why he would not at least *wish* it were true.)

Mill's hope, instead, was for earthly progress in education, economics, peace, and the relief of pain and sufferings such as poverty, disease, and cruelty. He was an optimist in seeing all these evils as **removable** and progress as quite possible and likely if we were sufficiently "enlightened."

He did not live to see the century of genocide.

Three Philosophers of Evolution:
Spencer, Bergson, and Teilhard de Chardin

If we were to pick the three philosophers in modern times whose popularity has most quickly and precipitously declined, it would probably be Herbert Spencer, Henri Bergson, and Pierre Teilhard de Chardin. Each was once the single most popular philosopher in the world (in Teilhard's case, the Catholic world, at least), and today they are so ignored that many students of the history of philosophy have never even heard their names, and almost no one reads them.

The reason for their popularity is clear, and I shall try to present that here. They are exciting, challenging, world-and-life-view-changing thinkers. The reasons for their decline are less clear. And they include the decline of the idea of progress after two world wars, for all three extended the idea of evolution from biology to all human experience and were therefore optimists about the future of mankind.

But the primary one is probably the popularity of analytic philosophy. For all three of these men were the polar opposite of analytic philosophers.

All three were synthesizers, universal cosmological system-builders, in the mold of Hegel though more empirical and less rationalistic. All three tried to synthesize modern science with some brand of traditional philosophy, morality, or religion. As prophets tell us to pray "Forgive us our sins," analytic philosophers tell us to pray "Forgive us our syntheses." Yet syntheses, like sins, continue to fascinate the human spirit, with its natural and perennial demand for a "big picture," a "metanarrative," like Christianity or Communism. All such "big pictures," like great works of art, have a single unifying center. For Christianity it is Christ Himself. For Communism it is the triumph of the international Communist Revolution and the classless society. For Spencer, Bergson and Teilhard, it was universal evolutionism.

84. Herbert Spencer (1820–1903)

Life

Like most modern philosophers, Spencer (1) had an intelligent but domineering father, (2) struggled with mental and physical ailments all his life (exacerbated by the morphine and opium he habitually took as medicine), (3) never married (he "married" his work), (4) was a bit prickly if not arrogant and egotistic in criticizing his critics, and (5) had pious but austere Christian parents and rejected all organized and Biblical religion at a young age. The most interesting fact of Spencer's life is that as a boy of 13 he ran away from the home of his uncle and tutor and walked 130 miles in 3 days to get home.

He practiced both teaching and engineering, but he was not a practicing scientist; and his science-based and science-exalting philosophy is typically criticized by actual scientists for lacking the patient methodical doubt and empirical testing used by real scientists, and for resembling, instead, a brilliant but hasty metaphysical system as ambitious as Hegel's. Huxley quipped that the plot of a tragic play written by Spencer would be "the slaying of a beautiful deduction by an ugly fact."

Metaphysics

The central principle of Spencer's *First Principles* is universal evolutionism and a consequent optimism about gradual but inevitable progress. He was a naturalist but not a materialist and an agnostic but not a dogmatic atheist. He rejected all absolutes (he argues that "the Absolute" would be so singular that it could have no relation to anything else), but believed in a first Cause of all phenomena in the universe. However, this was not the God of Judaism, Christianity, or Islam. Spencer believed that the Power which the Universe manifests to us is utterly inscrutable. He thought of religious sentiments (as distinct from doctrines) as worthy of respect, but not for scientific, logical or philosophical reasons; and he thought that all creeds and forms of worship were to be tolerated as infantile stages in man's mental evolution.

Spencer thus thought to reconcile science (to which he added his philosophical speculations) with religion (from which he subtracted all claims to divine revelation). By "religion" he meant especially the "perennial philosophy," as Aldous Huxley was to call it, the mystical religion of the Orient, especially Taoism, with its first principle of the transcendence of the Tao, the source of the universe, over not only nature but all possible human knowledge. (Thus the first line of Lao Tzu's *Tao Te Ching*: "The Way that can be known is not the eternal Way.")

Spencer labeled the undeniable elements of the universe as matter, motion, space and time. All were dependent on "Force" (equivalent to "energy" in later science). He argued that **The Persistence of Force,** or **the persistence of some Cause which transcends our knowledge,** was necessary to guarantee the uniformity of nature and the laws of nature which are presupposed by all science.

He tried to formulate the most abstract and general laws of the relationship and interchange of the fundamental forces of the universe on their different levels (physical, chemical, psychological and sociological) and in their different directions (along lines of least resistance and in undulating rhythms); and he deductively applied these principles to astronomy, geology, mechanics, biology, and sociology, claiming to explain all the phenomena of all the sciences by the same set of universal laws.

Though Spencer was not a materialist, he was a naturalist, not a supernaturalist. "Force" moves the universe but did not create it; and man is part of the universe, he does not transcend it by reason or will. Human social and historical evolution exemplify the same forces as the rest of the universe. For example, individuals in a society are moved by the "force" of their desires along lines of least "resistance" (pain) in a generational rhythm, so that **Life ... has progressed ... in immense undulations.** He called his comprehensive theory of all change and history (his "theory of everything") **the Law of Evolution.**

The most general formula for Evolution was that **Evolution is an integration of matter and concomitant dissipation of motion, during which the matter passes from an indefinite, incoherent homogeneity to a definite, coherent heterogeneity, and during which the retained motion undergoes a parallel transformation.** The teleological end of the process is **equilibration,** or equilibrium, or perfect adjustment, or homeostasis. Like Comte, he claimed that modern "industrial society" is progressing toward this goal and away from the violence and conflicts of past "military society."

Part of this "equilibration" is an equality of the economic forces of supply and demand, which he taught were natural and should not be interfered with by government. His name is closely associated with "Social Darwinism," a sociological and economic extension of Darwin's biological theory of evolution by "natural selection" of those organisms which were fittest to survive ("the survival of the fittest"). This contributed to the decline of his reputation, for he opposed many Liberal reforms, such as the equality of women and the abolition of child labor, and idealized the unregulated laws of supply and demand and existing social inequalities, since he believed that the "struggle to survive" was evolution's way of ensuring progress.

Psychology

Spencer was not a materialist. Although he was much more at home with the language of the material sciences than with any "spiritual" language, he tried to overcome the Cartesian dualism of matter and mind in his *Principles of Psychology.* He called psychical and physical changes "parallels" and "obverses" of each other. He thought his attempt to mediate between the a posteriori Empiricists like Mill and the a priori transcendentalists like Kant in this work would **ultimately stand beside Newton's *Principia.*** Freud and Pavlov were both impressed by this book. However, his scientist friend Julian Huxley, who respected him more than any other living philosopher, and William James, who was sympathetic with his attempt to affirm and unify matter and mind, were not convinced that he had succeeded.

One of the lasting insights of his psychology was that introspection was not true self-consciousness because it revealed only a past state of consciousness, not its present act itself. In other words, the subject and the object of consciousness could not be quite identical. mind in action had to transcend all its possible objects, mental as well as physical.[22]

Ethics

Spencer claimed that evolution applied to ethics too since our innate moral sense was evolution's means of guiding us to true happiness, in a very slow and gradual way, through history. He later added to this "moral sense" the **accumulated effects of inherited experiences** of pleasure and pain from good and bad actions respectively. Thus, he claimed to reconcile Kant and Mill, the a priori "innate intuitionist" and the a posteriori Utilitarian Empiricist, in ethics as he thought he had done in psychology.

Spencer is closer to Utilitarian ethics than to Kantian ethics, but there is also a great difference: Spencer called happiness the absolute and ultimate objective end, not just a relative and subjective one; and he objected to the Utilitarian standard of the calculation of pleasurable consequences, since it presumed far more knowledge than anyone had in predicting the consequences of our actions. Human rights, justice, and altruism, all of which were problems for Utilitarianism, he explained as "sentiments" produced by evolution as the teacher and by experience as its method. Eventually, he believed, the attraction of pleasant feelings would displace the moral coercion of conscience as the motivator for good behavior, through the inheritance of enough remembered experiences, and through social structures naturally improving so as to more consistently reward altruistic behavior. In other words, morality will become more and more like fun as society becomes less and less like war. This seems to make Spenser much closer to Mill than to Kant.

Philosophy of History

As an evolutionary optimist, Spencer thought morality, like man, was progressing, so that people were not as wicked as they used to be, and they no longer needed an a priori

---

22 Does this premise (look carefully at it again), coupled with the premise that man by science can know universal principles about the entire universe, logically entail the conclusion that man is not merely a part of the universe, or nature, but transcends the universe, as at least relatively super-natural? If not, why not? If so, why did Spencer not draw this conclusion?

imperative to judge their a posteriori feelings. He put much faith in scientific, technological, and industrial progress in evolving society into this more moral, more spontaneously-altruistic state—which helps explain both why he was so popular in the late Victorian Age and why his popularity declined so suddenly after two world wars and the rise of Nazism in the most scientifically, technologically, and industrially advanced society the world had yet seen

For Spencer, civilization is natural, not artificial; it is simply the latest stage in evolution, continuous with pre-human, pre-historical evolution, and exemplifies all the principles of evolution, such as differentiation and specialization. Society was like a complex organ or organism, and it evolved according to the same laws as biological organisms. The evolution of law itself—i.e., positive (human) law—was like the biological evolution of brains and nervous systems. Both were self-regulatory or "self-scanning" mechanisms. This legal and moral evolution, while continuous with biological evolution, is also different, for in society the cells (individual persons) are not in continuous contact but dispersed and individuated, and each has its own consciousness.

Subsequent thinkers rejected or ignored Spencer not because he was too materialistic but because he was not materialistic enough, or at least not empirical enough. After Hegel, comprehensive cosmic systems seldom arose, and when they did they quickly fell.

85. Henri Bergson (1859–1941)

Bergson was French, his mother was English and his father was a Polish Jew who taught and composed music. He had a happy, stable, faithful marriage and one daughter, who was deaf and became a painter. In many ways Bergson's philosophy, like that of Marcel, whom he influenced, moves like music rather than like mathematics: one sound (theme) reverberates with overtones and permeates others; mental spaces are shared rather than cordoned off by sharp definitions and distinctions, as in analytic philosophers, whose model is *mathematical* logic. For both Bergson and Marcel, as for Plato, "participation" is a key connecting theme.

Bergson was also an international diplomat to the U.S. during World War I, an elected member of the prestigious French Academy, and a recipient of the Nobel Prize for literature. Jacques Maritain (ch. 97) credited Bergson with saving him and his wife from a suicide pact and contributing to their religious conversion by his hopeful, positive rather than positivistic philosophy. In an age of cynicism, materialism, skepticism, reductionism, scientistic positivism, determinism, mechanism, materialism, and atheism, Bergson's positive alternative to these isms, as well as his personal example and inspiring lectures, rescued many ordinary and extraordinary people from despair.

Almost all of them used the same word for the effect of his philosophy: they called it a "liberation." From what were they liberated? From positivism, or scientism; from its denial of spirit, freedom, transcendence, and life after death; i.e., from imprisoning us in materialism, determinism, naturalism, and finite earthly time. The only mind that is content to live in a universe that is essentially a gigantic computer is a mind that thinks of itself as a computer.

In Bergson's last will, he wrote that he would have accepted baptism into the Catholic Church but for the rising popularity of anti-Semitism and his duty to stand with his persecuted people. He died in Nazi-occupied Paris, of pneumonia, which he contracted from standing in line for many hours to be registered as a Jew.

Like most anti-scientistic philosophers of the twentieth century, he had a profound interest, love, knowledge, and respect for science. One of his works was a debate with Einstein on the philosophical aspects of Einstein's theory of relativity.

Bergson's "Big Idea"

Most philosophers have one "big idea" that is central to all their ample and diverse writings. Bergson's central idea is about the nature of time—one of the most notoriously tricky and mysterious aspects of our experience. (Augustine famously said, "If you don't ask me what time is, of course I know, and so does everyone else; but if you ask me, I find that I really can't tell you, and neither can anyone else.")

149

For Bergson, time is not equally past, present and future, because the past and future does not really exist, except in our memory and anticipation. This is the polar opposite of the determinists' notion of time, which is a kind of a predestination from past and/or future, a necessary and predictable unrolling of the reel of a movie. For Bergson, time is open, not closed; unpredictably creative, not determined; and personal rather than impersonal. It is lived time, or experienced time rather than abstractly conceived time. He calls it *"duree* " ("dew-ray") which is usually translated, much too ambiguously, as "duration." It is very close to what the Greeks called *kairos* rather than *kronos*. It is really a very simple notion, because we all live it all the time, but we forget it when we objectify, abstract, and measure time, as we forget our own eyes when we look at what is in front of them.

Duree is the "internal" time of life rather than the "external" time we use to measure material things that change. Each present moment of this lived time (and these moments, though plural, cannot be sharply separated, counted or quantified) is different, and has a unique quality. In contrast, the merely-material, purely-objective, quantitatively-measurable time we usually think of is as homogeneous and indifferent as space. *Duree* is to clock time as concrete *place* is to abstract *space*. Our habitual mistake is to think of time as if it were a kind of space. But that kind of time is not real time, time as it exists; it is time as mentally frozen and "essentialized" or "thingified." It is only an abstraction made by our minds—the product of a lived but forgotten act of our own minds which are living in real time *(duree* or *kairos)*.

We can count areas of space, but we cannot do this to time, i.e., real, lived time—until we turn it into a kind of space. You cannot count the seconds as you live them, only when you step out of the continuous stream of life and look at it as an object, from outside, and "map" it as if it were space.

What is startling about this is not the distinction itself, for that distinction already exists in some languages, like Greek, and corresponds roughly, though not exactly, to the familiar idea of "lifetime," or "my biological clock," or "time *for*" something. What is startling is the consequence: that physical time, the time physical science measures, is not real.

We think it is real because we think of movement in time as if it were like movement in space. When we measure how far the distance is from New York to San Francisco, we abstract from everything concrete in between: we measure only the abstract space which we think, not the real places where we live. We think of it as "3000 miles," not as Chicago or the Mississippi or Nevada. It's not real, lived *places* that we measure but just "space," an abstraction that is characterless and homogeneous and infinitely divisible. But real time is not like space but like place. We make time into something unreal like space for practical purposes: in order to measure it, or to measure events by it. We abstract this kind of time *(kronos)* from real movement, or life, or events, and then we reify the abstraction. (Another example of this fallacy, from Aristotle's point of view, is Plato's Forms, which he treated as actual, independently-existing substances. Whitehead called this "the fallacy of misplaced concreteness.")

Our own experience shows us Bergson's distinction. Real, lived, experienced time, unlike this mental abstraction, is not divisible but continuous. It is not quantifiable but qualitative. It is not homogeneous and characterless, but each moment of it, and each lived event of it, is different and unique.

The reason each event is different and unique is because each event in our lives adds to a kind of memory-history: events happen to people who already have a history and a past, and this memory-history-past exists *now, in* the very event it is involved in, as an aspect of that event. The real, concrete past is an aspect or dimension of the real, concrete present.

Perhaps the best example of this is the death of Ivan Ilyitch, in Tolstoy's famous short story by that title. When Ivan realizes he is dying, he is in "denial" because he cannot believe that this unique person, *with all his past history,* this Ivan and not another, this Ivan who as a child played ball and loved the smell of his mother's gown, is now about to be no more. The Bergsonian point is that memory is not past, it is present. *The past is real because it is present.* The future is not real because it is not present. The past is full; the future is empty. This shows how different time is from space. Past and future are not equal. But left and right, east and west, up and down, north and south are all equal in space.

A startling consequence of this idea is that because the past is present, *nothing is lost.* The matter of the past may vanish but the "memory" of it does not. The past persists in the present. And this was for Bergson a metaphysical proof of the immortality of the human mind.

But memory is not just subjective, dependent on my conscious thought. It is in my very being. I may consciously forget, but my being never "forgets." I am like "memory foam." Every living being "remembers" because it acts, it changes, it lives; and "remembering" is an essential dimension of that living. Identity is always augmented, never diminished. This is true of every living thing. It is not true in the same way of mere matter, purely physical matter. But "mere matter" is another abstraction when it comes to anything alive.

With regard to time and its connection with memory, Bergson says that **we forget that we remember.** We forget lived time and reify conceptualized time, as both Empiricism and Rationalism "thingify" our ideas. This debate between Rationalism and Empiricism is an example not only of "the fallacy of misplaced concreteness" but also of a common pattern in philosophical disputes: a questionable assumption common to both parties of the dispute. Uncovering this common hidden false assumption is a favorite technique of Bergson's. He calls it *decoupage.* It is a way of answering Kant's "antinomies." (Ch. 64.)

Duree or lived time, for Bergson, is not confined to human minds. The universe itself, though it is not a personal subject, acts more like a mind than like the "matter" of modern physics which is one of our reified abstractions. (Abstractions are useful and even necessary for practical purposes, but that does not mean they are independently real.) The universe acts and changes not in a pre-set, deterministic, mechanical way, like a machine, but it evolves meaningfully, like an organism or a mind. It is propelled by some invisible "vital force" which Bergson called the *elan vital*.

This does not mean that there is a deistic divine mind *behind* or *above* the universe like a puppeteer, or like a man programming a very complex machine (think of Kristoff in "The Truman Show"), but that there is a mind-like meaning and identity and direction *in* the life and story of the universe, as the soul is "in" the body—or vice versa. (Aquinas says that the soul is *not* in the body, the body is in the soul, somewhat as a play's setting is *in* the play; and that is closer to Bergson's vision.)

Bergson is an evolutionist, but for him evolution is evidence against, not for, materialism; for Mind is not a late product of Matter, as a car is a product of a long production line in a factory; rather, Mind is that which is presupposed by the very idea of matter; for matter itself, and its 13.7 billion year past, and pastness itself, are all intelligible only as products of an act of mind, *viz.* the mental act of abstracting.

Thus in many ways Bergson turns our typically modern prejudices inside out. The very evolutionary science that seems to lead to materialism, atheism, and determinism really points in the opposite direction, to a spiritual metaphysics, to a kind of expansionism rather than reductionism. (The very act of reductionism is an act of *mind.)* Perhaps this helps explain his present unpopularity. He is a salmon swimming upstream. (But only living things can swim against the current; dead fish always move with it.)

Each of Bergson's books, as we shall see, has a single main point, which is always a critique of some popular positivistic reductionism, such as the Empiricist concept of psychology, the materialist concept of mind, the determinist and mechanist concept of evolution, and the naturalistic sociological and psychological concept of religion. Each Bergsonian critique is dependent on his central concept of *duree*. And each of his critiques makes the same point: that each of these typically modern reductionisms is just the opposite of what it claims to be: it is not open-minded and empirical, as a complete science should be, but prejudicial and ideological; that it ignores and then denies the very thing that alone brings it into being, namely the free, creative, living act of thinking, the very thought-act or thought-habit of turning away from the full, concrete data of experience and imposing upon it a useful scientific abstraction.

Bergson accused both the (a posteriori) positivists and the (a priori) Kantians, the two main philosophical alternatives in his day, of this same error. This is an example of his method of *decoupage* mentioned above. He sought to escape such dilemmas, and he saw his own philosophy, much as William James saw his "pragmatism" and as Husserl saw his "phenomenology," not as a theory or system at all, but as fidelity to the data. It was not a construction, like architecture or engineering, but an exploration, like spelunking. It did not claim to be systematic or final, but open to endless correction, revision, and addition. Therefore, even if we have serious objections to many things Bergson says, we can use and learn many other things from him. It is not a "take it or leave it" package deal, a "system."

152

We will explore the central idea of each of his seven major books, (1) Time and Free Will, *(2)* Matter and Memory, *(3)* Laughter, *(4)* Creative Evolution, *(5)* An Introduction to Metaphysics, *(6)* Duration and Simultaneity, *and (7)* Two Sources of Morality and Religion.

Time and Free Will: Refuting Determinism

Here is how Bergson's point about time refutes determinism: Only by (1) first objectifying and quantifying our subjective and qualitative mental life and time, and only by (2) thinking of time as space, can we (3) imagine separate mental states or acts to be like separate physical states or acts; and only by doing this can we (4) imagine a determinist explanation of those mental states or acts. Once again, the central point is *duree:* **Every demand for explanation in regard to freedom comes back, without our suspecting it, to the following question: "Can time be adequately represented by space?" To which we answer: "Yes, if you are dealing with time flown; No, if you speak of time flowing. Now the free act takes place in time which is flowing and not in time which has already flown. Freedom is therefore a fact, and among the facts which we observe there is none clearer. All the difficulties of the problem, and the problem itself, arise from the desire to endow duration** *(duree)* **with the same attributes as extension** (in space) . . .

Bergson applies his *decoupage* to both the opponents and the defenders of free will: **defenders and opponents of free will agree in holding that the action is preceded by a kind of mechanical oscillation between the two points X and Y. If I decide in favor of X, the former** (the defenders) **will tell me: You hesitated and deliberated, therefore Y was possible. The others will answer: You chose X, therefore you had some reason for doing so, and those who declare that Y was equally possible forget this reason** (which caused and determined the choice) . . . **both take up their position** *after* **the action X has been performed, and represent the process of my voluntary action by a path . . . which branches off . . . symbolizing two directions which abstraction distinguishes within the continuous activity of which X is the goal.** Both sides thingify the process and divide it into parts, like space. But *duree* is continuous and whole. That is where freedom lives: in the whole act and the whole actor. **It is the whole soul,**[23] **in fact, which gives rise to the free decision; and the act will be so much the more free the more the dynamic series** (of psychological acts) **with which it is connected is the fundamental self.** (By "the fundamental self" Bergson means the whole self, "I" or person rather than an abstracted part or element in the person's act, such as reasoning, desiring, etc.)

C. S. Lewis makes the same essential point about free will in reflecting on his conversion in his autobiography *Surprised by Joy:* "I chose to open, to unbuckle, to loose

---

23 He should say "person" or "I" instead of "soul," for he does not mean to exclude the body or to be a Cartesian dualist. The "I" is always whole and indivisible, like its time (*duree*).

the rein. I say, 'I chose,' yet it did not really seem possible to do the opposite. On the other hand, I was aware of no motives. You could argue that I was not a free agent, but I am more inclined to think that this came nearer to being a perfectly free act than most that I have ever done. Necessity may not be the opposite of freedom, and perhaps a man is most free when, instead of producing motives, he could only say, 'I am what I do' . . . Freedom, or necessity? Or do they differ at their maximum? At that maximum a man is what he does; there is nothing of him left over or outside the act."

Matter and Memory: Refuting Materialism

Determinists are usually materialists. Bergson refutes materialism in a single syllogism. He argues that the differences between any two material things or events can be quantified, but the differences between two mental states cannot, therefore mental states are not material.

He also offers a similar argument: One quantity or number (the greater one) contains another (the lesser one); but mental states, intellectual or emotional, do not *contain* each other. Therefore they are not quantifiable. When we claim to measure them as "greater" or "lesser" in "intensity," this is at best an analogy, not literal: the difference between "greater" and "lesser" here cannot in principle be quantified. As Aristotle would say, that is the fallacy of confusing fundamentally different categories, *viz.* quality and quantity; it is a "going-over-into-another-genus" *(metabasis eis allo genos).*

A third anti-materialist argument is that brain science cannot in principle explain the relation between body states (including brain states) and mental states in the two ways materialists always claim to do—either (1) that brain states are *identical* with mental states or (2) that they are the *sufficient causes* of mental states—because the brain is an organ for *selecting* mental states; it cannot at the same time *produce* them. It is like a valve, a faucet that determines how much water comes through; it does not produce the water. It works like a telephone message exchange system. There is indeed a relationship, which Bergson calls a "solidarity," and even a dependency, but **there is also a solidarity between clothes and the hook on which they hang; once we take away the hook, the clothes fall. Can we say that for this reason the form of the hook shapes the form of the clothes?** Thus the fact that certain lesions of the brain eliminate certain thoughts proves nothing.

A fourth argument is this: Bergson first defines a sense image as that which we perceive when our material senses are opened. We can have images of any bodily thing, and only of bodily things. Brains are bodily things, so we can have images of brains. Now materialism claims that the material brain is the sole cause of all our mental images. But nothing can cause itself. **To make of the brain the condition on which the whole image** (of the body, like all images) **depends, is, in truth, a contradiction in terms, since the brain is by** (this materialist) **hypothesis a part of this image** (i.e., a part of the body). Sense images can't be in the physical brain because an image of the brain is an image *of* the brain, not *in* it. An image of a thing is not a thing or a part of a thing. For instance, an image of a tree is not a tree or part of a tree, like a leaf.

This seems essentially the same as the point in Augustine's *Confessions* where he is finally freed from his materialism when he realizes that there is no image of the very act of forming a sense image: "I was so gross of mind, not seeing even myself clearly, that whatever was not extended in space . . . I thought must be nothing whatsoever. My mind was in search of such images as the forms my eye was accustomed to see; and I did not realize that the mental act by which I formed these images was not itself a bodily image."

An Introduction to Metaphysics: Two Ways of Knowing

Bergson makes a distinction between two kinds of knowing that is similar to Pascal's distinction between "the geometrical mind" and "the intuitive mind." The first kind of knowing produces *kronos* time rather than *kairos* time or *duree*. It is (1) as Einstein discovered, relative, or perspectival; it is limited to your perspective, in other words somewhat subjective; (2) external, (3) symbolic or verbal, (4) objective, or descriptive, (5) impersonal, (6) abstract, (7) conceptual, (8) analytical, (9) quantitative, and (10) spatial. (11) It reduces the object to what is already known by classifying it into pre-existing categories. The other kind of knowing, whose time is *duree,* is (1) absolute and objective, i.e., a knowledge of the thing itself, in itself, as it is in itself—which Kant declared impossible, (2) internal, or empathetic, (3) trans-lingual, (4) experiential, (what Russell called "knowledge by acquaintance" instead of "knowledge by description," *connaitre* rather than *savoir),* (5) personal, (6) concrete and lived, (7) pre-conceptual, (8) intuitive and synthetic or holistic, (9) qualitative, and (10) temporal rather than spatial. (11) It perceives the uniqueness and newness of the object, what Duns Scotus called its "thisness" or *hecceitas* and what the poet Gerard Manley Hopkins called "inscape."

The epistemic contrast is not between knowing and feeling but between two ways of knowing. Both kinds are fallible and partial. But modernity makes the more absolute kind of knowing (and thus the more absolute kind of time) subjective and relative to the other kind. Bergson seems to turn us upside down, but that is because we have been standing on our heads. It is really *kronos* time that is subjective and relative (as Einstein proved) and it is *kairos* or *duree* that is objective and absolute, not vice versa. Though *duree* is "*lived* time," that does not make it *subjective*; that makes it *real*. Though spatialized and conceptualized time is scientific and rational, that does not make it real; that makes it a creation of our subjective reason, not of objective nature.

The most fundamental difference, for Bergson, is that **analysis** (the scientific kind of knowledge and of time) **operates always on the immobile** ("fixed concepts"), **whilst intuition** (the lived kind of knowledge and of time) **places itself in mobility, or, what comes to the same thing, in duration** *(duree).*

Intuition is prior because **fixed concepts may be extracted by one thought from mobile reality; but there are no means of reconstructing the mobility of the real**

with fixed concepts. Once Humpty-Dumpty falls off the wall of the continuum of *duree,* and splits into pieces (separate concepts), all the king's horses and all the king's men can't put him back together again.

Intuition is prior also because it is "inside" the real, which is moving, while analysis is "outside" the real by being outside the moving life of its object and instead is in the fixed (i.e., concepts): **What is relative is the . . . knowledge by pre-existing concepts, which proceeds from the fixed to the moving, and not the intuitive knowledge which installs itself in that which is moving and adopts the very life of things**.

The issue here is not just epistemological but metaphysical. Bergson sets himself against the classical Greek metaphysical priority of the timeless over the changing. For him, the timeless is not the really real or the more real, as it was for Plato, and the changing relative to it, but vice versa. Plato contrasted "being" to "becoming," but for Bergson being *is* becoming. This is why God, for Bergson, is not eternal but the very force of all moving, the "elan vital" (see below).

This is one of the reasons the Catholic Church labeled his view of God heretical. But actually, Aquinas's theology, while not denying God's eternity, as Bergson did, is in one way closer to Bergson than to Plato, for he says that God is the dynamic (though not temporally changing) act of existence itself, not a static essence. And if love is an actual act rather than an abstract ideal or value, then "God is love" does not mean "God is the timeless ideal of love" but "God is the eternal *activity* of loving."

To explain the superiority of intuitive knowledge, Bergson gives the example of a character in a novel. You can know a lot *about* him by the first kind of knowledge but only the second kind—imaginatively sharing his *life* in the novel—enables you to know *him*. You "identify with" him. It is an intellectual empathy. This intuition alone enables you to know him as he is *as a whole*; the other kind of knowing, analysis, can only try to construct him out of analyzed-out fragments or parts or dimensions *of* him (like putting Humpty together again). But a person, real or fictional, cannot be constructed, like a machine, part by part, but can exist only as a whole, and can be known only as a whole, and can come into existence only as a whole. (How then could evolution alone possibly assemble a person out of previously existing impersonal parts?)

The same distinction applies to the knowledge of a pet, or a town, or a piece of music, or a poem. Bergson uses the fantasy parable of intelligent bees who are masters of the first kind of knowing and totally deficient in the second. (I have met some philosophers like that.) They claim to "know" everything about a painting by buzzing around it, analyzing it into all its parts, mathematically symbolizing the parts, and constructing a single enormous formula containing all the permutations and combinations of its parts in all their quantitative and spatial relationships. The bees cannot understand what they missed. They missed the whole thing.

Bergson describes this deeper kind of knowledge by "intuition" as a **kind of intellectual sympathy by which one places oneself within an object in order to coincide with what is unique in it and consequently inexpressible.** (Compare what Bergson calls "intuition" with what Wittgenstein calls "the mystical" and says can be only "shown," not "said"—ch. 90.) Bergson says that metaphysics uses "intuition" and science uses analysis. (That is probably an oversimplification of both metaphysics and science, but the distinction itself still holds.)

Laughter: Making Fun of Mechanism

Laughter, like music, is one of the most fascinating, delightful, and mysterious features of human life, and great philosophers and scholars seldom deal with it. (And when they do, their books are usually hilariously unhilarious.) It is also more central than it seems. Wittgenstein once said that you could write a whole philosophy book that consisted of nothing but jokes. Peter Berger, in *Redeeming Laughter,* called it one of the remaining and ineradicable "signals of transcendence" in our secular, naturalistic, materialistic world. We must transcend whatever we laugh at; and since we laugh at ourselves and at the whole world, we could not do this unless there was a point of view in us that transcends both. Humor also fosters faith and trust, especially in children, through games like peek-a-boo and jack-in-the-box.

Bergson's focus in his little book is not so much on the *effects* of laughter in the psyche or in the life of the one who laughs (that is relatively easy to see), but on its real but invisible *causes*. He says they cannot be reduced to a single one, but he notes three things that cause or occasion laughter have in common: (1) they are uniquely human (only humans find things funny); (2) they require emotional detachment (we laugh at others' pratfalls, not our own); and (3) they are social, or **stand in need of an echo,** an audience or a fellow-laugher, like a conspiracy, or a delightfully shared secret.

Bergson finds the commonest of the many causes of laughter to be rigidity or mechanism. (Here too his central notion of real time as *duree* and false time as static is the key.) Inelasticity, absent-mindedness, and the obstinacy of matter are examples. We laugh at people who try to act like angels or minerals or machines. For instance, practical jokes expose our being creatures of habit, and puncture our expectations. Persisting in prejudices, or out-of-date fashions, or stiffly ceremonious behavior, also illustrate rigidity and elicit laughter. Belching or farting during an important speech are examples of the rigid stubbornness of the body's matter. Another kind of laughable rigidity is people being treated as things, like bouncing balls or puppets.

Still other examples are role reversals, which surprise and discombobulate us because of our rigidity: e.g., prisoners judging judges, patients diagnosing doctors, students lecturing professors, or traps trapping the trapper, as on the old cartoons (Roadrunner and Wylie Coyote, or Tweetybird and Sylvester).

Ironic misunderstandings are also a classic plot device in comedies. **A situation is invariably comic when it belongs simultaneously to two altogether independent series of events and is capable of being interpreted in two entirely different meanings at the same time.**

Because comedy means laughing at ourselves, it is socially important in overcoming our vanity and pride, which are also forms of rigidity, since this rigidity is not only dehumanizing but contrary to the dynamism of being itself: it is a refusal to go along with the divine plot of the *elan vital*. In theistic terms, if "He that sitteth in the heavens shall laugh," then woe to him who refuses to laugh with Him.

Creative Evolution: Uniting Science and Religion

Creative Evolution was an instant best-seller and made Bergson famous. One reason was its bringing together of science and religion, like two divorced lovers.

Here too Bergson's view of time is central. It is the premise from which he both affirms "creative evolution" and criticizes mechanistic evolution—and equally criticizes "finalism," which is a kind of teleological predestination version of evolution. Both are deterministic: for the mechanist the past determines the future (and the present) and for the "finalist" the future determines the past (and the present). But for Bergson evolution is more like a man than like a machine: it is *free* and unpredictable. Its future is open. The force driving evolution is not a determinism, either from behind (mechanism) or from ahead (finalism), but what Bergson calls the *elan vital,* "force of life" or "vital impetus."

This force, though material, is also spiritual: **The life that evolves on the surface of our planet is indeed attached to matter. . . . In fact it is riveted to an organism that subjects it to the general laws of inert matter. But everything happens as if it were doing its utmost to set itself free from these laws.** In other words, evolution is "creative." Bergson is not saying that nature has the kind of freedom man has (free will), but it is not determined either. And it is certainly not merely materialistic, for entropy rules in the material world, but evolution moves in the opposite direction from entropy!

Bergson criticizes Darwin's explanation of evolution by mere natural selection, i.e., the emergence of genetic variations by random chance, some of which are adapted for survival. Against this he uses the same argument current "intelligent design" defenders use: that it cannot explain the evolution of complex organs like the eye, which function for survival only when fully developed, but not during the process of the gradual evolutionary emergence of its parts or primitive forms. Partial eyes would not have worked for survival at all. But in Darwin's theory an organ could not have appeared all at once, finished, and able to function to help the organism to survive. Thus evolution requires, if not a Creator-God, at least something like an inherent guiding design, a kind of immanent god, the *elan vital*.

Duration and Simultaneity: Bergson's Time and Einstein's Time

Bergson had an ongoing correspondence with Einstein to **find out to what extent our concept of duration was compatible with Einstein's views on time.** It centered on the "twin paradox." (If you don't know what this is, look it up.) The book based on this correspondence shows not only how interested Bergson was in physical science but also how honest and humble he was; for his final conclusion, after an exchange of correspondence with Einstein himself, was that he did not have the sophisticated mathematical ability to come to a final conclusion, and therefore he did not consent to republish it.

The Two Sources of Morality and Religion

In accordance with his distinction between the two kinds of time, Bergson makes two fundamental distinctions in this book: (1) between "closed" and "open" societies and (2) between "static" and "dynamic" religion. "Open" societies are universalistic and cosmopolitan; "closed" societies are provincial, "us" vs. "them." "Static" religion is basically rationalistic, rigid, "closed" religion; "dynamic" religion is basically mysticism, the ultimate openness, religion with an "undo" button. He rejected all unchangeable dogmas and creeds because they seemed to him to exemplify "static" rather than "dynamic" religion. (One wonders whether he would have accepted Newman's synthesis of these two apparently opposite dimensions in his notion of "the development of doctrine.")

Two different "takes" on Bergson are to be found in the same philosopher, Jacques Maritain: *Bergsonian Philosophy* is more critical and *On Bergson and St. Thomas Aquinas* more sympathetic

86. Pierre Teilhard de Chardin (1881–1955)

Teilhard's life was that of a pious, faithful Jesuit priest who was also a paleontologist—not a very good one, apparently, for he was fooled by the hoax of "Piltdown man" during his years of research in China. He was a war hero in World War I and awarded the Medal of Honor. The depth and sincerity of his prayer life and his love of God are very obvious from his letters. He prayed to die on Easter Sunday, and did. When the Church, after theological investigations, labeled him dangerous, forbade him to publish, and forbade its seminarians to read his books, he did not start a campaign, as most "dissenters" do, but obeyed. (Jesuits take a solemn vow of obedience to the Pope. Not all take it seriously. He did.)

Teilhard was a theologian by training and method rather than a philosopher, but he is included here, in a book of philosophers, because, even though his work's origins are more theological than philosophical, his work's philosophical implications and consequences are great. Also, because he is *interesting,* because he offers a very "big picture," both theoretical (a "world-view") and practical (a "life-view"). In fact, by William James's commonsense criterion of meaning—what *difference* does it make whether this idea is true or false?—Teilhard's ideas are arguably more meaningful than those of most other philosophers. This is so even if he is judged to be a dangerously naïve idealist and sentimentalist, a pseudo-scientific "crackpot," or a dangerous heretic. Hegel was called all three, yet he remains a formidable force in human intellectual history.

The difference his ideas make is why he is so controversial: he is either wonderfully right or disastrously wrong. He is both defended and attacked with great passion. Many "progressive" and a few traditional religious thinkers (notably Henri de Lubac) praise him for Christianizing the science of our age as St. Thomas Aquinas Christianized the philosophy of his, and for calling for a new expansion of Christianity, a "new Nicaea" which would define Christ's relationship to the universe as the first Nicaea defined his relationship to God the Father. Other traditional Christian thinkers, like C. S. Lewis, Jacques Maritain, Etienne Gilson, and Dietrich von Hildebrand, attack him for sacrificing religion on the altar of science and naively embracing the discredited idea of inevitable and unlimited progress. A third judgment is that of many non-religions scientists and philosophers who attack him for the opposite: for sacrificing real science and philosophy for the sake of religion. His intention was clearly to unite and synthesize the two, and to thereby expand rather than reduce both.

Teilhard effected something very much like what Bergson did from the opposite direction. Many who read or heard Bergson said they were "liberated" by his thought from materialistic scientism into a spiritual and even religious dimension, and into a larger world-view; and that this gave them a reconciliation or marriage of the scientific and the spiritual. Many who read Teilhard said they were "liberated" into this marriage from the opposite narrowness: a merely-spiritual, legalistic, moralistic, static or past-oriented religiosity (what Bergson called "static religion") into a larger, more cosmic one ("dynamic religion") that embraced evolution, science, and modernity. While Bergson added a religious dimension to science, Teilhard added a scientific dimension to religion. Bergson spiritualized evolution; Teilhard evolutionized spirituality. For him **Christianity and evolution are not two irreconcilable visions, but two perspectives destined to fit together and complement each other.**

His style of writing and thinking is visionary rather than critical. One can only imagine the frustration an "analytic philosopher" experiences when reading him: one finds no careful scientific or philosophical arguments or definitions, no critical logical dialectics. He is a painter, and his brush strokes are very broad. He summarizes the intent of his *magnum opus, The Phenomenon of Man,* simply as **an attempt to *see* and *to show.***

It is a religious vision, and expressed in religious language; but it is also a philosophy, a cosmology, a world-view, one that attempts to unite religion, science, and philosophy, mankind's three major enterprises, like longitude lines uniting as they approach the pole. ("Everything that rises must converge" was one of his oft-quoted sayings.) He did this both in his theoretical, scientific, and cosmological "world-view," in *The Phenomenon of Man,* and also in his practical, moral, religions, and mystical "life-view" in *The Divine Milieu.*

The two dimensions of his philosophy, his cosmological world-view and his moral and religious life-view, are closely connected; but many readers admire one of the two and not the other. (The same is true of the two main parts of Kant, the theoretical and the practical, the epistemology and the ethics.) But these two dimensions of his thought are unified by the central idea of "the cosmic Christ" of St. Paul, "in whom all things have been created, in whom all things hang together, and in whom all things are consummated." (Colossians 1:16–17).

Both books are arranged in a systematic, logical *order,* but the order is not that of logical *proof.* The order is that of seeing and showing, like music, poems or pictures that are presented for our contemplation and inspiration. We are drawn to them (or away from them) by the beauty (or lack of beauty) of the whole picture, not by a chain of proofs. The parts hang together in a kind of intuitive logic, like the logic of a drama. And the drama is as massive as the whole universe, the whole of history, and the whole of human life. Even one of his severest critics, Jacques Maritain, admires Teilhard's imagination, passion, and poetic vision, which he calls "extremely powerful."

Rather than looking at Teilhard through the eyes of his commentators, whether critics or defenders, we will summarize his two main books in his own words. They are works of art as much as philosophy, and talking *about* a work of art is not the best way to understand it; we must hear it or see it, or at least samples of it.

The Phenomenon of Man

(On Matter and Mind:) **In the eyes of the physicist, nothing exists legitimately, at least up to now, except the *without* of things. . . . This apparent restriction of the phenomenon of consciousness to the higher forms of life has long served science as an excuse for eliminating it from its models of the universe. A queer exception, an aberrant function, an epiphenomenon—thought was classed under one or other of these heads in order to get rid of it. But what would have happened to modern physics if radium had been classified as an "abnormal substance" without further ado? . . . .an irregularity in nature is only the sharp exacerbation, to the point of perceptible disclosure, of a property of things diffused throughout the universe . . . by reason of the fundamental unity of the world. Whither does this rule lead us if we apply it to the instance of human "self-knowledge"? Consciousness . . .** (therefore) **has a cosmic extension . . .** (and therefore) **matter is something more than the particulate swarming so marvelously analyzed by modern physics. . . . The *within, consciousness,* and then *spontaneity,* three expressions for the same thing. . . .**

Spiritual perfection (or conscious "centreity ") and material synthesis (or complexity) are but the two aspects or connected parts of one and the same phenomenon. . . . (This is) **the great *Law of complexity and consciousness.* . . .**

(The Problem of the Two Energies:) **Without the slightest doubt *there is something* through which material and spiritual energy hold together and are complementary. In the last analysis, *somehow or other,* there must be a single energy operating in the world . . .** (because of) **the refrain that runs all the way through this book:** *In the world, nothing could ever burst forth as final across the different thresholds successively traversed by evolution (however critical they be) which has not already existed, in an obscure and primordial way. . . .*

So, in a sense, we can no more fix an absolute zero in time (as was once supposed) for the advent of life. . . . **But to have realized and accepted once and for all that each being has and must have a *cosmic embryogenesis* in no way invalidates the reality of its *historic birth* . . . the liquid boils, the germ cell divides, intuition suddenly bursts on the piled up facts. . . . Critical points have been reached, rungs on the ladder, involving a change of state. . . .**

(On Man:) **If we wish to settle this question of the "superiority" of man over the animals. . . . I can only see one way of doing so . . .** *reflection* **. . . the power acquired by a consciousness to turn in upon itself . . . no longer merely to know, but to know that one knows. . . .**[24]

---

24 Teilhard is often misunderstood as a pantheist or monist, but he clearly affirmed God's transcendence over the universe and man's transcendence over mere matter, consciousness over pre-conscious stages of evolution. He wrote, in 1917, that **consciousness must not be re-**

Now the consequences of such a transformation are immense. . . . The being who is the object of his own reflection, in consequence of that very doubling back upon himself, becomes in a flash able to raise himself into a new sphere. In reality, another world is born. Abstraction, logic, reasoned choice and inventions, mathematics, art, calculation of space and time, anxieties and dreams of love—all these activities of *inner life* are nothing else than the effervescence of the newly-formed centre as it explodes onto itself. . . .

We are not astonished (because it happens to *us*) to see in each person around us the spark of reflection developing year by year. We are all conscious, too, at all events vaguely, that *something* in our atmosphere is changing with the course of history. If we add these two pieces of evidence together. how is it that we are not more sensitive to the presence of something greater than ourselves moving forward within us and in our midst? . . . . (*viz.* the further evolution of man as a species)

(The Noosphere:) We saw geogenesis promoted to biogenesis, which turned out in the end to be . . . . psychogenesis . . . Psychogenesis has led to man. Now . . . noogenesis . . . this irresistible tide of fields and factories, this immense and growing edifice of matter and ideas—all these signs that we look at, day in and day out—seem to proclaim that there has been a change on the earth and a change of planetary magnitude . . . the noosphere. . . .

(Unity:) Our habit is to divide up our human world into compartments of different sorts of "realities": natural and artificial, physical and moral, organic and juridical, for instance . . . (But) are not the artificial, the moral and the juridical simply the hominised versions of the natural, the physical, and the organic? . . .

The social phenomenon is the culmination . . . of the biological phenomenon . . . In the same beam of light the instinctive gropings of the first cell link up with the learned gropings of our laboratories . . .

(The modern crisis:) We are, at this very moment, passing through an age of *transition* . . . characterized by the birth pangs inevitable in another change of state . . . What has made us in four or five generations so different from our forebears, . . . so ambitious too, and so worried, is not merely that we have discovered and mastered other forces of nature. In final analysis it is, if I am not mistaken, that we have become conscious of the movement which is carrying us along . . . The discovery of evolution . . . (means that) what makes and classifies a "modern" man . . . is having become incapable of seeing anything otherwise—anything—*not even himself.* . . .

---

garded as a simple resultant…(but as) the appearance in the world of something entirely new…a new substance…(for) The unifying force of the multiple, (viz.) the spirit, cannot be composed *of* the multiple. (Compare Bergson's similar argument.)

The consciousness of each of us is evolution looking at itself and reflecting. . . . In addition it becomes free to dispose of itself—it can give itself or refuse itself . . . *we hold it in our hands,* responsible for its past to its future. . . .

What makes the world in which we live specifically modern is our discovery in it and around it of evolution And I can now add that what disconcerts the modern world at its very roots is not being sure, and not seeing how it ever could be sure, that there is an outcome—*a suitable outcome*—to that evolution. . . . If progress is a myth, that is to say, if faced by the work involved we can say: "What's the good of it all?" our efforts will flag. With that the whole of evolution will come to a halt—because we are evolution. . . .

Either nature is closed to our demands for futurity, in which case thought, the fruit of millions of years of effort, is stifled, still-born in a self-abortive and absurd universe; or else an opening exists—that of the super-soul above our souls. . . . Between these two alternatives of absolute optimism and absolute pessimism, there is no middle way. . . .

(The future of science:)[25] There was a time when the only part ascribed to knowledge lay in lighting up for our speculative (contemplative) pleasure the objects ready made and given around us. Nowadays . . . even (above all, in fact) in mathematics, is not "discovery" the bringing into existence of something new? . . . *Knowledge for its own sake.* But also, and perhaps still more, *knowledge for power. . . . Increased power for increased action.* But, finally and above all, *increased action for increased being. . . .*

. . . we appear to be on the eve of having a hand in the development of our bodies and even of our brains. With the discovery of genes it appears that we shall soon be able to control the mechanism of organic heredity. And . . . we may well one day be capable of producing what the earth, left to itself, seems no longer able to produce: a new wave of organisms, an artificially provoked neo-life. . . . The dream which human research obscurely fosters is fundamentally that of mastering, beyond all atomic or molecular affinities, the ultimate energy of which all other energies are merely servants, and thus, by grasping the very mainspring of evolution, seizing the tiller of the world.

I salute those who have the courage to admit that their hopes extend that far; they are at the pinnacle of mankind; and I would say to them that there is less difference than people think between research and adoration. . . . Religion and science are the two conjugated faces or phases of one and the same act of complete knowledge. . . .

So far we have certainly allowed our race to develop at random, and we have given too little thought to the question of what medical and moral factors *must*

25 If the reader was excitedly sympathetic up until this point and now begins to be excitedly terrified, the reader is one of many.

164

replace the crude forces of natural selection **should we suppress them. In the course of the coming centuries it is indispensable that a nobly human form of eugenics, on a standard worthy of our personalities, should be discovered and developed.**

Eugenics applied to individuals leads to eugenics applied to society. . . .

"Better not interfere with the forces of the world!" Once more we are up against the mirage of instinct, the so-called infallibility of nature. But is it not precisely the world itself which, culminating in thought, expects us to think out again the instinctive impulses of nature so as to perfect them?

(Collective consciousness:) (We should) **give to each and every element its final value by grouping them in the unity of an organized whole . . . we are faced with a harmonized collectivity of consciousness equivalent to a sort of super-consciousness. The idea is that of the earth . . . becoming enclosed in a single thinking envelope . . . the plurality of individual reflections grouping themselves together and reinforcing one another in the act of a single unanimous reflection . . . the unanimous construction of a** *spirit of the earth.* **. . .**

(Optimism vs. pessimism:) **The nineteenth century had lived in sight of a promised land. It thought that we were on the threshold of a Golden Age, lit up and organized by science, warmed by fraternity. Instead of that, we find ourselves slipped back into a world of spreading and ever more tragic dissension. Though possible and even perhaps probable in theory, the idea of a spirit of the earth does not stand up to the test of experience. . . . We have "mass movements" . . . and all this only ending up with Communism and National Socialism and the most ghastly fetters . . . the ant-hill instead of brotherhood. . . .**

In the presence of such a profound perversion of the rules of noogenesis, I hold that our reaction should not be one of despair but of a determination to re-examine ourselves. When an energy runs amok, the engineer, far from questioning the power itself, simply works out his calculations afresh, to see how it can be brought better under control. Monstrous as it is, is not modern totalitarianism really the distortion of something magnificent and thus quite near to the truth?[26]

(Personality and totality in the Omega point:) **All our difficulties and repulsions as regards the opposition between the All and the Person would be dissipated if only we understood that, by structure, the noosphere (and more generally the world) represent a whole that is not only closed but also** *centered.* **Because it contains and**

26 The reader's reaction to what Teilhard says about eugenics and totalitarianism here, will probably be either something like "This is a prophet inspired by the Holy Spirit" or "This is a fool in the grip of the deceptions of the Devil." Yet it might be wise to look for some gems of wisdom in the darkest mines and some inexcusable blind inexcusable spots on the sunniest heights.

engenders consciousness, space-time is necessarily *of a convergent nature.* Accordingly its enormous layers, followed in the right direction, must somewhere ahead become involuted to a point which we might call Omega, which fuses and consumes them integrally in itself. . . .

. . . what is the work of human works if not to establish, in and by means of each one of us, an absolutely original centre in which the universe reflects itself in a unique and inimitable way? And those centres are our very selves and personalities. The very centre of our consciousness, deeper than all its radii: that is the essence which Omega, if it is to be truly Omega, must reclaim. . . .

In any domain—whether it be the cells of a body, the members of a society or the elements of a spiritual synthesis—*union differentiates.* In every organised whole, the parts perfect themselves and fulfill themselves. . . . Egoism('s) . . . only mistake, but a fatal one, is to *confuse individuality with personality*[27] . . . . To be fully ourselves it is in the opposite direction, in the direction of convergence with all the rest, that we must advance—toward the "other." The goal of ourselves, the acme of our originality, is not our individuality but our person; and according to the evolutionary structure of the world, we can only find our person by uniting together. . . . The true ego grows in inverse proportion to "egoism."

(Love as energy:) love—that is to say the affinity of being with being—is not peculiar to man. It is a general property of all life. . . . If there were no internal propensity to unite, even at a prodigiously rudimentary level—indeed in the molecule itself—it would be physically impossible for love to appear higher up, with us, in "hominised" form. By rights, to be certain of its presence in ourselves, we should assume its presence, at least in an inchoate form, in everything that is . . . the universal gravity of bodies, so striking to us, is merely the reverse or shadow of that which really moves nature. . . . (Dante: "the love that moves the sun and the other stars")

Love alone is capable of uniting living beings in such a way as to complete and fulfill them, for it alone takes them and joins them by what is deepest in themselves. This is a fact of daily experience. At what moment do lovers come into the most complete possession of themselves if not when they say they are lost in each other? In truth, does not love every instant achieve all around us, in the couple or the team, the magic feat, the feat reputed to be contradictory, of "personalising" by totalizing? And if that is what it can achieve daily on a small scale, why should it not repeat this one day on world-wide dimensions?

Common sense is right. It is impossible to give oneself to anonymous number. But if the universe ahead of us assumes a face and a heart, and so to speak personifies itself . . . the formidable energies of attraction, still dormant between human molecules, will burst forth. . . .

27 Maritain makes the same distinction in *The Person and the Common Good*: see ch. 97.

(Omega's presence and transcendence of earth and death:) **To be supremely attractive, Omega** (God as the ultimate end of man's and the universe) **must be supremely present. . . . So long as our constructions rest with all their weight on the earth, they will vanish with the earth. The radical defect in all forms of belief in progress, as they are expressed in positivist credos, is that they do not definitely eliminate death. What is the use of detecting a focus of any sort in the van of evolution if that focus can and must one day disintegrate? To satisfy the ultimate requirements of our action, Omega must be independent of the collapse of the forces with which evolution is woven . . .** *the Prime Mover ahead . . .* **transcending time and space . . . evolution cannot attain to fulfillment on earth. . . .**

(The end:) **. . . mankind has enormous possibilities before it . . .** *we have as yet no idea of the possible magnitude* **of "noospheric" effects. . . .**

. . . mankind, *taken as a whole,* **will be obliged . . . to reflect upon itself at a single point. . . . This will be the end and the fulfillment of the spirit of the earth. . . . The end of the world . . . detaching the mind, fulfilled at last, from its material matrix, so that it will henceforth rest with all its weight on God-Omega.**

Not an indefinite progress, which is a hypothesis contradicted by the convergent nature of noogenesis, but an ecstasy transcending the dimensions and the framework of the visible universe. . . .

(Evil:) **We can entertain two almost contradictory suppositions** (about this end of history). **. . . According to the first . . . evil on the earth at its final stage will be reduced to a minimum. . . . The final convergence will take place in** *peace.* **. . . But there is another possibility . . . evil may go on growing alongside good. A conflict may supervene. In that case the noosphere . . . will . . . split into two zones each attracted to an opposite pole of adoration . . . this second hypothesis . . . is more in conformity with traditional apocalyptic thinking. . . .**

The Divine Milieu

This little book does no more than . . . teach how to see God everywhere. . . .

Is the Christ of the Gospels, imagined and loved within the dimensions of a Mediterranean world, capable of still embracing and still forming the centre of our prodigiously expanded universe?

Nothing is more certain, dogmatically, than that human action can be sanctified . . . But . . . how can the man who believes in heaven and the Cross continue to believe seriously in the value of worldly occupations? . . . According to the most sacred articles of his *Credo,* **the Christian believes that life here below is continued in a life of which the joys, the sufferings, the reality, are quite incommensurable with the**

present conditions in our universe. This contrast and disproportion are enough, by themselves, to rob us of our taste for the world and our interest in it; but to them must be added a positive doctrine of judgment upon, even disdain for, a fallen and vitiated world. . . .

. . . this conflict is in danger of finding its solution in one of the three following ways: either the Christian will repress his taste for the tangible . . . or else . . . he will dismiss the evangelical counsels . . . or else, again, and this is the most usual case, he will . . . never wholly belong to God nor ever wholly to things. . . . Whether we become distorted, disgusted, or divided, the result is equally bad. . . .

(An incomplete solution:) Human action has no value other than the intention which directs it . . . the immediate answer given by spiritual directors . . . will run along these lines . . . the material side of your actions has no definitive value . . . all that has no direct importance for heaven. None of these discoveries or creations will become one of the stones of which is built up the New Jerusalem. But what *will* count, up there, what *will* always endure, is this: that you have acted in all things *conformably* to the will of God . . . the things which are given to you on earth are given you purely as an exercise, a "blank sheet" on which you make your own mind and heart. . . .

. . . this attitude contains an enormous part of truth. It is perfectly right to exalt the role of a good intention as the necessary start and foundation of all else . . . it is the golden key which unlocks our inward personal world to God's presence. . . . The divinization of our endeavor by the value of the intention put into it pours a priceless *soul* into all our actions; but *it does not confer the hope of resurrection upon their bodies.* Yet that hope is what we need if our joy is to be complete. It is certainly a very great thing to be able to think that, if we love God, something of our inner activity, of our *operatio,* will never be lost. But will not the work itself of our minds, of our hearts, and of our hands—that is to say, our achievements, what we bring into being, our *opus*—will this, too, in some sense be "eternalised" and saved?

If I believed that these things were to perish forever, should I have given them life? The more I examine myself, the more I discover this psychological truth: that no one lifts his little finger to do the smallest task unless moved, however obscurely, by the conviction that he is contributing infinitesimally (at least indirectly) to the building of something definitive—that is to say, to your work, my G o d . . . .

. . . each soul exists for God . . . but all reality, even material reality, around each one of us, exists for our souls. . . . Hence, all sensible reality, around each one of us, exists, through our souls, for God. . . .

Where are the roots of our being? In the first place they plunge back and down into the unfathomable past. . . . In each one of us, through matter, the whole history of the universe is in part reflected . . . in each soul, God loves and partly saves the whole world which that soul sums up in an incommunicable and particular way. But this summing-up, this welding, are not given to us ready-made and complete with the first awakening of consciousness. It is we who, through our own activity, must industriously assemble the widely scattered elements. . . . We may, perhaps, imagine that the creation was finished long ago. But that would be quite wrong. It continues still more magnificently, and at the highest levels of the world. *Omnis creatura adhuc ingemiscit et parturit.* (All creatures are groaning and travailing in childbirth.) And we serve to complete it, even by the humblest work of our hands. That is, ultimately, the meaning and value of our acts. . . .

Our work appears to us, in the main, as a way of earning our daily bread. But its essential virtue is on a higher level: through it we complete in ourselves the (human) subject of the divine union; and through it again we somehow make to grow in stature the divine term of the one with whom we are united, our Lord Jesus Christ. Hence, whatever our role as men may be, whether we are artists, workingmen or scholars, we can, if we are Christians, speed toward the object of our work as though towards an opening on to the supreme fulfillment of our beings. . . .

We ought to accustom ourselves to this basic truth till we are steeped in it, until it becomes as familiar to us as the perception of shape or the reading of words: God, in all that is most living and incarnate in him, is not far away from us, altogether apart from the world we see, touch, hear, smell and taste around us. Rather he awaits us every instant in our action, in the work of the moment. There is a sense in which he is at the tip of my pen, my spade, my brush, my needle—of my heart and of my thought. By pressing the stroke, the line, or the stitch on which I am engaged to its ultimate natural finish, I shall lay hold of that last end towards which my innermost will tends . . . by virtue of the Creation and, still more, of the Incarnation, *nothing* here below is profane for those who know how to see. . . .

(The passivities of growth:) And so, for the first time in my life perhaps (although I am supposed to meditate every day), I took the lamp and, leaving the zone of everyday occupations and relationships where everything seems clear, I went down into my inmost self, to the deep abyss whence I feel dimly that my power of action emanates. But as I moved further and further away from the conventional certainties by which social life is superficially illuminated, I became aware that I was losing contact with myself. At each step of the descent a new person was disclosed within me of whose name I was no longer sure, and who no longer obeyed me. And when I had to stop my exploration because the path faded from beneath my steps, I found a bottomless abyss at my feet, and out of it came—arising I know not from where—the current which I dare to call *my* life. . . . In the last resort the profound life, and fontal life, the new-born life, escape our grasp entirely.

Stirred by my discovery, I then wanted to return to the light of day and forget the disturbing enigma in the comfortable surroundings of familiar things—to begin living again at the surface without imprudently plumbing the depths of the abyss. But then, beneath this very spectacle of the turmoil of life, there reappeared, before my newly-opened eyes, the unknown that I wanted to escape. This time it was not hiding at the bottom of an abyss: it disguised its presence in the innumerable strands which form the web of chance, the very stuff of which the universe and my own small individuality are woven. Yet it was the same mystery without a doubt: I recognized it. Our mind is disturbed when we try to plumb the depth of the world beneath us. But it reels still more when we try to number the favourable chances which must coincide at every moment if the least of living things is to survive. . . . At that moment, as anyone else will find who cares to make this same interior experiment, I felt the distress characteristic of a particle adrift in the universe, the distress which makes human wills founder daily under the crushing number of living things and of stars. And if something saved me, it was hearing the voice of the Gospel, guaranteed by divine successes, speaking to me from the depth of the night: *It is I, be not afraid. . . .*

(The passivities of diminishment:) It is easy enough to understand that God can be grasped in and through every life. But can God also be found in and through every death? That is what perplexes us deeply. . . . In death, as in an ocean, all our slow or swift diminishments flow out and merge. Death is the sum and consummation of all our diminishments. . . . We must overcome death by finding God in it. . . .

(The problem of evil): we must both (1) *struggle with God against evil . . .* and also (2) experience *our apparent failure and its transfiguration . . .* (1) At the first approach of the diminishments . . . the more we repel suffering at that moment . . . the more closely we cleave to the heart and action of God . . . it is God himself who, in the course of the centuries, awakens the great benefactors of humankind, and the great physicians . . . (2) Like an artist who is able to make use of a fault or an impurity in the stone he is sculpting or the bronze he is casting so as to produce more exquisite lines or a more beautiful tone, God, without sparing us the partial deaths, nor the final death, which form an essential part of our lives, transfigures them by, integrating them in a better plan—*provided we lovingly trust in him.* Not only our unavoidable ills but our faults, even our most deliberate ones, can be embraced in that transformation, provided always we repent of them. Not everything is immediately good to those who seek God, but everything is capable of becoming good: *all things work together for good. . . .*

God must, in some way or other, make room for himself, hollowing us out and emptying us, if he is finally to penetrate into us. And in order to assimilate us in him, he must break the molecules of our being so as to re-cast and re-model us. The function of death is to provide the necessary entrance into our inmost selves. . . .

(Seeing "the cosmic Christ" everywhere:) *O Lord, repeat to me the great liberating words, the words which at once reveal and operate:* This is My Body. *In truth, the huge and dark thing, the phantom, the storm . . . is you!* It is I, be not afraid. *The things in our life which terrify us, the things that threw you yourself into agony in the garden, are, ultimately, only the species or appearance, the matter, of one and the same sacrament. . . .*

As our humanity assimilates the material world, and as the (sacramental) **Host assimilates our humanity, the Eucharistic transformation goes beyond and completes the transubstantiation of the bread on the altar. Step by step it irresistibly invades the universe. It is the fire that sweeps over the heath, the stroke that vibrates through the bronze. In a secondary and generalized sense, but in a true sense, the sacramental Species are formed by the totality of the world, and the duration of the creation is the time needed for its consecration.** *In Christ we live and move and have our being.*

The Controversy

Did Teilhard sacralize the secular, as he intended to do, or did he secularize the sacred? Is Teilhardianism a fulfilment or a betrayal of historic Christianity? Is he a new Aquinas or a new Hegel? That is the essential theological question.

Is his world view credible to the intellect as well as to the imagination? Is it science or science fiction? That is the essential scientific and philosophical question.

The essential theological defense of Teilhard is that he did the same thing that was done by St. John and St. Paul in the Bible when they assimilated and used Greek thought, especially the "logos" of the Stoics, and wrote of a cosmic Christ (cf., e.g., Colossians 1:16–17), and later by the Eastern Church Fathers and by Augustine, who used Neoplatonism, and by Aquinas, who used Aristotle, to deepen and explore religious revelation by the science of their day; that Teilhard's frequent use of vague or unscientific terminology is excusable because of the newness of his project; that the wrongness of some of the details does not detract from the rightness of his "big picture"; and that we should judge him as a poet and prophet rather than as a scientist, careful philosopher, or rational theologian.

Every thinker's theoretical world-view and practical life-view are connected; yet it is often possible to accept either one of these without the other, as with Kant, e.g. Many good and wise people find much that is profound and inspiring in Teilhard. Sometimes nuggets of gold are to be found surrounded by mud.

The serious criticisms of Teilhard are:

(1) That he is either a heretical theologian or a heretical scientist because he confuses the supernatural with the natural, the Creator with the creature (pantheism), the impersonal with the personal, spirit with matter, Christ with the cosmos, science with religion, cosmic evolutionary progress with personal spiritual progress, and moral and spiritual evil with the slowness or retrograde direction of the process of evolution. Atheists and theists, materialists and spiritualists, scientists and theologians alike often voice this criticism.

(2) That he is ignorant of the history of philosophy; for instance, he neither knows nor uses either Augustine or Aquinas, the two giants of Christian thought; indeed, he

speaks only negatively of them. Dietrich Von Hildebrand writes that, naively expecting good things in conversation with Teilhard, "When our talk touched on St. Augustine, he exclaimed violently: 'Don't mention that unfortunate man; he spoiled everything by introducing the supernatural.'"

(3) That he is not a good scientist either in theory *(The Phenomenon of Man* is science fiction, not science) or in practice (remember his being fooled by the Piltdown hoax).

(4) That he does not love man as he is but only as he will be, and idealizes the technological manipulation of human nature itself, which he calls "the trans-human."

(5) That he has an inexcusable naïveté about human wickedness. His reaction to the atom bomb was a paean of praise. He speaks more about physical evil than moral evil. Claude Tresmontant protests, "Evil is not simply a temporary defect in a progressive arrangement (of matter). The death of six million Jews in concentration camps...are not the result of a wrong arrangement of the Multiple but of the perverse freedom of man, of wickedness, contempt for man, the taste for destruction, falsehood, the will to power, the passion, the pride of the flesh and of the spirit. Evil is the work of man, not of matter."

(6) That he is more in love with "Mankind" than with men; that he is a collectivist; that he neglects the single most important thing in the universe: individual human persons, and the greatest drama of all, played out in each soul, the spiritual war (moral and/or religious) between good and evil, with eternal life or death at stake. The cosmos seems more important to him than an individual soul. Contrast Leon Bloy's great line: "Life offers only one tragedy: not to have been a saint."

(7) That his naïve optimism about man and power and technology seems to blind him to the greatest danger of our time, perhaps of all time: that many intelligent scientists and technologists are now seriously and deliberately working to bring about a world in which we will

(a) create artificial life in the laboratory, harnessing the very force of evolution itself,

(b) create minds by creating artificial brains,

(c) create perfectly adjusted individuals by chemicals, a la *Brave New World,*

(d) create a perfectly stable society by sociological engineering, a la Skinner's *Walden Two,*

(e) create irresistibly attractive artificial religious experiences by psychedelics, and finally

(f) conquer death itself by genetically engineered artificial immortality. (See Osbourn Segerberg's *The Immortality Factor* and Robert Ettinger's *The Prospect of Immortality.*)

This is no longer science fiction. It is science. What is there in Teilhard's principles that would see through this "Brave New World" as *The Abolition of Man* and as *That Hideous Strength,* as C. S. Lewis did in those two prophetic titles of his? Is he confusing Hell on earth with Heaven on earth? Could any confusion be more disastrous and inexcusable?

"Analytic Philosophy"

Our next four philosophers all belong to a very distinctive movement called "analytic philosophy." Let me dare to say in print what most non-analytic philosophers believe but do not dare to say: This school, or style, or method, or definition, of philosophy, which has been by far the most popular and influential one everywhere in the English-speaking world for almost a hundred years, and still is—has been, in the main, a disease and a disaster for philosophy.

But it claims to be a *cure* for the intellectual diseases and errors of past philosophy. Yes; and that is precisely the problem: the arrogance, the dismissal of centuries of great minds by decades of little ones. For the "bottom line" of all the founders of this movement is that philosophy in the traditional sense, philosophy as nearly all great philosophers have conceived of it for twenty-four centuries, is fatally diseased. The enterprise is dead. The business is bankrupt.

But one may die either with a bang or with a whimper. Philosophy dies with a bang in Nietzsche. It dies with a whimper in the founders of analytic philosophy. Nietzsche is a hurricane: destructive but fascinating. Analytic philosophy is a viral infection: just as deadly, but boring.

The reason this history of philosophy text does not feature analytic philosophy more prominently, or use its method for explaining and evaluating other philosophers, is very simple. It is not because the author scorns the exact logical and linguistic analysis which its method calls for. After all, Socrates, after whom these four volumes are named, began that enterprise! But that was only a *dimension* of a larger and more humanly important thing that he called "the love of wisdom." Love and wisdom are two things that are very hard to find in the founders and famous names of this school. Thus they fail to practice the very first rule of the thing they preach, namely the use of correct language and correct definitions of terms. The word "philosophy," according to those who invented it and practiced it for 2400 years, meant something quite different from what these "philosophers" are doing. They are name-thieves. They steal an honorable title.

If these four greatest "analytic philosophers" are right, the whole history of philosophy before them (or at least before Hume) has consisted in little more than logical and linguistic mistakes made by no one about nothing. For Hume, there is no such thing as a substantial self, or person, or mind making the mistakes (thus "no one"); in fact there are no real substances or "things" or beings or entities at all in the world that we can know (thus "nothing"). Not all of the "analysts" would agree with that, but most of them see Hume as the first really "enlightened" philosopher.

College students who enroll in philosophy courses taught by "analytic philosophers" and who expect to find "the love of wisdom" in them typically find neither love nor wisdom but only the logical and linguistic analysis of others' confusions and mistakes. Perhaps ten per cent of these students are interested, about the same percentage who are interested in math. For analytic philosophy reduces philosophy to something very much like math.

A Harvard philosophy course was once advertised under the title of "The Meaning of Life." It drew over a hundred students. The professor explained, during the first class, that the course would be not about life but about meaning, and that he would show that the famous question of "the meaning of life" was strictly meaningless. Thirty students showed up for the second lecture.

My calling analytic philosophy a "plague" is ironic because the goal of all the early analytic philosophers was to *purge* philosophy of a plague: the plague Descartes tried to overcome by applying the scientific method to philosophy, *viz.* the plague of disagreements. Unlike all the other sciences, philosophy had made no progress toward agreement in its search for truth in Descartes's day—and there is still no agreement nearly 400 years later. There are still classicists and moderns, Platonists and Aristotelians, optimists and pessimists, atheists and theists, nominalists and realists, idealists and materialists. The analytic philosophers claimed to heal this plague by radically redefining philosophy itself. It was to be a much humbler thing: something like window washing rather than construction work on skyscrapers. All previous philosophers, they claimed, had confused these two jobs. They had claimed for philosophy the status of a science, or even a super-science. But according to the "analysts," only the "special sciences" (the other sciences than philosophy) could perform the actual construction work of finding truth. Philosophers were only their assistants, their cleanup crew. Scientists were the bullfighters, philosophers just cleaned up the bulls' anal products. Thus it is *analy*tic philosophy.

But there are some problems here.

(1) If it is a confusion of philosophy with science to make philosophy a super-science, is it not that same confusion to make it a sub-science?

(2) Most of the problems and disagreements were *not solved but dissolved* by the "analysts," i.e., were claimed to be rooted in logical and linguistic confusion by the new standards of the new mathematical logic. The patient's diseases were to be "cured" by killing the patient. It was philosophical euthanasia.

(3) Even after flushing the waste down the toilet, or euthanizing the patient, the analysts' promise to heal the plague of disagreement has not been fulfilled. There is as much disagreement among analytic philosophers as there ever was among other philosophers.

Analytic philosophy is a plague not because its method, the careful logical analysis of language, is in itself a bad thing. Saying that is as silly as saying that technology is "a bad thing." Nor is it bad simply because it is dull. Math and economics are dull to most people, but certainly not "bad." It has been a plague because wherever it takes over philosophy departments, it has almost always driven out all other ways of doing philosophy.

It has been like a cancer cell: it destroys all the other healthy cells. I would like to think that this is due merely to human folly and the lust for power on the part of its practitioners, but no other school of philosophy has been so "cancerous." There seems to be something intrinsically destructive about the enterprise itself, not just its practitioners.

Thus it is no surprise that the dispute between "analytic" philosophers and all others was a duel to the death. Unlike nearly all other philosophers (except Nietzsche—but at least he was *interesting),* the "analytic" philosophers set out on a mission of destruction. If they were right, *everybody* else was wrong. Either all the others should have stopped doing what they had been doing for 2400 years (*viz.* spouting nonsense), or the analytic philosophers should stop labeling it nonsense and telling them to stop. It was the cancer cells against all the other cells in the body. It was a war, an "us or them," an either/or, not a both/and.

That's the bad news. Here's the good news: All of the above has significantly changed in the last few decades. Bridges have been built between British ("analytical") and Continental (metaphysical, phenomenological, and existential) ways of doing philosophy. The Channel now has a "Chunnel." Most "analytic philosophers" today (but by no means all of them) are much more open-minded about past philosophers, about the history of philosophy and its traditional questions, than any of the great founders and early practitioners of the movement were. The window washers do not all bad-mouth the construction workers. They do not all dismiss the questions and answers of traditional philosophers as nonsense and muddleheaded thinking. Many of those who now accept and practice the positive task of "analytic philosophy," the careful analysis of language and meaning, do not accept the negative and destructive part of that task, especially the Positivist assumption that only empirical or mathematical science is meaningful and consequently that most of the history of philosophy is literally nonsense and at best subjective emotion misleadingly disguised as thought.

It is, after all, astonishingly arrogant to dismiss, as mere linguistic confusion, cognitive nonsense, and disguised emotion, nearly all of the most important thoughts—not only all the answers but also all the questions—of nearly all the greatest minds in human history except mathematicians and scientists—in other words *all* the great philosophers, sages, moralists, and religious thinkers as well as the thinking of all ordinary people who had the tragic bad luck to live and think in the muddy world outside of Oxford and Cambridge universities.

But the "fathers" of analytic philosophy *did* think that, as we shall see below. And among the later, more open and positive (rather than Positivistic) analytic philosophers, not a single great name stands out. These first doctors were all undertakers.

But where did the undertakers come from?

Analytic philosophy arose as a reaction against the then-popular Hegelianism of Hegel's disciples (Green, Bradley, and Bosanquet in England, Royce in America). Nearly everything in post-Hegelian philosophy is a reaction against Hegel: a remarkable tribute! But long before Hegel, from the time England first became a nation with a distinct identity, in the Middle Ages, nearly all her philosophers, from Ockham on, through Roger Bacon, Francis Bacon, Locke, Hobbes, Berkeley, Hume, Reid, Bentham, and Mill, have been Nominalists rather than Realists, pluralists rather than monists, and Empiricists rather than Rationalists, like nearly all analytic philosophers.

What is new about "analytic philosophy" is "the linguistic turn." The shortest way to explain what this means is that it reverses the previous relationship between philosophy and language. Ever since Socrates, philosophers have argued about language. But in analytic philosophy, instead of language being a subdivision of philosophy or an object of philosophy, philosophy becomes a subdivision or object of linguistics. We could also substitute "logic" (the new logic, symbolic logic) for "linguistics" to make essentially the same point.

Philosophy emerges radically skinnier from this liposuction. It is no longer a set of truths, teachings, or doctrines about reality, but only a kind of proofreading for modern science, which was assumed to be the only cognitively meaningful enterprise. After the scientists have done their work, there are no truths left over for the philosophers, no more facts or super-facts. Thus Wittgenstein says "the object of philosophy is the logical clarification of thoughts." The object of philosophy is not reality, as is the object of science. Nor is it even truth. It is "not a number of philosophical propositions, but to make propositions clear." Thus there *are* no "philosophical propositions." Philosophy is an activity, not a wisdom.

All the traditional divisions of philosophy except logic and linguistics are thus eliminated at one fell swoop: metaphysics, cosmology, philosophical anthropology, substantive as distinct from critical epistemology, ethics, political philosophy, aesthetics, philosophy of religion, philosophy of history, philosophy of education, etc. But philosophy of science remains, as a servant occupation. Only scientists can photograph the real world; philosophers can only photograph the photographs.

So there can be no philosophical systems any more, no "world views" or "meta-narratives," only individual philosophical problems to be worked at and solved one at a time.

Socrates, Plato and Aristotle all said that philosophy begins in *wonder* and ends in *wisdom*. Wonder explores *mysteries*. Its result is ever-increased understanding and appreciation. Analytic philosophy begins in puzzles, and ends (ostensibly) in definitive solutions. It resolves mysteries into confusions and then dissolves the confusions.

In other words, philosophy as traditionally conceived is a big mistake. Its source is linguistic confusion. It is Plato and his followers who are in the cave of shadows, and the anti-philosophers, the analysts, who alone escape this cave into the light.

The two different ways of escape proposed by the analytic philosophers were (1) the creation of a new, quasi-mathematical "ideal language" (Ayer, Russell, and the early Wittgenstein) and (2) the analysis of "ordinary language" (Moore and the later Wittgenstein). The latter are more lasting, more useful, more commonsensical, more humble, more sane, and more synthesizable with traditional philosophy.

87. G. E. Moore (1873–1958)

If any one philosopher can be said to have begun the "linguistic turn" that has so radically transformed English speaking philosophy, it was G. E. Moore. But there is no one "father" of this movement; nearly all of the early analytic philosophers influenced and were influenced by each other. They were more like scientists working on a joint project than artists each constructing his own product.

Moore resembles Socrates in that the most distinctive and unforgettable thing about him is not his content (he has only a few distinctive teachings and conclusions) but his style and method, which is easy to parody and hard to love. Reading him is a chore. It can feel like cleaning and polishing every surface of a battleship under the watchful eye of a fanatical, tyrannical, micro-managing commanding officer. He pursues tiny distinctions into every corner like an anteater pursuing ants. He seeks out vagueness, uncertainty, and equivocation like a Geiger counter searching for radioactivity, and with the passion of a pig snuffling for truffles. He takes many pages to say the simplest and most boring things. In fact, he is so boring that he is fascinating. But when he is done with you, you have not a scrap of warm mush left in your mouth. It must have been very uncomfortable, yet very useful, for the other philosophers at Cambridge to have a Moore around responding "But what, *exactly,* do you mean?" to your most innocent comments—as it must have been to have a Socrates around in Athens.

On his mission Moore took no weapons but common sense. He had no doctrinaire assumptions and principles, as nearly all the other analytic philosophers did (e.g., Ayer's "verification principle" or Russell's "logical atomism"). His tool was not an invented "ideal language" (like Russell or the early Wittgenstein), but simply the commonsensical analysis of ordinary language (like the later Wittgenstein).

Life and Character

Both his life and his character were atypical among modern philosophers. His childhood was not tragic or miserable. He never had a nervous breakdown or contemplated suicide. He was happily married to one woman. He was not a Lothario. Though he was an agnostic, he did not treat left-wing politics as his religion. He was not a snob. His philosophical colleague, C. D. Broad, summarized him this way: "He was a man of simple tastes and character, absolutely devoid of all affectation, pose and flummery. He thoroughly enjoyed the simple human pleasures of eating and drinking, walking, gardening, talking to his friends, playing with his children, and so on. It is because ordinary, unpretending Englishmen are so often muddle-headed, and intellectuals so often cracked and conceited, that Moore, who combined the virtues of both and had the vices of neither, was so exceptional and lovable a personality."

Broad adds: "It is doubtful that any philosopher known to history has excelled or even equaled Moore in sheer power of analyzing problems, detecting and exposing fallacies and ambiguities, and formulating and working out alternative possibilities. . . . Apart from his immense analytic power, Moore's most noticeable characteristic was his absolutely single-minded desire to discover truth and avoid error and confusion."

The *flavor* of a conversation with Moore—which is the most memorable and precious thing about him—can be tasted in C. S. Lewis's description of his first meeting with his tutor, W. K. Kirkpatrick, "Kirk" or "The Great Knock," in his autobiography, *Surprised by Joy*. Kirk was clearly a Moore imitator:

"'You are now,' said Kirk, 'proceeding along the principal artery between Great and Little Bookham . . . I began to 'make conversation' in the deplorable manner which I had acquired at those evening parties . . . I said I was surprised at the 'scenery' of Surrey; it was much 'wilder' than I had expected.

"' Stop!' shouted Kirk with a suddenness that made me jump. 'What do you mean by wildness and what grounds had you for not expecting it?'

"I replied I don't know what, still 'making conversation. ' As answer after answer was torn to shreds it at last dawned upon me that he really wanted to know . . . I was stung into attempting a real answer. A few passes sufficed to show that I had no clear and distinct idea corresponding to the word 'wildness,' and that, in so far as I had any idea at all, 'wildness' was a singularly inept word. 'Do you not see, then,' concluded the Great Knock, 'that your remark was meaningless?' I prepared to sulk a little, assuming that the subject would now be dropped. Never was I more mistaken in my life. Having analyzed my terms, Kirk was proceeding to deal with my proposition as a whole. On what had I based (but he pronounced it *baized)* my expectations about the flora and geology of Surrey? Was it maps, or photographs, or books? I could produce none. It had, heaven help me, never occurred to me that what I called my thoughts needed to be 'baized' on anything. Kirk once more drew a conclusion—without the slightest sign of emotion, but equally without the slightest concession to what I thought good manners: 'Do you not see, then, that you had no right to have any opinion whatever on the subject?'

"... If any man came near to being a purely logical entity, that man was Kirk. Born a little later, he would have been a Logical Positivist. The idea that human beings should exercise their vocal organs for any purpose except that of communicating or discovering truth was to him preposterous."

Stories abound about Moore's absent-mindedness, his preoccupation with philosophy, and his naïveté and innocence about the world. When the King awarded him the Order of Merit, the highest honor a British man of letters can receive, in a private audience, the first thing he told his wife about it, in an astonished tone of voice, was: "Do you know that the King has never heard of Wittgenstein?!"

Like William James, he was a lifelong agnostic who yet was interested in religion. He took religion to be like art in aiming at goodness and beauty, though not truth. He preferred art to religion because, he argued, beauty, unlike God, is easily attainable.

He was born in London and was a fixture at Cambridge all his life, as undergraduate, graduate, tutor, and eventually chaired Professor. He studied "Greats" (classics) as an undergraduate; but Russell, who discovered his intelligence, persuaded him to switch to philosophy, where he became fascinated with the absurd things the Hegelians were saying, such as that time and space were unreal. He asked the simple questions a child would ask, like "Does that mean I didn't really eat my lunch after I ate my breakfast, and that elephants aren't really bigger than mice?" Russell was his admiring colleague at first but soon departed from Moore's common-sense approach. (Russell wrote: "Science itself has shown that none of these common-sense notions will quite serve.") Moore was also a close friend of Wittgenstein, who was, at first, his student. He was also a member of the famous Bloomsbury group. (However, if you know anything about their politics, morality, and lifestyles, you know how much of a "fit" that was.)

The Nature of Philosophy and the Method of Analysis

Moore says that the purpose of philosophy is exactly what common sense thinks it is: to tell the truth about everything in the universe, i.e., to give a general description of the universe, which none of the special sciences do. And here is his common sense answer to this common sense question of "what *is* the universe?" I quote it at length to show why I do not quote Moore at length.

Firstly, that there certainly are in the Universe two very different kinds of things, namely material objects and acts of consciousness. And secondly, as to the relation of these two kinds of things, two points . . . (1) that conscious acts are attached to comparatively few of the material objects in the Universe; that the vast majority of material objects are unconscious . . . (2) that material objects are all of such a kind that they may exist even when we are not conscious of them, and that many do so in fact exist . . . (3) that there *may* have been a time when acts of consciousness were attached to *no* material bodies anywhere in the Universe, and (that in the future there) **may** **again be such a time; and that there almost certainly was a time when there were no human bodies, with human consciousness attached to them, upon this earth . . . (4) That all material objects and all acts of consciousness of ourselves and other animals upon the earth are in *time* . . . (5) That we know (1), (2), (3) and (4) to be true, and that we also know an immense number of details about particular material objects and acts of consciousness, past, present and future.**

Can you imagine Moore's students being astonished at this stunning revelation?

But his primary concern was not to defend this uncommonly commonsensical world view, but to analyze the statements of other philosophers. ("The definition of a philosopher is someone who disagrees with other philosophers.") He writes in his intellectual autobiography (entitled, startlingly, "Autobiography"): **What has suggested philosophical problems to me is things which other philosophers have said about the world or the sciences . . . the problems in question being of two sorts, namely, first, the problem of trying to get really clear as to what on earth a given philosopher *meant* by something which he said, and, secondly, the problem of discovering what really satisfactory *reasons* there are for supposing that what he meant was true, or, alternatively, was false. I think I have been trying to solve problems of this sort all of my life.**

In other words, Moore turned philosophy into metaphilosophy, i.e., into analysis. "Analysis" meant to Moore two different but similar things: (1) analyzing what we mean, i.e., what is in our mind, when we say something, by breaking it down into its smallest component parts, and (2) removing confused meanings, or equivocations, by distinguishing different meanings of propositions (truth-claims) and their terms.

He is at his Socratic best when writing critical studies of other philosophers, such as Berkeley, Hume, and James (he has essays in *Philosophical Studies* criticizing each of these). Though he has a distinctive method, he has no distinctive philosophical doctrine himself, except the doctrines of common sense.

Common Sense vs. Skepticism

Moore not only tried to refute Hegelian philosophers who departed from common sense by denying that such things as time, space, and individuality were real, at least in the way ordinary people thought they were, but also tried to defend common sense against the skeptical denials of his fellow analytic philosophers about such things as the existence of the external world. These philosophers worked themselves into knots worrying about such things as how you could know you were not really a brain in a vat only dreaming that the external world exists. No one, except perhaps Reid (ch. 63) has ever defended common sense as much as Moore. Most philosophers ignore or despise it (yes, most philosophers are intellectual snobs). The obvious fictional character to identify Moore with is the little boy in Hans Christian Andersen's "The Emperor's New Clothes."

In "A Defense of Common Sense" (1925), Moore argues, against skepticism, that the ordinary-language, common-sense meanings of "knowledge" and "certainty" are not identical; and this distinction *justifies* our claim to know the real world rather than putting it into question. For even to know x uncertainly, is *to know* x! (Most of Moore's points are "Duhs.") We can also know something without knowing *how* we know it. We don't need an epistemology of knowing a cat in order to know a cat. If we did, only philosophers could know cats.

He argues that propositions about material objects are not about sense data, or about our possible future perception of these objects, or about anything else than—those material objects. (Another "Duh!")

He argues that it is very easy to give proofs of things in the external world: for instance, holding up his two hands and saying "Here is one hand, and here is another." If you say you have six toes, you can prove this to me by removing your sock and letting me count them. This is what ordinary language means by "proving." So we can really prove, with certainty, "thousands of things" in the external world, contrary to the skeptical philosophers. (You don't need to go to Oxford or Cambridge to know this; you have to go there to doubt it.)

He also notes that we can know things that we cannot prove to others, e.g., that we are awake now and not dreaming. Just as things can exist without being known (contrary to Hegel's "idealism"), things can be known without being known with certainty (contrary to the skeptics), and things can be known with certainty without being proved (contrary to the Cartesian rationalists). There can also be proofs (like the sixth toe or the two hands) that are not strictly scientific proofs, or proofs by the scientific method (contrary to the Positivists).

He also points out that just as error presupposes truth, doubt presupposes certainty. (Josiah Royce, the Hegelian, made a similar point in "The Possibility of Error," in *The Religious Aspect of Philosophy.)* He convinced Wittgenstein that "the *questions* that we raise and our *doubts* depend on the fact that some propositions are exempt from doubt, as it were like hinges on which those (doubts) turn."

Moore was just as unsparing with Hegelian idealism as he was with the skepticism of his anti-Hegelian colleagues, since he thought that both philosophies departed radically from common sense. In "The Refutation of Idealism" he argued that all the arguments for idealism (which he defines as the identification of reality with objects of consciousness—to use Berkeley's formula, "esse est percipi") are fallacious. He argued, like the phenomenologists, that consciousness is essentially "intentional," i.e., is a "consciousness-*of*" some object *outside* of consciousness. It is this commonsensically obvious distinction between consciousness and the objects of consciousness that he claims the idealists deny. He argues that the contents known in your mind, or the objects of your mind, are not the *properties* of mind; or, to put it more simply, that what we know is not knowledge but known-things. The knowledge of a thing is not one of that thing's parts or properties. It is other than the thing. So matter, which is known by mind, is *other* than mind. It also seems to follow that mind, which knows matter, is other than matter; so this would seem to be a refutation of materialism as well as idealism, or immaterialism.

Ethics

Most of Moore's influential writings are essays. But he wrote two complete books on ethics *(Principia Ethica* (1903) and *Ethics* (1912)), in which he defended the view that "goodness," the fundamental term of ethics, (1) was an objectively real property of some

181

things and events in the world, (2) was indefinable by any more basic terms, and (3) was "non-natural." (By "non-natural" he did not mean "supernatural" but "not having a nature that can be defined.")

Start with point (2). We can argue about *what is good* but not about *what good is*. That is, we can show which things are good; but we cannot show what "good" means in any other terms. **That which is meant by "good" is, in fact, except its converse "bad," the only simple object of thought which is peculiar to ethics.** "Good' is simple and not analyzable into more basic parts; that is why it is not definable. We can apprehend it but we cannot define it.

Moore labeled philosophers' attempts to define the good in terms of a 'natural property' (a 'what') "the naturalistic fallacy"—e.g., the hedonistic identification of good with pleasure, the Stoic identification of good with virtue, the Aristotelian identification of the good with happiness, or the Kantian identification of the good with moral duty. Pleasure, virtue, happiness, and duty may well all be good, in fact, but they are not *goodness*.

So the question "What is goodness?" cannot be answered. But two other fundamental questions of ethics can; and Moore claimed that most moral philosophers have confused these two different questions. These other two questions are: (a) **"What kinds of things ought to exist for their own sakes?"** (i.e., what things are good in themselves, and not just good for something else?) and (b) **"What actions ought we to perform?"** He argues that answers to question (b) can be proved, but answers to question (a) can only be directly "intuited," like a simple color like "yellow":

My point is that "good" is a simple notion, just as "yellow" is a simple notion; that, just as you cannot, by any manner of means, explain to any one who does not already know it, what yellow is, so you cannot explain what good is. . . . You can give a definition of a horse, because a horse has many different properties and qualities, all of which you can enumerate. But when you have enumerated them all, when you have reduced a horse to his simplest terms, then you can no longer define those terms. They are simply something which you think of or perceive, and to any one who cannot think of or perceive them, you can never, by any definition, make their nature known.

88. A. J. Ayer (1910–1989)

Ayer's importance stems mainly from a single book, *Language, Truth and Logic* (first published in 1936), which became one of the most influential and best-selling philosophy books of modern times even though its philosophy, "Logical Positivism," is one of the only philosophies in history that has been almost universally agreed to have been so conclusively refuted that philosophers who profess to be Logical Positivists are almost as hard to find today as Massachusetts Republicans.

Life

Like most philosophers, Ayer was intellectually precocious and physically delicate, clumsy, and incompetent as a boy. He could never learn to ride a bike. According to all his biographers except himself, he grew up in a joyless and loveless household. At Eton, he writes, he **got on badly with the other boys in College. This was very largely my own fault. I was too pleased with my own cleverness and I had a sarcastic tongue.** He abandoned whatever nominal religion he had at 12, when prayer failed to get him entrance onto his school's cricket team.

At Oxford he discovered Moore, Russell, and Wittgenstein. He modeled himself especially on Russell, both philosophically and personally, in a life of leftist activist politics and sexual conquests. (Why do they always seem connected?) His wife's son was fathered by Stuart Hampshire, another philosopher at Oxford. He continued his Russell imitation by marrying four times and having so many affairs that one Englishwoman claimed in print that she was the only pretty woman in England who had *not* had an affair with either Russell or Ayer.

On his teacher Gilbert Ryle's recommendation, he went to Vienna (on his honeymoon!) to study with the "Vienna Circle" of analytical philosophers there (Schlick, Neurath, Waismann, Goedel, and occasionally Wittgenstein and Quine) who together were constructing a new and powerful tool for analyzing and evaluating all other philosophies and finding them defective in meaningfulness. They called it "Logical Positivism."

The Vienna Circle broke up in 1939 as a result of the Nazi annexation of Austria and the murder of Schlick by one of his students. Wittgenstein, by far the most influential of all "analytic philosophers," performed an analogous termination service in the intellectual dimension when he repudiated his own earlier philosophy which had been influenced by the Vienna Circle.

Ayer returned to Oxford and wrote *Language, Truth and Logic,* a powerful missionary manifesto which did for Logical Positivism what *The Communist Manifesto* did for

Communism. The two manifestoes were very different, of course, but also similar in that (1) both were radical critiques of everything that had happened before them; (2) both became enormously successful (because they were such powerfully destructive weapons); and (3) both were thoroughly discredited by subsequent history.

Ayer himself admitted as much. On a TV interview in 1979, he was asked what he thought were the main defects of his earlier work, and he replied, **I suppose the most important of the defects was that nearly all of it was false.**

Ayer wrote a two-volume autobiography which the *Times* called "vain" and "arctic," "all fact and no feeling." His biographer judges it, like his life, to have "no center," just like Ayer's Humean view of the self as a literally insubstantial bundle of desires and perceptions.

He became quite famous and popular because of *Language, Truth and Logic,* and appeared on many TV interviews. He wrote 13 books, over 300 essays, and thousands of letters to the editor.

At age 77 he rescued a woman who was being assaulted in a bedroom at a fashionable party by Mike Tyson, the world heavyweight champion, by enticing Mike into a dialog. It was the single most heroic and the second most interesting thing he ever did.

At 88 he had a near-death experience, and wrote: **I was confronted by a red light, exceedingly bright, and also very painful even when I turned away from it. I was aware that this light was responsible for the government of the universe. Among its ministers were two creatures which had been put in charge of space. These ministers periodically inspected space and had recently carried out such an inspection. They had, however, failed to do their work properly, with the result that space, like a badly fitting jigsaw puzzle, was slightly out of joint. A further consequence was that the laws of nature had ceased to function as they should. I felt that it was up to me to put things right.**

That was the most interesting thing he ever wrote.

The Point: The "Verification Principle"

Some philosophers, like Plato and Heidegger, center on one "big idea"; others, like Aristotle and Leibnitz, have many. The "big idea" (or *little* idea) Ayer is famous for, the central thesis of *Language, Truth and Logic,* is what he called "the Verification Principle"

A philosophical doctrine is most meaningful when we see what question it means to answer or what problem it means to solve. The problem that analytic philosophy in general, and Ayer in particular, tries to address is the one that motivated Descartes, "the father of modern philosophy," to invent a new method to solve it. The problem was that philosophers, unlike scientists, have not progressed to any agreement; that the same questions are being asked, the same answers are being given, and the same uncertainty about which answer is right, characterizes philosophy now just as much as when it first began in ancient Greece.

It is reasonable, or at least tempting, to think that this is because there is some false assumption at the root of both sides—of *all* sides—of the disputes among philosophers, and that if this assumption could be exposed and refuted, philosophy could finally begin to progress like the other sciences. That is what Ayer thought:

The traditional disputes of philosophers are, for the most part, as unwarranted as they are unfruitful. The surest way to end them is to establish beyond question what should be the purpose and method of philosophical inquiry.

And that is the radical turn recommended by the fathers of analytic philosophy. The purpose of philosophy is not truth but meaning; not world-views but word-views; not profundity but clarity. And the method is the logical analysis of language.

The first step in doing this is to introduce into our language a severe "principle of parsimony," or Ockham's Razor; to refuse to admit any kind of propositions as meaningful except the following two kinds:

Like Hume, I divide all genuine propositions into two classes: those which, in his terminology, concern "relations of ideas," and those which concern "matters of fact." The former class comprises the *a priori* propositions of logic and pure mathematics, and these I allow to be necessary and certain only because they are analytic. That is, I maintain that the reason why these propositions cannot be confuted in experience is that they do not make any assertion about the empirical world, but simply record our determination to use symbols in a certain fashion. Propositions concerning empirical matters of fact, on the other hand, I hold to be hypotheses which can be probable but never certain. . . .

To test whether a sentence expresses a genuine empirical hypothesis . . . some possible sense-experience should be relevant to the determination of its truth or falsehood. If a putative proposition fails to satisfy this principle, and is not a tautology (= an analytic proposition), **then I hold that it is metaphysical, and that, being metaphysical, it is neither true nor false but literally senseless. It will be found that much of what ordinarily passes for philosophy is metaphysical according to this criterion.**

This is almost exactly what Hume said at the end of his *Enquiry:* "If we go over libraries persuaded of these principles, what havoc must we make? If we take into our hand any volume of metaphysics or school divinity, let us ask: Does it contain any abstract reasoning concerning quantity and number? No. Does it contain any statements about matter of fact and existence? No. Commit it then to the flames, for it can contain nothing but sophistry and illusion."

Ayer simply accepts all of this from Hume and aims this new weapon at nearly the whole history of philosophy, with the result that all the philosophers are lined up like prisoners before a firing squad and dispatched with a single bullet each. It is a philosophy to end philosophy, an intellectual suicide mission, a death wish. Since the only meaningful statements are empirical, to be evaluated by scientists, or tautological, to be evaluated by logicians and mathematicians, there is nothing left for philosophers to do except analyze the statements of science and math. Philosophy says nothing. It has nothing to do with truth, much less wisdom. It has argued itself out of its job.

The only thing Ayer adds to Hume is to translate the claim about the limitations of our *knowledge* into a claim about the limitations of our *meaningful language.* This is essentially Hobbes's ploy in answer to Descartes in their debate about Hobbesian materialism vs. Cartesian dualism. To Descartes's arguments Hobbes answered not with a logical refutation but with the claim that they were meaningless. This must have frustrated Descartes, and the same frustration appears when analytic philosophers argue with traditional philosophers today.

In the passage quoted above Ayer seems to assume, rather than prove, that metaphysics is meaningless. That is really the premise of his argument, rather than its conclusion. For his argument is a *reductio ad absurdum* and "metaphysics" is used as the "absurdity." The argument is that if the verification principle were not true, we would have to admit metaphysics, which is unthinkable.

What reason does he give for the assumption that metaphysics is unthinkable? It is the further assumption of strict Empiricism:

We may begin by criticizing the metaphysical thesis that philosophy affords us knowledge of a reality transcending the world of science and common sense. . . . One way of attacking a metaphysician who claimed to have (such) knowledge . . . would be to inquire from what premises his propositions were deduced. Must he not begin, as other men do, with the evidence of his senses? (But) . . . surely, from empirical premises nothing . . . super-empirical can legitimately be inferred.

The last sentence is the key one. Many "soft empiricists" like Aristotle, and even critics of Empiricism like Kant, would agree that all our knowledge *begins* with experience, but not that it ends there or is limited to experience. That is the difference between "hard empiricism" and "soft empiricism."

Hume deduces from his "hard empiricism" a "soft skepticism," or probabilism. This is an *epistemological* skepticism. Ayer translates this into a *linguistic* skepticism through his "Verification Principle":

The criterion which we use to test the genuineness of apparent statements of fact is the criterion of verifiability. We say that a sentence is factually significant to any given person, if, and only if, he knows how to verify the proposition which it purports to express—that is, if he knows what observations would lead him, under certain conditions, to accept the proposition as being true, or reject it as being false. If, on the other hand, the putative proposition is of such a character that its truth, or falsehood, is consistent with any assumption whatsoever concerning the nature of his future experience, then, as far as he is concerned, it is . . . a mere pseudoproposition. The sentence expressing it may be emotionally significant to him, but it is not literally significant.

The Vienna Circle's earlier "Verification Principle" had claimed that "the meaning of any proposition *is* its mode of verification." Ayer modified this to make verification the *criterion* of its meaning. He also modified his own principle in two other ways. "Verified" in Ayer's original, simple version, meant "proved with certainty"; but in his later, modified version it was softened to "rendered at least probable." Also, instead of simply "verified" Ayer wrote "verified in principle." The number of grains of sand on Mars cannot be verified in practice but it can in principle.

Ayer then added Hume's principle of "hard empiricism," that "verified" could mean only two things, the only two ways Hume said we could verify any proposition: by empirical verification or by showing that it is, or can be reduced to, a tautology. So every meaningful proposition must be either empirically verifiable or tautological.

Critique

(1) The most obvious objection to this principle is that it is self-contradictory, self-refuting, self-eliminating. For it itself is neither a tautology nor is it empirically verifiable. Thus the philosophical proposition that eliminates most philosophical propositions as meaningless is, by its own standards, meaningless!

Ayer responded to this objection by saying that the Verification Principle was not a proposition at all but a proposal, a practical rule, a method, and enunciating it was not saying "This principle is *true*" but "*Let's* accept this principle." To use a technical distinction in logic, it was not a real definition but a stipulative definition. It is a practical proposal rather than a theoretical principle.

The obvious question then is why any metaphysician would ever adopt this proposal, in fact why anyone at all *should* ever adopt it. Ayer's only answer is that it works. It attains a goal. But what goal? The elimination of metaphysics. But why is this goal good? Because metaphysics is meaningless. But why is metaphysics meaningless? Because it violates this proposal. And that, of course, is simply arguing in a circle, or begging the question.

(2) Thus it seems more like an ideological weapon than a philosophical argument: justified not by its truth but by its applications, its consequences, in eliminating metaphysics (and also, as we shall see, morality), which is the taken-for-granted end. Thus it is metaphysics rather than meaninglessness that is assumed to be the intrinsic intellectual evil, the self-evidently bad kind of thinking. Since the Verification Principle is neither tautological (self-evident), nor empirical (you can't *see* a "principle"), and since it is not deduced from any more fundamental premises, its only justification is its consequence, which is the elimination of metaphysics. It is a case of "the end justifies the means."

That this (the elimination of metaphysics) was indeed Ayer's fundamental goal becomes evident from his later statement about needing something more than the principle itself to accomplish that end: **I confess, however, that it now seems to me unlikely that any metaphysician would yield to a claim of this kind; and although I should still defend the use of the criterion of verifiability as a methodological principle, I realize**

that for the effective elimination of metaphysics it needs to be supported by detailed analyses of particular metaphysical arguments.

Further evidence that the elimination of metaphysics was Ayer's *summum bonum* is his description of meaningful propositions. They are not statements about *real things,* since both "real" and "thing" are metaphysical concepts. They are only statements about our observation of sense data. E.g., "That table is white" means "If you look at that in daylight, it will look the same color as this paper." Categorical statements ("It is . . . ") are really hypothetical statements ("If you . . .then . . ."). Statements that seem to be about real things, for Ayer, are really only statements about us, about our sensing.

But why change what people actually *mean* by statements like "That table is white" into something obviously different than what they mean or say? The answer is clear: Because what they say is metaphysical. If metaphysics is an error, it is a natural and universal error, not a specialized superstition invented by absent-minded philosophers. Ayer implicitly admits this when he says that if we do not agree to change the meaning of such statements about real things into statements about our sensations, this means that we are **unaware of the hidden logical complexity of such statements, which our analysis, has just brought to light. And, as a result,** (if we do not follow this new analysis,) **we may be led to adopt some metaphysical belief in the existence of material substances. . . .** In other words, we would fall into the terrible trap of believing that the chairs we sit on actually exist!

All this reduces the philosophy ultimately to an arbitrary act of will rather than an act of reason. It is a weapon to win the war against metaphysics by force: it is a bombardment by the Ayer force.

(3) The Verification Principle would eliminate as meaningless many other kinds of propositions which everyone finds obviously meaningful, but are neither tautological nor empirically verifiable. The list is very long:

(a) Statements about the past. These are, strangely, reinterpreted to mean statements about the future—e.g., "Kennedy was assassinated in 1963" is supposed to really mean that if you looked at the books in the library you would find that they said that.

(b) Statements about yourself. Remember, there *is* no substantial self—that's too metaphysical.

(c) Statements about other persons. These are reinterpreted to mean statements about their bodies (without anyone in or behind these bodies, as if persons were self-moving mannequins). And statements about these bodies of "ours" (who?), in turn, are interpreted to mean statements about our own sense perceptions of their appearances (since there is no substance behind either bodies or minds). **Just as I must define material things . . . in terms of their empirical manifestations, so I must define other people in terms of their empirical manifestations—that is, in terms of the behavior of their bodies, and ultimately in terms of sense-contents.**

(d) Statements about other minds. Even if "sensation" is expanded to include our own "inner sensation" or immediate awareness of our own minds, this does not account for our meaningful statements about other minds.

(e) Statements about geometry. These are not mere tautologies, yet they are universal a priori necessary truths.

(f) Statements about moral values, or ethical statements. See section 4 below.

(g) Statements about beauty, or aesthetic statements. These cannot be reduced to subjective expressions of emotion, since they refer to a quality (*viz.* "beauty") in things that elicits or *causes* our aesthetic emotions.

(h) Statements about will and intention and choice. Empirical categories simply fail to contain the meaning these statements have in ordinary minds and ordinary conversation, because they deny the whole *dimension* they express, the non-empirical. That elimination is not Empiricism but Rationalism, the imposition of an a priori rational scheme upon ordinary experience. It is a blind man declaring that sight is an illusion.

(i) Statements about religion. Ayer has the same unquestioned a priori assumption against religion that he has against metaphysics. Nietzsche was at least candid enough to confess it, and even to give some explicit arguments for it.

(j) Scientific statements, universal formulas and predictions. Statements like "If two bodies occupy a common space, the quantity of their gravitational attraction will increase with mass and decrease with distance" predict an infinite number of future sense experiences which could not, even in principle, be verified except by God. So science itself, which was Ayer's model and the source of his attack on supposedly unscientific statements, is eliminated. It is Hume's problem all over again.

(k) Inductive reasoning. This is a related Humean problem, the problem of the justification for induction, which requires the unverifiable principle of the uniformity of nature. Fortunately, it is only a universally Humean problem, not a universally human problem.

(l).Empiricism itself, which is Ayer's first premise, is an "ism," not an empirically verifiable statement. Thus it seems to contradict itself. There is no possible empirical proof of Empiricism.

(m) And besides eliminating all these things, it also eliminates itself (point (1) above), like a mass murderer who then commits suicide.

(n).There is also a pragmatic problem with this philosophy. What happens if you live it? What if you actually believe it and act as if it is actually true, instead of just playing philosophical games with it? A philosopher's ex-wife once said (and this is not a joke, but an actual story), "My ex-husband was a logical positivist, and it was logical positivism that broke up our marriage, because everything I said, whatever it was, he kept telling me was meaningless."

(4) Particularly troubling is the elimination of all moral language as cognitively meaningless. Ayer devotes a whole chapter to this in *Language, Truth and Logic* and says that **The presence of an ethical symbol in a proposition adds nothing to its**

factual content. Thus if I say to someone, "You acted wrongly in stealing that money," I am not stating anything more than if I had simply said, "You stole that money." In adding that this action is wrong I am not making any further statement about it -even though I *think* I am doing that, and I *intend* to do exactly that, and *mean* to do that. So Ayer is telling us what we "really" mean when we mean to mean something else: that we are really meaning what *he* means rather than what *we* mean. This sounds like not only obfuscation rather than clarification but personal megalomania rather than impersonal analysis. He continues:

I am simply evincing my moral disapproval of it. It is as if I had said, "You stole that money," in a peculiar tone of horror, or written it with the addition of some special exclamation marks. The tone, or the exclamation marks, adds nothing to the literal meaning of the sentence. It merely serves to show that the expression of it is attended by certain feelings in the speaker.

If I now generalize my previous statement and say, "Stealing money is wrong," I produce a sentence which has no factual meaning—that is, expresses no proposition which can be either true or false . . . ethical concepts are pseudo-concepts and therefore unanalyzable.

If you ask Ayer how it is possible that people have moral arguments and disagreements about moral statements, he replies not by altering his theory to fit the fact (that people do dispute quite meaningfully about moral values) but by altering the facts to fit his theory: the theory that insists, in the face of the empirical facts of observation, that **it is impossible to dispute about questions of value. . . . If a man said that thrift is a virtue, and another replied that thrift is a vice, they would not . . . be disputing with one another. One would be saying that he approved of thrift, and the other that he didn't; and there is no reason why both these statements should not be true.**

So all the billions of people that have engaged in billions of moral arguments over thousands of years were just confused. No one was ever really right or wrong, not even Gandhi or Hitler, and no one ever uttered a true or false statement about right or wrong, because they lived in the dark world outside of the Vienna Circle and the philosophy departments at Oxford and Cambridge.

More traditional philosophers have called the Logical Positivist theory of values "the boo-hooray theory." Like the Verification Principle itself, it seems self-refuting. For it is difficult to see why, if one adopts this theory toward all values, one should not apply the theory to the value of the theory itself and simply "boo" it rather than "hooraying" it as Ayer does.

There is a serious practical as well as theoretical problem with the "boo-hooray theory." It is an extremely attractive philosophy for tyrants. Mussolini, who lived in practical Italy rather than theoretical Oxford, saw more clearly than the "analysts" did the logical corollary of this moral relativism in practice. He wrote: "Everything I have said and done in these last years is relativism...there is nothing more relativistic than fascistic attitudes and activity...From the fact that all ideologies are of equal value, that all ideologies are mere fictions, the modern relativist infers that everybody has the right to create for himself his own ideology and to attempt to enforce it with all the energy of which he is capable."[28]

---

28 This is from Benito Mussolini's *Diuturna*, pp. 374–77. Ayer does not, of course, use his moral relativism to defend tyrants—but why? Only because he is an English philosopher rather than an Italian politician. But if the "boo-hooray" theory is true, then force (military or emotional) rather than rational persuasion is the only way to resolve moral disputes, individually or globally.

89. Bertrand Russell (1872–1970)

Russell was three things no other analytic philosopher was: an eloquent writer, a political activist, and (therefore) the most famous philosopher in the world.

His eloquence won him the Nobel Prize for literature. To begin with a concrete example of his eloquence, consider the following typical passage. No atheist in history, not even Nietzsche, has ever written such powerful and provocative words as these:

To Dr. Faustus in his study Mephistopheles told the history of the Creation, saying:

"The endless praises of the choirs of angels had begun to grow wearisome; for, after all, did he not deserve their praise? Had he not given them endless joy? Would it not be more amusing to obtain undeserved praise, to be worshipped by beings whom he tortured? He smiled inwardly, and resolved that the great drama should be performed.

"For countless ages the hot nebula whirled aimlessly through space. At length it began to take shape, the central mass threw off planets, the planets cooled, boiling seas and burning mountains heaved and tossed; from black masses of cloud hot sheets of rain deluged the barely solid crust. And now the first germ of life grew in the depths of the ocean, and developed rapidly in the fructifying warmth into vast forest trees, huge ferns springing from the damp mould, sea monsters breeding, fighting, devouring, and passing away. And from the monsters, as the play unfolded, Man was born, with the power of thought, the knowledge of good and evil, and the cruel thirst for worship. And Man saw that all is passing in this mad, monstrous world, that all is struggling to snatch at any cost, a few brief moments of life before Death's inexorable decree. And Man said: 'There is a hidden purpose, could we but fathom it, and the purpose is good; for we must reverence something, and in the visible world there is nothing worthy of reverence.' And Man stood aside from the struggle, resolving that God intended harmony to come out of chaos by human efforts. And when he followed the instincts God had transmitted to him from his ancestry of beasts of prey, he called it Sin, and asked God to forgive him. But he doubted whether he could be justly forgiven, until he invented a divine Plan by which God's wrath was to have been appeased. And seeing the present was bad, he made it yet worse, that thereby the future might be better. And he gave God thanks for the strength that enabled him to forego even the joys that were possible. And God smiled; and when he saw that Man had become perfect in renunciation and worship, he sent another sun through the sky, which crashed into Man's sun; and all returned again to nebula.

"'Yes,' he murmured, 'it was a good play; I will have it performed again.'"

Such, in outline, but even more purposeless, more void of meaning, is the world which Science presents for our belief. Amid such a world, if anywhere, our ideals henceforward must find a home. That Man is the product of causes which had no prevision of the end they were achieving; that his origin, his growth, his hopes and fears, his loves and his beliefs, are but the outcomes of accidental collocations of atoms; that no fire, no heroism, no intensity of thought and feeling, can preserve an individual life beyond the grave; that all the labours of the ages, all the devotion, all the inspiration, all the noonday brightness of human genius, are destined to extinction in the vast death of the solar system, and that the whole temple of Man's achievement must inevitably be buried beneath the debris of a universe in ruins— all these things, if not quite beyond dispute, are yet so nearly certain that no philosophy which rejects them can hope to stand. Only within the scaffolding of these truths, only on the firm foundation of unyielding despair, can the soul's habitation henceforth be safely built.

Life

Who was this man? His life was much more interesting than his philosophy. He was an English Lord (an Earl), grandson of a Prime Minister. He was a liberal, a radical, and a Socialist. (When a critic asked him why, as a Socialist, he did not practice what he preached and give his fortune to the poor, he replied, (We) **are Socialists. We do not pretend to be** *Christians.)* John Stuart Mill was his godfather, intellectually as well as officially.

He summed up the intellectual history of his life in three stages by saying that when he became too stupid for mathematics he took up philosophy and when he became too stupid for philosophy he took up history and political activism.

(1) At the beginning of his career, in 1910, he wrote, with Whitehead, his former teacher at Cambridge, one of the most difficult, technical, and abstract books in the entire history of philosophy, *Principia Mathematica,* which laid the foundations for the whole movement of "analytic philosophy" in constructing a new logic, symbolic or mathematical logic.

(2) His philosophical "bottom line," like that of all the important early analytic philosophers, was a commitment to Ockham's Razor and reductionism, and a scientific Positivism, assuming that **science is innocent unless proved guilty, while philosophy is guilty unless proved innocent.** Thus philosophy's role is mainly to support and clarify science.

(3) Toward the end of his career he became a popular political activist, radical, and agitator for Leftist causes, especially nuclear disarmament and anti-Americanism. He wrote, **Either man will abolish war, or war will abolish man.** (So far, neither of these two disjunctives has proved true.) He called J.F.K. **much more wicked than Hitler** and

accused Americans of **organizing the massacre of the whole of mankind. . . . They are the wickedest people that ever lived in the history of man**.

He lived for 98 years. He was born when Grant was elected President and lived to see and support the student revolts of 1968. He wrote 60 books and over 2000 articles. His friends often said that he looked exactly like the Mad Hatter in the *Alice* books. He had a haughty look but an impish grin and twinkly eyes. He was physically as well as mentally strong. He survived a plane crash at age 76 by swimming through freezing sea water. He married four times, the fourth time at age 80, and sired his last child at 66. He had a lifelong reputation as a seducer and womanizer. Outside France (where Sartre reigned) he was the single most famous philosopher in the world for most of the twentieth century.

Famous and brilliant people often feel a deep inner loneliness, which in Russell's case was also a natural effect of his being both an orphan and an aristocrat. His continuous experiments with his philosophy, his politics, and his loves, all failed to fill this void. He kept changing all three, so that it became a stock joke in England to guess what philosophy, what political system, and what woman Russell was with today. He founded a progressive school for underprivileged children but left his own children feeling neglected and unloved.

His childhood, like most philosophers', was unhappy, although (or perhaps *because)* he never had to lift an aristocratic finger, being surrounded by 11 servants. To the end of his life he was incapable of the simplest physical tasks, like boiling water for tea (literally!). His father died when he was 2, his mother when he was 4, his grandfather when he was 6. He was brought up by a Puritanical and legalistic grandmother, whose religion he rejected early, substituting mathematics for God as his paradigm of perfection when, at age 15 he discovered two things: (1) Euclidean geometry, which he called **one of the great events of my life, as dazzling as first love. I had not imagined that there was anything so delicious in the world;** and (2) a purported logical fallacy in Aquinas's "first cause" argument for God. The fallacy was the contradiction between its premise, that everything must have a cause, and its conclusion, that there is something that does not have a cause, *viz*. God the uncaused First Cause. (But Aquinas does *not* assume that everything must have a cause, only that every *change* must have a cause.)

At the International Congress of Philosophy in Paris in 1900, he met the Italian logician Peano, who had invented an ideal artificial language, a kind of x-ray of the logical structure of ordinary language. This, together with the writings of Frege, was the inspiration for his *Principles of Mathematics* (1903) and, later, the epochal *Principia Mathematica* (1910–1913), which proved that all of arithmetic could be derived from logic. (Be still, my heart!)

Like most child prodigies, he received much admiration and little affection, resulting in his lifelong loneliness and insatiable need for love. Money and women came into and out of his life like torrents in a desert, with no stability, predictability, or law. Thus his love of mathematics. He wrote: **I like mathematics because it is *not* human.** He was always something of a snob philosophically, and deplored G. E. Moore's concentration on ordinary language and common sense, writing that **common sense embodies the metaphysics of savages.** The heart of his philosophy is the demand for an "ideal language" that imitated the precision of mathematics, so that by its standards, most of philosophy and all of metaphysics, religion, and morality (except for Utilitarianism) could be dismissed as linguistic confusion.

He was a tireless political activist, fined and jailed twice (mildly and comfortably) for public anti-war protests. Unlike most Leftists, he was never snookered by Russian Communism. He visited Russia in 1920 and met Lenin, whom he immediately saw through as a phony. He wrote of him that **he despises the populace and is an intellectual aristocrat.** (It takes one to know one.)

In *Marriage and Morals* he attacked the Christian view that demanded fidelity to your spouse, and he had the consistency to preach what he practiced. In 1940 he was prevented from accepting an appointment to teach at City College of New York by Mayor LaGuardia and the clergy of the city, whose lawyer described his works as "lecherous, libidinous, lustful, venerous, erotomaniac, aphrodisiac, irreverent, narrow-minded, untruthful, and bereft of moral fibre." This, of course, only fanned the flame of his fame rather than dampening it. He found himself in America without a job and unable to return to England because of the war. John Dewey helped support him here.

He was a lifelong "feminist," an activist for women's rights, yet his actual treatment of women was abominable, even by the standards of his "freethinking" friends. Sidney Hook wrote that Russell, "despite his advanced age, was pursuing anything in skirts that crossed his path . . . he was carrying on flagrantly even with the servant girls, not behind (his wife's) back but before her eyes and those of his house guests." In middle age, he and his second wife started a "progressive" school where after two hours of lessons the students could "run wild." After a few years it declared itself a failure and closed its doors, unlike the philosophy that spawned it.

What the New Logic Does to Philosophy

Russell, more than any other individual, is responsible for the popularity of analytic philosophy, which changed the meaning and task of philosophy more than any other philosophy in history. It is essential that we understand not only the cognitive content of this new concept of philosophy, or philosophical language, or philosophical method, but also its motivation, its appeal, its evangelistic and missionary excitement. For the human head, even among philosophers, is always driven by the heart.

The new logic and the new philosophy it spawned is an instrument of great power, like the computer. (It also resembles a computer in many other ways.) Its power is like that of laser light: by sacrificing scope and breadth, it achieves a new intensity, exactness and concentration. It is like a spotlight rather than a floodlight. Not only does it enable logic to deal more clearly than ever before with certain kinds of propositions and

propositional relations that are more complex than the simple subject-predicate propositions of Aristotelian logic, but, much more important, it cuts like a powerful lawnmower
through centuries of mysterious and confusing weeds. Little is left. It radically reduces
the height of the weeds (i.e., the traditional problems of philosophy).

The new language that Russell and Whitehead pioneered in *Principia Mathematica*
is, like mathematics itself, not a natural language, not a human language. It is an artificial
language, an "ideal language." There is no ambiguity in it—like mathematics. Russell
says: **In a logically perfect language the words in a proposition would correspond
one by one with the components of the corresponding fact, with the exception of
such words as 'or,' 'not,' 'if,' 'then,' which have a different function. In a logically
perfect language, there will be one word and no more for every simple object. . . . A
language of that sort will be completely analytic. . . . The language which is set forth
in *Principia Mathematica* is intended to be a language of that sort. . . . Actual languages are not logically perfect in this sense, and they cannot possibly be, if they
are to serve the purposes of daily life.**

The idea that all natural languages, though practical and necessary, are deceptive and
lead us astray, especially when we use them in philosophy, and the idea that this new
"ideal" language does not, gives rise to the exciting program of ending forever all philosophical disputes, as the scientific method can in principle end all scientific disputes. If
only we translated all philosophical questions into this one ideal language, they would
all be solved, or rather dissolved. That is a heady project: to be philosophy's final, definitive Messiah. You can see why "analysts" almost always replace rather than supplement
traditional philosophers, the way the Jewish God replaced all the idols of pagan polytheism.

It was Wittgenstein who, even more than Russell, famously summarized and sys-
tematized the philosophical application of this new language and new logic in one great
philosophical classic, his *Tractatus Logico-Philosophicus* (which he later repudiated),
in which he claimed that all previous philosophy is based on confusion and misunderstanding. He wrote: "The book deals with the problems of philosophy and shows, I believe, that the reason why these problems are posed is that the logic of our language is
misunderstood. The whole sense of the book might be summed up in the following words:
what can be said at all can be said clearly, and what we cannot talk about we must pass
over in silence . . . The right method of philosophy would be this: to say nothing except
what can be said, i.e., the propositions of natural science, i.e., something that has nothing
to do with philosophy; and then always, when someone else wished to say something
metaphysical, to demonstrate to him that he has given no meaning to certain signs in his
propositions. This method would be unsatisfying to the other—he would not have the
feeling that we were teaching him philosophy—but it would be the only strictly correct
method. . . . Whereof one cannot speak, thereof one must be silent." That was Russell's
program as well as the early Wittgenstein's.

The touchstone, standard, and ideal for Russell's philosophy was mathematics. Thus the language of philosophy ought to be the new mathematical logic rather than the old Aristotelian logic which was based on ordinary language. But the new logic prevented you from saying anything beyond the empirical or the tautological, and therefore prevented you from saying anything metaphysical, and thus anything really interesting, like "What is the meaning of life?" or "Does God exist?" or "What kind of person should I be?" The new purpose of philosophy, for Russell and all the early analytic philosophers, should be not truth but meaning, not discovery but clarification. It was not the thing Socrates, Plato, and Aristotle invented and named, the thing that began in wonder and aimed at wisdom.

Mathematical Logic and "Logical Atomism"

Since the elements of mathematics are numbers, mathematics is the only language that is totally computer-like, i.e., univocal, non-analogical. All its terms are totally clear and distinct (non-overlapping). Descartes would be proud of it. And as the new logic, for Russell, took its standards from mathematics, philosophy should take its standards from the new logic. (The title of ch. 2 of *Our Knowledge of the External World* is "Logic as the Essence of Philosophy.") Therefore Russell, consistently, entitled his philosophy "Logical Atomism." Since the elements of math were numbers, the elements of logic were elementary propositions, and the elements of the world, deduced from his logic, were "atomic facts" that could not be further analyzed into parts.

Russell wrote: **the kind of philosophy that I wish to advocate, which I call logical atomism, is one which has forced itself upon me in the course of thinking about the philosophy of mathematics.** Insofar as Russell has a metaphysics, or a world-view (essentially, scientific Positivism), the structure of the world is deduced from the structure of his logic. He explicitly connected them this way: he said he taught **a certain kind of logical doctrine and on the basis of this a certain kind of metaphysics** (i.e., answer to the question what is real?).

Russell assumed that **facts, since they have components, must be in some sense complex, and hence must be susceptible to analysis.** The new logic was to be the tool of this analysis. **In a logically perfect language, the words in a proposition would correspond one by one with the components of the corresponding facts** as stated by propositions.

The new logic was not a logic of *terms,* like Aristotelian logic, for terms usually referred to universals (like "man" or "mortal"), and real universals were eliminated by Russell's Nominalism (which, in turn, was dictated by Ockham's Razor). Since for Nominalism there were no essences or natures, you could not distinguish essential from accidental predicates, as in the old logic. Instead, the new logic was a "truth-functional" logic which began with simple ("atomic") *propositions* and calculated "molecular" truths on a "truth-table" from the assumptions of the truth or falsity of the "atomic propositions" of which the molecular propositions were composed. (This is the logic taught by 99% of all logic texts now in print. For the alternative, see the author's *Socratic Logic.)*

The new logic was not an extension of or an addition to the old but an eliminator of it. It was a war to the death with only one survivor. According to Russell, Aristotle's commonsensical analysis of propositions into subject and predicate, i.e., "two term relations," had **vitiated almost everything that has hitherto been written on the theory of knowledge.**

The new logic, being Nominalistic, cannot account for, or test the truth of, universal statements like "all men are mortal." For they are not provable either as tautologies or as empirical statements (for no one can observe "all men"). All universals, or "abstractions," are mere "logical fictions."

Nor could the new logic justify or account for itself. For the relation between words and facts is neither a word nor a fact. If only language about facts is meaningful, then language about the relation between language and facts is not meaningful. The early Wittgenstein answered this problem in his *Tractatus* by admitting that "my propositions are elucidatory in this way: he who understands me finally recognizes them as senseless, when he has used them to climb out beyond them. (He must so to speak throw away the ladder after he has climbed up on it.)"

Puzzles the New Logic Solves

(1) But Russell's new logical language enabled him to solve some famous puzzles and paradoxes very neatly. One of the puzzles was how to express relational propositions which did not fully translate into the Aristotelian subject-predicate format. The new logic made better room for them.

(2) Another is his solution to the old "liar paradox": "All Cretans are liars," said a Cretan. If he spoke the truth about all Cretans, then he, being a Cretan, lied. And if he lied when he said he *was* a liar, then he was *not* a liar but a truth-teller. "Russell's paradox" is a more complex example of the same apparently logically self-contradictory statement: "There is a village in which there is a barber who shaves all and only all the men who don't shave themselves." So does the barber shave himself or not? Work it out: it is self-contradictory either way. A third version of the paradox is the concept of "a class that contains all classes that do not contain themselves." Does it contain itself or not?

Russell's simple solution was his "theory of types," which decrees that no proposition, and no class, may refer to itself, so that such self-referential questions have no true *or* false answers. A bag of balls can neither contain itself nor fail to contain itself. The referring proposition is like the bag and the referred-to proposition is like the balls.

Russell's solution is a decree of the will, not a discovery of the mind: a forbidding, a refusal, to any class that wants to be self-referential, to include itself as a member. The puzzle in the mind is solved by the will. It is not solved by the mind, but remains in the mind unless commanded to leave by the will.

There is another problem: Russell's solution to the self-contradiction of the liar paradox also entails a self-contradiction, since the "theory of types" defines and limits all classes that are permissible by the decree of this theory; but this class of "permissible classes" contains itself, and therefore by its own law is not permissible. And if you didn't follow that, you are less than fully human and you are putting the survival of Western civilization in jeopardy.

Any alternative solution would have required a return to Aristotelian logic and an abandonment of the new Frege-Russell Nominalistic logic in which a "class" is no longer a "species" or "nature" or "form" or "logos" with meaning, intension, or comprehension, but is purely quantitative and extensional and content-free—in fact meaning-free. The new logic abstracts from all meaning, since meaning is understood intuitively, by an act of intellectual intuition, *intellectus,* rather than by an act of calculation, *ratio,* which can be done purely mechanically and materially, by computers. Computers understand absolutely nothing. They are machines. The new logic assumes that we are too, or tries to turn us into them. It enables us to do logic and mathematics brilliantly, cleverly and effectively without *understanding* any real thing at all.

(3) Another puzzle about truth and falsity was solved by Russell's "theory of descriptions." The puzzle was that a sentence like "The present king of France is bald" is neither true nor false, since there is no present king of France. According to the traditional logical "law of excluded middle," every proposition must be either true or false, but this one is neither. Another way to put the puzzle is this: the law of excluded middle says that the contradiction of any false proposition must be true, so if it is false that the present king of France is bald, then it must be true that he is not. Yet that proposition is false too.

Traditional logic solved this puzzle by labelling it the material fallacy of "complex question," a question with a hidden false assumption. But there are no material fallacies in the new logic.

Russell constructed a language that more clearly distinguished questions of existence and questions of properties, by distinguishing "reference" (which assumed existence) and "meaning" (which did not). Russell's new logic solves puzzles about existence by excising existence from descriptive propositions. For instance, the puzzle about a sentence like "The golden mountain does not exist" seems to attribute some kind of existence to its subject in the same proposition as it denies it in the predicate. Russell's solution was to invent a language in which such puzzles about existence could not be uttered because existence had been distinguished from and analyzed out of the description. His "theory of descriptions" requires us to translate "The golden mountain does not exist" into "There is no entity, C, such that the sentence 'X is golden and mountainous' is true if and only if X = C."

The medievals accomplished the same thing without twisting language into pretzels by their metaphysical distinction between essence and existence, which is the metaphysical basis for Russell's quite commonsensical distinction between meaning and reference. Yet Russell claimed that his solution **clears up two millennia of muddle-headedness**

about "existence." (Like most aristocrats, Russell was *not* usually a snob in dealing with ordinary people, but like most analytic philosophers, he was a supreme snob when dealing with nearly all previous philosophers.)

Russell's Metaphysics

In one sense Russell was against metaphysics; in another sense he did metaphysics.

Like other early analytic philosophers, Russell dismissed traditional metaphysics as unscientific and unverifiable. "On the rebound" from his early infatuation with the rationalistic metaphysical systems of the English Hegelians, he became convinced that the only way to know the nature of the world was through sense experience and logical analysis, not by any system or synthesis or by any intellectual intuition. (Nominalists deny that there is such a thing as intellectual intuition because there are no real universal forms to intuit. It thus reduces reason to reasoning, the "third act of the mind.") Like the Logical Positivists, Russell believed that philosophy's job was not any "big picture" synthesis, but analysis—the analysis of the complex into the simple "logical atoms."

But this "logical atomism" is itself a "big picture" synthesis, a metaphysics. It is a picture of the structure of the whole of reality. In fact, it is a highly rationalistic metaphysics because it deduces the structure of the world from the structure of logic rather than vice versa.

However, the "atoms" of "logical atomism" were not *physical* atoms, as in the ancient materialists Democritus and Lucretius, but *logical* atoms: atoms of meaning, not matter. Russell replaced Hegel's monism with pluralism, or atomism, but this was meant merely as a logic, not a metaphysics. For it is not about any substance, or essence, or being behind appearances. There *is* no such thing, for Russell.[29]

In fact, there is no such thing as Russell if Russell is right. For, following Hume, Russell believed that there are no substances; therefore persons are no more than the sum total, or collection, or sequence, of experiences.

How a mere collection or sequence of experiences can know itself as a whole, and how the word "I" can be meaningful, are two questions that Russell's "logical atomism" has no experientially verifiable answer to. The common sense of the "savages" outside Oxbridge believes that things with proper names, like "Bertrand Russell," are real entities, or substances with attributes. Russell disagrees and calls them "logical fictions." You need a new logic— a fictional logic—to explain how a logical fiction can know itself to be a logical fiction.

Russell argued against Moore's "common sense" and "ordinary language" because he believed that "common sense is for savages" and that ordinary language is hopelessly confused, deceptive, and vague. Yet it has worked pretty well for the rest of us human

29 But isn't such a claim, that "there *is* no 'is,'" itself a statement about what is?

beings for many millennia, including "savages" like Aristotle, Aquinas, Descartes, Galileo, and Newton. In fact there has never been a single great scientist or philosopher who wrote a great book in Russell's "ideal language."

Russell's Epistemology

Russell was a phenomenalist (not a phenomenologist), an Empiricist, and a skeptic in his epistemology.

As a phenomenalist he limited what we could know to phenomena, or "sense-data." Like Locke, he believed that these, and not real things, are the immediate objects of our sense experience. But when he tried to infer the nature of the world from them, he realized, as Hume did, that we could never attain certainty about anything in the real world in this way. Thus Russell, like Hume, embraced skepticism as the logical consequence of his phenomenalism. Thus we cannot even be certain that the world outside our experience, the world of planets and birds and other people, really exists!

Another source of Russell's skepticism is his belief that logical certainty was truth-functional only, and therefore only hypothetical: we could not be certain of p or q, only that *if* p implied q and *if* p was true, *then* q was certainly true. (Contrast Moore's epistemological realism and his arguments against skepticism.) Epistemological certainty, as distinct from probability, was impossible. Only psychological certainty, i.e., the subjective *feeling* of certainty, was possible. But it is an unjustified feeling. The only two things that can be known with certainty are immediate sense data and analytic propositions, i.e., tautologies. Thus Russell set the stage for Ayer's Logical Positivism's "verification principle."

Also factoring into Russell's skepticism were his acceptance of Clifford's Rule as a philosophical as well as a scientific principle of method. Clifford's Rule says that it is always wrong to accept any idea for any other reason than evidence sufficient to prove its truth. (Compare William James's criticism of Clifford's Rule in his "Will to Believe.")

Still another source of Russell's skepticism was his acceptance of Cartesian universal methodic doubt, i.e., that we must begin with doubt, not knowledge, intuition, faith, common sense, or any certainty, and accept only that which can be conclusively proved. He thought Descartes was right to begin with doubt but wrong to think that he had any logically justified escape from his deepest levels of doubt, *viz.* whether we are hallucinating, or dreaming, or being deceived by an evil spirit.

Still another source of skepticism for Russell was his argument that we all see the world from different perspectives—e.g., the table looks tan and smooth to me, who see it in a bright light, but brown and rough to you, who see it in a darker light—so none of us sees the world as it really is in itself. And this subjectivity that is true of sensation is even truer of thought.

A major epistemological problem for Russell was the problem of justifying induction, which is the primary form of reasoning for an Empiricist. He follows Hume here both in worrying about the question and in having nothing but a skeptical answer to it. The question is: Why do we think that the fact that the sun has risen every morning makes it more likely that it will rise tomorrow morning? Only because we expect nature tomorrow to be the same as today. Why do we expect nature tomorrow to resemble nature today? What grounds our belief in "the uniformity of nature" which is the assumption of all induction? We can't use experience to prove it because that would beg the question, using induction (from experience) to justify the *principle* of induction. Russell's only solution, like Hume's, is a semi-skepticism or probabilism. But even probability is not justified unless the uniformity of nature is assumed.

Russell's Anthropology

Distinguishing sensation and thought brings us to the mind-body problem, which was the primary problem in philosophical anthropology for Russell.

Russell was not a materialist because materialism is a metaphysics and Russell was skeptical of metaphysics. Because he was skeptical of metaphysics, he believed we had no reason to believe in substances, as distinct from their appearances, and this included not only mental substances (minds) but also material substances (bodies).

What then is a self, an "I"? It is a logical and grammatical fiction! Where Descartes began with "I think, therefore I am" as his prime certainty, Russell ends his analysis with "Substances do not exist and therefore neither do I." Personal identity is an illusion. There is no persistent individual substance behind my acts of thinking, sensing, and other activities; there is only a causally connected stream of events united by memory. So the word "I" can be simply eliminated from the philosopher's vocabulary. The philosopher's vocabulary for Russell suspiciously resembles Orwell's "Newspeak" in *1984:* a new language invented not by creating new words but by destroying old ones that are found undesirable. And "personal selfhood" and "free will" are two of those undesirable words for both Orwell's and Russell's new languages.

Russell's scientific Positivism insisted on reducing all unscientific words to scientific ones. In practice this entailed what common sense would call materialism. But materialism is in theory self-contradictory since it is an "ism," a thought, not the material object of a thought. In other words, the materialist idea that there are no mental events but only material events is self-contradictory, for that idea, like all ideas, is a mental event. So Russell calls his denial of any mind distinct from the body not "materialism" but "physicalism," and defines it as the idea that "all events whatsoever are subject to the laws of physics." He contrasts this with what he calls "eliminative materialism" because it at least admits that there *are* mental events. But it says that these too are subject to the laws of physics. There is no "mind" as distinct from "brain." Thus, concepts like "soul," "spirit," "free will," and "life after death" are not only false but meaningless.

Russell's Ethics

Like most Empiricists and physicalists, Russell was a Utilitarian. This meant essentially two things: that the test of the moral goodness of any act is its consequences, and that the test of whether the consequences were good is pleasure, i.e., the satisfaction of desires.

Russell argues that the only epistemological alternative to Utilitarian Empiricism is intuitionism, the view that there is a mental power, usually called "conscience," which is neither sensory nor mathematical—in other words, that man is something other than an ape plus a computer. Russell admits that we do have moral intuitions, but he reduces them to feelings and asks how we can ever know which intuition is right when they conflict with each other. Arguments will never convince anyone in morality, he says; only consequentialist calculation based on observational premises, can ever do that.

Thus morality is not based on any kind of knowledge or truth, only on desire. And the only moral law and limit on my desires is to not interfere with the satisfaction of others' desires. (But *why* even that restriction?) That is the only distinction between good and bad desires. Have your orgy, or suicide, or addiction if you wish, just don't interfere with mine.

Russell's ethics is similar to that of Hume and Logical Positivism. He judges that judgments of value, and terms like "good," "right," "justice" and "duty" are neither objectively true nor false. They do not express facts, they express only feelings. They do not tell us truths about how people do in fact behave. They claim to tell us truths about how people ought to behave. But they do not do what they claim to do. They tell us only feelings that some people have about how they would like other people to behave. "There is nothing right or wrong, but thinking (or feeling) makes it so." One is tempted to call this a convenient philosophy for philanderers, but one "ought" not to use such cheap *ad hominems*—but, then again, "oughts" are just feelings, so why not?

Russell's fundamental assumption in ethics concerns the very nature of philosophy. It is something like this: Philosophers used to believe that their moral disagreements were inevitable and natural because of the profound nature of the subject matter. Science has shown that they were wrong. For scientists, once they distinguished themselves from philosophers, developed the scientific method and ended their disagreements. They did this by narrowing their subject matter to the empirical and narrowing their method to the mathematical. Philosophers now "ought" to imitate scientists in every division of philosophy, including ethics, and thus resolve their long-standing disagreements by the scientific method. If they unite in the methods of analytic philosophy, they will soon come to unite in their content, their conclusions, and finally end their disagreements. The price for this is the end of philosophy itself, i.e., the end of almost everything that used to be called philosophy, the reduction of "the love of wisdom" to the logical analysis of the language of science.

Russell's Attack on Religion

Russell discarded belief in free will and life after death at age 15, and in God at 18. He had a personal interest in mysticism, but held it in check with his reason. A popular story has him on his deathbed visited by a preacher who asked him what he would say to God if after death he found out that He actually existed. Russell replied: "I suppose I should call him 'Sir,' and I should say something like this: Evidently, You exist, and evidently my atheistic hypothesis was erroneous. Would You mind answering one wee little question? Why the hell didn't You give us more *evidence?* " Clifford's Rule to the end![30]

Russell was much more opposed to Christianity than to any other religion. He argued that Christ may never even have existed, and that if he did exist, he was not even especially wise or good. He was not wise because he made an error about the end of the world. (Russell interpreted Mt. 24:34–35 literally, even though that interpretation contradicts the very next verse, 36.) He was not good because he believed in Hell, and **no even moderately good person would attempt to instill such fears and terrors.** (But what if it actually existed? Would it not be good to warn us?) Russell accused Christianity of being responsible for retarding science and social progress and causing enormous human suffering. For him its three main impacts on history seem to have been the Inquisition, the Crusades, and witch hunts. **Every single bit of progress in humane feeling has been opposed by the Church, which still is the principal enemy of moral progress in the world.** (Compare Hobbes's *Leviathan* here, the whole second half of which is an extended attack on the Catholic Church as "The Kingdom of Darkness.") Russell believed not only that Christianity was *untrue* but that Christian morality was *wicked* and Christian faith was irrational. Christian morality was wicked and inhumane because it required more than the easy and comfortable Utilitarian principle of "Do whatever you desire except interfering with others' desires." It thus lessened rather than increased the sum total of human happiness (pleasure) in this world. And Christian faith was irrational because it is unscientific: it cannot be empirically or mathematically verified.

As all those statements, of course, can.

Russell, unlike most philosophers, is worth reading just for his writing style. His most important books include:

The Principles of Mathematics (1903)
Principia Mathematica (1910–1913) with Alfred North Whitehead, 3 vols.
The Problems of Philosophy (1912)
Our Knowledge of the External World (1914)
Mysticism and Logic (1918)

30 For a reasonable answer to this very reasonable of Russell's question, see Pascal, ch. 56 on "Why God Hides."

89. Bertrand Russell (1872–1970)

The Analysis of Mind (1921)
What I Believe (1925)
On Education (1926)
Why I Am Not a Christian (1927, 1957)
Marriage and Morals (1929)
A History of Western Philosophy (1945)
Philosophy and Politics (1947)
Human Knowledge: Its Scope and Limits (1948)
Unpopular Essays (1950)
The Autobiography of Bertrand Russell (3 volumes: 1967, 1968, 1969)

90. Ludwig Wittgenstein (1889–1951)

A personal note, to begin. Of the 100 philosophers in this 4-volume work, none has demanded of me as much qualitative rethinking and reappraisal, and as much quantitative expansion of pages, as Wittgenstein. One reason for this is that few philosophers, and certainly no "analytic philosophers," are as fascinating *persons* as he. And none, except perhaps Nietzsche, more drastically and seriously challenged the very existence and essence of philosophy itself.

Life and Personality

Wittgenstein was born in Vienna into a wealthy, educated, and aristocratic family. Vienna was a primary source of modernism in the arts, and Wittgenstein's philosophy shares this style: spare, sparse and fragmentary. The style of his only published work, the *Tractatus Logico-Philosophicus,* reminds us of a play by Samuel Beckett.

His father was an engineer and an industrialist, his mother a musician, and these were his two influences—the scientific, technological, and practical on the one hand and the poetic, aesthetic, and mystical on the other hand. He studied engineering in Berlin and in Manchester, England, before deciding on philosophy instead; and the philosophy of his only published book (the *Tractatus Logico-Philosophicus,* or just the *Tractatus* for short) could be described as an engineer's theory of language. He virtually identified philosophy with logic and mathematics. In contrast, his greatest personal passions were music and what he called "the mystical" (which included aesthetics, ethics, and religion).

Like so many modern philosophers, he was a troubled and conflicted soul, perpetually on the brink of neurosis. Three of his brothers committed suicide. He was a homosexual who never "came out." He was small and thin, with bright blue eyes and an intense face. (He actually looked very much like Samuel Beckett.) His colleague Norman Malcolm wrote that Wittgenstein lived "in perpetual torment," yet in the end he judged his own life to be "wonderful." Contrast Russell, who lived "the high life," yet judged his life to be meaningless (see the long quotation at the beginning of the previous chapter, on Russell). Wittgenstein is to Russell what Job is to Ecclesiastes.

He was as compelling a personal presence at Cambridge as Socrates was in Athens. His lectures were always ad hoc, noteless, and passionate, delivered while pacing up and down and thinking on his feet, like a dog gnawing a bone or a cat harrying a mouse, and with religious intensity even when dealing with trivial problems.

He told his students to throw away all their philosophy books. Literally. No philosopher in history was ever so totally ignorant of the history of philosophy. He knew only

Frege and Russell. He boasted to his friends that he had never read a single word of Aristotle. (He softened this later.)

His fascination with mathematics led him to Frege, the first founder of modern mathematical logic. Frege advised him to go to Cambridge to study under Russell. (This was 1911.) Russell describes their meeting memorably: "He came to me and said, 'Will you please tell me whether I am a complete idiot or not?' I replied, 'My dear fellow, I don't know. Why are you asking me?' He said, 'Because if I am a complete idiot, I shall become an aeronaut (pilot), but if not, I shall become a philosopher.' I told him to write me something. . . . After reading only one sentence, I said to him, 'No, you must not become an aeronaut.'"

Russell found Wittgenstein "obstinate and perverse, but I think not stupid . . . very argumentative and tiresome. He would not admit that it was certain that there was not a rhinoceros in the room."

Russell thought of Wittgenstein as his protégé and the most brilliant philosopher in the world, and wrote a laudatory preface to his *Tractatus.* But Wittgenstein thought Russell radically misunderstood him and he refused to print his preface until the publisher insisted. After one year of friendship, he wrote Russell a letter saying that they could never be friends because their values and their philosophies of life were total opposites. Later, he repudiated not only Russell's but also his own earlier philosophy of the *Tractatus,* which had made him famous. No philosopher in history ever more completely disowned his own major work.

Also, no other philosopher in history has been the primary example and most famous instance of *two* so diametrically opposite philosophical movements. These were the two opposite versions of "analytical philosophy," first the Logical Positivism, logical atomism, and "ideal language" philosophy of the *Tractatus* and then the "ordinary language" philosophy of his later work, which was unpublished in his lifetime but posthumously collected as *Philosophical Investigations.* First he was a Russell, or an Ayer, then he was a Moore. But he was a much more difficult version of both.

When World War I broke out in 1914 he enlisted in the Austrian army. (Russell, meanwhile, became a pacifist and was imprisoned for it.) He made repeated requests to be sent to the front to fight. He was captured (philosophers are not usually very effective warriors), and spent a year in an Italian prisoner of war camp. After his release, he gave away his whole very considerable inheritance from his father, and lived in an austere, monastic style for the rest of his life. He probably contemplated a monastic vocation; he was a kind of Catholic agnostic Jew. He was baptized as a Catholic (his mother was Catholic), and publicly listed that as his religion. Though his father was racially (but not religiously) Jewish, he never identified himself as Jewish. His philosophy is closer to agnosticism than to any substantive religious beliefs, but he was deeply haunted by religious *questions.*

During the war he picked up a copy of Tolstoy's version of the New Testament, was deeply impressed with it, and kept it with him everywhere. Russell wrote, in 1919, "I had felt in his book a flavor of mysticism, but was astonished when I found he had become a complete mystic. He reads people like Kierkegaard and Angelus Silesius, and he seriously contemplates becoming a monk. . . . He reads Tolstoy and Dostoyevski, especially *Karamazov* . . . it all started when he read William James's *Varieties of Religious Experience* . . . I think (though he wouldn't agree) that what he likes best in mysticism is its power to make him stop thinking." In Tolstoy's introduction to the New Testament there is this famous line: "The more we live by our intellect, the less we understand the meaning of life." That is perhaps the ultimate point, the "bottom line," for Wittgenstein too. (See the later subsection on "The Mystical.")

After writing the *Tractatus* he claimed to have solved (or rather dissolved) all the problems of philosophy. And since, unlike most philosophers, he was ruthlessly honest with himself and actually practiced what he preached, he left Cambridge and philosophy to teach children in a remote Austrian village and to work in a monastery as a gardener. He also worked as an architect; the house he designed for his sister still stands, as austerely modernistic as his philosophy. While in Austria he also attended meetings of the Vienna Circle of Logical Positivists (see the previous section on Ayer), with which he had both serious agreements and serious disagreements. Like Russell, the Vienna Circle were scandalized when they realized that his true passion was for what he called "the mystical." In fact, this was the main point of the *Tractatus,* according to Wittgenstein himself, though it is mentioned only in one line, the very last one! ("Whereof one cannot speak, thereof one must be silent.") In a sense the whole book is a very long shaggy dog story.

He came to believe his earlier philosophy was radically mistaken, so he returned to philosophy to correct it. On Russell's recommendation, Cambridge invited him back to occupy the chair of the retiring G. E. Moore (whom Wittgenstein had befriended) and to lecture there; and Cambridge, out of homage to his genius, accepted the *Tractatus* in lieu of a doctoral dissertation. He never published anything else in his lifetime. Student notes of his lectures circulated clandestinely.

He left Cambridge for a while and moved to Norway, living alone in a cottage he built in the woods in order to think through, in solitude, the same philosophical problems that he had thought about in dialog with other philosophers at Cambridge. At Cambridge he ate alone, not at Commons with the other dons, since conversation there was academic chatter which was (in his own words to his colleague John Wisdom) "neither of the head nor of the heart." He lived alone in his monastically spare room. Instead of entering a monastery he turned his world into one.

The New Logic

When Wittgenstein first arrived at Cambridge, Russell and Whitehead had just published the Bible of the new logic, *Principia Mathematica,* and Wittgenstein accepted this as the standard and model for all philosophical language. His *Tractatus* deduces the philosophy that logically follows from this assumption. It could be regarded as an unintended *reductio ad absurdum* argument *against* the principles of Russell rather than a successful application of these principles; indeed, that is how the later Wittgenstein himself came to regard it.

The difference between the old Aristotelian logic and the new, mathematical logic is a crucial indicator of, and cause of, the enormous difference between nearly all previous philosophies and the new "analytic philosophy" in all its forms: (a) G. E. Moore's "common sense" "ordinary language analysis," (b) The Vienna Circle's and Ayer's "Logical Positivism," (c) Russell's "ideal language" philosophy of "logical atomism," (d) Wittgenstein's version of "logical atomism" in the *Tractatus,* and also (e) Wittgenstein's later substitution of many flexible, pragmatic "language games" for one ideal language in the *Philosophical Investigations.* All five kinds of "analytic philosophy," and all "analytic philosophers" today, use the new logic instead of the old. Wittgenstein believed the new logic had simply replaced the old. He called it a progress **comparable only to that which made Astronomy out of Astrology and Chemistry out of Alchemy.**

What are the differences between the two logics and why are they so important?

(1) The new logic is mathematical: quantitative rather than qualitative and extensional rather than intentional or comprehensional.[31] It is computer logic, abstracted from all form, i.e., *logos,* specific meaning, or content. The new logic is a machine. Indeed, every machine is an embodied logical procedure: if x is done, y will happen, if A is put in, B will come out. Machines understand nothing whatsoever, and computers are only machines, therefore computers understand nothing whatsoever. (That's Aristotelian logic, by the way: a syllogism.) They store and retrieve and relate data, like libraries. Is your library conscious? Do the books in it understand themselves? Does a library become conscious when it reaches a certain size or complexity of structure in its parts?

(2) There are no *analogical terms* in the new logic. Every term must be clear and distinct, like a number. Nothing fuzzy. No *range* of meanings. In teaching logic for fifty years, I have found a spectacularly strong correlation between students who study the new logic rather than the old, and who also feel great familiarity, comfort and even love for computers, on the one hand, and on the other hand their inability to recognize or understand analogies, metaphors, images, and symbolic language. The new logic is a logic for the hard sciences but not for the humanities. It is significant, and quite natural, that logicians before Frege were almost all classicists, i.e., writers and readers, while logicians after Frege were almost all mathematicians.

(3) It is a logic that begins not with terms, and with what traditional logic called the "first act of the mind," *viz.* the intellectual intuition into the meaning of terms, but with propositions (which are the expressions of judgments, traditional logic's "second act of the mind"). The new logic abstracts completely from the term-content of propositions,

31 A term's "intention" or "comprehension" is its inner meaning, all the qualities it contains, or "comprehends." Its "extension" is its population, so to speak: all the real things it refers to, all its concrete instances.

then it combines these "atomic propositions" into molecular arguments. (Arguing, or reasoning, or inference, is "the third act of the mind" in traditional logic.) The old logic began with terms like "man" and "mortal," then combined them into propositions like "All men are mortal," then connected *them* in arguments like "All men are mortal, and I am a man, therefore I am mortal."

(4) Because it abstracts from the content of propositions, the new logic also reinterprets the proposition itself as a mere extensional class-inclusion of the members of the subject class in the predicate class rather than interpreting the predicate of the proposition as revealing some aspect of the *nature* of the subject. It is a Nominalistic logic without universal natures, forms or *logoi*. When it says that S is P it does not mean that S is P *because it is S,* but only that all instances of S are to be labeled also as instances of P. There is no real intrinsic relation between them. And, as we shall see in the next point, there is also no intrinsic relation between premise and conclusion.

(5) Logical implication (the premise-to-conclusion or "if.. .then . . . " relationship) in the new logic has nothing to do with any real connection or relation in the world. "If it rains, you will get wet" does not mean that you will get wet *because* rain *causes* you to get wet, but merely that all cases of it raining are also cases of you getting wet. In the old logic the relation between premise and conclusion mirrors some kind of causal relation in the world—e.g., rain makes you wet. But in the new logic a premise entails a conclusion quite irrespective of content.

This results in a counter-intuitive (anti-commonsensical) paradox, which is called the "paradox of material implication." (It really ought to be called the paradox of *non-*material implication because it results from abstracting from the matter or content of a proposition.) "Material implication" means that according to the rules of the new logic, a false proposition implies or entails any and all propositions. For instance: If Antarctica is not cold, then the moon is blue and also the moon is not blue. And every true proposition implies every other true proposition. For instance: If Antarctica is cold, then the moon is not blue, and if 2+2=4, then I exist. (Poor Descartes didn't really have to search that hard to prove anything!)

These paradoxes result from the fact that the new logic is simply a set of formal rules for the manipulation of contentless symbols on a "truth table"; it is not from, about, or for the real world. It does not tell us either *what* anything is or *why* anything is. It abstracts from all real causality, all real *relationships* between facts. If this atomistic logic pictures the real world, as Russell and the early Wittgenstein believed, then the real world is a world of "logical atomism" in which, as Hume said, everything is "loose" from everything else. In other words, a world that is empty of meaning.

This is why Wittgenstein says in the *Tractatus* that **Any one fact** (in the world, which is the sum of all facts) **can either be the case, or not be the case, and everything else remains the same. . . . From the existence or non-existence of one state of affairs, it is impossible to infer the existence or non-existence of another.** This is obviously not true of the real world; there, things cause other things to happen, and we can infer one thing from another. For instance, if you have sex, you might have a baby. (Those who have gone through sufficient "sex education" of the currently fashionable type call a baby an "accident"—which is like calling growth an accident of eating.) But what is true of the new logic and what is true of the real world are quite different. The question is whether logic should match the world (as the old logic tried to do) or whether "the world" must match the new logic.

Russell had claimed that logical atomism *is* true in the real world. Although he says one cannot deduce one thing in the real world from another, he claims to deduce the structure of the whole real world from the structure of the new logic. Facts must be atomic in the world because propositions are atomic in the new logic. And Wittgenstein follows this in the *Tractatus*. A wag famously said that Russell described the world as if God had created it after reading *Principia Mathematica*. (Only a philosopher as brilliant as Wittgenstein could possibly believe such an absurdity. And only a philosopher as passionately honest and truth-seeking as Wittgenstein could later repudiate it.)

The new logic thus expresses (and reinforces) the fragmentation and meaninglessness of modern life. It is the logic of "Waiting for Godot" or "ulysses" rather than the logic of "It's a Wonderful Life," or "Schindler's List" ("He who saves one life, saves the world"), or *The Brothers Karamazov* ("We are each responsible for all"). This new world is flat. Nothing has any more significance than anything else. There is no value in this world, only loose, free-floating facts.

(6) In the new logic **any given propositions . . . are . . . truth-functions of simpler propositions.** The new logic is simply a system of rules for the transformation of propositions and relations between propositions, rules for saying the same thing but changing one expression into another. That is what a "tautology" literally means: "saying *(logos)* the same thing *(to autos)*." In the new logic, all of logic is tautologous. Predicates say no more than subjects, and conclusions say no more than premises. In the new logic, propositions are declared true not because of their content mirroring the real world but because of their relation to each other on a truth table irrespective of their content. And thus logic can say absolutely nothing about the real world.

(7) The new logic is the logic of mathematics, which is a powerful instrument of the scientific method, which itself is the most powerful and important scientific discovery of all time because it makes possible so many other new discoveries. Although analytic philosophers usually disagree radically with Descartes, they all accept the single most foundational idea in his philosophy, the idea that philosophy should be done by the scientific method (that's the point of his title *Discourse on the Method);* and the hope that this would end forever 2400 years of disagreements in philosophy, just as it had resolved disagreements in the sciences. (Needless to say, this hope has never materialized, even among analytic philosophers, who disagree as much as anyone else.)

(8) The new logic is Nominalistic. There are no real universals, kinds, or natures, only arbitrarily invented "classes." Russell wrote that "Hitherto the people attracted to philosophy have been mostly those who loved the big generalizations, which were all wrong." *(That* is quite a big generalization! So it must be wrong.)

(9) The new logic is totally impersonal and uncreative, like a computer. It follows a mechanical technique. It does not invent or refute syllogistic arguments; it does not engage in Socratic dialog; it simply sets up "truth tables." It is a logic for "artificial intelligence" (computers), not "natural intelligence" (human beings).

(10) It is wholly analytic, not synthetic; left-brain, not right-brain. It deconstructs statements into their atomic logical parts. It reduces mysteries to problems and solves them by logical form alone.

(11) It is a closed system. You have a closed system whenever there is some infallible mechanical means for determining truth and falsity. By truth tables you can determine whether any set of logical statements is true, consistent, and tautological, or false, inconsistent, and self-contradictory. Those are the only two possibilities. In traditional logic this is only a small part of logic, the "calculus of sentences." In the new logic, it is the whole.

Kurt Goedel refuted this "formalist" notion of a closed system even in the simplest mathematical system, arithmetic. "Goedel's Proof" shows that no system can prove all of its own assumptions or premises, and must either borrow them from another system or simply postulate them without proof. Because of Goedel, even logic and mathematics turned out to be open rather than closed systems.

The choice of Russell's new logic is a strange one for Wittgenstein, for he is the polar opposite of a typical "analytic" philosopher temperamentally. His mind is deeply intuitive. He is constantly inventing new and arresting images, metaphors, and models. He habitually looks at the most familiar things from a remarkably unfamiliar point of view. He is "creative"—a poet, not a "techie." Philosophy becomes in his hands a way of seeing, not just calculating.

Thus it is useful to regard the whole *Tractatus* as a brilliantly consistent fiction, a work of art rather than science, a thought-experiment, a fantasy world based on a hypothesis much more fantastic than the hypothesis of magic, elves and dragons: the hypothesis of logical atomism.

The Main Point of the *Tractatus*

According to Wittgenstein himself (but not according to most "analytic philosophers" who admire and use the *Tractatus)* the main point of the *Tractatus* was *not*

(1) the use of the new logic to create a new philosophy; nor

(2) its "picture theory" of language, in which the atomic parts of any statement simply reflect the atomic parts of a fact, as a mirror reflects each part of the real things in front of it; nor

(3) the picture of the world as "logical atomism," the confidence that the world consists of atomic facts because the new logic consists of atomic propositions; nor even

(4) the claim to solve all philosophical problems by dissolving them in the acid of the new logic.

(5) It was *ethics*, of all things. The logic is there only to point to the trans-logical ethics, which Wittgenstein calls "the mystical."

To understand what this means, consider a typical Chinese or Japanese landscape painting. Western painting typically uses space to frame the things, people or events that the painter wants to direct the viewer's attention to. Thus the space is filled. It is exactly the opposite in the Orient: the few things or people are there to set off the space, the emptiness, and *that* is the whole point of the picture. What is *not* shown is more important than what is shown; in fact it is the whole point.

Or take a haiku. The severe 17-syllable form gives you only a few strokes of the verbal brush, and the rest is silence. "An old pond. A green frog jumps into it. The sound of moving water." The sound of the frog jumping into the water is the frame around the silence. The silence is not the frame around the sound.

Or take a *koan* in Zen. There is no solution, no answer, to the puzzle of a koan. That is its whole point. "What is the sound of one hand clapping?" "Define the indefinable Buddha." The words of the puzzle point not forward to the solution to it, but back to the emptiness out of which it emerges.

The *Tractatus* is like that. Its most important line is its last one, its culminating point 7: **Whereof one cannot speak, thereof one must be silent. (*Wovon Mann nicht reden kann, davon muss Mann schweigen.*)** For Wittgenstein, all that is worth saying is unsayable.

Lao Tzu began the most popular book in the Orient with that point, in the first line of the *Tao Te Ching:* "The Way that can be spoken is not the eternal Way." The last line of the dying protagonist in the greatest play ever written ("Hamlet") is: "The rest is silence." Pascal said that the whole of philosophy was not worth a half hour's trouble. Aquinas refused to finish his "Summa" because all that he had written was only "straw" compared with what he saw. (Cf. Wittgenstein's distinction between *saying* and *showing.)*

But why is *ethics* not sayable but only showable for Wittgenstein?

It is the ethical *dimension* that is not sayable in indicative propositions, because imperative conclusions cannot be derived from indicative premises alone. Value is not a kind of fact but another dimension, as color is not a kind of shape, or even a shade of grey, but another dimension.

The first line of the *Tractatus* is: **1. The world is all that is the case.** In other words, the world is the sum total of all facts, all true propositions, all declarative sentences. But ethics is not factual. It does not tell us how we do in fact behave. It tells us something wholly outside of facts: values, oughts rather than isses, imperatives rather than indicatives.

But for Wittgenstein ethics, not logic, is the meaning of life. Thus he says **that The sense (*Sinn,* meaning) of the world must lie outside the world. In the world everything is as it is and happens as it does happen. *In* it there is no value. . . . If there is a value which is of value, it must lie outside all happening and being-so. . . . Hence also there can be no ethical propositions** (indicative statements, declarative sentences).

Ethics cannot be expressed (if expression requires propositions). **Ethics is transcendental.** . . .

And, a little later, **The solution to the riddle of life in space and time lies** *outside* **space and time . . . even if** *all possible* **scientific questions be answered, the problems of life have still not been touched at all Is this not the reason why men to whom after long doubting the sense** (meaning) **of life became clear, could not then say wherein this sense consisted?**

And, a little later, **Not** *how* **the world is, is the mystical, but** *that* **it is.**

Thus we have three examples of "the mystical": (1) the ethical, (2) the meaning of life, and (3) existence itself. All three transcend propositional language: **There is indeed the inexpressible. This** *shows* **itself; it is the mystical.**

The *Tractatus* is a "show and tell"; and the "telling," which is scientific and logical, is there only to set off, by contrast, the "showing, which is *not* in the book." When a real mystic is actually "shown" a vision—the "beatific vision"—he does not write beautiful poems, as Dante did. (Dante was only a would-be mystic. Real mystics can't talk.) When Peter saw Christ's "transfiguration," he babbled nonsense about building three churches. When Pascal saw God as "fire," all he could say was "God of Abraham, Isaac and Jacob, *not* the God of philosophers and scholars." When Job saw God, he stopped his complaints and questions and simply said "I had heard about You with the hearing of the ears, but now I see You with my eyes." It's showing versus saying. Showing can't be said.

But it *can* be said that showing can't be said. Enter Wittgenstein.

The New Definition of Philosophy

What then can philosophy do? Not much. Wittgenstein's conception of philosophy is as tiny as that of the Logical Positivists and Logical Atomists. But his conception of reality is much larger. Philosophy is merely polishing the eyeglasses of the prisoners in the Cave. But reality is much larger than the Cave, unsayable, and unendurably bright.

Philosophy aims at the logical clarification of thoughts. Philosophy is not a body of doctrine but an activity. A philosophical work consists essentially of elucidations. Philosophy does not result in "philosophical propositions," but rather in the clarification of propositions.

The right method of philosophy would be this. To say nothing except what can be said, i.e., the propositions of natural science; i.e., something that has nothing to do with philosophy; and then always, when someone wished to say something metaphysical,[32] **to demonstrate to him that he has given no meaning to certain signs in**

---

32 Wittgenstein used "metaphysical" to mean not "more universal than physics" but "not physical at all." This is, of course, to accept California bookstores as your lexicographer, rather than Aristotle.

his propositions. This method would be unsatisfying to the other—he would not have the feeling that we were teaching him philosophy—but it would be the only strictly correct method. . . .

Most of the propositions and questions to be found in philosophical works are not false but nonsensical. Consequently we cannot give any answer to questions of this kind, but can only establish that they are nonsensical. Most of the propositions and questions of philosophers arose from our failure to understand the logic of our language.

As a matter of historical fact, Wittgenstein invented the whole program of Logical Positivism, in his twenties, before the Vienna Circle was even formed and long before Ayer wrote his *Language, Truth and Logic*. Yet his own personal philosophy, his concept of the most important purpose of philosophy, his values, his personality, and his temperament are all very far from that of any of the Positivists, none of whom had any sense of wonder and mystery whatsoever, much less mysticism. Yet the Positivist side of Wittgenstein was there too. He was a deeply divided man, like the Grand Canyon. Essentially, he gave philosophy up to the Positivists as something relatively trivial, and cared incomparably more about the trans-philosophical, which for him meant the trans-Positivistic. It included things like teaching children in rural Austria, and gardening in a monastery. His was an extreme version of Kant's claim to have shrunk reason to make room for faith. It was deeply respectful of faith, but it was far from the synthesis of reason and faith that was the main task of medieval philosophy.

Like Pascal, Wittgenstein had a philosopher's disdain of (what he saw as) philosophy. He once told a student, "A bad philosopher is like a slum landlord. It's my job to put him out of business." And Wittgenstein thought that pretty much all previous philosophers had been slum landlords.

So the right method of philosophy would make it impossible to write a book on philosophy. Yet the *Tractatus* is a book on philosophy. Did he not see that self-contradiction? Of course he did. So what did Wittgenstein claim for it? Two things: first, that it put all the "slum landlords" out of business; and second, that after that had been done it could lead us to the border of something higher than philosophy, a "seeing" and a "showing" rather than a "saying":

My propositions are elucidatory in this way: he who understands me finally recognizes them as senseless, when he has climbed out through them, on them, over them. (He must so to speak throw away the ladder after he has climbed up on it.)

He must surmount these propositions; then he sees the world rightly.

Whether (1) philosophy is only the logical analysis of language, as the Russell of the *Principia Mathematica* thinks, or whether (2) it leads to the "seeing" at the top of the "ladder" when it transcends itself, as Wittgenstein thinks, or whether (3) it is the

SOCRATES' CHILDREN, VOLUME IV: CONTEMPORARY PHILOSOPHERS

reflection on and clarification of unlimited, flexible "language games," as the later Wittgenstein came to believe, in all three of these cases philosophy is not any kind of science. The new logic prevents it from being that. It is not even anything *like* a science. It teaches nothing. It seeks not truth or wisdom but only clarity. It is an activity, not a result. It is a servant to science and perhaps other enterprises that use language. It is not the love of wisdom but the logical analysis of language. That is the view common to the early and the later Wittgenstein. That is his single most popular and influential legacy among all divisions of "analytic philosophers." The main function of philosophy is to be a *therapy* for the disease of linguistic confusion; and "linguistic confusion" means pretty much all of preanalytic philosophy.

The preface to the *Tractatus* begins by asserting that philosophy is an activity that analyzes problems rather than a doctrine that synthesizes answers, when it says:

The book deals with the problems of philosophy and shows, I believe, that the method of formulating these problems rests on the misunderstanding of the logic of our language. Its whole meaning could be summed up somewhat as follows: What can be said at all can be said clearly; and whereof one cannot speak, thereof one must be silent.

Thus the *Tractatus* begins with the same point it ends with, like the book of Ecclesiastes: "Vanity of vanities, says the preacher, all is vanity." And the content of the main points of these two books is similar too, as well as the form. Silence reigns both at alpha and omega.

The book will, therefore, draw a limit to thinking, or rather, not to thinking, but to the expression of thoughts; for in order to draw a limit to thinking we should have to be able to think both sides of this limit (we should therefore have to be able to think what cannot be thought).

The limit can, therefore, only be drawn in language and what lies on the other side of the limit will be simply nonsense.

Notice how similar this project of "drawing a limit to thinking" is to Hume's. It is the polar opposite of Plato's project, as symbolized in his parable of the "cave." It is also similar to Kant's project, which his successors logically criticized as self-contradictory, as Wittgenstein points out here. For in limiting thought by thought, Kant has to think the unthinkable, the "things-in-themselves."

It is effing the ineffable.

But Wittgenstein does not escape the same self-contradiction merely by transferring the limit from language to thought, for instead of thinking the unthinkable he has to say the unsayable. Russell waggishly put the problem thus: "After all, Mr. Wittgenstein manages to say a good deal about what cannot be said." And that is pretty much the same thing as thinking the unthinkable, especially if, as Wittgenstein himself argues in his later

Investigations, there is no thought without public language, there is no "private language."

But this apparent self-contradiction is the problem all the mystics struggled with, and Wittgenstein is quite aware of it, and, with total logical consistency, embraces the logical consequence that his own words about sense versus nonsense are nonsense, or "senseless"; but they are *useful* nonsense: **My propositions are elucidatory in this way: he who understands me finally recognizes them as senseless, when he has climbed out through them, on them, over them. (He must so to speak throw away the ladder, after he has climbed up on it.)** As Aquinas did to his "straw," which was piled much higher than Wittgenstein's.

This "useful nonsense" is not only nonsense, it is also useful. This severe limiting of thought (and language) is not wholly negative for Wittgenstein, as it was for Hume. For the sentence that immediately follows is: **He must surmount these propositions;** *then he sees the world rightly.* (Italics mine.) One renounces "saying" for the higher "seeing," as a saint would renounce the world for God, or as a mystic would renounce the clarity of reason for the "dark night" of faith.

The "saying" and the "showing" are exclusive of each other: **What can be shown cannot be said.** Yet one way in which what cannot be said (in words) can be shown is through words, at least negatively and indirectly (as Kierkegaard said, "by the *absence* of a system"). It is by showing the *failure* of words to express what can only be shown— in other words, by the "useful nonsense" of the *Tractatus* itself. It cannot say what cannot be said, nor can it show what cannot be shown, but it can show what cannot be said—or if not that, it can at least *say* that "what can be shown cannot be said."

So Wittgenstein is a wisdom-seeking, and even contemplative, person after all. He is even in a sense a wisdom-seeking and contemplative *philosopher,* even though he believes that philosophy itself cannot seek wisdom or contemplate. For his philosophy points beyond itself, invites us to climb a ladder, and at the top of the ladder we find not more analysis of language but an attempt, by Wittgenstein, to "show" and, on our part, to "see," something beyond language and analysis, some other dimension, some synthetic or intuitive vision that this analysis sets off as a frame sets off a picture or as darkness sets off light. Wittgenstein calls this "the mystical."

And the great surprise is that the relation between it and philosophy is exactly the opposite of what Russell and the other analytic philosophers think: It is not that philosophy is the light as opposed to "the mystical" as the darkness, but that philosophy is the darkness (the "nonsense") that sets off "the mystical" as the light.

Thus the whole rest of the *Tractatus* exists only to point to its last sentence, its single main point: **Whereof one cannot speak, thereof one must be silent.**

Wittgenstein wrote to Russell that he had missed the whole point of the *Tractatus:* **Now I'm afraid you haven't really got hold of my main contention, to which the whole business of logical propositions is only a corollary. The main point is the theory of what can be expressed** (gesagt) **by propositions—i.e., by language—(and,** which comes to the same, what can be *thought)* and what cannot be expressed by propositions, but only shown (gezeigt); which, I believe, is the cardinal problem of philosophy.

Wittgenstein had said in the *Tractatus* that **What can be shown cannot be said. And this is *real:* There is indeed the inexpressible. This *shows* itself; it is the mystical.**

For the last century, since the *Tractatus,* most analytic philosophers, even those who think of themselves as disciples of Wittgenstein, have been more disciples of Russell than of Wittgenstein.

Repudiating The *Tractatus*

The later Wittgenstein repudiated five important claims of the *Tractatus:*

(1) He repudiated its demand for a single ideal logical language (the language of *Principia Mathematica)* which would clear up all the confusions, ambiguities and errors inherent in ordinary natural languages that had seduced previous philosophers and that arose from **the misunderstanding of the logic of our language.** In the *Investigations* he admitted that **the crystalline purity of logic was, of course, not a *result of investigation*: it was a requirement.** It was a willed ideology that dictated the logic, not vice versa.

(2) He repudiated its simple "picture theory" of thought, according to which each thought is a picture that corresponds to the fact in the world that it pictures.

(3) He repudiated the "logical atomism" that this implies: analyzing "molecular" facts and statements into "atomic" ones, so that each "atom" is independent of the other. In the *Tractatus,* **The world divides into facts. Anyone can either be the case or not be the case, and everything else remains the same.** But in the *Investigations,* he argues: **What are the simple constituent parts of a chair? . . . it makes no sense at all to speak absolutely of the "simple parts of a chair."**

(4) And he repudiated the claim that this solved all the problems of philosophy once and for all. He had written in the *Tractatus:* **the truth of the thoughts communicated here seems to me unassailable and definitive. I am, therefore, of the opinion that the problems have in essentials been finally solved.** I think I hear Socrates gently laughing, from Heaven, when he reads this, and preparing to ask Wittgenstein a few little questions when he arrives. That would simultaneously be part of Socrates' Heaven and Wittgenstein's Purgatory.

(5) Perhaps the most important repudiation is an implicit one, but the one that is the most pervasive: whereas in the *Tractatus* logic contained life and dictated to life all its forms, in the *Investigations* it is the opposite: life contains logic and dictates to it what its forms shall be. Logic is a human instrument, a "language game" used for human purposes. It is a technique which, like all techniques, is invented and used for an end that has already been chosen, and chosen not by a computer but by a concrete human being

with desires, will and emotions and with a prior philosophy, an at least implicit world-view and a set of values. The technique cannot determine the philosophy because the philosophy has determined the technique. William James would be proud of this inversion.

However, the conception of philosophy as linguistic therapy remained. Wittgenstein wrote in the *Investigations* that **philosophical problems ... are, of course, not empirical problems; they are solved, rather, by looking into the workings of our language ... the problems are solved not by giving new information ... philosophy is a battle against the bewitchment of our intelligence by means of language.**

The *Philosophical Investigations: Übersicht*

One of the events that convinced Wittgenstein that the *Tractatus'* theory of language was mistaken was a conversation with an Italian economist at Cambridge, Piero Sraffa. According to the "picture theory of thought" in the *Tractatus,* every proposition must have the same "logical form" as the fact it pictures. When Wittgenstein explained this idea to him, Sraffa made the Neapolitan gesture of brushing his chin with his fingertips, a contemptuous gesture that implies something like "the F-word," something stronger than "baloney." Sraffa asked, "What is the logical form of *that?* " The history of modern British philosophy suddenly tottered.

What Wittgenstein was beginning to discover was something like what the Greeks meant by *logos.* Wittgenstein called it *Übersicht.* Translators rendered it "perspicacious representation." It was something "seen" by the mind as a whole, like a *Gestalt,* especially "seeing connections." It was synthetic rather than analytic. Wittgenstein learned the notion from Goethe. Goethe was repelled by the vision of the dead, mechanistic universe depicted by Newtonian science, where everything was as separate from everything else as one number was separate from another number. Goethe sought instead to "recognize living forms as such ... to perceive them as manifestations of something within" and to see the connections, similarities, or analogies between one living thing and another. Spengler, the anti-modernist German historian who wrote *The Decline of the West,* and who also influenced Wittgenstein, applied this to culture and formulated this contrast: "The means whereby to identify dead forms is mathematical law. The means whereby to identify living forms is analogy."

Analogy, remember, is the one human thought form computers simply cannot deal with. Analogy is also the key to both our theological language and the universe's cosmic hierarchy according to Thomas Aquinas. Wittgenstein was repudiating Russell's scientism and was learning that poetry could be as true as science. He said, **I am in a sense making propaganda for one style of thinking as opposed to another. I am honestly disgusted with the other. ... People nowadays think that scientists exist to instruct them, but poets, musicians, etc. to give them pleasure. The idea *that these have something to teach them*—that does not occur to them.**

Real life certainly taught Wittgenstein that the logical atomism of scientific propositions was not the way anyone learns language. **When we first begin to *believe* anything, what we believe is not a single proposition, it is a whole system of propositions. (Light dawns gradually over the whole.)**

Philosophical Investigations: "Imponderable Evidence"

A concept similar to, or perhaps a subdivision of, or even perhaps identical to, *Übersicht* in the *Philosophical Investigations* is the concept of "imponderable evidence." This is one of the many aspects of the *Investigations* that Wittgenstein must have learned from his real-life experiences teaching children in rural Austria rather than in intellectual arguments with professional academics at Cambridge.

Is there such a thing as "expert judgment" about the genuineness of expressions of feeling? —Even here there are those whose judgment is "better" and those whose judgment is worse.

Correcter prognoses will generally issue from the judgments of those with better knowledge *(kennen,* not *wissen)* of mankind.

Can one learn this knowledge? Yes; some can. Not, however, by taking a course in it, but through "experience."—Can someone else be a man's teacher in this? Certainly. From time to time he gives him the right *tip.*—This is what "learning" and 'teaching' are like here.—What one acquires here is not a technique;[33] one learns correct judgments. There are also rules, but they do not form a system, and only experienced people can apply them right. Unlike calculating rules.

It is certainly possible to be convinced by evidence that someone is in such-and-such a state of mind, that, for instance, he is not pretending. But "evidence" here includes "imponderable" evidence. . . .

Imponderable evidence includes subtleties of glance, of gesture, of tone.

I may recognize a genuine loving look, distinguish it from a pretended one (and here there can, of course, be a "ponderable" confirmation of my judgment). But I may be quite incapable of describing the difference. And this is not because the languages I know have no words for it. For why not introduce new words?—If I were a very talented painter I might conceivably represent the genuine and the simulated glance in pictures.

Ask yourself: How does a man learn to get a "nose" for something? And how can this nose be used?

This "imponderable evidence" is the kind of power of judgment we all have and use in both life and the arts, as distinct from the sciences. Wittgenstein has overcome the

---

33 See the book recommended in the last sentence of ch. 79, William Barrett's *The Illusion of Technique.*

"bewitchment" that the success of modern science has used to lure so many modern philosophers into the fly-bottle.

Wittgenstein's favorite novel was Dostoyevski's *The Brothers Karamazov.* He wrote of its hero the wise old Father Zossima: **It was said that, by permitting everyone for so many years to come to bare their hearts and beg his advice and healing words, he had absorbed so many secrets, sorrows, and avowals into his soul that in the end he had acquired so fine a perception that he could tell at the first glance from the face of a stranger what he had come for, what he wanted and what kind of torment racked his conscience.** Wittgenstein added: **There really have been people like that, who could see directly into the souls of other people and advise them.** Remember, Wittgenstein lived among monks, as their gardener.

Philosophical Investigations: "Language Games"

The most obvious change from the *Tractatus* to the *Investigations* is the change from (A) trying to solve philosophical problems by transforming ordinary language into a single ideal logical language, the language of Russell's "logical atomism" in *Principia Mathematica,* to (B) trying to solve philosophical problems by (1) a more flexible and pragmatic approach (2) not in an artificial "ideal language" but an analysis of ordinary language (3) based on the theory that language is like a game and that (4) there are many useful "language games," in which (5) **the meaning is the use.** (These are not five distinct points but five aspects of the same one.)

Notice that although the means has changed very sharply, the end is the same: the solving of philosophical problems by dissolving them, showing that they arise from a misunderstanding of language.

Wittgenstein used the image of the fly in the fly bottle as an image for his philosophical program. (He is uncanny at finding arresting and unforgettable images.) In his native Austria flies were often caught not by flypaper but by putting some honey in an open vinegar bottle to lure the fly in. It then either drowns in the vinegar or kills itself dashing itself against the walls of the bottle to try to get out. Wittgenstein said that his philosophical strategy was to **show the fly the way out of the fly bottle,** which was the same way it came in, through the neck—which symbolizes the **bewitchment** (misunderstanding) **of language.**

Can the great philosophical questions be resolved this way? That's questionable. *Have* they been? That's not questionable. They haven't.

To explain his new theory of "language games," and the idea that meaning is relative to use, Wittgenstein used a number of analogies. (Analogies, remember, are something Russell's logic makes no room for). One of them was the idea of games as such. Languages are humanly invented activities, not objectively given entities like planets, and therefore **A word or sentence *has the meaning it has because someone has given it* that, and not because it has some power independent of us. If we wish to know or**

comprehend its significance, we must examine . . . how this word or sentence is actually used. It's empirical and a posteriori, not theoretical and a priori. Meaning is discovered only by observation: **Don't think, but look!** We use the same item—a ball, e.g.—in different games, and the different rules of each game result in different uses for the ball, and therefore different meanings for the ball. The meaning is inside the game, not outside it. Wittgenstein wrote: **The question: "What is a word really?" is analogous to "What is a piece in chess?" . . . the meaning of a piece is its role in the game.**

He also used the analogy of a tool box. **Think of the tools in a tool-box: there is a hammer, pliers, a saw, a screwdriver, a rule, a glue-pot, glue, nails and screws. The functions of words are as diverse as the functions of these objects.** Words are tools, and each tool has a different function. So do words. The meaning of a tool is its function, and its function is its use. Thus we use words, as we use tools, for a great variety of "games," for **language is part of an activity, or a form of life. Review the multiplicity of language-games in the following examples, and in others: Giving orders, and obeying them—Describing the appearance of an object, or giving its measurements—Constructing an object from a description (a drawing)—Reporting an event—Speculating about an event—Forming and testing a hypothesis—Presenting the results of an experiment in tables and diagrams—Making up a story; and reading it—Play-acting—Singing catches** (rounds)**—Guessing riddles—Making a joke; telling it—Solving problems in practical arithmetic—Translating from one language to another—Asking, thanking, cursing, greeting, praying.**

Since "the meaning is (in) the use," we communicate the meanings of our words to each other by use, and therefore by *showing,* not simply by *saying.* I do not *explain* the word by other words, as the dictionary does—that is just linguistic tautology, like the new logic. That is not how we in fact learned the meaning of our language. I *show* you the meaning by what I do, how I live and act, how I follow the implicit rules of my "language game." Augustine makes a similar point in *On the Teacher.*) In real life, pragmatics determines semantics and semantics determines syntax, rather than the other way round. But it is the other way round in the new logic of analytic philosophy.

Wittgenstein uses another memorable image for the theory of language: **Our language can be seen as an ancient city: a maze of little streets and squares, of old and new houses, and of houses with additions from various periods; and this surrounded by a multitude of new boroughs with straight regular streets and uniform houses.** Descartes had used the very same analogy, at the beginning of his *Discourse on the Method,* to make the exactly opposite point: the need to level out all the crooked streets and old houses, which had accumulated in layers of tradition, and to create a single perfectly clear, rational, streamlined city of philosophy by the new scientific method. The attitude toward that project is the difference between the *Tractatus* and the *Investigations.*

One sign of this difference is the amazing number of *questions* in the *Investigations.* No other great book in the history of philosophy not written in dialog form contains such a large percentage of questions among its propositions, except Augustine's *Confessions.*

Philosophical Investigations: "Family Resemblances"

What Aquinas meant by "the analogical use of terms" is what Wittgenstein calls "family resemblances." This is a crucial addition to the limitations on language imposed by his earlier theory. The meanings of a single word in different "language games" are neither simply the same (what the old logic called "univocal") nor simply different (what it called "equivocal") but partly the same and partly different (this is what it called "analogical"). And we cannot simply separate out the samenesses from the differences, the constants from the variables, and come up with some parts of the meaning that are simply the same, or univocal, and others that are totally different, or equivocal:

Instead of producing something common to all that we call language, I am saying that these phenomena have no one thing in common which makes us use the same word for all—but that they are *related* to one another in many different ways.[34] And it is because of this relationship, or these relationships, that we call them all "language." I will try to explain this. Consider for example the proceedings that we call "games." I mean board-games, card-games, ballgames, Olympic games, and so on. What is common to them all?—Don't say: "There *must* be something common, or they would not be called "games"—but *look and see* whether there is anything common to all.—For if you look at them you will not see something that is common to *all*, but similarities, relationships, and a whole series of them at that. To repeat: don't think, but look!— Look for example at board-games; here you find many correspondences with the first group, but many common features drop out, and others appear. When we pass next to ball-games, much that is common is retained, but much is lost. . . .

And the result of this examination is: we see a complicated network of similarities overlapping and criss-crossing: sometimes overall similarities, sometimes similarities of detail.

I can think of no better expression to characterize these similarities than "family resemblances"; for the various resemblances between members of a family: build, features, colour of eyes, gait, temperament, etc. etc. overlap and criss-cross in the same way.—And I shall say: 'games' form a family. . . .

One might say that the concept "game" is a concept with blurred edges.

This is "fuzzy logic," something absolutely necessary for real-life conversation. But it applies to *terms,* not propositions; while the "non-fuzzy," "black-or-white," "either

---

34 Aquinas give the example of "healthy," which can be predicated of a body, as *having* health, or a good food or climate, as *a cause* of bodily health, or healthy urine as an *effect* and *sign* of bodily health. And Plato used "healthy" analogically when he called justice "health of soul." Justice is to the soul what health is to the body.

true or false" law of non-contradiction, the fundamental law of all logic, applies to propositions, not terms.

That is why Descartes's insistence on "clear and distinct ideas" (terms) is such a mistake, and leads to such "fly in the bottle" puzzles as the "mind-body problem." The problem was produced by the fly's entrance into the bewitching bottle of mathematically-clear, computer-like, univocal language and its demand for "clear and distinct ideas," namely the clear concept of mind as "non-spatial, thinking substance" vs. the clear concept of body as "spatial, non-thinking substance"—two concepts that do not come from our actual use of those words, and experience of these things, in life. They came from ignoring Wittgenstein's advice: *Look,* **don't think**—or, in other words, be a novelist, not a mathematician.

Another example is the term "religion." We all intuitively understand that Buddhism and Confucianism are religions while Platonism and Communism are not; yet Platonism admits a God while Buddhism and Communism do not, so "religion" can't mean "belief in a God." That's too narrow. But it can't mean "belief in some absolute" either, because that's too broad, and applies to Communism at least as much as to Confucianism. The term is analogous.

Philosophical Investigations: the "No Private Language" Argument

This argument is the part of the *Investigations* that has become the most famous and the most universally accepted among analytic philosophers. And the very probable reason for this is that it is often misunderstood as not merely denying Cartesian dualism (which it does) but as affirming materialism and behaviorism instead—which was definitely *not* Wittgenstein's intention or belief. In denying that there is a private language and a private meaning, a room in the mind like a private cinema, that is unconnected to the public world, Wittgenstein is not denying that mind exists, any more than he is denying that language exists, only that either one is wholly "private."

What he means by a "private language" is not a private code, or a language spoken by only one person to himself, like a hermit. He means a language that cannot be shared with others because it refers to the individual subject's private experiences. That would not be a *language* at all. He does not deny private experiences, like pain; he denies that there is no way to communicate them. There is. Even "the mystical" can be communicated, though not defined. Mysticism is *not* a "private language."

Since Descartes, we have tended to think that the private is prior to the public in time, because the existence of the private self or mind was *proved* prior to proving the existence of the public world, by Descartes's "Cogito ergo sum." Wittgenstein, like most psychologists, says that the process of knowing works in exactly the opposite way: we know ourselves and other selves only as a function of knowing our common public world. This is what Thomas Aquinas taught too: that we, unlike angels, can know ourselves only after we first know things in the world; then we reflect on the act of knowing, and finally on the self behind it.

(Actually, Descartes's proof of the self *before* proving the world did not purport to be a descriptive psychology of the process of knowing, only a logical process of proving. Often, we prove at the end what came first in time—e.g., from the fingerprint we claim to prove the finger, or from the creation we claim to prove a Creator.)

The idea that there is no private language is closely connected with the idea that "the meaning is the use." We know invisible mental meanings only by publicly visible bodily uses of these meanings. It's not that thought *is* merely bodily behavior, but it is *known* only through bodily behavior.

That Wittgenstein was not a materialist or a behaviorist is evident from such quotations as these: **Why should I deny that there are mental processes?** And **My attitude toward him is an attitude toward a soul.** His point is simply that we know these mental processes or souls only through the visible behavior they inspire and structure. They "show" themselves rather than "say" themselves.

Wittgenstein is concerned to reject the notion that thoughts are things (as in Locke: "idea = object of knowledge"). This is an example of "the fallacy of misplaced concreteness," treating something we have abstracted from a concrete thing or action as if it were itself a concrete thing or action. And this is the point taught by Aquinas (in ST I, 85, 2): that an idea is not the first object understood but the mode or way or instrument for understanding real things.

The Dimensions of "the Mystical"

So how to sum up Wittgenstein's main positive point? The point is not something we can put into propositions (declarative sentences), but it is something we can use propositions to point *to*. And there are many examples or instances of this "point," which Wittgenstein calls "the mystical":

(1) The personal, knowing subject. **The subject does not belong to the world;**[35] **rather, it is a limit of the world. The philosophical self is not . . . the human body or the human soul, with which psychology deals, but rather the metaphysical subject, the limit of the world, not a part of it.**

(2) Music. Beauty, especially in music, was an important part of "the mystical" for Wittgenstein. He once said: **It is impossible for me to say one word in my book about all that music has meant in my life. How then can I hope to be understood?**

(3) The ethical, i.e., all value, including "the meaning (or value) of life." This too transcends the world, for the world is simply all facts, and values are not facts. **When *all possible* scientific questions have been answered, the problems of life remain completely untouched. . . . The solution to the problem of life is seen in the vanishing of**

---

35 This is a startling point. If "the world" means Nature, this means that the self is supernatural. For the world is the sum total of objects, and the subject is not an object, not one of those things in the world.

the problem. **(Is not this the reason why those who have found after a long period of doubt that the sense** *(Sinn,* "meaning") **of life became clear to them have then been unable to say what constituted that sense? There are indeed things that cannot be put into words. They** *make themselves manifest.* **They are what is mystical. . . .**

The sense of the world must lie outside the world. In the world everything is as it is, and everything happens as it does happen: *in it* **no value exists—and if it did exist, it would have no value. If there is any value that does have value, it must lie outside the whole sphere of what happens and is the case. And so it is impossible for there to be propositions of ethics . . . ethics cannot be put into words. Ethics is transcendental**.

Wittgenstein wrote to the publisher for the *Tractatus:* **My book's point is an ethical one. I once meant to include in the preface a sentence which is not in fact there now but which I will write out for you here, because it will perhaps be a key to the work for you. What I meant to write, then, was this: My work consists of two parts: the one presented here plus all that I have** *not* **written; and it is precisely this second part that is the important one.**

(4) The aesthetic in general, which is in some sense equal to ethics: **Ethics and aesthetics are one and the same.** They are both *values* (though not wholly the same kind).

(5) The eternal, which is another commonality between the aesthetic and the ethical: **The work of art is the object seen** *sub specie aeternitatis* (under the aspect of eternity from an eternal perspective)**; and the good life is the world seen** *sub specie aeternitatis.* **This is the connection between art and ethics.**

(6) The present moment, which is more like eternity than like past-to-future time. To live in the present is to live "sub specie aeternitatis."

(7) The peace and happiness this life brings: **Whoever lives in the present lives without fear and hope . . . I will mention another experience straight away which I also know and which others of you might be acquainted with: it is what one might call the experience of feeling** *absolutely safe.* **I mean the state of mind in which one is inclined to say "I am safe, nothing can injure me whatever happens"** (because one is living in the present only, or because one is transcending time altogether and seeing from a God's-eye point of view).

(8) Wonder at existence, which Wittgenstein also connects with what he (strangely and perhaps misleadingly) calls the aesthetic: **Aesthetically, the miracle is that the world exists. That what exists does exist . . .** *I wonder at the existence of the world.* **And I am then inclined to use such phrases as "how extraordinary that anything should exist" or "how extraordinary that the world should exist."** (Compare Heidegger's "fundamental question" "Why does anything exist rather than nothing?")

In other words, "the mystical" is just about everything interesting in human life.

A final proof of Wittgenstein's distance from the positivism and materialism typical of analytical philosophers is his critique of the technological civilization they loved. This was written in 1930 for a forward to *Philosophical Remarks* but not published. The first sentence recalls Augustine's reluctance to publish his *Confessions* because most readers "have not their ear to my heart where I am what I am." **This book was written for those who are in sympathy with the spirit in which it is written. This is not, I believe, the spirit of the main current of European and American civilization. The spirit of this civilization makes itself manifest in the industry, architecture and music of our time, in its fascism and socialism, and it is alien and uncongenial to the author . . . the spectacle which our age affords us is not the formation of a great cultural work, with the best men contributing to the same great end** (as in the Middle Ages), **so much as the unimpressive spectacle of a crowd whose best members work for purely private ends. . . .**

I have no sympathy for the current of European civilization and do not understand its goals, if it has any. So I am really writing for friends who are scattered throughout all the corners of the globe.

It is all one to me whether or not the typical western scientist understands or appreciates my work, since he will not in any case understand the spirit in which I write. Our civilization is characterized by the word "progress". . . . It is occupied with building an ever more complicated structure. And even clarity is sought only as a means to this end, not as an end in itself. For me on the contrary clarity, perspicuity are valuable in themselves (as in the classical tradition of Aristotle and Aquinas, where contemplation of Truth is the *summum bonum).*

So I am not aiming at the same target as the scientists and my way of thinking is different from theirs.

"Analysts" cannot endure such words from their hero, so they ignore or discount them. Wittgenstein's supreme achievement may have been this: to have been as radically misunderstood as any philosopher since Socrates

91. Edmund Husserl (1859–1938)

Husserl was the founder of a very popular new school (or rather, a new method) of philosophy, "phenomenology," which dominated the continent of Europe throughout the twentieth century almost as much as analytic philosophy dominated English-speaking countries. Like Existentialism and analytic philosophy, phenomenology is more a method than a doctrine or set of results, so that we find it used by different philosophers with very different results, for instance realists and idealists, religious and non-religious, more rationalistic and more skeptical philosophers.

Unfortunately, phenomenologists are not usually much fun to read. This is especially true of Husserl. He is agonizingly careful. He invents a new technical terminology. He concentrates not on the most interesting divisions of philosophy: ethics, politics, aesthetics, and the philosophy of religion, the realms of values and practice, or even anthropology or metaphysics in the traditional sense, but rather epistemology.

Life

Husserl was born in Moravia in what is now the Czech Republic (then the Austro-Hungarian Empire) to a non-religious Jewish family. Unlike most philosophers, he was not a child prodigy or even a good student at school. His early interests were in mathematics, which he studied at the University of Vienna. The neo-Scholastic Franz Brentano turned him toward philosophy, and to the idea that philosophy should be a rigorous science that explored and justified the foundations in consciousness for all the other sciences. From Brentano Husserl also picked up the crucial notion that all cognition is intentional, i.e., a sign of something other than itself—a notion implicit in medieval Scholastic philosophy, with its epistemological realism.

Husserl influenced a very large number of major Continental philosophers in the first half of the twentieth century, including Sartre, Heidegger, Marcel, Levinas, Ricoeur, Von Hildebrand, Dilthey, Scheler, Edith Stein, Merlou-Ponty, Blondel, Koyre, and Gadamer, all of whom used some version of his phenomenological method.

In 1936 he was deprived of his teaching license by the Nazis because of his Jewish ancestry, with the approval of his former student Heidegger, who became rector of the University of Freiburg. He died in Freiburg in 1938.

The Search for Certainty and the Crisis of Reason

Bergson says that every philosopher, throughout his lifetime, says only one thing in all his works. Husserl's essential quest was for the same thing Descartes sought above all:

certainty. He sought the absolutely unquestionable and indubitable foundations of all human knowledge. (Thus Husserl's first major work is called *Cartesian Meditations.)* However, Husserl did not agree that the Cartesian program or system attained that certainty, though he would classify his earlier philosophy, like Descartes's, as a kind of Rationalism.

This was not only a theoretical quest for Husserl. He thought that the crisis of reason which had developed in modern philosophy, with its scientific Positivism, naturalism, and materialism in its implied metaphysics (or anti-metaphysics) and its skepticism, subjectivism, and historical or psychological relativism in its epistemology, would spell the doom of Western civilization. (Though he was not a political theorist or activist, it is obvious that he was thinking of the lack of rational foundations to combat irrational totalitarianisms of both Right and Left.) The title of his last book was *Philosophy and the Crisis of European Man* (1935). The "crisis" was the loss of faith in any absolutely certain objective truth. Not only was rational certainty necessary for society, it was also necessary for the individual "existentially." Husserl wrote that without certainty, **I cannot love, I cannot bear life unless I believe that I shall achieve it.** Phenomenology was essentially the attempt to re-establish that certainty on a new basis, with a new method.

Husserl's own eventual verdict on his passionate attempt was that it was a failure. Though the phenomenological method proved very useful for a wide variety of philosophers and a wide variety of topics, it did not give the absolute certainty Husserl sought, nor could it establish the foundations of all the other sciences as he had hoped. During the last part of his life he used it for a different end: to explore the "life-world" *(Lebenswelt)* of ordinary experience, a more modest task for which it has proved to be much more useful, especially for the value dimensions of human experience.

"To the Things Themselves"

The central slogan of Husserl's "phenomenology" at the beginning is "to the things themselves." This means essentially an objective rather than a subjective look, following the intentionality of cognition and carefully describing the essential natures of things as they appear immediately to consciousness. It opposes (1) Locke's Empiricism, which makes ideas the *objects* of consciousness, thus cutting us off from any immediate knowledge of "things in themselves," *and* (2) Hume's consequent skepticism, *and* (3) Kant's "Copernican Revolution" and its "transcendental idealism."

The *Epoche*

Husserl's alternative is a purely descriptive analysis of what is immediately given in our primary experience, the "phenomena" or "appearances." Husserl means by "phenomena" not merely empirical, sensory phenomena but also what immediately "appears" to the mind.

Husserl disagrees with Descartes's "clear and distinct" separation of mind from body. That is a construct of reason that is not *immediately given* in consciousness. In fact, all such theoretical constructs—all concepts, judgments, and causal reasoning that can be imposed on phenomena—are "bracketed" or set aside (Husserl uses the Greek word *epoché* for this "bracketing"), including the crucial question of epistemological realism vs. idealism, i.e., the question whether consciousness receives and knows real things as they are, as most pre-Kantian philosophers assumed, or constructs or constitutes its objects, as Kant contended. Like Descartes, Husserl insisted on beginning with *no presuppositions*.

"Eidetic Reduction"

Since he is trying to map the essential structures of consciousness, Husserl focuses especially on the *universals,* or "essences" ("forms") that are the immediate objects of the question "what is it?" Plato did the same; each Platonic dialog is about "what" something essentially is (justice, knowledge, love, etc.). However, Husserl does not construct a theory about the metaphysical status of these "essences" as Plato did in his Theory of Ideas, or Theory of Forms.

For Husserl, as for Plato, Aristotle and Aquinas, "form" means not the surface but the depth, not mere geometrical shape but essential nature. The test for whether any feature belongs to the essential form or is merely accidental is the intellectual imagination. Can we imagine x without y? If not, then y is the essence, or part of the essence of x; if so, then y is not essential but accidental to x. We can imagine a man without hair but not without reason; we can imagine color without redness but not without spatial extension. Husserl called this focus on essential forms *eidetic reduction* (from *eidos,* the Greek word for "form"). It tries to isolate what is constant and unchangeable, necessary, and universal in our knowledge as distinct from what is variable and changeable, contingent, and particular.

Intuition of Universals

Kant had made the same distinction and sought the same necessary and universal *a priori* forms in our experience; but what distinguishes Husserl from Kant is his acceptance of intellectual intuition. Kant had maintained that intuition—the immediate grasp of a cognitive object—is only sensory, not intellectual, while Husserl's phenomenological method seeks the intellectual "intuition" of "essences."

Most modern philosophers had been skeptical of the very notion of essences, forms, or universals, and our ability to know them—mainly because they had shrunk the notion of "reason" to reasoning or calculating (what the Scholastic philosophers called the "third act of the mind"). And since it is the "first act of the mind" ("simple apprehension" or intellectual intuition) that knows universals, most modern philosophers were skeptical of universals, which they reduced to names: they were Nominalists.

Like Hume, Husserl saw that Nominalism was compatible only with skepticism, not with certainty. Unlike Hume, he saw skepticism as intolerable and certainty as necessary. Like Descartes, Husserl began with a kind of *methodological* skepticism—the "bracketing"—precisely in order to overcome skepticism.

Like Descartes, he thought that if we begin with doubt, we may hope to end with certainty; but if we begin with certainty, unless we stop thinking we will end with doubt. Thus Husserl insists on beginning with no kind of presuppositions at all, whether from the history of philosophy, or from religious faith, or from the results of the natural sciences, or from any cultural or ideological or personal assumptions or orthodoxies.

The Phenomenological Method

Such phenomenological analysis is slow, careful, painstaking, and unlimited in scope. It cannot be finished. It does not produce "systems" of philosophy. It is like archeology rather than engineering; it explores the details in the earth of our experience rather than building skyscrapers or cities of ideas.

The method does not focus on singular concrete events or things that exist, but on essences, on universals. This requires a disciplined effort: "bracketing" not only the philosophical assumptions of both realism and idealism but also all the concrete things that seem at first most real and most interesting to our natural, uncritical way of thinking. We naturally prefer the concrete to the abstract. But "the abstract" and "the universal" here does not mean *theories*. Husserl seeks not *theories* but *data*. He would have agreed with Wittgenstein's advice: "Don't think; look!" Look for the *eidos*. Most people do not find this much "fun." If philosophers were rated by how much of a "fun read" they were, Husserl would be far from the top of the list.

Idealism or Realism?

Later in life Husserl changed his phenomenology from merely a method to a system that he called "transcendental phenomenology." It was somewhat like Kant's "transcendental " idealism. Kant explicitly rejected Berkeley's *metaphysical* idealism, but he was an *epistemological* idealist because his "Copernican Revolution" denied our access to the real ("things-in-themselves") and restricted our knowledge to the ideational, or what our consciousness had constructed and formed. Husserl thus chose to open the "brackets" that earlier had bracketed, contained and quarantined the realism-vs.-idealism question. Some other phenomenologists, like Von Hildebrand, opened the brackets the opposite way, not to idealism but to an epistemological realism.

Until he turned in this idealist direction, many of Husserl's discoveries coincided with what had become commonplace in medieval Scholastic, especially Thomistic, philosophy, e.g.,

(1) the distinction between logical and psychological laws,

(2) the logical distinction between meaning (comprehension) and reference (extension),

(3) the "moderate metaphysical realism" of universals,

(4) the epistemology of abstraction (of the universal from the particular and accidental), which is essentially what Husserl calls the "eidetic reduction,"

(5) the distinction between essence and existence (on the phenomenal level, though not the metaphysical level),

(6) intentionality (cf. *Summa Theologiae* I, 85,2), and

(7) the related distinction between the mental act and the mental object.

Overcoming Solipsism: Empathy

One of the most interesting issues in the later Husserl is how we know other minds, a problem philosophers had largely ignored until recently. The method of *epoche* puts us into a starting point that is like Descartes's, *viz.* a kind of solipsism (from *sole ipse,* "only oneself"). If we begin only with our own consciousness, how do we get out of it and into an epistemological realism and the real world?

There are two problems here. 1) In general, how do we build a bridge from the self and its immediate consciousness, which is the only thing that we start with, to other selves, and to the world? (2) And among all the things that appear to our consciousness, how do we distinguish other subjects, or persons, from mere objects, or things, without going beyond the phenomena and imposing a belief or theory upon the phenomena?

Husserl's answer to both questions is *empathy.* The other self presents itself to me through its body as another subject and not a mere object of my own subjectivity. By "empathy" I enter into that other's subjectivity, not by any special psychological gifts but by the simple realization that what is presented to me is another ego, another subject and not merely a phenomenon. "Empathy" is not a special talent or an emotion or a choice; it is a mode of consciousness given immediately and naturally to all of us.

This transcendence of solipsism depends on the fact that the other ego's *time* is not the same as my time, whereas all the other phenomena of my consciousness are. (Husserl is speaking of time now as Bergson did, as what Bergson called *duree:* as the lived time of experience, not the measured time of matter's movement through space.) I know that the other is other because I know that the "now" of my act of empathy with the other is not the same as the "now" of the other. Though they may occur at the same moment of objective and impersonal clock time *(kronos)* as measured by physics, they are subjectively different in real, lived time or personal time *(kairos).* My lived time and the other's lived time are two, not one; they *meet* at a common point of objective time. Simone Weil, Husserl's closest student and associate, who died in Auschwitz, explored and developed this notion of "empathy," which is close to the heart of what Buber called "the I-thou relationship" and what Levinas called "the Face-to-face."

91. Edmund Husserl (1859–1938)

"Life-world"

In concentrating on the "life-world," Husserl in his own later life-world expanded phenomenology from its original, more Cartesian, individual-ego-oriented perspective into an also intersubjective one, and finally into a holistic one in which the entire communal "life-world" becomes his new perspective. This would need to eventually include social, political, cultural, and global dimensions, though Husserl did not have time to pursue these. As phenomenology expanded, like a floodlight, it abandoned the "spotlight" hope of laser-like concentration on *eidos* and on scientific certainty. Husserl wrote, eventually: **Philosophy as science, as serious, rigorous, indeed apodictically rigorous science—the dream is over.**

So Husserl, like Wittgenstein and Heidegger (perhaps the three most original and important philosophers of the century), ends on a note of honest confession of failure.

92. Dietrich von Hildebrand (1889–1977)
(by Dr. Steven Schwarz)

Von Hildebrand took Husserl's phenomenology in two new directions: into an exploration of moral values and into a realist epistemology.

Life and Personality

Born in Florence of German parents, Von Hildebrand spent most of his young adult years in Germany, where he taught philosophy at the University of Munich. He was one of the first to see the evils of the Nazi ideology, and spoke out forcefully against it. When Hitler came to power he fled to Vienna because he refused to live in a country headed by a monstrous criminal. There he continued his uncompromising fight by founding a newspaper devoted to uncovering the evils of Nazism. With the fall of Austria, he fled through several European countries, the Nazis on his heels. He was at the top of Hitler's "hit list." He came to the United States in 1940, where he was professor at Fordham University until his retirement in 1959.

He was the most dynamic personality imaginable, full of life, always eager to engage others in sharing what he loved: religion, beauty (especially the music of Bach, Mozart and Beethoven), deep and important truths, and his extensive knowledge of history, literature and culture.

He was a member of the "Munich school of phenomenology," the realist version of the philosophy inspired by the early Husserl, whose motto was "Back to the things themselves." It is a philosophy consistent with common sense, based on the premise that we can know the things of the world as they are in themselves; that philosophizing means receptivity and faithfulness to reality as given to us in our immediate experience. It stands opposed to skepticism, reductionism, subjectivism, and relativism.

Husserl praised him as "a philosophical genius." However, von Hildebrand and other like-minded phenomenologists later broke with Husserl when the latter abandoned his earlier realism and turned toward a subjective idealism.

Big Idea #1: Three Basic Kinds of Good and Evil

It is often said that when we are motivated, it is always by the good (at least the apparent good). Von Hildebrand says this is not enough; the key question is: What *kind* of good is it that motivates us? He identifies three essentially different kinds of good and corresponding evil.

The first is *the merely subjectively satisfying.* For one person, who enjoys smoking, a cigarette is seen as a good because it is satisfying to him; for another person, who detests smoking, that same cigarette is seen as an evil because he finds it repulsive. From the point of view of this kind of "good," neither person is correct or mistaken, for in each case the "good" or "evil" is merely subjective. Objectively, of course, the cigarette is medically bad for the person who smokes it. But that shows exactly what this category of motivation is: it consists in ignoring the question of what is really, objectively good or bad. It is an approach to things concerned only with subjective satisfaction. Again, why does a person feel satisfied when a competitor suffers great harm, such as the loss of a job? Why does a person relish hurting another in order to "get even" with him? Why does revenge taste sweet to him? Far from being really good, all these things are really evil, but they can all seem attractive to a person, as subjectively satisfying.

But not all things in this category are evil; many are legitimate pleasures, such as delicious chocolate, a swim in cool water on a hot day, and a good rest when we are exhausted.

That is, for the merely subjectively satisfying, nothing in this category is good in itself. It is only an approach we can take, a way of being motivated, a point of view. It is the approach which sees its object exclusively as something satisfying or pleasing, either physically (e.g., overeating just because it tastes so good) or psychologically (e.g., relishing power over another). Not being good in itself, it is only good for the person who relishes it, not for another person; and perhaps good only now and not at another time. Again, not being good in itself, or objectively good, it is always something else: either really morally evil (revenge) or bad for the person (smoking), or good for the person (food that is not only tasty but nutritious), or neutral in all respects (tasty and merely harmless food).

The second, and by far the most important, kind of good is what von Hildebrand calls *value.* By this he does not mean what we usually associate with the term, a subjective element, as in what a person happens to value. Quite the opposite: he means what is good in itself, good objectively, that is, *intrinsic value.* He gives as an example of this **a generous action, a man's forgiving of a grave injury.** Another example of intrinsic value is the dignity of a human person. The value of his being as a person exists entirely in itself, independently of whether it is recognized and respected or not. If a person is shamefully mistreated in a Nazi concentration camp, the objective, intrinsic value he has as a person remains untouched. In this example we are struck by the terrible disharmony: his dignity, the objective value inherent in it, calls for an adequate response of respect—while the actual response given to him is directly opposite of this. This disharmony goes far beyond any suffering he may endure, or even whether he cares about his mistreatment; it is an objective, ethical, and even metaphysical, disharmony.

Von Hildebrand distinguishes two different value domains. one he calls ontological values: the value of being a person; the value of the being of an animal, which is higher than that of a plant, which in turn is higher than that of a rock. Another domain he calls qualitative values: above all, moral values, such as self-giving love, gratitude, forgiveness, compassion, generosity, moral courage, honesty, and humility; intellectual values, as in a genius; and aesthetic values, as in the beauty of nature, music, paintings, sculptures, and architecture. Unlike ontological values, qualitative values always have a negative counterpart or opposite, a disvalue such as injustice, meanness, hatred, and cruelty.

The third kind of good is *the objective good for the person.* Consider your health. What kind of good is it? It is a real good, an objective good, and not merely subjectively satisfying. And it is a good for you, and not an intrinsic value which has no "for you" in its essential nature as a good. Another example is a deep and loving friendship.

This category of good is closely related to that of value, in that some things are objective goods for you *because* they are first and foremost and in their nature intrinsic values. Being a loving person is primarily an intrinsic value, but if you are such a person this is *also* a great good *for you.* Other things, like health, do not have this character of intrinsic value; they are primarily and in their nature simply objective goods for the person.

We can see the meaning of this category by thinking about gratitude and forgiveness. What can I be grateful for? Not simply a value, but a real good *given to me.* What is the object of my forgiveness? Not a moral disvalue as such, but a real evil *inflicted on me.* So the subjectively satisfying is merely a subjective good, the intrinsically valuable is an objective good, and the objective good for the person contains both subjective and objective aspects.

For each of these categories of good there is a corresponding evil. Winning a game is subjectively satisfying; losing it, *subjectively dissatisfying.* Sickness, losing a friend, and being imprisoned are *objective evils for a person.* Injustice, dishonesty, and betraying a friend are moral evils; they are *intrinsic disvalues.* To be morally evil is also an objective evil for a person; the moral evil that is primarily and *in itself* a disvalue also has its effect *on that person.*

Von Hildebrand's treatment of good distinguishes sharply between two questions: how we may be *motivated* and what something is *objectively.* Each of the three categories of "good" represents a specific point of view in regard to how we may be motivated. Revenge can be seen as a "good" only from the point of view of the subjectively satisfying motivation; objectively it is an evil. To be lovingly disciplined is in reality an objective good for a child, but probably not a "good" to him from the point of view of his motivation. Someone gives me delicious chocolates: my point of view may see them as subjectively satisfying, or as objective goods for me for which I am grateful, or as expressions of the intrinsic value of the love the other person has for me, or all three. (The second and third kind of good—value and the good for me—correspond to what they are objectively.)

The notion of different points of view is crucial for understanding moral evil. Von Hildebrand's thesis is that moral evil is not, as has often been thought, a mistaken preference for a lower good over a higher good; it does not result from ignorance regarding what is really good (as Plato says). Rather, he says, it typically results from choosing what appeals to us as merely subjectively satisfying but is in reality morally evil. We adopt the point of view of the merely subjectively satisfying rather than that of what is objectively good. When Macbeth chooses to murder Duncan, he is not ignorant of the intrinsic value of his life; rather, he disregards this value and adopts the point of view of the merely subjectively satisfying. He is motivated by his intense desire to be the king, the satisfaction of his pride, ambition, and lust for power.

Big Idea #2: Value Response

Imagine the following: a child is trapped in a burning building. A stranger risks his life to save him. I am moved by the nobility of this deed, its objective, intrinsic value. My response is what Von Hildebrand calls *value response,* a response motivated by the objective value and importance of the deed. This notion is at the core of his ethical philosophy, in some way even at the core of his whole philosophy. **It is the fundamental fact that every being endowed with a value calls for a due and adequate response.** A contrasting example, equally a value response, is my being indignant at a terrible injustice. Here my value response is directed to the objective importance of a disvalue, something that should not be. But like the first case, my response is the response that *should be given,* that is *called for* by the value or disvalue. If it is not given, there is an objective disharmony. Another example of value response is our natural desire that truth be honored, that what we say should correspond to reality, expressed in the simple phrase that we should *tell it as it is.* The evil of lying stems largely from the violation of this "call to give the right response."

Giving the response due, the response called for by a value, brings into being a new value: the value of the value response itself. **Every value response is itself endowed with a value.** Where the value responded to is a *morally relevant value* such as a human person, justice, or truth, the new value is *a moral value.* When seeing the beauty of a majestic mountain or hearing sublime music, we can also recognize the call to respond in accordance with the value before us, even though there is no *moral* requirement to do so.

A value response can come from the heart, as when I am moved by the heroic deed of the rescuer; or it can come from the will, as when I resolve to resist doing a tempting moral evil. It should be noted again that a response to a value is a value response only if it is *motivated* by the objective and intrinsic importance of the value itself. If I refrain from doing a tempting moral evil out of respect for the value of moral integrity, it is a value response. However, if my motive in not doing the evil is simply a desire not to get in trouble, it is not a value response. In being motivated by the objective importance of a value in my value response, I *transcend* myself, I go beyond myself, I "step outside" myself. For Von Hildebrand the capacity to do this is one of the deepest and most significant features of human persons.

Von Hildebrand not only taught the idea of value response and its significance for ethics, indeed for all of life; he also *lived value response* in his daily life. His glowing kindness to others, his reverent listening to sublime music, and perhaps above all his courageous fight against the Nazis all attest to the concrete reality of value response in the person and life of Dietrich von Hildebrand.

The Three Spheres of Morality

In many ethical systems, morality is seen primarily, sometimes exclusively, as a matter of actions. In other systems, the focus is on moral virtues, such as being a loving, a generous, and a just person. For von Hildebrand these ethical systems are incomplete. Morality includes both these spheres, and even another one, so that there are three spheres in all.

(1) *The sphere of physical actions:* I rescue a drowning person. My action is the carrying out of an inner response, a value response motivated by the value of his continuing to be alive.

(2) *The sphere of spiritual responses:* This includes acts of will, such as renouncing evil or asking for forgiveness. It also includes affective responses, voices of the heart, such as a deeply felt gratitude or compassion for a suffering person. All these are value responses.

(3) *The sphere of virtues:* In contrast to the other two spheres, these go beyond the concrete moment in that they are lasting characteristics of a person, and are responses to an entire realm of goods. We say of someone that he is generous, grateful, humble, and loving.

In each of these spheres there is both a positive good and a negative evil counterpart. Murder is an evil and wrong action. Malicious joy at the suffering of another is an evil response. Vices such as stinginess, ingratitude, pride, and meanness are evil counterparts of moral virtues.

Each of these spheres is significant in itself. Virtues are not simply means to good actions, and actions are not simply signs of virtues or vices. Each is meaningful in itself.

Having a virtue implies ease in acting according to it. Think of the generous person who gives easily, in the sense that he does not need to struggle against contrary tendencies. This ease is radically different from the ease of a habit or skill. The virtue of generosity is a victory of value response, and represents a heightening of consciousness, a fully personal response. Habits and skills, in contrast, involve no value response and are a lessening of consciousness, something semi-automatic.

The Different Sources of Moral Values and Disvalues

How do moral values and disvalues arise? What is the source of their coming into being? In most of his writings von Hildebrand gave a single answer to these questions. Moral values arise from value responses to morally relevant values and disvalues, such as human persons, justice, and injustice. And moral disvalues arise from the failure to give an adequate value response or from giving a contrary response, as in cruelty, murder, and lying. But towards the end of his life he realized that there are actually other sources as well; that value responses and responses contrary to the call of values do not constitute the whole of morality. He enumerated a set of nine sources, starting with value response as the most important and basic source:

(1) Value response to morally relevant values. I rejoice at the conversion of an evil person. I respond to the value of justice by indignation at a great injustice.

(2) Treasures of goodness: forgiving a person who has injured me; showing mercy.

(3) The objective good for a person: for *another* person; concern for him for his sake.

(4) The objective good for a person: for *my own* person; gratitude for what I have received.

(5) Obedience to legitimate authority.

(6) Freely binding myself by promising something to another person.

(7) The sphere of rights: respecting the rights of a person because they call for such a response.

(8) The metaphysical situation of man. This refers to the limits each person has as a creature under the sovereignty of God. Thus mercy killing might be considered a value response of compassion to another who is suffering, but it is wrong because it violates this norm.

(9) Motives and actions: different combinations of morally good and non-moral *motives* with morally right and wrong *actions;* for example, a wrong action done from a morally good motive. Thus, not all moral evil is motivated by the merely subjectively satisfying.

As noted, the first of these sources—value response—is the most important, and it is implied in all the others. These others are rooted in the first, and they form supplementary sources.

Substitutes for Real Moral Norms and Virtues

Von Hildebrand adds a whole new dimension to ethics with his discovery that there is a realm of norms and qualities situated somehow in between what is genuinely morally good and right and what is morally wrong and evil. That is, people are sometimes guided in their moral thinking by various norms and qualities which may look genuinely moral but which are really only *substitutes* for real morality. They are a mixed bag. They each retain some moral element, some link to the moral sphere. Thus they may keep us from doing wrong, as when a person says "No, I can't do this. It would go against my honor." In such a case it is better that the wrong action is omitted, but the motive is here misplaced. And in other cases honor may not prevent a wrong action, and it may even prompt a wrong action, as in "honor killings." Such substitutes, even when they correlate with genuine moral norms and qualities, are a severe restriction of the whole of genuine morality. Some important substitutes are the following: pseudo-norms, seen as providing a code regarding what one ought to do and not to do:

(1) Honor: it can prevent some evils, but it does not prevent other evils, and it may even prompt some evils.

(2) Tradition: it can coincide with true morality, but it can also diverge, even dramatically, as in the claim by some of racial superiority over others.

(3) Laws of the state: the same applies here as with tradition (can coincide; can also diverge).

(4) Identifying morality with doing one's duty as the hard thing to do. (Kant and the Stoics: resisting "inclination.") This leaves out giving generously to another person, from one's heart, out of love, and delighting in doing so.

Pseudo-virtues, features of the character of a person that are good but not real moral virtues:

(5) Warmth of heart: as a value response it is a real moral value, but it is not the only one.

(6) Self-control: a necessary element in real morality but not a guarantee (a thief can have it).

(7) Courage: genuine moral courage is a real moral value but not the only one.

(8) Nobleness: avoiding what is mean and base is a real moral value but not the only one.

(9) Being genuine and sincere: necessary but not sufficient; one can be sincere about a wrong cause.

(10) Being broad-minded and tolerant: not always a moral value and surely not the only one.

Von Hildebrand's expose of these substitutes for true morality takes us beyond the realms of traditional ethics and provides us with a new clarity in showing us something that is really "relative" in the sense claimed by ethical relativism. By seeing that it is the substitutes that are really relative, we can better understand true morality.

The Heart: Spiritual Affectivity — Feelings

What is essential for being a human person? Is it intellect and will? Certainly, but Von Hildebrand adds that there is a third spiritual center: the heart as the seat of affective responses, spiritual feelings. Think of a deeply felt compassion for people who are suffering; a deeply felt gratitude to a person who saves your life; a deeply felt love for a child; being moved by the love another has for you; being moved by the beauty of sublime music. All these are just as spiritual and personal as an intellectual act of understanding or an act of will in resolving to do something. Animals are incapable of them just as they are incapable of abstract reasoning or free choice.

Like acts of the intellect and acts of the will, these are "intentional" responses: meaningfully directed at some reality. A judgment is implied. Just as I am convinced *that* people are suffering, so too I am horrified *that* they are suffering, indignant *at* the injustice that caused their suffering, and filled with compassion *for* them. All these terms—*at, for, that*—indicate the meaningful direction to the object. In this, spiritual feelings differ from bodily feelings. I am just tired; I am not tired at or about something. They also differ essentially from such non-spiritual feelings as euphoria or a jolly mood after drinking a bit too much. These are merely caused by certain factors; they do not incorporate a meaningful relation to an object such as gratitude to a person for a loving deed. They are not *about* anything objective outside themselves.

Consider compassion. There is the compassion of the person who *acts* to help suffering people but *feels* nothing; he does it purely from a sense of duty. Then there is the compassion of the person who acts and also feels deeply for the suffering people. His heart goes out to them, he is moved in the depth of his soul, he suffers with them. Doesn't the second add something of great significance? Granted, the feeling is not necessary for the action; and the feeling alone, with no action where action is called for, is not sufficient. Still, isn't the feeling also morally important? Can we not say that the fullness of compassion contains in its very nature a feeling, which is a type of response that is equal in its personal value and dignity to a response of the intellect or the will?

Von Hildebrand's incorporation of affectivity into ethics contradicts the philosophy of the Stoics, but not the (reliably commonsensical) philosophy of Thomas Aquinas: see *ST* I—II, 26–28, 59. No mere rationalist could ever have written those passages.

Freedom

In addition to freedom of action, which means I bring about a change in the world, Von Hildebrand identifies also another type of freedom. This consists in the stand I can take toward thoughts and feelings that arise within me.

Suppose feelings of hateful anger towards another person come over me. They arise on their own, not by my free choice; and I do not have the power to just annihilate them. But I can take a stand towards them; I can *disavow* them, saying an inner No to them, comparable to telling an unwelcome person to get out of my house. It is similar with feelings of envy, jealousy, and a thirst for revenge. They are in themselves morally evil positions; but since their arising in me is not in my direct free power, I am not morally responsible for their coming into being. However, I should disavow them, thereby creating an inner distance from them. This has the effect of "decapitating" them, thereby sparing me guilt. Failing to disavow them results in guilt by implicitly allowing them to become my own actual responses.

On the positive side, suppose a feeling of joy over the conversion of an evil person arises in me. I can and should explicitly *sanction* it to make it fully and consciously my own. Only then does such a feeling achieve its true significance and full moral worth.

The application of this principle especially to *sexual* feelings and desires would clarify much confusion today. The basic premise is that we are responsible *only* for what we have some control over, but we are responsible for *all* that we have some control over, whether it is internal or external.

Personalism

For Von Hildebrand, the greatest difference in the realm of concrete beings, apart from the incomparable difference between God, the Absolute, Infinite Being, and all finite beings, is that between persons and all impersonal beings. A person is a being who in his

241

very nature has the basic, inherent capacities to say "I," to have free will, to be morally good or evil, to know and understand, and to have spiritual response feelings such as joy and sorrow, love and compassion. This means that a person is a "spiritual" being in the true sense, in radical contrast to what is merely non-physical, as in an abstraction such as "humanity." A person has these basic capacities as a person, whether he can exercise them or not (e.g., a person in a coma or a pre-born child).

Each person is like a world unto himself in his conscious inner life, his thoughts and feelings. But von Hildebrand says a person realizes himself most fully in *self-transcendence:* when he "steps outside" himself, goes beyond himself, especially in value response. Though a person is the highest form of individual being, he is also called to go beyond himself and exist in communities with other persons on many different levels, such as marriage and family, friendships, religious communities, and nations. This is particularly true of the deep union with another person through love. Such a union is something far more profound and significant than the mere "fusion-union" of a drop of water that falls into the sea. The drop of water *loses* its entire individual being in the process; a *person's* being is *heightened* through a love union.

Love

To understand von Hildebrand's rich and original teaching on love, think of a deep friendship love, a deep love of a mother for her child, the sweet love of a child for his mother, or the deep love between a man and a woman that we call "being in love" or "falling in love." Von Hildebrand's view of love centers on four main things:

First, love is a *value response.* **It is essential for every kind of love that the beloved person stands before me as precious, beautiful, lovable,** and **as objectively being worthy of love.** This stands in contrast to seeing another person as *useful* to me.

Second, love is *a response from the heart.* **Love is essentially a voice of the heart.** In all forms of love **we always find this element of giving one's heart.** When the preciousness, beauty, and loveableness of the other touches me and engenders a response from me, it is my heart that is touched, and the ensuing response is from my heart. If my heart is not touched I do not really love the other person.

That love is a response from the heart does not mean there is no role for the will to play. (Aquinas defines the essence of love as "the will to the good of another.") Let us recall Von Hildebrand's notion of freedom. As applied to love it means that I can freely choose to say an inner yes or no to the love that is in my heart. By saying an inner yes I identify myself with that love and make it explicitly my own response. My love thus achieves a new character. It is my love in a new way, since it is now not merely the voice of my heart but of my whole being. What is originally given to me in my heart as gift now becomes fully my own active choice through the explicit inner yes of my will. The response of my will joins the response of my heart to form a new reality.

Third, love includes a yearning for union. Von Hildebrand calls this the *Intentio Unionis*. **Whoever loves also desires a spiritual union with the beloved person. He desires not only the presence of the other, not only knowledge of his life, his joys, his sufferings, but above all else a union of hearts that only mutual love can grant.**

The *Intentio Unionis* of love is not only a yearning for union with the beloved; it is also the power to bring about such a union, to make it a reality. The union of love is a union of mutual self-donation, or self-giving. And this mutual self-donation of love shows that my desire for union and the happiness it brings me is not something selfish. The self-donation of a value-responding love is the opposite of anything selfish; and the happiness I seek in love is sought equally for the other and for myself.

Fourth, there is the *Intentio Benevolentiae*. This means that my love desires all that is good for the happiness of the other, including my desire that I bring about that happiness by my love. And, like the other intention, it is also a power by which the good for the other is actually accomplished.

The *Intentio Benevolentiae* of love brings about a remarkable change in what I experience as objective goods for me. Von Hildebrand distinguishes here between two kinds of objective goods for me: direct and indirect. Direct objective goods for me are things such as my own health, beauty as I experience it, and the deepening of my own understanding of reality. Indirect objective goods for me are these kinds of good as they directly affect the person I love. That is, in being objective goods for the other (direct), they also become objective goods for me (indirect). This is part of the solidarity of love. That is, through the solidarity of love I have the same relation to goods and evils for the other person as I naturally have to the goods and evils that directly affect me in my own person. If a person I love deeply loses her child, it is a heavy loss primarily for her, but it is also, indirectly, a heavy loss for me. (Compare Aristotle and Augustine here, who both called a friend "the other half of my soul.")

A List of Some Major Original Insights

(1) Value response: Every objective, intrinsic value (and disvalue) calls for an adequate response, motivated by the importance of the value itself. Such responses are at the core of morality, and of everything deeply meaningful in human life.

(2) Three basic kinds of good: the merely subjectively satisfying; intrinsic, objective value; and the objective good for a person.

(3) Moral evil: It is not a mistaken preference for a lower good over a higher good. Rather, it is typically the choosing of an evil that appeals to us as merely subjectively satisfying.

(4) The three spheres of morality: actions, responses, and virtues.

(5) Substitutes for true morality: always a severe restriction of the whole of true morality.

(6) The heart: spiritual affectivity, spiritual feelings, meaningfully directed to an object.

(7) The super-actual: At a particular moment I think of a person I love; my love is actualized. But when I turn my attention to other matters and focus on them, my love does not cease to exist in me. It is still fully real, fully there; it continues to exist neither merely potentially nor actually but super-actually. It colors my every experience and tends towards actualization in thought, word and deed. other examples of the super- actual include sorrow over the death of a loved one, gratitude, and religious faith. The super-actual differs essentially from the unconscious and from mere abilities, like the ability to play the piano. A key application of this notion is the thesis that moral virtues are super-actual value responses to a whole sphere of goods.

(8) Superabundance. A medicine may be effective in restoring health. We have here a means-end relationship. The significance of the means lies entirely in its capacity to bring about the end. In contrast, a deep friendship may also be an effective means in enriching a person's life, but the relation here is radically different: the friendship is first of all significant in itself, as an intrinsic value. It then also *superabundantly* enriches a person's life. This an effect beyond its original meaning, and it will have that effect only if it is seen in this original meaning as a value. Seeing it as a mere means would destroy both its meaning and such an effect.

(9) Active/passive/receptive. When I do something, I'm being active. In contrast, when I lie on the table undergoing surgery, I'm being passive. There is a third case: receptivity, as when I listen intently to beautiful music and let it fill my soul. Receptivity is not passivity.

(10) *Objectivity* is not the same thing as *neutrality*. Objectivity calls for giving the right response, such as deep feelings of sorrow and indignation at the killing of young children. Neutrality here would be the opposite of objectivity. Neutrality is called for in some cases, such as a trial judge; here it would be the right response, and because of this it is *also* objective.

In all these original insights, von Hildebrand, though he begins with traditional philosophies, takes us beyond what they have shown us, providing us with a new clarity about these important topics.

Von Hildebrand's most important works include:
Ethics
Graven Images: Substitutes for True Morality
The Heart: An Analysis of Divine and Human Affectivity
The Nature of Love
Man and Woman
Morality and Situation Ethics
The New Tower of Babel
What is Philosophy?
See also the biography by his wife Alice von Hildebrand (also an important philosopher in her own right), *The Soul of a Lion (2000).*

93. Paul Ricoeur (1913–2005)

Ricoeur was one of many philosophers after Husserl who used his phenomenological method. A second major influence was Marcel. One of the most wide-ranging of all modern philosophers, Ricoeur had lasting influence on hermeneutics, literary criticism, Biblical interpretation, the study of mythology, philosophy of history, politics, law, linguistics, psychoanalysis, and psychology.

He was an enormously popular teacher at the Sorbonne, and helped found a new university at Nanterre, where he was forced to call in the police to quell violent riots by radical left-wing students. This hurt his reputation and his relation with the government, and he was forced to resign (though he himself was a moderate left-wing socialist and a pacifist). He then taught in Belgium (Louvain), America (Chicago), and Canada (Toronto), returning to Nanterre later. He lived and worked well into his nineties and many of his most influential works were written after his retirement.

Because of his positive, hopeful, and implicitly religious perspective, he appeared to many in France as a counter-cultural light in dark places, as Bergson had done to the previous generation. His approach was always to affirm, to include, to build bridges, rather than to confront, to refute, or to destroy (or deconstruct). He is iconoclastically counter-cultural precisely by *not* being an iconoclast like Derrida. Instead of "a hermeneutic of suspicion" or Descartes's "universal methodic doubt," he used a kind of universal methodic trust. Like the ancients, he thought philosophy should begin in wonder rather than doubt. But he used the very careful and critical detailed method of phenomenology to establish his positive conclusions.

I here summarize not all of Ricoeur—that would require too many pages—but a few of his "big ideas" which readers are likely to find both memorable (because surprising) and useful (in fact, possibly life-changing). Like most phenomenologists, he specializes in careful, detailed descriptions, or "maps," of experience which, although they are as useful as road maps, are usually also as dull as road maps. That is one reason I do not detail them here.

If there is a single "big idea" or unifying principle in all Ricoeur's works, it is a method of hermeneutics (the science of interpretation) which, instead of "deconstructing" the meaning of words to find them deceptive, draws out their depths of hidden meanings. His attitude toward language is Hamlet's attitude toward the universe: there are "more things in heaven and earth than are dreamed of in your philosophy." For a "hermeneutic of suspicion," there is less.

A fundamental problem of hermeneutics (perhaps *the* fundamental problem) is often called "the hermeneutical circle": it is that the assumption behind the act of interpreting any text or discourse is that it points to some meaning outside of itself (that it is "intentional," as Husserl would say), and *that,* in turn, assumes that the real world, or real life, which the meaning of the text intends, is itself inherently meaningful. The text can encompass and define the world only if the world encompasses and defines the text.[36] Ricoeur's solution to this logical problem of arguing in a circle is simply to accept it; that it is not a "vicious circle" but a "virtuous circle." We live in this circle and should not demand to escape from it.

Philosophy of the Will is a phenomenological addition and correction to Husserl, who, Ricoeur claims, like Descartes, failed to understand the passions and the dependence of the mind on the body. Ricoeur defends the freedom of the will but insists that this freedom is always limited and confronted by some "necessity," which is caused by the body's influence on all spiritual acts, even the purely intellectual "I think."

Ricoeur tries to demonstrate that in this world a human soul is impossible without a body. He uses Marcel's notion of the body: I do not *have* a body, as Descartes thought, I *am* a body, just as I am a soul. The "mind-body problem" cannot be not an objective "problem" to be solved but can only be a "mystery" that I cannot detach myself from and observe as if I were out of my body (or out of my mind!).

This helps Ricoeur explain evil. Human nature is not inherently evil but it is inherently fallible, or able to fall into evil, because of the potentially unstable relation within it between free and voluntary reason and will on the one hand and the involuntary body and passions on the other hand. Ricoeur describes this relation by the geological analogy of a "fault line," an inherent weakness in the makeup of our earthy nature that allows (but does not necessitate) conflict and rebellion.

Another memorable theme in this long book is the use of phenomenology to explain *feelings* in an illuminating way. Feelings are a topic that philosophers, being "intellectuals," tend to ignore. Human feelings are at the same time both intentional, actively directed outward at something other than myself, and also "affective" or passive (they "affect" me). It is only by an act of mental abstraction that we can separate either one of these two dimensions of feelings from the other. When I feel love for you, I cannot love without directing my love to *you,* but I also cannot be conscious of you without being affected by my feeling of love.

There is an important application to ethics: to be a fully good person we need to be rightly affected, to *feel* love (Ricoeur calls it "a preferential outlook") for what is truly good and lovable, as well as to actively and freely direct love to the right objects and persons. Even though this aspect of feeling is not directly voluntary and free, it is part of

---

36 This is similar to the "gnoseo-ontological circle," or the dialectic of realism and idealism: we cannot affirm being independent of knowing because "affirming" *is* knowing; and we cannot affirm knowing independent of being because knowing must *be* in order to know.

a whole human goodness. Saints have not only deliberate rational charity but also spontaneous compassion. Von Hildebrand also took up this theme, an important addition to the more rationalistic picture of the ethical person that we find in classical moralists like Plato, Aristotle, and the Stoics.

In *The Symbolism of Evil* Ricoeur explores the "fall" into the "fault line," which moves us from our inherent potentiality for evil to actual evil. He distinguishes three dimensions of evil, which he identifies with three historical stages in man's spontaneous understanding of his own evil, and with three different kinds of mythical symbols which show three different understandings of evil in these three historical stages of human cultures. He calls these **defilement, sin,** and **guilt.**

(1) *Defilement* is an objective, impersonal thing: impurity, dirt. Punishment is needed to remove it. Justice here means restoring a cosmic order of purity. There is no concept of a personal relationship with God or of self-conscious personal responsibility. This is the "archaic" or primitive stage. It is a necessary beginning to progress to the later, more self-aware stages.

(2) *Sin* is a religious term. It means breaking the relationship with God; a free, personal choice of the will to disobey God's will. It is both subjective and objective, for there is always both a subjective and an objective dimension in a personal relationship. Sin is like divorce from God, and justice here means restoring the relationship. It is not a matter of degree, but an either/or. As one is never half pregnant, one is never half married or divorced.

(3) *Guilt* is subjective, and follows the typically modern "turn to the subject" as a natural psychological development of the human psyche. It is the self-awareness of having devalued ourselves by sin, the awareness of our deserving punishment for our sins. It is a movement from religion to ethics. Guilt is a matter of degree, while sin is not. Guilt is a relationship not just with God but with oneself, and also with other people. It is the result of free will having bound itself to unfreedom by evil choices.

Ricoeur is best known for hermeneutics, the study of interpreting texts, and in Ricoeur's case especially symbols. This may seem rather specialized, esoteric, and far from the center of philosophy; but Ricoeur sees the world as the primary text and human life as its primary interpretation. He maintains that modernity has forgotten the power and meaning of symbols because now that we have science, we no longer use myth to explain the world. But science's **dissolution of the myth as *explanation* is the necessary way to the restoration of the myth as *symbol* . . . by a criticism that is no longer reductive but restorative.** The difference between a "reductive" and "restorative" interpretation of symbols is the difference between seeing-*through* the symbols as codes *hiding* some more philosophical and rational meanings, and seeing and bringing out the meaning *inherent* in them. It is in many ways the exact opposite of the hermeneutics of Deconstructionism (ch. 95). Symbols have to be understood by a kind of faith, or receptive, naïve immediacy, to which Ricoeur tries to return us. Ricoeur reformulates the "hermeneutical circle" in these terms: **We must understand in order to believe, but we must believe in order to understand.** This is **a living and stimulating circle.** It "elevates" our understanding of life; so the "circle" is really an upward *spiral*.

One of Ricoeur's most interesting applications of his phenomenological method is *Freud and Philosophy,* which is sympathetic even though critical. He is led to Freud because he sees psychoanalysis as a kind of hermeneutics.

A more specialized linguistic study is *The Rule of Metaphor,* which centers on metaphor as a kind of "seeing-as": metaphor helps us see something familiar in a new and unfamiliar way. It is the means by which "imitation" of life becomes a meaningful story with a plot, which transcends simple factual description. It is Aristotle's meaning of *mimesis* rather than Plato's: an imitation of human actions, especially in drama, rather than the static "imitation" of an archetype or "Platonic Idea" by a material thing.

Ricoeur does not see language as a kind of limitation on our consciousness, as if only a small portion of consciousness could be expressed in the strait-jacket of language, but as expanding and liberating our mental horizons, especially when the language is metaphorical or figurative. Thus he calls literature the highest human art. He calls Nietzsche and Derrida **philosophers of suspicion** because of their reduction of *logos* or language to something dead and oppressive. Instead, for Ricoeur, creative metaphors (as distinct from dead metaphors which have become clichés) invite us to interpret them, and thus to do hermeneutics, expanding our consciousness rather than contracting it.

Time and Narrative extends this study of language to the notorious philosophical problem of time. Time, he says, is not a series of present points that pass away as soon as they arrive. That is the rationalistic, detached notion of time (kronos), the time measured by chronometers. Real time, in contrast, is lived time (*kairos*), which creates the pastness of the past by memory and the futurity of the future by anticipation—a notion of time first taught by St. Augustine and also used by Bergson and by the phenomenology of Husserl and Heidegger. We organize time into a narrative, a story; we interpret our lives as stories, or turn them into stories by interpreting them. Thus we "know thyself" by understanding our lives as narratives. The "meaning of life" is not an abstract, static idea but the very narrative of life itself; the meaning of a good story is the story!

History, for Ricoeur, is also to be understood as narrative. Though it is not fiction, it is not just a chronology, a series of events or "facts." History is not a science, it is one of the humanities, like philosophy. Yet, like science, it is a form of inquiry: it explains events by causes.

The reality of the past comes to us in the form of what Ricoeur calls **traces**—people and the works of people (documents, stories). Our writing and studying history is **the payment of our debt** to the past which brought us here and put us into a meaningful narrative.

History thus has ethical dimensions. It is a moral duty to do history. We are morally obliged never to forget horrors like Nazism or triumphs like its defeat. This remembering is central to justice. Justice consists not first of all in retribution but in remembering.

Thus reading history and fiction changes historical and social reality by changing our lives and actions for the better. Fiction can do this as well as history, and it is typically the works of fiction that are most "fantastic" and least "realistic" that change the world the most, because they require us to enter a whole new world imaginatively. (Think of *The Lord of the Rings,* ranked by four popular polls as "the greatest book of the twentieth century.")

Ricoeur's ethics is classical: its main themes are teleology (which he calls **aim),** "the good life," the primacy of the person, virtues, and character (especially promise-keeping). Our "narrative journey" is the frame for the whole ethical picture. Ricoeur defines a good life as a life worthy of being remembered and recounted in a good story. (Thus in *The Lord of the Rings* Sam formulates the question "What is the meaning of life?" this way: "I wonder what kind of a story we're in.")

For narrative is inherently ethical; in fact **there is no ethically neutral narrative.** Narrative is evaluation, not just facts. How can we tell whether a life has been good? By reading it as a story. Ricoeur prioritizes "ethics" (thus conceived as life-narrative) over "morality" (conceived as abstract norms or rules).

Seeing life as a narrative forces us out of egotism and isolation; this is necessary to give us personal identity and character.

Central to character is faithfulness, or constancy, being true to one's word: **Self-constancy is for each person that manner of conducting himself or herself so that others can *count on* that person. Because someone is counting on me, I am *accountable for* my actions before another. The term "responsibility" unites both meanings: "counting on" and "being accountable for." It unites them, adding to them an idea of a *response* to the question "Where are you?" asked by another who needs me. This response is the following: "Here I am!"** As Woody Allen said, "Ninety percent of life is just showing up."

Eight of the most interesting points in Ricoeur's *political* philosophy are the following:

(1) **The problem of the control of the state consists in this: to devise institutional techniques especially designed to render possible the exercise of power and render its abuse impossible.** Power inherently tempts us to perversion; yet it is necessary to complete politics, which is necessary to complete human happiness. This is **the political paradox.**

(2) Marxism's fundamental error is to confuse economics with politics. Economic equality does not equal political equality because the governing of things is not the same as the governing of persons. But socialist economics, even of a semi- or soft-Marxist kind, is compatible with liberal politics.

(3) The truly liberal state is a rule of law, not of will. Thus the law must be above the

state. The rule of justice is prior, not posterior, to politics; justice is not the creature of the state but its creator. On this issue Ricoeur strongly sides with pre-modern rather than typically modern political philosophy.

(4) Justice is necessary but vengeance is not. In justice, the punishment, though it *fits* the crime, is *less* than the crime. "An eye for an eye, a tooth for a tooth" is not justice but vengeance. Another difference is that unlike vengeance, justice must be administered by a judge who intervenes, a third party.

(5) Higher even than justice, with its "golden rule" ("Do unto others what you would have them do unto you"), is the "new commandment" of love, generosity, and forgiveness. Love is directed against the process of victimization that utilitarianism sanctions when it proposes as its ideal the maximization of the average advantage of the greatest number at the price of the sacrifice of a small number, a sinister implication that utilitarianism tries to conceal. (Cf. the problem of the cannibals in Mill, ch. 83.)

(6) Forgiveness is not merely amnesty. Amnesty **purports to erase the debt and the fact. Amnesty . . . is an institutionalized form of amnesia.** "Forgive" does not mean "forget." In fact it means a kind of remembering. Amnesty erases the criminal's responsibility, and this dehumanizes him.

(7) *Authority* is distinguished from *power.* It is a rule of law and justice. It is right, not might. The state itself, with its might (power), is answerable to law (right). The law has authority *not* because authority has been given to it by the power of the state; the law founds the state, not vice versa. (See point 3 above.) This implies the existence of some kind of a "natural law," not just positive (man-made, man-posited, artificial) laws.

(8) Law, and a constitution, means the replacement of violence by reasoned discourse *(logos).*

All this is part of what Europeans used to be called "liberalism" and Americans used to call "conservatism."

94. Emmanuel Levinas (1906–1995)

If Martin Buber had been a deconstructionist, he probably would have sounded like Levinas. Much of Levinas's *content* is similar to Buber's; the " big idea" common to both is that the primordial source of meaning for man, especially ethical meaning, is the I-Thou encounter (which Levinas calls **the Face-to-Face).**

Both thinkers explore this encounter, but their methods and styles are very different. Buber is fairly clear and direct, even though he uses poetic language; while Levinas tortures French (and English) prose as much as Derrida, or even more, if possible. If Buber's language is beautiful, Levinas's is *ugly.* Yet one never gets the impression, or the suspicion, that he is just playing a game with us to shock us, as one does with Derrida, the "Deconstructionist" with whom Levinas had a long, friendly association and much correspondence. Levinas is not trying to deconstruct, but to construct—to construct a more fundamental phenomenology than either Husserl or Heidegger.

Here are some typical examples, chosen almost at random, of his philosophical prose. Please do not linger over them or try to figure them out. They make Hegel and Heidegger look easy and clear:

Responsibility is substitution . . . it is . . . obsession . . . persecution . . . recurrence . . . too tight in its skin . . . exile . . . maternity . . . love . . . expiation . . . and kenosis. . . . Remorse is the trope of the literal sense of sensibility. In its passivity is erased the distinction between being accused and accusing oneself. *(Otherwise than Being)*

Being is the verb itself. Temporalization is the verb form to be. Language issued from the verbalness of a verb would then not only consist in making Being understood, but also *in making its essence vibrate. (Totality and Infinity)*

The ipseity ("itselfness") has become at odds with itself with its return to itself. The self-accusation of remorse gnaws away at the closed and firm core of consciousness, opening it, fissioning it . . . to measure the pre-ontological weight of language . . . interpreting the fact that essence exposes and is exposed, that temporalization is stated, resounds and is said, does not give priority to the word said over the saying. It is first to awaken, in the said, the saying which is absorbed in it.

Mercy! This chapter will be mercifully short.

Levinas was born in Lithuania to a family of observant Jews who had to endure persecution from both the Bolshevik and the National Socialist revolutions. He studied phenomenology under both Husserl and Heidegger in the 1920s. During World War II he lost almost all his relatives to the Nazis, who killed 91% of Lithuanian Jews; but his wife and daughter were saved by Maurice Blanchot, a right-wing French monarchist, who hid them in a Catholic monastery. Levinas himself survived a Nazi work camp during the war.

His most enduring philosophical legacy is (A) his claim that "first philosophy" is not metaphysics but ethics, and (B) his attempt to found ethics neither on (1) pre-modern virtue and natural law, nor on (2) a Utilitarian calculation of pleasure, nor on (3) any Kantian a priori legislated by autonomous rational freedom of will, but on (4) the primal face-to-face encounter between persons, which is embodied ("sentience") and affective ("emotion") rather than conceptual.

How do I relate to the world? I master it, I consume it and enjoy it. But I cannot do that to another self. The other self is an **interruption** or **disruption** into my consciousness: not an object but another subject; and his **expression,** i.e., his look, his bare face, naked and defenseless, speaks to me a wordless imperative: **"Do not kill me."** If this sounds like Hobbes's "state of nature," that is an illusion, because I experience at that moment the fundamental, primordial ethical experience of **responsibility.**

Three features emerge in this primordial experience, which Levinas labels **fraternity, discourse,** and **transcendence.**

Fraternity means that he is my brother, we can form a "we"-subject, the very thing Sartre declares impossible.

Discourse means language, communication, which is rooted in this "Face-to-Face" and which then becomes more abstract as it moves farther away from the original, concrete, affective, pre-verbal and pre-conceptual Face-to-Face encounter.

Transcendence means **escape** from self: **Escape is the need to get out of oneself, that is, to break that most radical and unalterably binding of chains, the fact that the I** *(moi)* **is oneself** *(soi-meme).* Levinas uses "escape" positively here, not negatively. It is a need, but need is not an emptiness or privation or lack but a fullness. (The sentimental song line "People who need people are the luckiest people in the world" takes on a profound meaning here.)

"Transcendence" also means **infinity.** We encounter infinity *in* the ordinary Face-to-Face, not above it or outside it. We meet something that is *not* a finite, definable thing or object when we meet another Face (person). We have no positive *concept* of infinity, yet the Face-to-Face offers us unlimited realities in the positive affective qualities of joy, love of life, and sociality or hospitality.

We can interpret this "infinity" as the presence of "God," but that word is no more definable than is the other human person, subject, or "Face." Levinas stays with Moses Maimonides' purely negative theology: we can know what God is not, but not what He is. (Aquinas says the same thing—we have no positive univocal concept of God—but unlike Maimonides and Levinas, he also adds analogical positive knowledge.)

Rather than try to outline Levinas's more tortured explorations of consciousness, I add just a few scattered points that strike me as interesting, comprehensible, and memorable:

• Labor is defined not as mastery of nature but as the creation of goods with which to welcome the other and a space or home into which to receive him.

• Justice is not found primarily in the state but in the family, where we first find Face-to-Face responsibility.

• Levinas was harshly criticized by the Left for being right-wing, apolitical, "Judaeo-Christian," and antifeminist; for defending Israel's right to be a Jewish state; and for recommending to France that it add "religion" to its three values of "liberty, fraternity, equality."

• He recognized the threat of Hitler before Hitler came to power, in his prophetic 1932 article *The Philosophy of Hitlerism,* published in a Catholic journal, in which he said that **the source of the bloody barbarism of National Socialism** was not a momentary madness but **the essential possibility of elemental Evil . . . against which Western philosophy had not sufficiently inured itself** and that it is **Nietzsche's will to power which modern Germany is rediscovering and glorifying..**

• The Face-to-Face relationship is non-reciprocal. It is not a relationship of equality in the sense of sameness, but of *otherness*. Levinas speaks of the other as **the mystery of the feminine** which is ungraspable, unique, and unmasterable. This is also the feminine "other" through which the future "other" of the child comes into being, who incarnates hope. French "feminists" (many of them men) never forgave him for this, especially for praising "the feminine" for her virtues of "welcoming," "reservedness," and "discretion."

• In contrast to Derrida, Levinas admired Plato, especially his metaphysics of "the Good beyond Being."

• Most of Levinas's later works are not philosophical but expositions of the Talmud.

95. Jacques Derrida (1930–2004)

I must begin with a personal, confessional note. I have tried to do justice to every one of the 100 philosophers and philosophies in this long book, but I cannot do justice to Derrida and his philosophy of "Deconstructionism" for two reasons. First of all, I cannot catch it. I must compliment Derrida for writing the most remarkably unreadable prose in the history of philosophy. If "the Godfather" became a Deconstructionist, he'd make me an offer I couldn't understand. Compared with Derrida, Lucky's single three-page-long diarrhetic sentence in Beckett's "Waiting for Godot" is lucidly clear. Second, I cannot do justice to Deconstructionism because according to Deconstructionism itself, justice is impossible, in fact justice is injustice.

The fundamental principle of Deconstructionism is a peculiar form of the denial of the law of non-contradiction. Everything is what it isn't and isn't what it is. In one place Derrida described Deconstructionism as an attack on Platonism, and in another as an attack on the notion of "purity," i.e., the purity of an essence, a Platonic Form, such as Justice, or Goodness. It is equally an attack on Aristotelian forms, and most especially on the idea of any kind of value hierarchy, such as good vs. evil, truth vs. falsehood. It is also an attack on Husserl's phenomenological notions of pure consciousness (or "transcendental ego") and pure essences as that which consciousness intends in the "eidetic reduction."

In Derrida all boundaries, identities, and hierarchies are attacked. Deconstructionism is an attack on the fundamental foundation not only of all Western philosophy but also of all sanity. Its sanity is (as Derrida would probably cheerfully admit) in-sanity and its in-sanity is sanity. (Derrida has the habit of inserting hyphens into words as one would insert pins into voodoo dolls, and for similar reasons.)

And therefore, of course, the philosophy whose "is" isn't and whose "isn't" is, is the most fashionable philosophy in the humanities departments of universities throughout Western civilization. Derrida was famous, a media darling. Two movies were made about him, one by Woody Allen. Thousands of Frenchmen filled auditoriums to hear him, as they did for Sartre. There seems to be something deliciously decadent about French tastes in philosophers, as in foods. Think of pigs snuffling in the dirt for truffles, or a master chef's use of carefully selected waste products of one food to flavor another. In fact, that is a perfect example of Derrida's central notion of *differance*, the presence of the opposite in everything, of the impure at the heart of the "pure." (Arbitrarily changing the e to an a in the word that labels the practice is an example of the practice: the practice of making each thing not-itself.)

One way of summarizing the central impetus of everything in Derrida is to compare him to the Bible. St. Paul wrote: "Finally, brethren, whatsoever things are true, whatsoever things are honest, whatsoever things are just, whatsoever things are pure, whatsoever things are lovely, whatsoever things are of good report, if there be any virtue, and if there be any praise, think on these things." (Phil. 4:8) Derrida asks us to do exactly the opposite, to *stop* thinking on these things, or to see their opposites at the heart of them. If the Bible asks for childlike faith, Derrida asks for super-sophisticated suspicion.

Deconstructionism does to our ideas, i.e., the ideas of common sense and of the traditional philosophy that begins with common sense, what death does to our bodies. It is a kind of decomposing.

(Unfair but funny gibe: When he was alive, Mozart spent his time composing; when he died, he spent his time decomposing. In other words, he became a Deconstructionist.)

Born a Sephardic Jew in Algeria, Derrida experienced the anti-Semitism of the collaborationist Vichy regime in his *lycee* (high school). He moved to Paris, where he studied philosophy, especially Husserl, Foucault, Heidegger, Hegel, and Levinas—probably the five most difficult and unreadable philosophers who ever lived. He outdid them all. The most charitable way to describe his writing style is "evocative rather than logical." He called his style **an intransigent, even incorruptible, *ethos* of writing and thinking . . . without concession even to philosophy, and not letting public opinion, the media, or the phantasm of intimidating readership frighten or force us into simplifying or repressing. Hence the strict taste for refinement, paradox, and aporia.**

Derrida first became famous, in the seventies, for "deconstructing" the Platonic hierarchy of speech over writing as something that is prior in time, in value, and in causality. According to this Platonic tradition, writing is a kind of frozen speech, or directions for speech, as sheet music is directions for music. Derrida maintained, on the contrary, that speech is a form of writing rather than vice versa, and that writing has priority over speech both historically and logically.

The same pattern of turning traditional hierarchies on their heads recurs in everything Derrida writes about: see the list of 16 examples below. Derrida's analyses of these polarities is clever, though his language is maddeningly obscure. He finds the "other," or the opposite, in everything that has an identity. He calls this *differance,* changing one letter of the word "difference" as a girl coyly changes one letter in her name to be cute and to get attention (e.g., "Robin" becomes "Robyn").

Thus Derrida attacks Plato's idea of Absolute Goodness and of God (what Aristotle developed into the idea of the unmoved Mover, or Thought Thinking Itself). He argues that **immortality and perfection . . . would consist in having no relation at all with any outside** and is therefore impossible. He argues that Plato's Ideas are relative, not absolute, for they are able to be copied or imaged by material things, and therefore they are relative to that possibility, so that the "impurity" of matter and plurality is already inherent in the pure idea of the Idea. (This is a rare example of traditional logic in Derrida.)

Some of the dualisms or polarities Derrida applies this notion of *differance* to include:

(1) monolinguism vs. bilinguism, (2) speech vs. writing, (3) unpredictable singularity vs. mechanical repeatability, (4) particular vs. universal, (5) present vs. past or future, (6) justice vs. injustice, (7) openness, or "hospitality" vs. borders, (8) freedom vs. violence and coercion, (9) self-love vs. other-love (auto-affection vs. hetero-affection), (10) concealing (secrets) vs. revealing—in fact for him in a real sense truth-telling is lying and lying is truth-telling, (11) democracy vs. sovereignty, (12) essence vs. accident, (13) reality vs. appearance, (14) law and order vs. violence, (15) presence vs. absence, and (16) certainty vs. uncertainty. He finds the presence *(and* absence) of each opposite at the heart of the other.

Rather than go into the details of his analysis of each of these 16 particular cases, I will let Derrida himself define his principle of deconstructionism, his one "big idea":[37]

Each time that I say "deconstructionism and X (regardless of the concept or the theme)," this is the prelude to a very singular division that turns this X into, or rather makes appear in this X, *an impossibility* **that becomes its proper and sole possibility, with the result that between the X as possible and the "same" X as impossible, there is nothing but a relation of homonymy. . . . For example . . . gift, hospitality, death itself (and therefore so many other things) can be possible only** *as impossible,* **as the im-possible, that is, unconditionally.**

And this is one of his *clearest* paragraphs.

However, to try to be as fair and charitable as we can to Derrida, we could admit that this essential notion of Deconstructionism, this *differance,* which finds the "other," the excluded, in the heart of everything, could quite easily be constructive rather than destructive, positive rather than negative, even though Derrida himself calls it an "attack" on everything "pure." This is so not merely for the logical reason that if we extend *difference* to everything, including *differance* itself, its refusal of purity and identity becomes its opposite, *viz.* purity and identity. It is true also for the substantial reason that in practice this search for the "other" and the opposite at the heart of everything can be quite creative and mind-expanding, as in Hegel's dialectic or even as in the Socratic questioning of popular opinions or in the Chestertonian habit of turning clichés inside out and upside down. The fact that it is destructive and "a hermeneutic of suspicion" in Derrida's hands rather than the positive and expansive thing it is in Hegel, Socrates, and Chesterton indicates that a deeper principle than *differance* itself is at work in Derrida. And this is Derrida's attack on *logos,* on all real, objective order everywhere, the idea he calls "logocentrism." That is his primary enemy. He is a modern Gorgias (see ch. 22).

The battle began not in philosophy but in literature. Deconstructionism arose first in

37 Derrida would say that that very dualism, between his single "big idea" and his many examples or applications, must also be deconstructed, and not distinguished, opposed and separated.

reaction to a movement called "structuralism," which, like Deconstructionism, began as a theory of literature and literary criticism, then expanded into a whole philosophy. Structuralism sought unchanging structures, or forms (what Husserl called "essences") first in language, then in society, and eventually in consciousness and in being. Derrida's subversive mission is the destruction of all such structures.

This is why he is rightly classified as a disciple of Nietzsche, and a nihilist. (The fact that Nietzsche inveighed *against* nihilism no more proves he was not one than the fact that Communist China called itself "the People's Republic of China" proves that it was. Remember Hitler's insight into the power of "the Big Lie.") Nietzsche called himself "the philosopher with a hammer." If you see yourself as a hammer, you tend to see everything as a nail.

In his own words, Derrida deconstructs, by his own admission, **the very concepts of knowledge and truth.** (The word *logos* can mean both "knowledge" and "truth.") He is a striking confirmation of Camus's observation that the fundamental philosophical question is the question of suicide. Camus was thinking of bodily suicide; Derrida applies the noose to the reason.

In literary criticism, the most famous of Derrida's ideas is the deconstruction of the difference between text and word, or word and referent: **There is nothing outside of the text.** Therefore no text is a true or false interpretation of the world and there is no true or false interpretation of a text, for there is no text prior to interpretation of it; all reading *is* interpretation. Language is not "intentional," not a series of signs "about" a world. As Archibald MacLeish put it, in "Ars Poetica," "A poem should be palpable and mute/ Like globed fruit;/ A poem should not *mean*/ But *be.* "The medievals saw even many of the *things* in the world as *signs* (of their Creator); deconstructionists see even signs as things.

Things can be used as weapons, and contemporary Deconstructionists see *words* as weapons (and as things rather than signs) which are used to impose power for the sake of race, class, or gender, rather than true or false labels for objectively real things, like the word "poison" on a bottle. One man's ecstasy is another man's poison.

Deconstructionism, and the vaguer movement called Postmodernism, of which it is a central part, insists on the impossibility of "meta-narratives," i.e., true and meaningful overviews of the meaning of all of human life and history—the very thing Paul Ricoeur focuses on, and the thing common to all the religions of the world. For Deconstructionism, as for Sartre and Nietzsche, human life is not a story with an Author. Man is merely, in the words of Macbeth, "a poor player who struts and frets his hour upon the stage and then is heard no more . . . (Life) is a tale told by an idiot, full of sound and fury, signifying nothing."

Thus Deconstructionism provides an indirect argument *for* religion. As Freud said, in *Civilization and its Discontents,* "only religion can answer the question of the meaning of life. The very possibility of life having a meaning stands and falls with the religious system." If "God is dead," as Nietzsche said, then meta-narratives are dead too, and the very question of "the meaning of life" is meaningless. Meaning is merely whatever we make it. So the answer to this most profound of questions is the banality of the jaded and cynical teenager: "Whatever."

It is impossible to disprove Deconstructionism because it does not claim to prove itself, but to create itself (and to uncreate itself). It is voluntaristic rather than rationalistic. It is a choice, an act, a method, rather than a doctrine. Its words are not pens but swords, and it practices what it preaches, that the pen is *not* mightier than the sword. Trying to refute Deconstruction- ism as irrational is like trying to threaten a masochist with pain. Derrida would welcome, and be in total agreement with, the obvious logical criticism that Deconstructionism is self-contradictory since it itself must also be deconstructed. His "big idea" cannot be destroyed because it is the very idea of universal destruction and therefore also of self-destruction. It is like the Devil that way.

I never thought anything could make me fall in love with analytic philosophy—until I discovered Deconstructionism.

96. Etienne Gilson (1884–1978)

We conclude with five different examples of the only traditional philosophical school that has remained popular, alive and growing, in various directions, like the branches of a tree, *viz.* Thomism.

Gilson's discovery of medieval philosophy, and St. Thomas in particular, at the Sorbonne before World War I, gave him his intellectual and professional identity. He was primarily a historian of medieval philosophy, but also an original philosopher in his own right, writing in a lively, elegant style that, like Thomas, combines clarity and profundity, and which shows the influence of Chesterton. His magisterial *History of Christian Philosophy in the Middle Ages* is to its subject what Euclid's *Elements* was to geometry, Ptolemy's *Almagest* was to astronomy, and Newton's *Principia* was to physics. Unlike these three, however, his primacy has remained.

He is largely responsible for saving the real Aquinas from his rationalistic, essentialistic, conceptualistic, and scholastic commentators, and for the "school" of "existential Thomism" which centers on the insight that being, for Aquinas, is the very act of existing (*esse*). Being is not the most general and abstract *concept* that can be predicated of all things. Nor is it an *accident* that is added to some possible beings but not others, to make them actual. Nor is the mere *fact* that some beings (like horses) exist while others do not (like unicorns or mental constructs like the "parts of speech"). It is the supreme act rather than the supreme fact.

Gilson reminds us that for Aquinas there is a "real distinction" between essence and existence in all finite, created beings. It is a real distinction but not a distinction between two distinct realities, but between two co-principles of reality.

God alone is existence itself by His essence; that is why His being is eternal and ontologically necessary. Every being has a sufficient reason why it exists; every other being finds its reason in its extrinsic causes, not in its intrinsic essence, while God's reason for existing is in His essence, not in extrinsic causes.

And this central thesis of the act of existence, Gilson shows, makes a difference to every major division of Aquinas's philosophy, as he demonstrates in *The Christian Philosophy of St. Thomas Aquinas* and *The Elements of Christian Philosophy*. The metaphysical point of the primacy of existence even structures Aquinas's ethics, as Gilson shows in *Moral Values and the Moral Life*. In fact ethics is so essentially grounded in metaphysics that Gilson formulates the first question of Aquinas's ethics as: "What happens to Being when it enters the realm of human free choice?"

This is the first of Gilson's three most distinctive, original and controversial "big ideas": the metaphysics of the primacy of the act of existence. It runs like a guiding thread through all his many books on St. Thomas, and it contrasts most sharply with the alternative concepts of being in Plato, Aristotle, Plotinus, Avicenna, and Kierkegaard (as essence, form, unity, accident, and subjectivity respectively), as Gilson shows in *Being and Some Philosophers.*

Gilson's second "big idea" is St. Thomas's epistemological realism. This is presented and argued for primarily in *Thomistic Realism and the Problem of Knowledge,* where Gilson argues that the very question of Descartes and his modern followers, the question of the "critique of reason," the demand to rationally justify reason itself, is illegitimate and impossible to answer. The starting point of philosophy, for Thomas, is not Descartes" "I think" but the fact that "something exists."

In other words, we must move from reality to thought, from metaphysics to epistemology, rather than vice versa, as Descartes and nearly every modern philosopher after him assumes we must do, no matter how much they disagree with Descartes in other ways. The Cartesian program of deriving being from thought cannot be carried out; the "bridge" between the two cannot be built by thought but only by being. Or, better, there is no bridge because there is no gap. Once we open such a gap in our philosophy, we cannot close it.

A third distinctive Gilsonian thesis is the legitimacy of "Christian philosophy." The philosophers of the "Enlightenment" had assumed that between Aristotle and Descartes there had been no philosophy, only theology, and that Christianity could not possibly have a legitimate influence on philosophy without corrupting it. In other words, that faith and reason are like fire and water, or like matter and antimatter, rather than like man and woman or like positive and negative polarities. Gilson refuted this in such classic and readable works as *God and Philosophy, Reason and Revelation in the Middle Ages,* and *The Spirit of Medieval Philosophy*

Gilson also put Aquinas in dialog with modern philosophers, especially In *The Unity of Philosophical Experience,* which shows the consequences of reducing philosophy to some other science, an error common to thinkers as diverse as Abelard and Comte. It should be read together with Thomist Mortimer Adler's *Ten Philosophical Mistakes* as a critique of the major systems of modern philosophy, especially in epistemology.

Gilson also wrote distinctively valuable books on St. Augustine, Dante, St. Bonaventura, and Heloise and Abelard.

A good introduction to Gilson is the anthology of representative short essays collected in *A Gilson Reader.*

97. Jacques Maritain (1882–1973)

Maritain was the most famous and influential Thomist since Thomas. Five ways he differed radically from most modern academic philosophers are the following: (1) He thought "against the current" of modernity, yet out of honest love, openness and respect for it. (2) He wrote on a very wide range of practical as well as theoretical subjects both in and out of philosophy. (3) He lived a full, interesting, socially and politically engaged, multifaceted life. (4) He remained not only married and faithful but deeply in love with his wife Raissa all his life. (5) Above all, he passionately agreed with the oft-repeated central theme of Leon Bloy, that "there is in the end only one tragedy: not to have been a saint." Indeed, there is an ongoing process for his canonization.

Since there are more memorable and personally illuminating biographical facts about Maritain than about most philosophers, I submit no less than 22 of them. Nearly everyone who met Maritain said the man was even more impressive than his many writings—a rarity among philosophers. (Marcel is another such rarity.)

(1) His grandfather, Jules Favre, a freethinker (a nineteenth-century euphemism for "atheist"), was one of the most famous and influential politicians in France.

(2) His father, Paul Maritain, was a lawyer, libertine, and lapsed Catholic who divorced his wife and later committed suicide.

(3) Maritain became a left-wing socialist at a young age, and passionately defended the innocent Dreyfus against the political Right who condemned him, in the case that deeply divided France.

(4) He studied at the Sorbonne, where me met and fell in love with his future wife Raissa, a Russian Jewess.

(5) Jacques and Raissa made a suicide pact based on their philosophical agreement that if, as most modern philosophers said, truth was unattainable, then life was meaningless. He wrote: **We wanted to die by a free act if it was impossible to live according to the truth.**

(6) Bergson saved them from their metaphysical despair by convincing them that truth was knowable by the human mind.

(7) As an agnostic Jacques prayed daily, "God, if you exist and are the truth, let me know."

(8) Jacques and Raissa read, then met, Leon Bloy, whose personal holiness sparked their conversion to Catholicism and convinced them that the meaning of life was simple: to become a saint.

(9) They made a vow to live together as brother and sister. (What does your reaction to that fact say about your open-mindedness, tolerance and pluralism?)

(10) They became Benedictine oblates, praying at least an hour a day, usually more. "To be a saint" was no vague ideal but the most literal, passionate necessity of their lives.

(11) First Raissa, then Jacques, discovered Thomas Aquinas. It was a second marriage of minds. He wrote: **As it was for her, it is a deliverance, an inundation of light. The intellect finds its home.**

(12) Raissa, dying, was apparently miraculously healed by the intercession of Our Lady of LaSalette.

(13) Jacques joined and supported a conservative, "restorationist," monarchist Catholic political movement, "Action Française." When the Church condemned it, he submitted to the Church's judgment. His political opinions changed from socialist to monarchist to liberal, but he did not let his religion follow his politics, but vice versa. When he came to America he befriended Saul Alinsky, the radical Leftist antipoverty organizer.

(14) He began a Thomistic study center at his home. Friends and visitors included Maeterlinck, Gilson, Bloy, Peguy, Edith Stein (since canonized), Cocteau, Gide, Berdyaev, Mauriac, Claudel, Bernanos, Julien Green, Charles Maurras, Garrigou-Lagrange, Yves Simon, Chenu, and Marcel.

(15) The Right accused him of being a Marxist when he issued manifestos condemning the war in Ethiopia and the bombing of Guernica.

(16) He and Raissa (and her sister Vera) moved to America in 1940, where he was vice president of French exiles. He was a weekly voice on the "Voice of America."

(17) In 1944 he was appointed French ambassador to the Vatican.

(18) He became close friends with Msgr. Montini, the future Pope Paul VI, who as Pope called himself Maritain's grateful student.

(19) He was the president of the UNESCO conference in Mexico in 1947, and together with Charles Malik helped draft the united Nations' universal Declaration of Human Rights in 1948.

(20) He taught at Princeton, Notre Dame, Chicago, and Hunter College. Notre Dame set up a Maritain Study center during his lifetime.

(21) At the close of Vatican Council II, the Pope sent a "message to intellectuals" of the world through Maritain.

(22) After Raissa died, Jacques took monastic vows as one of the Little Brothers of Jesus. He died in France in 1973.

What kind of a Thomist was he? He summarizes his relation to Thomas in eight points:

(a) . . . a Thomistic philosophy, not a neo-Thomist philosophy.

(b) Thomism does not imply a return to the Middle Ages.

(c) Thomism seeks to use reason . . . not to destroy modern thinking but to purify and to integrate all the truths that were discovered after St. Thomas.

(d) Thomism is neither Right nor Left; it is not positioned in space but in the spirit.

(e) To judge Thomism as if it were a style of clothing that was worn in the 13th century but that today is no longer fashionable, as if the value of metaphysics was a function of time, is a truly barbaric mindset.

(f) Ongoing interchanges must take place between it and the particular forms of culture, but Thomism in its essence is strictly independent of these particular forms of culture.

(g) There is nothing more childish than to judge the value of metaphysics in the light of a social state that must be retained or destroyed.

(h) The philosophy of St. Thomas in itself is independent of the information derived from faith and depends only on its principles and its structuring of experience and reason. While remaining, however, completely distinct from such data of faith, this philosophy is still in vital communication with the superior wisdoms of theology and contemplation.

Maritain's essential Thomistic critique of modern philosophy and the modern world is that **The disease afflicting the modern world is above all a disease of the intellect. . . . The due order between the intellect and its object was . . . shattered. We have difficulty in realizing the frightful significance, charged with blood and tears, of these few abstract words; we have difficulty in realizing the tremendous upheaval, the tremendous inevitable catastrophe, to which they point. The intellect! That "divine" activity, as Aristotle termed it, that prodigy of light and life, that glory and supreme perfection of created nature, through which we become spiritually all things, through which we shall one day possess our supernatural beatitude, from which here on earth all our acts (insofar as they are *human* acts) proceed, and on which the rectitude of all we do depends! Can we conceive how ruinous for man is the disturbance of that life—a participation in the divine light—which he bears within him?**

Indocile to the object, to God, to being, the intellect becomes also and to the same extent a rebel against any kind of tradition and spiritual continuity. It retires within itself. . . .

The fact is that Saint Thomas—and this is the most immediate benefit he confers—brings the intellect back to its object, orientates it toward its end, restores it to its nature. He tells it that it is made for being. How could it possibly not give ear? It is as if one told the eye that it is made to see, or wings that they are made to fly. . . .

Saint Thomas . . . teaches us how to triumph over both anti-intellectualism and rationalism, over the evil which degrades reason below, and the evil which exalts it above, the real. . . .

Maritain's writings are remarkably many and diverse. I list the ones readers are likely to find the most useful, in alphabetical order

Approaches to God exemplifies its title.

Art and Scholasticism shows Thomism's relevance to aesthetics (1) by focusing on beauty as a transcendental property of all being, (2) by tracing analogies between the work of the artist and those of the moralist, the saint, and the mystic, and (3) by paralleling the artist's natural affinity (or "connaturality") for his object with the philosopher's natural "intuition of being."

On Bergson and St. Thomas Aquinas is a more mature and balanced treatment of the philosopher whose counter-cultural, anti-reductionistic, and anti-Positivistic philosophy had saved Jacques and Raissa from suicide and saved Maritain's later Thomism from the ossification and essentialism of the Scholastic manuals.

Bergsonian Philosophy is an earlier severe critique of Bergson's anti-intellectualism.

Christianity and Democracy is a balanced treatment showing how this relation is neither a contrast nor an identity.

Creative Intuition in Art and Poetry includes some striking wisdom about the need to love *and suffer* for both life and art—e.g., Dante's "wound" upon seeing Beatrice. The main point of this book is the analogy, rather than the contrast, between artistic creativity and sanctity: both imitate God in *loving* new things into existence. It is a striking contrast to the typically modern opposition between the artist as non-conformist and the saint as conformist, both errors forgetting the centrality of creative love to both art and sanctity.

Distinguish to Unite; or, The Degrees of Knowledge is Maritain's masterpiece, on epistemology, which is at the center of modern philosophy, its primary questions, and its contrast with pre-modern philosophy. More on this book below. It is similar in subject, scope and depth to Lonergan's *Insight*. (ch. 98)

The Dream of Descartes: It is not widely known that Descartes's whole philosophy was motivated by a dream, supposedly sent by "the Spirit of Truth." The key to Descartes, says Maritain, is that he is an "angelist": what he says about the mind is true, but it is true only of the mind of angels.

An Essay on Christian Philosophy defends the Thomistic marriage of faith and reason against the typically modern assumption that it is an impossibility, like mating a fish with a bird.

Existence and the Existent contrasts modern existentialism and Thomistic existentialism. Maritain argues that Thomas is the true "existentialist." But he attempts to extract some profoundly true insights about human distinctiveness, subjectivity, and freedom even from modern anti-intellectualist and atheistic existentialisms like Sartre's.

Education at the Crossroads: The authentic goal of education, for Maritain, is not mere information or training for social action and technological success but the personal and moral wisdom of self-mastery, **the conquest of individual and spiritual freedom. liberation through knowledge and wisdom, good will and love.**

God and the Problem of Evil is a brief Thomistic and metaphysical answer to this strongest argument for atheism.

Human Rights and Natural Law and *Man and the State* both attempt to reconcile pre-modern natural law ethics and the modern ethics of rights.

Integral Humanism contrasts a humanism based on eternal values and truths with one based on ideology and human autonomy. It argues that philosophy, and especially metaphysics, is essential for the preservation of true humanism, and that its absence has caused **the progressive loss, in modern ideology, of all the certitudes coming either from metaphysical insight or from religious faith, which had given foundation and granted reality to the image of Man in the Christian system. The historic misfortune has been the failure of philosophic Reason. . . . Human Reason lost its grasp of Being, and became available only for the mathematical reading of sensory phenomena.**

An Introduction to Philosophy is a somewhat over-simple but clear and well-organized introduction, for beginners, to the themes and historical sources of Thomism. Its guiding thread is Thomas's avoidance of opposite extremes and errors on each major philosophical question.

Introduction to Logic is a philosophical account of traditional Aristotelian logic.

The Meaning of Contemporary Atheism (1948) traces atheism not to rational inquiry but to a prior fundamental moral choice against all subordination or "submission." Yet it sees positive religious themes in the "absolute atheism" which will sacrifice itself to the future for others.

Moral Philosophy is an evaluative tour of the history of ethics.

The Peasant of the Garonne, written shortly after Vatican II, is a prophetic critique of the forthcoming hijack of the Council by the so-called "liberals."

Man and the State argues that even though religious faith is the best guarantee of tolerance and pluralism, and even though secular, autonomous justifications of human rights (e.g., Rousseau's or Kant's) are idolatrous, Christians and secularists can agree in practice on the existence and defense of these rights.

The Person and the Common Good distinguishes the *person* from the *individual*. The individual is only an abstracted aspect of the concrete person, and exists both *for* and *from* the community and the common good, just as the community exists both for individuals and from individuals. Maritain sees the separation between the person and the common good as the source of both totalitarianism, whether Right or Left, and bourgeois autonomous individualism.

A Preface to Metaphysics introduces Thomistic metaphysics to intelligent beginners.

Reflections on America follows DeTocqueville's tradition of Frenchmen falling in love with America and its democratic spirit yet warning Americans not to be naïve about it and its fragility.

The Rights of Man and Natural Law affirms and synthesizes these two notions, one quintessentially modern and the other quintessentially medieval.

The Range of Reason stakes out a Thomistic ground between rationalism and irrationalism.

Scholasticism and Politics shows the relevance of Aquinas's political philosophy for modernity.

St. Thomas Aquinas is a rambling, readable, and popular philosophical biography of St. Thomas.

The Twilight of Civilization is a rejection of both optimistic presumption and pessimistic despair and a call for a true humanism which is both natural and supernatural.

Three Reformers: Luther, Descartes, Rousseau sees the common theme in all three of these important founders of the modern world as the anti-intellectualism of the solitary, uprooted individual judging the whole of the past and its traditions by his own personal experience (Luther), self-consciousness (Descartes), or emotions (Rousseau). Despite the personal religiosity of all three, their individualistic arrogance led to the secular humanism that exalted man's autonomy over and against God. All three, especially Descartes, opened an abyss between the subjective mind and objective being, and deprived the intellect of its proper object. Where Descartes's "angelism" ignored the *body,* Luther and Rousseau opposed *reason.*

Raissa Maritain's *We Have Been Friends Together* is a personal autobiographical diary of their spiritual life.

The Degrees of Knowledge is Maritain's magnum opus. What other major work in modern epistemology takes as its starting point the fact that man's ultimate end is supernatural? (Only Thomas Merton's *The Ascent to Truth* comes to mind, but that is more theological than philosophical.) But this starting point is totally reasonable, in Maritain's mind; for how could a philosophy direct us to our true end if it did not even claim to know what it is? Philosophy is not a game; **to philosophize, man must put his whole soul into play.**

Maritain distinguishes three "degrees" or levels of wisdom:

(1) philosophical wisdom, as defined at the beginning of Aristotle's *Metaphysics,* as including natural theology, which Aristotle calls "the divine science" in two senses: it is the knowledge of God by human reason and it is human reason's best approximation to the knowledge that God Himself has;

(2) revealed theological wisdom, taught by God Himself and therefore most certain; and

(3) contemplative mystical experience, as exemplified by St. Augustine, St. Thomas, and St. John of the Cross, who was a philosopher and a Thomist as well as a saint and mystic.

On all three levels Maritain speaks of personal knowledge, or "knowledge by connaturality," the knowledge that comes from a real presence of the object in the knowing subject. Lacking this, modern philosophy is doomed to end in subjectivism and skepticism.

In mystical contemplation, Maritain explains, we know the very existence, i.e., the actual *act* of existing (*esse*), not the mere fact that it exists, of things and of ourselves. This *esse* is a participation in, though not identical with, the *esse* of God. In the "void" of mystical knowledge, where all forms and concepts are transcended, the act of existing, which transcends all essences, natures, forms and concepts, is known in a way that cannot be expressed in inner or outer words. (Compare Wittgenstein's idea of "the mystical.")

Maritain, following Aquinas, insists that *wisdom,* not *certainty,* is the epistemic goal; and that even *certainty* is more than *proof.* It is impossible to prove, or demonstrate, the existence of the external world, yet we can be certain of it, for this is the beginning of all our knowledge.

A crucially important technical point in the book is the discussion of the concept as a "formal sign," i.e., purely a sign and not a thing, and therefore *not* the first and immediate object of knowledge, as in Descartes, Locke and Hume (the crucial text here is *Summa Theologiae* I,85,2). This is the central claim of epistemological realism; and it alone, for Maritain, as for Gilson, guarantees the knowledge of being and avoids the unsolvable modern problem of building a bridge between knowledge and reality, between concepts or percepts and real things. A concept **is not known by "appearing" as object but by "disappearing" in the face of the object, for its very essence is to bear the mind to something other than itself.** Once the concept is treated as the first object of knowledge, skepticism or subjectivism are inevitable.

See also, in ch. 99, Fr. Clarke's use of Maritain's concept of "ontological generosity" (everything that exists gives something of itself to other beings) in his little classic *Person and Being,* as a concept that unites ethics and metaphysics, human love and "the love that moves the sun and other stars."

98. Bernard Lonergan, S.J. (1904–1984)

"Of all the major figures in contemporary theology (and philosophy), Bernard Lonergan still remains the least known." What David Tracy wrote in 1970 is still true. Of very few other contemporary philosophers does anyone claim he is the most important thinker since Kant, or Descartes, or even Aquinas. Yet many of Lonergan's disciples (who are philosophers, not fanatics) claim that for him.

Lonergan's life (born in Canada, lived mainly in America and Rome) was as unspectacular as you would expect of a priest, an academic, a theologian and a philosopher. (Contrast Maritain here.) The drama is in the ideas.

Like Maritain, Lonergan discovered Aquinas after years of philosophizing, and he spent eleven years studying him. This study, he said, **changed me profoundly,** especially since he saw how much more profound and dynamic the actual Aquinas was than the fossilized rationalism taught in the scholastic manuals.

But there were two major developments in philosophy since Aquinas that needed to be addressed in ways impossible for Aquinas because his "horizons" were different. One was the development of modern science, and the other was the consciousness of history. Thus, in two words, Kant and Hegel had to be assimilated, but critically. Lonergan uses Kant's "transcendental method" but not Kant's epistemological idealism (the "Copernican revolution in philosophy"), and he embraces a historical dialectic like Hegel and is very sensitive to the depth of the historical changes in human consciousness, but he does not accept the content of Hegel's "absolute idealism" or his pantheistic "process theology."

Lonergan's central question, like the central question of modern philosophy, is epistemological. He became convinced that neither the medieval Scholastic, the Cartesian, the Humean, the Kantian, or the Hegelian epistemologies were adequate. This is what he tried to remedy in his magnum opus, *Insight, A Study of Human Understanding,* in 1958.

Like all modern Thomists, Lonergan attacks modern philosophy's denial that the human mind can know being, or objective reality as it really is. But his realism is not a "naïve" or "common sense" realism but a very careful, phenomenological, detailed, sophisticated, critical realism. He accepts modern philosophy's "turn to the subject" but not its subjectivism. One of his most quoted sayings is that **genuine objectivity is the fruit of authentic subjectivity.**

He begins with questioning, or **the pure, unrestricted desire to know,** to know all that there is to know about all that there is. This desire is implied in all human questioning, and it orients all other human conscious acts. **Prior to the neatly formulated**

questions of systematizing intelligence, there is the deep-set wonder in which all questions have their source and ground. This is the life and task that Socrates, Plato, and Aristotle all affirmed for philosophy when they said that philosophy begins in wonder.

The assumption inherent in questioning is that there are true, intelligible answers, and this fact turns out to be an argument for God, when Lonergan asks: **Why should the answers that satisfy the intelligence . . . yield anything more than a subjective satisfaction? Why should they be supposed to possess any relevance to knowledge of the universe? Of course, we assume that they do. We can point to the fact that our assumption is confirmed by its fruits. So implicitly we grant that the universe is intelligible and, once that is granted, there arises the question whether the universe could be intelligible without having an intelligent ground. . . .**

To deliberate about deliberating is to ask whether any deliberating is worth while. Has "worth while" any ultimate meaning? . . . Is the universe on our side or are we just gamblers, and, if gamblers, are we not, perhaps, fools, individually struggling for authenticity and collectively endeavoring to snatch progress from the ever mounting welter of decline? The questions arise and, clearly, our attitudes and our resoluteness may be profoundly affected by the answers. Does there or does there not necessarily exist a transcendent, intelligent ground of the universe? Is that ground, or (instead) are we, the primary instance of . . . consciousness? Are cosmogenesis, biological evolution, (and) historical process . . . cognate to us . . . or are they indifferent and so alien to us?

Insight is a difficult book, rather like Kant's *Critique of Pure Reason*. What would motivate us to read it? Well, suppose we knew next to nothing about the bank into which we put all our money and valuables; would we be satisfied with that? But understanding is our mind's bank. So Lonergan tells us to Thoroughly understand what it is to understand, and not only will you understand the broad lines of all there is to be understood but also you will possess a fixed base, an invariant pattern, opening upon all further developments of understanding.

Cultural tradition, common sense, and science are not sufficient. History and our cultural traditions give us a mixture of truth and bias (of which Lonergan helpfully distinguished four basic kinds), so we need a way to distinguish them. **There are precise matters in which common sense can be expected to go wrong; there are definite issues on which science is prone to issue extra-scientific opinions,** especially on questions of value, morality, philosophy, and religion. The modern "turn to the subject" means that we must be more critical about ourselves and our questioning.

The three basic questions of *Insight* are: **What am I doing when I am knowing? Why is doing that** *knowing?* **and What do I know when I do it? The first answer is a cognitional theory. The second is an epistemology. The third is a metaphysics.**

Metaphysics is not easy, especially because, according to Lonergan, Maritain and Husserl are wrong when they affirmed that we have a direct intuition of being. Lonergan says we have a "notion" of being but not a "concept" of being. For a concept contains the essence of its object, and only God can have such a concept of being itself. But since we do have a "notion" of being, we can affirm that being is intelligible—intrinsically (essentially), universally, and completely. We implicitly affirm that in our unrestricted desire to know all that there is to know about all that there is. We cannot affirm a desire and at the same time not affirm its object.

Lonergan, contrary to Gilson and Maritain, maintains that a metaphysics that follows, rather than precedes, a cognitional theory and an epistemology is a more dynamic one, and therefore a more complete one, than that of classical pre-modern metaphysics. The reason for that is not just epistemological but metaphysical: **Being is the unknown that questioning intends to know, that answers partially reveal, that further questioning presses on to know more fully. The notion of being, then, is essentially dynamic, proleptic, an anticipation of the entirety, the concreteness, the totality, that we ever intend and, since our knowledge is finite, never reach.** For Lonergan the dynamism of metaphysics necessarily follows from the dynamism of the knowing subject.

Lonergan distinguishes three essential steps in all human inquiry, or questioning: (1) experiencing, (2) insight (understanding), and (3) judging.

Like Aquinas, Lonergan sees the proper use of the intellect as the key to morality and the good life. He summarizes the five great commandments of the mind this way: **Progress proceeds from . . . subjects being their true selves by observing the transcendental** (universal) **precepts: Be attentive, Be intelligent, Be reasonable, Be responsible, Be loving.**

The ultimate goal of philosophical understanding for Lonergan, as for Aquinas, is the ultimate reality: **Our subject has been the act of insight or understanding, and God is the unrestricted act of understanding, the eternal rapture glimpsed in every Archimedean cry of Eureka.**

After *Insight* Lonergan turned to Husserl and other phenomenologists, focused on feelings and values, and spoke of the **world mediated and constituted by meaning and motivated by value.** *Method in Theology* gives carefully worked-out critical criteria for making value judgments about our culture's past and present, for discriminating between the wheat and the chaff that our history gives us. The two fundamental ways this is to be done are: first, the development of our nature, and second, our response to the supernatural:

Human development is of two different kinds. There is development from below upwards, from experience to growing understanding, from growing understanding to balanced judgments, from balanced judgment to fruitful courses of action, and from fruitful courses of action to the new situations that call forth further understanding, profounder judgment, richer courses of action.

But there is also development from above downwards. There is the transformation of falling in love: the domestic love of family, the human love of one's tribe, one's city, one's country, mankind; the divine love that orients man in his cosmos and

expresses itself in his worship. Where hatred only sees evil, love reveals values. . . . Where hatred reinforces bias, love dissolves it . . . a religion that promotes self- transcendence to the point, not merely of justice, but of self-sacrificing love, will have a redemptive role in human society inasmuch as such love can undo the mischief of decline and restore the cumulative process of progress.

Despite his concentration on the intellect (like both Augustine and Aquinas), Lonergan prioritizes love (also like both Augustine and Aquinas) when it comes to God and neighbor: **it is primarily a question of decision. Will I love God . . . or will I refuse? Will I live out the gift of His love, or will I hold back, turn away, withdraw? Only secondarily do there arise the questions of God's existence and nature, and they are the questions either of the lover seeking to know Him or of the unbeliever seeking to escape Him. Such is the basic option of the existential subject.**

Lonergan is a polymath; his interests are wide-ranging (mathematics, evolution, economics, art, language, method, theology, Thomism, phenomenology) but integrated in a system that I have not even attempted to outline in a fair or comprehensive way. Instead, I have offered samples of the wisdom of both his questions and his answers to entice further exploration.

99. W. Norris Clarke, S.J. (1917–2008)

My penultimate philosopher is a surprising choice, because he is relatively little-known: W. Norris Clarke, S.J. Yet I predict that his central idea may be, and certainly should be, the most fruitful wave of the future if philosophy is to fulfill its essential original task, the love of wisdom. The central idea is the marriage of the best of the old with the best of the new, i.e., the ancient objective metaphysics of Aquinas with the modern philosophy of the subject, or Personalism, especially Buber, Marcel, Levinas, and Kant's second categorical imperative. This was done also by Maritain and by two other thinkers who were theologians more than philosophers but who also happened to be popes: Karol Wojtyla and Joseph Ratzinger.

Fr. Clarke, a native New Yorker and a Jesuit who taught at Fordham University and wrote hundreds of landmark articles on the intersections between Thomism and modern philosophy, was both a Thomist and a Personalist. He integrated into traditional Thomism not only Personalism but also many of the other positive themes of modern philosophy, e.g., in *The One and the Many,* a creative and exciting metaphysics textbook. (That description is not, as it seems, an oxymoron!). His "big idea" in *Person and Being,* from which we quote below, is to explicitly unite the two most fundamental, and fundamentally different, positive philosophical traditions, the ancient and the modern, the objective and the subjective, the metaphysical and the phe- nomenological.

Others have contributed to the same synthesis. Karol Wojtyla united Thomism, personalism, and phenomenology, though not nearly as clearly as Clarke. Dietrich Von Hildebrand united personalism and phenomenology in ethics. In a very different way, Levinas did the same, and also (in still another different way) Buber in *I and Thou.* Lonergan also combined traditional Thomism and modern thought, especially "the turn to the subject."

Just what is "personalism"? We should take time to define it, since it is such an influential and lasting, yet flexible, strand in contemporary philosophy.

Emmanuel Mounier in France and Edgar Brightman in America are often credited with inventing this philosophy, since they coined the term (and Mounier's short but clear *Personalism* is a very readable introduction to it), but the philosophy itself extends considerably beyond these two into both earlier and later thinkers.

Leszek Kolakowski, in his excellent *A History of Contemporary Philosophy,* provides a useful double list of the tenets of personalism:

Traditional theses:

(1) It promotes a worldview that is ontological or metaphysical . . . the world is a reality external to man, which has its own consistency. In it there are entities with varying degrees of perfection, among which the person stands out. (Cf. Aquinas's remark that "'Person' designates that which is noblest in all nature.")

(2) Man has the capacity to know a truth that, at the same time, transcends him. Personalism allows the possibility of objective knowledge of reality, which is accessed subjectively. However, man is not capable of knowing the whole truth, leaving the door open to mystery and transcendence.

(3) The person is free, with the capacity for self-determination—man has self-mastery—and the capacity to change the world.

(4) The person is a substantial reality, not merely a succession of experiences.

(5) A human nature exists, which changes accidentally over the course of history but remains specifically identical to itself within these changes.

(6) Man has an ethical dimension and a religious dimension, which arise from his spiritual and free nature.

(7) There should be a union between faith and culture. yet we must **distinguish between the supernatural and natural realms . . . there are revealed truths, but it** (philosophy) **carries out a strictly philosophical labor.**

Modern theses:

(1) The insurmountable distinction between things and persons and the need to treat them as distinct philosophical categories. (Existentialism's point.)

(2) The foundational importance of emotions, seen as an essential part of the person. Feelings, emotions, the "heart"—these things should be the subject of philosophical reflection just as intelligence and free will have long been. (Von Hildebrand's point.)

(3) The person has an essential calling for interpersonal, family and social relationships. The person realizes himself through giving, dialogue, and communion with other persons. (Buber's point.)

(4) Personalism maintains the absolute primary of moral and religious values over those that are purely intellectual. (Kierkegaard's point.)

(5) It turns human corporeality and sexuality into a topic of philosophical reflection. A person is an embodied, sexed spirit. (The point of the "Theology of the Body" of Karol Wojtyla, Pope St. John Paul II.)

(6) Personalism must be communitarian, given the relational characteristics of the human person . . . political philosophy should help overcome the choice between totalitarian collectivism and capitalist individualism. (Ricoeur's point.)

(7) Philosophy cannot be reduced to an academic and erudite knowledge but must interact with cultural and social reality. (Maritain's point.)

(8) Personalism sees the development of a modern philosophy that values subjectivity as a positive turn and yet **criticizes the modern trends of relativism and subjectivism. Personalists do not position themselves as "outside" of Modernity.** (Lonergan's point.)

Fr. Clarke's marriage of Thomistic metaphysics and Personalism is presented most centrally in his *Person and Being*—a little book but a potentially revolutionary one. It "sparks" like flint and steel (or man and woman) coming together. He calls it **a creative retrieval and completion of St. Thomas's own thought on the metaphysics of the person,** and he wrote it out of the need **to draw out and highlight a dynamic and relational notion of the person which seems to us clearly implied in St. Thomas's own metaphysics of being as existential act.** In other words, he grounds Buber in Gilson.

Professor Joseph Ratzinger (later Pope Benedict XVI) wrote that "in the relational notion of person developed within the theology of the Trinity . . . lies concealed a revolution in man's view of the world . . . that *in* its self-being it does not belong to itself." This central theme has historical roots that are nearly 2000 years old and deeply embedded in Christian Trinitarian theology, specifically in the distinction between "person" and "nature," the fundamental philosophical distinction that came to light from the theological controversies about the nature of God. That fact about the historical origin of the idea will automatically disqualify it in many minds; but it rests not on religious but on philosophical grounds that are verifiable in universal human experience. Its ultimate ontological foundation, however, is the nature of God, the ultimate being, as revealed in the divine name itself: "I AM": the unity of the "I-ness" and the "am-ness."

There is another urgent reason for undertaking this "creative completion" today. The second part of our century has seen a rich development of the relational aspects of the person, worked out by existential phenomenologists and personalists of various schools. . . . Yet these valuable analyses have almost without exception been suspicious of, or even positively hostile towards the notion of person as *substance,* **which was so heavily stressed in the classical tradition. . . .**

The single text in Aquinas that anchors the synthesis is that "Person is that which is most perfect in all of nature (reality, being)." (ST I,29,3)

Thus, Clarke points out, both being and the person are

(a) active,

(b) receptive (which is *not* an imperfection except accidentally, because of time),

(c) self-communicative, and

(d) relational.

"Being" means above all "existence" (the central thesis of Gilson and Maritain).

And "existence" means "actuality.'

And "actuality" ("first act") always issues forth in some "activity" ("second act").

And "activity" means relationship, self-communication, self-giving, and, ultimately love. "The act of existence *(esse)* is not a state, it is an act, the act of all acts, and therefore must be understood as act and not as a static definable object of conception. *Esse* is dynamic impulse, energy . . . a restless, striving force," says Gilsonian Gerald Phelan. Maritain calls it "the basic generosity of existence." Dante called it "the love that moves the sun and the other stars," in the last line of the "Divine Comedy."

The act of existence is not merely the actualization from without, so to speak, of the perfections somehow already present potentially in the essence in its own right; it is rather the whole positive core and content of *all* the perfection that is actualized in the essence. Thus the essence (in a finite created being) is really only a particular limiting mode of existence, which constricts the all-embracing fullness of perfection that is existence itself down to some determinate, limited participation.

Of both the act of existence and of the person can it be said that it is "most perfect." Like *esse,* the **person is not some special mode of being, added on from the outside, so to speak. It is really nothing but the fullness of being itself . . . when not restricted by the limitations proper to the material mode of being.** Personality is to matter what existence is to essence.

If all the perfection of being a person comes to it from its act of existence, proportioned of course to its nature, then we can transfer all the attributes characteristic of existence itself over into the person as such, where they will be found at enhanced degrees of intensity . . . . The higher the form of intrinsic existence, the more developed becomes the relatedness with reality. . . . And paradoxically, the more intensely present to myself I am at one pole, the more intensely I am present and open to others at the other. And reciprocally, the more I make myself truly present to the others as an "I" or self, the more I must also be present to myself, in order that it may be truly *I* that is present to them, not a mask. We are moving towards a metaphysics of love . . . love is not a passing pleasure or emotion, but the very meaning of being alive, the basic generosity of existence.

This very abstract metaphysical point has cutting practical and even political consequences: **It is worth noting how far this conception of the human person is from the excessively autonomous, individualistic one of John Locke and so many modern Western political thinkers since Descartes, where the primary value is not put on relationship and communion but on self-sufficiency . . . (but) it is impossible to make justice alone the foundation for a viable social order. Only friendship, altruistic love of some kind, can supply the positive cohesive energy required, as St. Thomas himself maintains.** (And so did Aristotle!)

100. G. K. Chesterton (1874–1936)

He was not a professional philosopher. As far as I know, he is not included in any other anthology of "great philosophers." Yet when you read him I think you will see why I have included him here, in fact given him the very last place, the final say, even though he wrote 100 years ago.

The reasons are, in three words, that he was prophetic, profound, and practical, i.e., commonsensical.

How can I claim he is commonsensical when what he is the most famous for is his paradoxes, his habit of standing things on their heads?

Because that posture is an illusion: it is we who are standing on our heads, not he. He is simply looking at our upside-down world right side up, speaking the common sense of a child to those who have lost it. When you read him, you see most other philosophers—and yourself—as exposed naked emperors.

For this, and for his constant cheer and joy, for his playful personality and his poet's love of juggling words, as well as for his philosophy, I love him. I also understand how it is that some readers passionately hate him: because he leaves you feeling really stupid! But you can cultivate the habit of being grateful for being shown how stupid you are. It really helps your education.

Because he is not a professor—he never even went to university—he talks about real things rather than philosophical abstractions; and it may seem a "stretch" for me to outline his thoughts under the traditional divisions of philosophy, as I have done here. But I have done it because it is doable: for he is as much of a philosopher as Socrates, and similar enough in spirit to justify ending the book with him, the book that bears Socrates' noble name in its title.

Bartlett's Familiar Quotations lists more quotations from him than from anyone else outside the Bible except Shakespeare. And Chestertonianisms are as addictive as potato chips: you can't eat just one. You will probably underline more of his quotations than anyone else's in this book.

These quotations are only a small sample. I have chosen only *philosophical* quotations; the ones about religion are even more numerous and even more radical.

His philosophy is best summarized in *Orthodoxy,* one of the most unorthodox books ever written, and in *St. Thomas Aquinas, the Dumb Ox,* which Thomists like Gilson insist is the best book ever written by anyone about Aquinas. *The Everlasting Man* is his other masterpiece, a magisterial history of religion unlike any other. (It, more than any other book, converted C. S. Lewis.)

Because his last name is so large, like himself (he weighed over 300 pounds), he is habitually nicknamed GK, as Kierkegaard is nicknamed SK.

We will look at his answers to ten great questions of philosophy: questions of method, metaphysics, cosmology, anthropology, epistemology, general ethics, applied ethics, political philosophy, philosophy of history, and aesthetics. Philosophy of religion is omitted only to prove he can hold his own with the philosophers without it, and because it would require another twenty pages.

Method

Part of GK's charm is his striking clarity with words. This, plus the habit of "telling it like it is" and exposing popular fallacies with paradoxes, constitutes his method. It is unfortunately rare among philosophers. Here is a good example of his style in speaking about style:

Long words go rattling by us like long railway trains. We know they are carrying thousands who are too tired or too indolent to walk and think for themselves. It is a good exercise to try . . . to express any opinion one holds in words of one syllable. If you say "The social utility of the indeterminate sentence is recognized by all criminologists as a part of our sociological evolution towards a more humane and scientific view of punishment," you can go on talking like that for hours with hardly a movement of the gray matter inside your skull. But if you begin "I wish Jones to go to gaol and Brown to say when Jones shall come out," you will discover, with a thrill of horror, that you are obliged to think.

Metaphysics

(1) In metaphysics, as everywhere, the best question to begin with is the beginning. GK begins, as Aquinas does, with our awareness of being:

There is at the back of our lives an abyss of light more blinding and unfathomable than any abyss of darkness; and it is the abyss of actuality, of existence, of the fact that things truly are.it is unthinkable, yet we cannot unthink it. . . .

The whole system of St. Thomas hangs on one huge and yet simple idea, which does actually cover everything there is, and even everything that could possibly be. He represents this cosmic conception by the word *Ens.. .*Unfortunately there is no satisfying translation of the word *Ens . . .* the word "being," as it comes to a modern Englishman, through modern associations, has a sort of hazy atmosphere that is not in the short and sharp Latin word. Perhaps it reminds him of fantastic professors in fiction, who wave their hands and say, "Thus do we mount to the ineffable heights of pure and radiant Being"; or, worse still, of actual professors in real life,

who say, "All Being is Becoming, and is but the evolution of Not-Being by the law of its Being." Perhaps it only reminds him of romantic rhapsodies in old love stories: "Beautiful and adorable being, light and breath of my very being." Anyhow it has a wild and woolly sort of sound, as if only very vague people used it. . . . Now the Latin word *Ens* has a sound like the English word *End*. It is final and even abrupt. . . .

Ever since Descartes, modern philosophers have begun not with metaphysics but with epistemology, with the critique of reason. GK praises Thomas for doing the opposite:

St. Thomas's work has a constructive quality absent from almost all cosmic systems after him. For he is already building a house, while the newer speculators are still . . . quarrelling about whether they can even make the tools that will make the house.

(2) Granting that being comes first, what comes first in our reaction to it? For GK, as for Socrates, Plato, Aristotle, Augustine, and Aquinas, the answer is *wonder and gratitude:*

I would maintain that thanks are the highest form of thought, and that gratitude is happiness doubled by wonder.

I invented a rudimentary and makeshift mystical theory of my own. It was substantially this: that even mere existence, reduced to its most primary limits, was extraordinary enough to be exciting. Anything was magnificent as compared with nothing . . . (we should) dig for this submerged sunrise of wonder, so that a man sitting in a chair might suddenly understand that he was actually alive, and be happy.

(3) But what is being? GK rejects equally the two easy answers of monism and pluralism, pantheism and Nominalism, that have seduced so many philosophers:

(Pantheism) means that there is no such thing as a thing. At best, there is only one thing, and that is a flux of everything and anything. This is an attack not upon the faith but upon the mind; you cannot think if there are no things to think about. You cannot think if you are not separate from the object of thought.

(Pantheism) is the doctrine that we are really all one person; that there are no real walls of individuality between man and man. If I may put it so, (it) does not tell us to love our neighbors; (it) tells us to be our neighbors. . . . I never heard of any suggestion in my life with which I more violently disagree. I want to love my neighbor not because he is I, but precisely because he is not I. . . . If souls are

separate, love is possible. If souls are united, love is obviously impossible. . . . The oriental deity is like a giant who should have lost his leg or hand and be always seeking to find it; but the Christian power is like some giant who in a strange generosity should cut off his right hand so that it might of its own accord shake hands with him.

There is an opposite attack on thought: that every separate thing is "unique" and there are no categories at all. This is also merely destructive. . . . Thinking means connecting things, and stops if they cannot be connected. A man cannot open his mouth without contradicting it. Thus when Mr. Wells says (as he did somewhere), "All chairs are quite different," he utters not merely a misstatement, but a contradiction in terms. If all chairs were quite different, you could not call them "all chairs."

. . . the Nominalist declared that things differ too much to be really classified, so that they are only labeled. Aquinas was a firm but moderate Realist, and therefore held that there really are general qualities: as that human beings are human, amid other paradoxes. . . . Mr. H. G. Wells had an alarming fit of Nominalist philosophy, and poured forth book after book to argue that . . . a man is so much an individual that he is not even a man.

(4) One of the most pervasive and important terms in Aquinas's metaphysics, and the one most consistently misunderstood by moderns, is the Aristotelian term "form."

It is not really very difficult to learn the meaning of the main terms (of Thomas's metaphysics); but their medieval meaning is sometimes the exact opposite of their modern meaning. The obvious example is in the pivotal word "form." We say nowadays, "I wrote a formal apology to the Dean," or "The proceedings when we wound up the Tip-Cat Club were purely formal." But we mean that they were purely fictitious; and St. Thomas, had he been a member of the Tip-Cat Club, would have meant just the opposite. He would have meant that the proceedings dealt with the very heart and soul and secret of the whole being of the Tip-Cat club; and that the apology to the Dean was so essentially apologetic that it tore the very heart out in tears of true contrition. For "formal" in Thomist language means actual, or possessing the real decisive quality that makes a thing itself. . . . Every artist knows that the form is not superficial but fundamental; that the form is the foundation. Every sculptor knows that the form of the statue is not the outside of the statue but rather the inside of the statue.

(5) If Aquinas is right, the most obviously and disastrously erroneous metaphysics is materialism, which GK refutes with a reductio ad absurdum:

The great human dogma is that the wind moves the trees. The great human heresy is that the trees move the wind ... the trees stand for all visible things and the wind for the invisible ... When people begin to say that the material circumstances have alone created the moral circumstances, then they have prevented all possibility of serious change. For if my circumstances have made me wholly stupid, how can I be certain even that I am right in altering those circumstances?

As an explanation of the world, materialism has a sort of insane simplicity.... He understands everything, and everything does not seem worth understanding.

(6) What makes anything worth understanding is its value, its good, its purpose, its end, its final causality, its teleology. GK affirms this feature of the world, which is intuitively and commonsensically obvious to everyone but atheists, and he immediately shows us its obvious anti-atheist implication, thus showing why atheistic Darwinian fundamentalists see the very idea of "intelligent design" as Christians see the forbidden fruit:

I had always felt life first as a story; and if there is a story there is a story-teller ... if there has been from the beginning anything that can possibly be called a Purpose, it must reside in something that has the essential elements of a Person. There cannot be an intention hovering in the air all by itself, any more than a memory that nobody remembers.

Cosmology

(1) When we turn to cosmology we again find GK starting with the single most obvious and universal feature of the cosmos, its contingency.

Until we realize that things might not be, we cannot realize that things are.... Until we picture nonentity, we underrate the victory of God ... we know nothing until we know nothing.

(We) discover that the rhinoceros does exist and then take pleasure in the fact that he looks as if he didn't.

My first and last philosophy ... are the things called fairy tales. They seem to me to be the entirely reasonable things.... It might be stated this way. There are certain sequences or developments (cases of one thing following another) which are, in the true sense of the word ... necessary. Such are mathematical and merely logical sequences. We in fairyland (who are the most reasonable of all creatures) admit that reason and that necessity. For instance, if the Ugly Sisters are older than Cinderella, it is (in an iron and awful sense) *necessary* that Cinderella is younger than the Ugly Sisters.... But as I put my head over the hedge of the elves and began to take notice of the natural world, I observed an extraordinary thing. I observed that

learned men in spectacles were talking of the actual things that happened—dawn and death and so on—as if *they* were rational and inevitable. They talked as if the fact that trees bear fruit were just as *necessary* as the fact that two and one trees make three. But it is not. There is an enormous difference, by the test of fairyland, which is the test of the imagination. You cannot *imagine* two and one not making three. But you can easily imagine trees not growing fruit; you can imagine them growing golden candlesticks or tigers hanging on by the tail. . . . These tales . . . make rivers run with wine only to make us remember, for one wild moment, that they run with water . . . the fairy-tale philosopher is glad that the leaf is green precisely because it might have been scarlet. He feels as if it had turned green an instant before he looked at it. He is pleased that snow is white on the strictly reasonable ground that it might have been black. Every colour has in it a bold quality as of choice: the red of garden roses is not only decisive but dramatic, like suddenly spilt blood. He feels that something has been *done*. . . .

We cannot say why an egg can turn into a chicken any more than we can say why a bear could turn into a fairy prince. As *ideas,* the egg and the chicken are further off from each other than the bear and the prince; for no egg in itself suggests a chicken, whereas some princes do suggest bears. . . . When we are asked why eggs turn to birds or fruits fall in autumn, we must answer exactly as the fairy godmother would answer if Cinderella asked her why mice turned to horses or her clothes fell from her at twelve o'clock. We must answer that it is *magic* . . . It is not a necessity. . . . We do not count on it; we bet on it. We risk the remote possibility of a miracle.

. . . repetition made the things to me rather more weird than more rational. It was as if, having seen a curiously shaped nose in the street and dismissed it as an accident, I had then seen six other noses of the same astonishing shape. I should have fancied for a moment that it must be some local secret society. So one elephant having a trunk was odd; but all elephants having trunks looked like a plot. . . .

All the towering materialism which dominates the modern mind rests ultimately upon one assumption; a false assumption. It is supposed that if a thing goes on repeating itself it is probably dead; a piece of clockwork. People feel that if the universe was personal it would vary; if the sun were alive, it would dance. This is a fallacy . . . it might be true that the sun rises regularly because he never gets tired of rising. His routine might be due, not to a lifelessness, but to a rush of life. The thing I mean can be seen, for instance, in children. . . . Because children have abounding vitality, because they are in spirit fierce and free, therefore they want things repeated and unchanged. They always say, "Do it again"; and the grown-up does it again until he is nearly dead. For grown-up people are not strong enough to exult in monotony. But perhaps God is strong enough to exult in monotony. It is possible that God says every morning, "Do it again" to the sun, and every evening "Do it again" to the moon. It may not be automatic necessity that makes all daisies alike; it may be that God makes every daisy separately, but has never got tired of making them. . . . Heaven may *encore* the bird who laid an egg.

"Robinson Crusoe" . . . owes its eternal vivacity to the fact that it celebrates the poetry of limits. . . . Every kitchen tool becomes ideal because Crusoe might have dropped it in the sea. It is a good exercise, in empty or ugly hours of the day, to look at anything, the coal-scuttle or the book-case, and think how happy one could be to have brought it out of the sinking ship onto the solitary island. But it is a better exercise still to remember how all things have had this hair-breadth escape: everything has been saved from a wreck. Every man has had one horrible adventure . . . every man in the street is a Great Might Not Have Been.

(2) As in metaphysics, so in cosmology GK moves from the first fact, of the existence of contingent things, to our first reaction to that fact, which is gratitude and wonder:

If one could see the whole universe suddenly, it would look like a bright-coloured toy, just as the South American hornbill looks like a bright-coloured toy.

If a man saw the world upside down, with all the trees and towers hanging head downwards as in a pool, one effect would be to emphasize the idea of dependence . . . he would be thankful to God Almighty that it had not been dropped. . . . He who has seen the whole world hanging on a hair of the mercy of God has seen the truth . . . he who has seen the vision of his city upside-down has seen it the right way up.

The prerequisite for this wonder is humility: **Alice must grow small if she is to be Alice in Wonderland.**

It is too little to say that GK accepts, or even loves, the cosmos: he exults in it. He calls himself not an optimist but a "higher optimist": **These higher optimists, of which Dickens was one, do not approve of the Universe; they do not even admire the universe; the fall in love with it.**

The same is true of our human cosmos, our city: **Men did not love Rome because she was great; she became great because men loved her.**

But what is cosmological optimism? **An optimist could not mean a man who thought everything right and nothing wrong. For that is meaningless; it is like calling everything right and nothing left. . . . My acceptance of the universe is not optimism, it is more like patriotism. It is a matter of primary loyalty. The world is not a lodging house at Brighton, which we are to leave because it is miserable. It is the fortress of our family, with the flag flying on the turret. . . . What is the matter with the pessimist? I think it can be stated by saying that he is the cosmic anti-patriot.**

What is the cosmos, then? Again, an image says more than a concept: **Nature is not our mother; Nature is our sister. We can be proud of her beauty, since we have the same father; but she has no authority over us. . . . To St. Francis, Nature is a sister, and even a younger sister: a little, dancing sister, to be laughed at as well as loved.**

(3) Ever since Hegel, the fundamental feature of the modern cosmos has been Evolution. GK is skeptical of this as a universal philosophical theory, as distinct from a humble merely biological hypothesis:

There is something slow and soothing and gradual about the word . . . evolution really is mistaken for explanation. . . . But this notion of something smooth and slow, like the ascent of a slope, is a great part of the illusion . . . an event is not any more intrinsically intelligible or unintelligible because of the pace at which it moves. . . . The Greek witch may have turned sailors to swine with a stroke of the wand. But to see a naval gentleman of our acquaintance looking a little more like a pig every day, till he ended with four trotters and a curly tail, would not be any more soothing. . . . Man is not merely an evolution but rather a revolution. . . .

They are obsessed by their evolutionary monomania that every great thing grows from a seed, or something smaller than itself. They seem to forget that every seed comes from a tree, or from something larger than itself. . . . According to the real records available, barbarism and civilization were not successive stages in the progress of the world. They were conditions that existed side by side, as they still exist side by side. . . .

The world does not explain itself, and cannot do so merely by continuing to expand itself . . . it is absurd for the evolutionist to complain that it is unthinkable for an admittedly unthinkable God to make everything out of nothing and then pretend that it is *more* thinkable that nothing should turn itself into everything.

(4) GK's cosmos is open, not closed. Thus miracles, whether actual are not, are possible:

For some extraordinary reason, there is a fixed notion that it is more liberal to disbelieve in miracles than to believe in them. Why, I cannot imagine, nor can anybody tell me. . . . The man of the nineteenth century did not disbelieve in the Resurrection because his liberal Christianity allowed him to doubt it. He disbelieved in it because his very strict materialism did not allow him to believe it.

(5) The cosmos is also, for GK, as for the medievals, not just a thing, or the sum of things, but a sign. It is significant. It points beyond itself to something else, something mysterious:

There was a time when you and I and all of us were all very close to God, so that even now the color of a pebble . . . the smell of a flower . . . comes to our hearts with a kind of authority and certainty; as if they were fragments of a muddled message, or features of a forgotten face.

(6) This world is mysterious because there are more connections in it than we can know, not fewer. We might call this Synchronicity:

Suppose somebody in a story says: "Pluck this flower and a princess will die in a castle beyond the sea," we do not know why something stirs in the subconsciousness, or why what is impossible seems almost inevitable. Suppose we read "And in the hour when the king extinguished the candle his ships were wrecked far away on the coast of Hebrides." We do not know why the imagination has accepted that image before the reason can reject it; or why such correspondences seem really to correspond to something in the soul. Very deep things in our nature, some dim sense of the dependence of great things upon small, some dark suggestion that the things nearest to us stretch far beyond our power, some sacramental feeling of the magic in material substances, and many more emotions past finding out, are in an idea like that of the external soul.

Epistemology

(1) Unlike most modern philosophers and like St. Thomas, GK is neither a Rationalist nor an Irrationalist. His practical common sense tells him that **Those who use the intellect never worship it; they know too much about it. Those who worship the intellect never use it, as you can see by the things they say about it.**

Three things keep reason humble: imagination, mysticism and faith.

First, imagination: **Imagination does not breed insanity. Exactly what does breed insanity is reason. Poets do not go mad; but chess-players do. . . . Poetry is sane because it floats easily in an infinite sea; reason seeks to cross the infinite sea, and so make it finite. The result is mental exhaustion. . . . The poet only asks to get his head into the heavens. It is the logician who seeks to get the heavens into his head. And it is his head that splits. . . . The madman is not the man who has lost his reason. The madman is the man who has lost everything except his reason. . . . If a man says (for instance) that men have a conspiracy against him, you cannot dispute it except by saying that all the men deny that they are conspirators, which is exactly what conspirators would do. . . . Curing a madman is not arguing with a philosopher, it is casting out a devil . . . his mind moves in a perfect but narrow circle. A small circle is quite as infinite as a large circle; but, though it is quite as infinite, it is not so large. . . . How much larger your life would be if your self could become** smaller in it. . . . **How much happier you would be, how much more of you there would be, if the hammer of a higher God could smash your small cosmos, scattering the stars like spangles, and leave you in the open, free like other men to look up as well as down!**

Second, mysticism: **Mysticism keeps men sane. As long as you have mystery, you have health; when you destroy mystery you create morbidity. The ordinary man has always been sane because the ordinary man has always been a mystic. . . . The whole secret of mysticism is this: that man can understand everything by the help of what he does not understand. . . . The mystic allows one thing to be mysterious, and everything else becomes lucid. . . . The one created thing which we cannot look at is the one thing in the light of which we look at everything. Like the sun at noon-day, mysticism explains everything else by the blaze of its own victorious invisibility.**

Third, faith: **It is significant that in the greatest religious poem extant, the Book of Job, the argument which convinces the infidel is not (as has been represented by the merely rational religionism of the eighteenth century) a picture of the ordered beneficence of the Creation; but, on the contrary, a picture of the huge and undecipherable unreason of it. . . . (God's) exuberant independence of our intellectual standards and our trivial definitions is the basis of spirituality as it is the basis of nonsense. Nonsense and faith (strange as the conjunction may seem) are the two supreme symbolic assertions of the truth that to draw out the soul of things with a syllogism is as impossible as to draw out Leviathan with a hook.**

(2) The happy relation between faith and reason is a second Thomistic theme in GK's epistemology:

It is idle to talk always of the alternative of reason and faith. Reason is itself a matter of faith. It is an act of faith to assert that our thoughts have any relation to reality at all.

In fact, **In so far as religion is gone, reason is going. For they are both of the same primary and authoritative kind. . . . The whole modern world is at war with reason; and the tower already reels.**

The first line of GK's autobiography satirizes faithless reason: **Bowing down in blind credulity, as is my custom, before mere authority and the tradition of the elders, superstitiously swallowing a story I could not test at the time by experiment or private judgment, I am firmly of the opinion that I was born on the 28th of May, 1874. . . .**

Thus **there are only two kinds of people: those who accept dogmas and know it, and those who accept dogmas and don't know it.**

(3) Once reason is accepted, so is objective truth; and this is another radical alternative to typically modern epistemologies: it entails rejection of pragmatism, subjectivism, relativism, and skepticism:

I agree with the pragmatists that apparent objective truth is not the whole matter; that there is an authoritative need to believe the things that are necessary to the human mind. But I say that one of those necessities precisely is a belief in objective truth. . . . Pragmatism is a matter of human needs; and one of the first of human needs is to be something more than a pragmatist.

(4) Subjectivism fares no better than pragmatism:

When a child looks out of the nursery window and sees anything, say, the green lawn and the garden, what does he actually know? . . . (Modern epistemology says) **that the child does not see any grass at all, but only a sort of green mist reflected in the tiny mirror of the human eye. . . . If he is not sure of the existence of the grass, which he sees through the glass of the window, how on earth can he be sure of the existence of the retina which he sees through the glass of the microscope?**

(5) Ditto for relativism:

The modern habit of saying, "Every man has a different philosophy; this is my philosophy and it suits me": the habit of saying this is a mere weak-mindedness. A cosmic philosophy is not constructed to fit a man; a cosmic philosophy is constructed to fit a cosmos. A man can no more possess a private religion (or philosophy) **than he can possess a private sun and moon.**

(6) And skepticism is the easiest of all to refute. To the skeptic's objection that dogmas inhibit thought, GK replies that **Trees have no dogmas. Turnips are singularly broad-minded.**

To the objection that we must have an open mind, GK replies, **I opened my intellect as I opened my mouth, in order to shut it again on something solid.**

To the objection that we are all biased, GK replies: **It is useless to argue at all if all our conclusions are warped by our conditions. Nobody can correct anybody's bias if all mind is all bias.**

To the idea that bigotry is the only alternative to skepticism GK replies: **It is not bigotry to be certain we are right; but it is bigotry to be unable to imagine how we might possibly have gone wrong . . . bigotry is an incapacity to conceive seriously the alternative to a proposition.**

To the universal doubter GK replies: **In dealing with the arrogant asserter of doubt, it is not the right method to tell him to stop doubting. It is rather the right method to tell him to go on doubting, to doubt a little more . . . until at last, by some strange enlightenment he may begin to doubt himself.**

To the objection that doubt is humble GK replies: **What we suffer from today is humility in the wrong place. . . . A man was meant to be doubtful about himself, but undoubting about the truth; this has been exactly reversed.**

(7) For GK, as for Aquinas, the central question of modern philosophy, the refutation of skepticism, is a fake question. St. Thomas, he says, **does not deal at all with what many now think the main metaphysical question: whether we can prove that the primary act of recognition of any reality is real. . . . St. Thomas recognized instantly what so many modern sceptics have begun to suspect rather laboriously: that a man must either answer that question in the affirmative or else never answer any question. . . . I suppose it is true in a sense that a man can be a fundamental sceptic, but he cannot be anything else: certainly not even a defender of fundamental skepticism. . . . St. Thomas says emphatically that the child is aware of Ens. Long before he knows that grass is grass, or self is self, he knows that something is something. . . . That is as much monkish credulity as St. Thomas asks us to believe at the start.**

Rejection of skepticism and affirmation of being must be our starting point, not our demonstrated conclusion. **To this question "Is there anything?" St. Thomas begins by answering "Yes." If he began by answering "No," it would not be the beginning but the end. That is what some of us call common sense. Either there is no philosophy, no philosophers, no thinkers, no thought, no anything; or else there is a real bridge between the mind and reality.** Has any single modern epistemologist put that primary point so clearly? Have many of them even seen it?

There is a deeper human issue here, and not just a logical one, in the modern ingrown eyeballs. GK's alternative is the human and happy and natural one: **I was never interested in mirrors; that is, I was never primarily interested in my own reflection, or reflections. I am interested in wooden posts, which do startle me like miracles. I am interested in the post that stands waiting outside my door to hit me over the head, like a giant's club in a fairy tale. . . . For the amazing thing about the universe is** that it exists, not that we can discuss its existence . . . All my mental doors open outwards into a world I have not made.

That *strangeness* of things which is the light in all poetry, and indeed in all art, is really connected with their otherness, or what is called their objectivity. What is subjective must be stale.

GK habitually reverses our subjective perspective: **Grant Allen had written a book about the evolution of the idea of God. . . . It would be much more interesting if God wrote a book about the evolution of the idea of Grant Allen.**

The study of subjectivity is not yet subjectivism, but it is dangerous: **It is always perilous to the mind to reckon up the mind. A flippant person has asked why we say, "As mad as a hatter." A more flippant person might answer that a hatter is mad because he has to measure the human head.**

(8) GK affirms Aquinas's view that knowledge, like sex, is both active and passive, thus avoiding both typically modern epistemological errors of passive empiricism and active rationalism: He says that St. Thomas **avoids both pitfalls: the alternative abysses of impotence. The mind is not merely receptive in the sense that it absorbs sensations like so much blotting paper; on that sort of softness has been based all that cowardly materialism which conceives man as wholly servile to his environment. On the other hand, the mind is not purely creative, in the sense that it paints pictures on the windows and then mistakes them for a landscape outside. . . . In other words, the essence of the Thomist common sense is that the two agencies are at work: reality and the recognition of reality; and their meeting is a sort of marriage. Indeed it is very truly a marriage because it is fruitful . . . the external fact *fertilizes* the internal intelligence.**

According to Aquinas, the object becomes a part of the mind; nay, according to Aquinas, the mind actually becomes the object. But . . . it only becomes the object and does not create the object. In other words, the object is an object; it can and does exist outside the mind, or in the absence of the mind. And *therefore* it enlarges the mind of which it becomes a part. The mind conquers a new province like an emperor, but only because the mind has answered the bell like a servant.

(9) GK distinguishes two kinds of knowing: by acquaintance and by description, or *kennen* and *wissen,* or *connaitre* and *savoir,* or *mysteries* and *problems.* **Science can analyse a pork-chop, and say how much of it is phosphorous and how much is protein; but science cannot analyse any man's wish for a pork-chop, and say how much of it is hunger, how much custom, how much nervous fancy. . . . All attempts, therefore, at a science of any human things, at a science of history, a science of folk-lore, a science of sociology, are by their nature . . . hopeless.**

(10) GK's epistemological touchstone is common sense. That is why he is a Thomist. He says **The fact that Thomism is the philosophy of common sense is itself a matter of common sense. . . . Since the modern world began in the 16ᵗʰ century, nobody's system of philosophy has really corresponded to everybody's sense of reality; to what, if left to themselves, common men would call common sense.**

Anthropology

(1) GK affirms the intrinsic dignity of man. It is based on his uniqueness in nature: **Man is an exception, whatever else he is. If he is not the image of God, then he is a disease of the dust. If it is not true that a divine being fell, then we can only say that one of the animals went entirely off its head. . . . Alone among the animals he is shaken with the beautiful madness of laughter.**

The simplest lesson to learn in the cavern of the coloured pictures (at Lascaux) **. . . is the simple truth that man does differ from the brutes in kind and not in degree; and the proof of it is here: that it is like a joke to say that the most intelligent monkey drew a picture of a man. . . . Art is the signature of man. . . . This creature was truly different from all other creatures because he was a creator as well as a creature.**

(2) This uniqueness is universal, and it stems from our divine origin and end: **All human beings, without any exception whatever, are specially made, were specially shaped and pointed like shining arrows, for the end of hitting the mark of Beatitude.**

Our dignity is not refuted by our tininess in the universe: **Why should a man surrender his dignity to the solar system any more than to a whale?**

Our immanent dignity in the world is based on our transcendence of the world. Thus **Thoroughly worldly people never understand even the world.**

And our transcendence is based on God's: **Insisting that God is inside man, man is always inside himself. By insisting that God transcends man, man has transcended himself.**

Thus the modern cult of self-worship is deadly: **That Jones shall worship the god within him turns out ultimately to mean that Jones shall worship Jones. Let Jones worship the sun or moon, anything rather than the Inner Light; let Jones worship crocodiles, if can find any in his street, but not the god within.**

The men who really believe in themselves are all in lunatic asylums.

This does not contradict human dignity, for **One can hardly think too little of one's self. One can hardly think too much of one's soul.**

Thus humility is needed for humanity, self-forgetfulness for self-transcendence. GK shares the wisdom of Lao Tzu when he says: **A bird is active because a bird is soft. A stone is helpless because a stone is hard. . . . Hardness is weakness. The bird can of its nature go upwards because fragility is force. In perfect force there is a kind of frivolity. . . . Angels can fly because they can take themselves lightly.**

(3) GK distinguishes three philosophies of man, corresponding to rationalism, empiricism, and realism; or spiritualism, materialism, and common sense:

Man is not a balloon, going up into the sky, nor a mole burrowing merely in the earth, but rather a thing like a tree, whose roots are fed from the earth while its branches seem to rise almost to the stars.

(4) He also distinguishes three kinds of people: **Roughly speaking, there are three kinds of people in the world. The first kind of people are People; they are the largest and probably the most valuable class. We owe to this class the chairs we sit on, the clothes we wear, the houses we live in; and, indeed (when we come to think of it), we probably belong to this class ourselves. The second class may be called for convenience the Poets; they are often a nuisance to their families, but, generally speaking, a blessing to mankind. The third class is that of the Professors or Intellectuals, sometimes described as the thoughtful people; and these are a blight and a desolation both to their families and also to mankind.**

GK's odd wisdom is for ordinary people: **Oddities only strike ordinary people. Oddities do not strike odd people. This is why ordinary people have a much more exciting time; while odd people are always complaining of the dullness of life.**

(5) GK sees voluntarism as self-contradictory:

The worship of will is the negation of will. To admire mere choice is to refuse to choose. If Mr. Bernard Shaw comes up to me and says "Will something," that is tantamount to saying, "I do not mind what you will," and that is tantamount to saying, "I have no will in the matter."
They always talk of will as something that expands and breaks out. But it is quite the opposite. Every act of will is an act of self-limitation. To desire action is to desire limitation. In that sense every act of will is an act of self-sacrifice. When you choose anything, you reject everything else.

(6) Being a Christian, GK differs from modern anthropologists and psychologists by the key principle that could be called abnormalism:

The ordinary condition of man is not his sane or sensible condition . . . the normal itself is an abnormality.

(7) This fallenness came about by free will:

God had written not so much a poem, but rather a play; a play he had planned as perfect, but which had necessarily been left to human actors and stage-managers, who had since made a great mess of it.

(8) And free will is still in force. Thus GK rejects determinism as literally unlivable:

Determinists will tell me, with a degree of truth, that Determinism makes no difference to daily life. That means that although the Determinist knows men have no Free Will, yet he goes on treating them as if they had.
      . . . that no man should be blamed for anything he did because it was all (determined by) **heredity and environment . . . would stop a man in the act of saying "Thank you" to somebody for passing the mustard. For how could he be praised for passing the mustard if he could not be blamed for not passing the mustard?**
      To a Christian, existence is a story which may end up in any way. In a thrilling novel (that purely Christian product) the hero is not eaten by cannibals, but it is essential to the existence of the thrill that he might be eaten by cannibals. The hero must (so to speak) be an edible hero. So Christian morals have always said of the man, not that he would lose his soul, but that he must take care that he didn't.

(9) One of the sharpest differences free will makes is to penology:

. . . this is the real objection to that torrent of modern talk about treating crime as a disease. . . . The whole point indeed is perfectly expressed in the very word which we use for a man in hospital: "patient" is in the passive mood; "sinner" is in the active. If a man is to be saved from influenza, he may be a patient. But if he is to be saved from forging, he must be not a patient but an *impatient.* He must be personally impatient with forgery.

(10) GK always maintained that mankind's most important relationship is the family:

. . . revolting against the family . . . (is) revolting against mankind. Aunt Elizabeth is unreasonable, like mankind. Papa is excitable, like mankind. Our youngest

brother is mischievous, like mankind. Grandpa is stupid, like the world; he is old, like the world.

Family is also the greatest adventure and drama, for **When we step into the family, by the act of being born, we do step into a world which is incalculable, into a world which has its own strange laws, into a world which could do without us, into a world which we have not made. In other words, when we step into the family we step into a fairy tale.**

The best way that a man could test his readiness to encounter the common variety of mankind would be to climb down a chimney into any house at random, and get on as well as possible with the people inside. And that is essentially what each one of us did on the day that he was born.

(11) Defending the traditional family means also defending traditional marriage and rejecting

The dreamy old bachelor notion—that notion that the unity of marriage, the being one flesh, has something to do with being perfectly happy. . . . I tell you, an ordinary honest man is part of his wife even when he wishes he wasn't. I tell you, an ordinary good woman is part of her husband even when she wishes him at the bottom of the sea. I tell you that, whether the two people are for the moment friendly or angry, happy or unhappy, The Thing marches on, the great four-footed Thing, the quadruped of the home. . . . I tell you they are one flesh even when they are not one spirit.

They have invented a phrase, a phrase that is a black-and-white contradiction in two words—"free-love"—as if a lover ever had been, or ever could be, free. It is the nature of love to bind itself, and the institution of marriage merely paid the average man the compliment of taking him at his word . . . the liberty for which I chiefly care (is) the liberty to bind myself. . . . To take an obvious instance, it would not be worth while to bet if a bet were not binding. . . . Christian marriage is the great ex- ample . . . that is why it is the chief subject and centre of all our romantic writing . . . I ask . . . to have my oaths and engagements taken seriously . . . (to) have real obligations, and therefore real adventures. . . . The man who makes a vow makes an appointment with himself at some distant time or place.

(12) And therefore divorce is a superstition:

If Americans can be divorced for "incompatibility of the temper" I cannot conceive why they are not all divorced. I have known many happy marriages, but never a compatible one. The whole aim of marriage is to fight through and survive the instant when incompatibility becomes unquestionable. For a man and a woman, as such, are incompatible.

(13) GK is also a feminist in the true, traditional sense:

The father of a family has never been called "the king of the house" or . . . "the pope of the house". . . . He was called "the head of the house." The man is the head of the house, while the woman is the heart of the house. . . . The head of an arrow is not more necessary than the shaft of it . . . but the head of an axe and arrow is the thing that enters first; the thing that speaks. If I kill a man with an arrow I send the arrow-head as an ambassador, to open the question.

GK sees women as liberated precisely by being mothers: liberated from narrow male specialization: **Woman is generally shut up in a house with a human being at a time when he asks all the questions that there are, and some that there aren't. It would be odd if she retained any of the narrowness of a specialist. . . . How can it be a large career to tell other people's children about the Rule of Three and a small career to tell one's own children about the universe? How can it be broad to be the same thing to everyone, and narrow to be everything to someone? No; a woman's function is laborious, but because it is gigantic, not because it is minute . . . even the male child is born closer to his mother than to his father. No one, staring at that frightful female privilege, can quite believe in the equality of the sexes.**

Feminists would probably agree with me that womanhood is under shameful tyranny. . . . But I want to destroy the tyranny. They want to destroy womanhood. . . . . Ten million young women rose to their feet with the cry, *We will not be dictated to*—and proceeded to become stenographers.

(14) GK even has commonsensical things to say about sex, and the main thing is the one thing that modern sex education courses make us forget:

The creation of a new creature not ourselves, of a new conscious centre, of a new and independent focus of experience and enjoyment, is an immeasurably more grand and godlike act even than a real love affair; how much more superior to a momentary physical satisfaction. If creating another self is not noble, why is pure self-indulgence nobler?

GK was a sexual prophet. He wrote, a century ago: **The next great heresy is going to be simply an attack on morality, and especially on sexual morality. . . . The madness of tomorrow is not in Moscow but much more in Manhattan.**

General Ethics

(1).When we turn to ethics, GK again focuses on the central, the commonsensical:

The vast and shallow philosophies, the huge syntheses of humbug, all talk about ages and evolution and ultimate developments. The true philosophy is concerned with the instant. Will a man take this road or that?—that is the only thing worth thinking about. (This is exactly what Kierkegaard would say if he read Teilhard de Chardin.)

(2) Morality gets its absoluteness from its origin:

Morality did not begin by one man saying to another, "I will not hit you if you do not hit me"; there is no trace of such a transaction. There *is* a trace of both men having said, "We must not hit each other in the holy place." Thus the "social contract" theories of both Hobbes and Rousseau are refuted at a single stroke.

(3) This is why moral values are objective and absolute:

Right is right, even if nobody does it. Wrong is wrong, even if everybody is wrong.... Men spoke of the sinner breaking the law, but it was rather the law that broke him.

(4) Thus conscience transcends feelings, and judges them:

The (modern) **critic instinctively avoids the admission that Hamlet's was a struggle between duty and inclination, and tries to substitute a struggle between consciousness and subconsciousness. He gives Hamlet a complex to avoid giving him a conscience.**

(5) But subjective conscience is not infallible and absolute:

Why should your conscience be any more reliable than your rotting teeth?

(6) And the good is not historically relative either:

... the false theory of progress ... maintains that we alter the test instead of trying to pass the test. It said, for instance, "What is right in one age is wrong in another." This is quite reasonable if it means that there is a fixed aim, and that certain methods attain it at certain times and not at other times. But ... if the standard itself changes, how can there be improvement, which implies a standard? .... Progress itself cannot progress. Progress should mean that we are always changing the world to suit the vision. Progress does mean (just now) that we are always changing the vision. ... We are not altering the real to suit the ideal. We are altering the ideal: it is easier.

(7) GK affirms Kant's second categorical imperative:

. . . all evil comes from enjoying what we ought to use and using what we ought to enjoy.

(8) Rational and moral law are the guardians, not the enemies, of freedom and joy:

. . . doctrine and discipline may be walls, but they are the walls of a playground.

Special Ethics: Virtues and Vices

(1) GK has much to say about particular virtues, but the most important thing is about virtue in general: that it is not a generality but has a character, like a person. As an artist GK knew **that white is a colour. It is not a mere absence of colour. It is a shining and affirmative thing, as fierce as red, and as definite as black . . . (similarly) Virtue is not the absence of vices or the avoidance of moral dangers. Virtue is a vivid and separate thing, like a pain or a particular smell.**

(2) Here is GK's take on justice and mercy, or truth and pity:

The modern world is full of the old Christian virtues gone mad. The virtues have gone mad because they have been isolated from each other and are wandering alone. Thus some scientists care for truth, and their truth is pitiless. Thus some humanitarians only care for pity; and their pity (I am sorry to say) is often untruthful.

(3) Justice comes first, as childhood comes first. Thus GK explains why children love fairy tales that end with villains being punished: because **children are innocent and love justice, while most of us are wicked and naturally prefer mercy.**

(4) Presupposed in all virtues is humility; and this is not small-minded but great-minded; it enables us to soar like eagles, while egotism makes us creep like worms:

Humility is the mother of giants. One sees great things from the valley, only small things from the peak. . . . If I had only one sermon to preach, it would be a sermon against Pride . . . all evil began . . . when, as we might say, the very skies were cracked across like a mirror, because there was a sneer in Heaven.

(5) Christian virtues are wild and dramatic and happy:

. . . the pagan virtues, such as Justice and Temperance, are the sad virtues . . . Faith, Hope and Charity are the gay and exuberant virtues . . . the pagan virtues

are the reasonable virtues. Faith, Hope and Charity are unreasonable. . . . Charity means pardoning what is unpardonable, or it is not virtue at all. Hope means hoping when things are hopeless, or it is not virtue at all. And Faith means believing the incredible, or it is no virtue at all.

(6) The virtue of love entails also the virtue of proper hate:

. . . hatred is beautiful when it is hatred of the ugliness of the soul . . . as if there were any inconsistency between having a love for humanity and having a hatred for inhumanity!

(7) Gratitude is another primary and wild virtue:

. . . the man who really knows he cannot pay his debt will be forever paying it. . . . He will be always throwing things away into a bottomless pit of unfathomable thanks.

(8) Connected with this is GK's caution against idolizing control, especially by technology, and the consequent boredom of modern life:

A man has control over many things in his life; he has control over enough things to be the hero of a novel. But if he had control over everything, there would be so much hero that there would be no novel. And the reason why the lives of the rich are at bottom so tame and uneventful is simply that they can choose the events. They are dull because they are omnipotent. They fail to feel adventurous because they can make the adventures. The thing which keeps life romantic and full of fiery possibilities is the existence of these great plain limitations which force all of us to meet the things we do not like or do not expect. . . . (For) an adventure is only an inconvenience rightly considered. An inconvenience is only an adventure wrongly considered.

(9) How often GK uses words like "vivid," "wild," and "adventure." How happy he was! Perhaps his best short summary of the good life is this: **The secret of life lies in laughter and humility. Self is the gorgon.**

The case for his canonization as a saint is presently proceeding.

(10) On the Aristotelian Golden Mean: **It is always simple to fall; there are an infinity of angles at which one falls, only one at which one stands.**

(11) Finally, not success but effort is primary: **If a thing is worth doing, it is worth doing badly.**

Applied Ethics

Issues in applied ethics that GK addressed, controversially and prophetically, included suicide, euthanasia, abortion, and birth control.

(1) On suicide: **The man who kills a man, kills a man. The man who kills himself, kills all men; as far as he is concerned he wipes out the world. . . . Obviously a suicide is the opposite of a martyr. A martyr is a man who cares so much for something outside him that he forgets his own personal life . . . he sets his heart outside himself: he dies that something may live. . . . A suicide is a man who cares so little for anything outside him that he wants to see the last of everything.**

(2) On euthanasia: **We call in the doctor to save us from death; and, death being admittedly an evil, he . . . has not the right to administer death as the cure for all human ills.**

(3) On why abortion will doom Western civilization: **In the New Town, which the Romans called Carthage, as in the parent cities of Phoenicia, the god who got things done bore the name of Moloch, who was perhaps identical with the other deity whom we know as Baal, the Lord . . . the worshippers of Moloch were not gross or primitive. They were members of a mature and polished civilization, abounding in refinements and luxuries; they were probably far more civilized than the Romans. And Moloch was not a myth; or at any rate his meal was not a myth. Those highly civilized people really (did) invoke the blessing of heaven on their empire by throwing hundreds of their infants into a large furnace. . . . It is common enough to blame Rome for not making peace. But it was a true popular instinct that there could be no peace with that sort of people . . . *Delenda est Carthago* . . . Hannibal, the Grace of Baal, marched down the road to Rome, and the Romans who rushed to war with him felt as if they were fighting with a ma- gician. . . . The name of the New City remains only as a name. There is no stone of it left upon the sand. . . . Carthage fell because she was faithful to her own philosophy and had followed out to its logical conclusion her own vision of the universe. Moloch had eaten his children.**

(4) On birth control vs. lust control: **If everything that is natural is right, why in the world is not the birth of a baby as natural as the growth of a passion? If it is un- natural to control appetite, why is it not unnatural to control birth? They are both obviously parts of the same natural process, which has a natural beginning and a natural end. . . . If nature is infallible, we must not question what progeny she produces. If Nature is not infallible, we have a right to question the passions that she inspires.**

Political Philosophy

(1) GK loved both democracy and tradition. He said, **I have never been able to understand where people get the idea that democracy was in some way opposed to tradition. It is obvious that tradition is only democracy extended through time. . . .
Tradition may be defined as an extension of the franchise. Tradition means giving
votes to the most obscure of all classes, our ancestors. It is the democracy of the
dead. Tradition refuses to submit to the small and arrogant oligarchy of those who
merely happen to be walking about. All democrats object to men being disqualified
by the accident of birth; tradition objects to their being disqualified by the accident
of death.**

Our civilization has decided, and very justly decided, that determining the guilt
or innocence of men is a thing too important to be trusted to trained men. . . . **When
it wants a library catalogued, or the solar system discovered, or any trifles of that
kind, it uses up its specialists. But when it wishes anything done which is really serious, it collects twelve of the ordinary men standing round. The same thing was
done, if I remember right, by the Founder of Christianity.**

In short, the democratic faith is this: that **the most terribly important things
must be left to ordinary men themselves—the mating of the sexes, the rearing of
the young, and the laws of the state. But men in a state of decadence employ professionals to fight for them, professionals to dance for them, and a professional to rule
them.**

(2) GK opposed both capitalism and socialism: **There is less difference than many
suppose between the ideal Socialist system, in which the big businesses are run by
the State, and the present Capitalist system, in which the State is run by the big
businesses.**

But he was most adamantly opposed to socialism: **The Socialist says we have too
many capitalists. I say we have too few.**

What he hated about Socialism was centralization. He believed in the neglected but
crucial principle of subsidiarity: **I am one of those who believe that the cure for centralization is decentralization. It has been described as a paradox. There is apparently something elvish and fantastic about saying that when capital has come to be
too much in the hand of the few, the right thing is to restore it into the hands of the
many. The Socialist would put it in the hands of even fewer people; but those people
would be politicians, who (as we know) always administer it in the interests of the
many. For there are far more blunders in a big shop than ever happen in a small
shop, where the individual customer can curse the individual shopkeeper.**

Communism is the silliest solution of all: **Communism . . . only reforms the pick-
pocket by forbidding pockets.**

(3) GK opposed what nearly all take for granted today, government education: **State education is simply conscription applied to culture.**

(4) He always put the family above the state: **The huge fundamental function upon which all anthropology turns, that of sex and childbirth, has never been inside the political state but always outside it. The state concerned itself with the trivial question of killing people, but wisely left alone the whole business of getting them born.**

For . . . **the commonwealth is made up of a number of small kingdoms, of which a man and a woman become the king and queen and on which they exercise a reasonable authority, subject to the commonsense of the commonwealth, until those under their care grow up to found similar kingdoms and exercise similar authority. This is the social structure of mankind, far older than all its records and more universal than any of its religions, and all attempts to alter it are mere talk and tomfoolery.**

On government and marriage, he wrote: **Government grows more elusive every day. But the traditions of humanity support humanity; and the central one is this tradition of Marriage. And the essential of it is that a free man and a free woman choose to found on earth the only voluntary state; the only state which creates and which loves its citizens. So long as these real responsible beings stand together, they can survive all the vast changes, deadlocks and disappointments which make up mere political history. But if they fail each other, it is as certain as death that "the State" will fail them.**

(5) He was skeptical of both liberalism, or libertarianism, and conservatism. He wrote: **A liberal may be defined approximately as a man who, if he could, by waving his hand in a dark room, stop the mouths of all the deceivers of mankind forever, would not wave his hand.** On the other hand, he wrote about conservatism: **one reason offered for being a progressive is that things naturally tend to grow better. But the only real reason for being a progressive is that things naturally tend to grow worse. The corruption in things is not only the best argument for being progressive; it is also the only argument against being conservative . . . conservatism is based upon the idea that if you leave things alone you leave them as they are. But you do not. If you leave a thing alone you leave it to a torrent of change. If you leave a white post alone it will soon be a black post. If you particularly want it to be white you must be always be painting it again; that is, you must be always having a revolution.**

(6) He was all for rules: **A strict rule is not only necessary for ruling; it is also necessary for rebelling.**

(7) Yet society was fundamentally not about rules but about happiness: **If we can make men happier, it does not matter if we make them poorer, it does not matter if we make them less productive, it does not matter if we make them less progressive.**

Philosophy of History

(1) GK defended traditionalism, and therefore the poor, for **Few except the poor preserve tradition. Aristocrats live not in traditions but in fashions.**

Traditionalism is commonsensical: **Let us say, for the sake of simplicity, that there is a fence or gate erected across a road. The more modern type of reformer goes gaily up to it and says, "I don't see the use of this; let us clear it away." To which the more intelligent type of reformer would do well to answer, "If you don't see the use of it, I certainly won't let you clear it away. Go away and think. Then, when you can come back and tell me that you *do* see the use of it, I may allow you to destroy it."**

But modernity scorns tradition: **If the modern man is the heir of all the ages, he is often the kind of heir who tells the family solicitor to sell the whole damned estate. . . . He is certainly not the kind of heir who ever visits his estate . . . he is a very absentee landlord.**

This is unreasonable even from the premises of progressivism because **Real development is not leaving things behind, as on a road, but drawing life from them, as from a root.**

Our anti-traditionalism, our scorn of "the permanent things," really makes us barbarians, for **There is above all this supreme stamp of the barbarian: the sacrifice of the permanent to the temporary.**

Modernity has turned concrete things into abstractions: **So long as the village is merely the ancient human village, it is dealing with elemental and universal things; with water and fire and the watching of stars and winds, the rearing of children, the mourning for the dead. . . . But as soon as it becomes a modern industrial city . . . it shrinks and dwindles to little and local things, things peculiar to a particular and already passing epoch: the particular mechanical toys of our time. . . . Men are not talking about Land . . . they are talking about Real Estate.**

(2) GK attacked Progressivism back when people still believed in the myth of progress:

. . . they are always saying, "You can't put the clock back." The simple and obvious answer is "You can." A clock, being a piece of human construction, can be

restored by the human finger to any figure or hour. In the same way, society, being a piece of human construction, can be reconstructed upon any plan that has ever existed. . . .

The worst argument in the world is a date. For it is actually taking as fixed the one thing that we really know is fugitive. . . .

How can anything be up to date? A date has no character. . . .

He who marries the Spirit of the Times will soon be a widower. . . .

Some dogma, we are told, was credible in the twelfth century but is not credible in the twentieth. You might as well say that a certain philosophy can be believed on Mondays but cannot be believed on Tuesdays. . . . What a man can believe depends upon his philosophy, not upon the clock or the century. . . .

Progressivism is stupidest of all regarding morality: "Away with your old moral formulas; I am for progress." This, logically stated, means, "Let us not settle what is good, but let us settle whether we are getting more of it."

Do not be proud of the fact that your grandmother was shocked at something which you are accustomed to seeing or hearing without being shocked. . . . It may be that your grandmother was an extremely lively and vital animal and you are a paralytic.

(3) GK's philosophy of history divided history into three eras by the standard of Christianity that came in the middle. Here is all of history in three sentences:

Paganism was the largest thing in the world, and Christianity was larger, and everything else has been comparatively s ma ll. . . .

I freely grant that the pagans, like the moderns, were only miserable about everything—they were quite jolly about everything else. I concede that the Christians of the Middle Ages were only at peace about everything—they were at war about everything else. . . . Man is more himself . . . when joy is the fundamental thing in him and grief the superficial. . . . Yet, according to the . . . pagan or the agnostic, this primary need of human nature can never be fulfilled.

What modern man has lost is not merely the true end but hope that there is one: **Man has always lost his way . . . But . . . for the first time in history he begins to doubt the object of his wanderings on earth. He has always lost his way, but now he has lost his address.**

(4) Modern man is not more rational and critical: **Only a very soft-headed, sentimental and rather servile generation of men could possibly be affected by advertisements at all . . . If you had said to a man in the Stone Age, "Ugg says Ugg makes the best stone hatchets,". . . .**

Aesthetics

(1) GK's aesthetics was not just a theory of art but of life. Thus art for art's sake works no better than any other kind of idolatry: **you never work so well for art's sake as when you are working for something else.**

That "something else" is life. **Art indeed copies life in not copying life, for life copies nothing.**

(2) Art is no more a friend of anarchy than science is:

It is impossible to be an artist and not care for laws and limits. Art is limitation; the essence of every picture is the frame. If you draw a giraffe, you must draw him with a long neck. If, in your bold and creative way, you hold yourself free to draw a giraffe with a short neck, you will really find that you are not free to draw a giraffe. . . . You can free things from alien or accidental laws, but not from the laws of their own nature. You may, if you like, free a tiger from his bars, but you do not free him from his stripes. Do not free a camel of the burden of his hump; you may be freeing him from being a camel. Do not go about as a demagogue, encouraging triangles to break out of the prison of their three sides.

(3) But art, unlike science, is symbolic:

Every great literature has always been allegorical—allegorical of some view of the whole universe. The "Iliad" is only great because all life is a battle, the "Odyssey" because all life is a journey, the Book of Job because all life is a riddle.

(4) Sometimes the best art is wordless:

When I had looked at the lights of Broadway by night, I made to my American friends an innocent remark that seemed for some reason to amuse them. . . . I said to them, in my simplicity, "What a glorious garden of wonders this would be to anyone who was lucky enough to be unable to read."

(5) Like many philosophers, GK found music especially exhilarating, but, unlike them, drew the logical conclusion that it should be universalized:

If reapers sing while reaping, why should not auditors sing while auditing and bankers while banking? . . . the work of bank clerks when casting up columns might begin with a thundering chorus in praise of Simple Addition: "Up, my lads, and lift the ledgers; sleep and ease are o'er. Hear the Stars of Morning shouting: "Two and

**Two are Four! Though the creeds and realms are reeling, though the sopists roar,
Though we weep and pawn our watches, Two And Two are Four!"**

(6) GK's saw all life as art, and therefore as joy. And here is an immensely practical
philosophical wisdom for us:

**I believe that the great source of the hideousness of modern life is that lack of
enthusiasm for modern life. If we really loved modern life we should make it beautiful. For all men seek to make beautiful the thing which they already think beautiful. The mother always seeks to deck out her child in what finery she possesses. The
owner of a fine house adorns his house; the believer beautifies his church. . . . If we
regarded the engineering of our age as the great Gothic architects regarded the engineering of their age we should make of the ordinary steam engine something as
beautiful as the Christian cathedral.**

I conclude on a personal note: If our doddering civilization can recapture that childlike joy that Chesterton both says and shows, both in his philosophy and in his personality, it will be saved; if not, not. Chesterton, I firmly believe, shows us, better than any
mere philosopher, the alternative to decadence and decay. And even if we cannot sell it
to our civilization, we can certainly sell it to ourselves and transform our lives. And that
is the highest function of the love of wisdom, which is what philosophy is supposed to
be.

Selected Bibliography:

Chesterton, *Orthodoxy*
The Everlasting Man
The Man Who Was Thursday

Conclusion

After studying the thoughts of many minds—no less than 100!—all probably greater than your own, you are tempted to a skeptical despair. "How could ordinary little I possibly play this giants' game of philosophy? How could this Jack climb this beanstalk into their country in the sky? How could I compete with these superior minds, or judge them? The superior must judge the inferior, not vice versa. They have every advantage over me."

Not so. You have a great advantage over almost every single one of these philosophers that qualifies you to judge them. You are alive; and you are firmly planted in the very same soil that was the first foundation of all of the great jungle growths of ideas that grew from them, namely common sense.

If you judge them from that point of view (common sense), you probably see some truth in all or nearly all of the philosophers, and total truth in none of them. And so you are learning different things from different philosophers—e.g., Ideas from Plato, the four causes from Aristotle, the "restless heart" from Augustine, essence and existence from Aquinas, methodic doubt from Descartes, the wager from Pascal, the consequences of empiricism from Hume, the categorical imperative from Kant, dialectic from Hegel, the three stages from Kierkegaard, the Dionysian vs. the Apollonian from Nietzsche, "the mystical" from Wittgenstein, the I-thou relationship from Buber, and the authority of common sense from Reid or G. E. Moore. You thus can see more than most of these philosophers have seen, because you have climbed on all their shoulders for a more comprehensive view. You may be a dwarf, and they may be giants, but you are a dwarf who has climbed onto the shoulders of giants. (The image is from Bernard of Chartres, a wise medieval "dwarf.")

And you have done that, you have learned from them all, not because you are a great philosopher but because you are not one: you are an ordinary human being living where every philosopher once lived: not in a philosophical system but in the real world, in real life, in ordinary human experience and common sense. Every philosophy must begin there, at least, no matter how far it may eventually depart from it. Every abstraction, every bit of technical terminology, every question, every project, every thought experiment, however far it rises from this soil, rises from this soil, and depends on it, and is rightly called to judgment by it to be tested there by the likes of *you*.

Philosophers write for you, not for each other. There are not enough of them as readers to pay for publishing their books as writers. They claim to be your teachers, they try to lead you out of your cave. It is up to you to decide whether they are just leading you into their own caves. The teachers cannot choose their students, but the students can choose their teachers. Choose well. You are in the driver's seat. Drive well: drive safely, but also drive adventuresomely.

Appendix I: A Doable Do-It-Yourself Course in the Classics of Philosophy

Many people have asked me for a recommended booklist for a teach-yourself philosophy course. Many beginning philosophy teachers have asked me for a similar list for an introductory course in philosophy.

I know of no more effective way to teach philosophy, to yourself or others, than the apprenticeship to the masters that is called "The Great Books." The "canon" of Great Books is certainly not fixed, or stuffy, or irrelevant to today's world. The list is pragmatic: it is a list of what has "worked."

Based on my own experience of what "works," i.e., what (a) is comprehensible to beginners and (b) inspires them to think and perhaps even to fall in love with philosophy, here is my list.

There is a primary list and a secondary list for each of the four periods in the history of philosophy. For a high school course, one of these eight lists would seem to fit into one semester; for a college course, two; and for a graduate course, three or four. The lists are deliberately short and selective; far better to spend much time with a few great friends than a little time with many little ones.

Ancient Philosophy, Basic List:

Solomon, *Ecclesiastes*
Plato, Meno and *Apology*
Plato, *Republic,* excerpts. (If you use the Rouse translation *(Great Dialogs of Plato)* and mentally divide each book into 3 parts, A, B and C, you could cover Book I, IIA, VB through VIIA, IXC, and Rouse's helpful summary of the rest).
Aristotle, *Nicomachean Ethics.* Select your own excerpts, but be sure to cover Books I and VIII.
Plotinus, "Beauty"

Ancient Philosophy, Additional List:

Parmenides' poem
The rest of Plato's *Republic*
Plato*, Gorgias*
The rest of the *Nicomachean Ethics*

A secondary source summary of Aristotle, either Adler's *Aristotle for Everybody* (easy) or Ross's *Aristotle* (intermediate)

Medieval Philosophy, Basic List:

Augustine, *Confessions 1–10* (Sheed translation; Hackett pub.)
Boethius, *The Consolation of Philosophy* (Hackett pub.)
Anselm, *Proslogium*
Aquinas, *Summa Theologiae,* at least I, 2, 3 ("on God's existence") & I—II, 1, 2 ("On Those Things in which Happiness consists"). These and more, with explanatory notes, are included in my *A Shorter Summa.*

Medieval Philosophy, Additional List:

Bonaventure, *Itinerary of the Mind to God*
Aquinas, more of the *Summa.* My *Summa of the Summa* anthology is 500 pages, with many footnotes.
Nicholas of Cusa, *Of Learned Ignorance*

Modern Philosophy, Basic List:

Machiavelli, *The Prince*
Descartes, *Discourse on Method*
Hume, *Enquiry Concerning Human Understanding*
Kant, *Foundations of the Metaphysics of Morals*

Modern Philosophy, Additional List:

Pascal Pensées *(or my Christianity for Modern Pagans: Pascal's Pensées edited and outlined)*
Descartes, *Meditations*
Leibnitz, *Monadology*
Kant, *Critique of Pure Reason, excerpts*

Contemporary Philosophy, Basic List:

Sartre, Existentialism and Human Emotions *(or Existentialism and Humanism)*
James, "What Pragmatism Means" and "The Will to Believe"
Marx, *The Communist Manifesto*
C. S. Lewis, *The Abolition of Man*
Buber, *I and Thou*

Contemporary Philosophy, Additional List

Mill, Utilitarianism
Russell, *The Problems of Philosophy*
Ayer, *Language, Truth and Logic*
Wittgenstein, *Tractatus Logico-Philosophicus*
Chesterton, *Orthodoxy*
Clarke, *Person and Being*

Appendix II: A Bibliography of Books on the History of Philosophy by the Author:

(1) Solomon: ch. 1 of *Three Philosophies of Life* (Ignatius Press)

(2) Shankara: "Philosophy of Religion" (taped lectures, Recorded Books)

(3) Buddha: *op. cit.*

(4) Confucius: *op. cit.*

(5) Lao Tzu: *op. cit.*

(6) *Socrates:* Philosophy 101 by Socrates: An Introduction to Philosophy via Plato's "Apology " *(Ignatius Press, St. Augustine's Press)*

(7) *Plato:* The Platonic Tradition *and* A Socratic Introduction to Plato's Republic *(St. Augustine's Press)*

(8) Aristotelian logic: *Socratic Logic* (St. Augustine's Press)

(9) Jesus: *The Philosophy of Jesus* (St. Augustine's Press)

(10) Jesus: *Socrates Meets Jesus* (InterVarsity Press)

(11) Jesus: *Jesus Shock* (St. Augustine's Press)

(12) Muhammad: *Between Allah and Jesus* (InterVarsity Press)

(13) Aquinas: "The Philosophy of Thomas Aquinas" (taped lectures, Recorded Books)

(14) Aquinas: *A Shorter Summa* (Ignatius Press)

(15) Aquinas: *Summa of the Summa* (Ignatius Press)

(16) *Aquinas:* Practical Theology: The Spiritual Wisdom of St. Thomas Aquinas *(Ignatius Press)*

(17) Machiavelli: *Socrates Meets Machiavelli* (St. Augustine's Press)

(18) *Pascal:* Christianity for Modern Pagans: Pascal's *Pensées (Ignatius Press)*

(19) Descartes: *Socrates Meets Descartes* (St. Augustine's Press)

(20) Hume: *Socrates Meets Hume* (St. Augustine's Press)

(21) Kant: *Socrates Meets Kant* (St. Augustine's Press)

(22) Marx: *Socrates Meets Marx* (St. Augustine's Press)

(23) Kierkegaard: *Socrates Meets Kierkegaard* (St. Augustine's Press)

(24) Freud: *Socrates Meets Freud* (St. Augustine's Press)

(25) Sartre: *Socrates Meets Sartre* (St. Augustine's Press)

(26) Tolkien: *The Philosophy of Tolkien* (Ignatius Press)

(27) *Lewis:* C. S. Lewis for the Third Millennium *(Ignatius Press)*

(28) Modern philosophers systematically argued with from a Thomist perspective: *Summa Philosophica* (St. Augustine's Press)

(29) The history of ethics: "What Would Socrates Do" (recorded lectures, Recorded Books)

(30) Ethical classics: *Ethics for Beginners* (St. Augustine's Press)